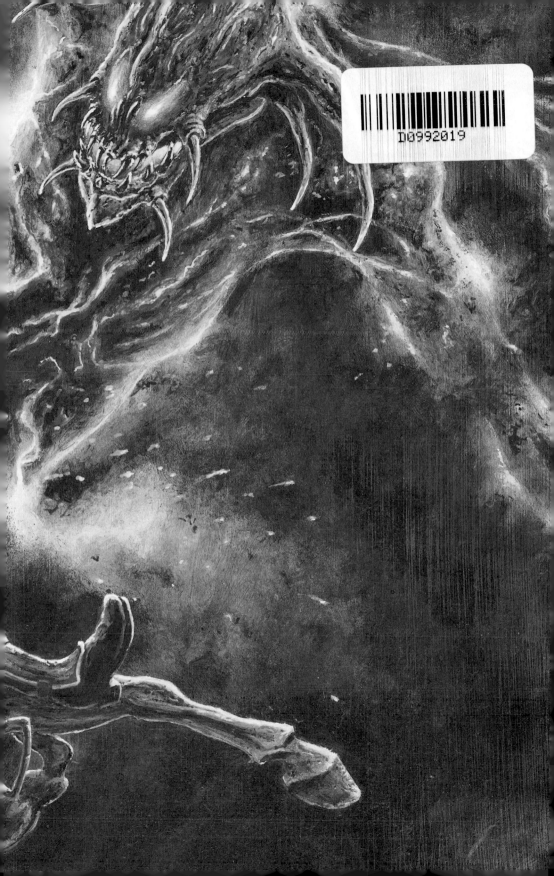

AN
ENCYCLOPEDIA
OF TOLKIEN

San Diego, California

Durin in the Long Sleep

AN
ENCYCLOPEDIA
OF TOLKIEN

THE
HISTORY AND MYTHOLOGY
THAT INSPIRED
TOLKIEN'S WORLD

DAVID DAY

San Diego, California

Canterbury Classics
An imprint of Printers Row Publishing Group
10350 Barnes Canyon Road, Suite 100, San Diego, CA 92121
www.canterburyclassicsbooks.com • mail@canterburyclassicsbooks.com

Printers Row Publishing Group is a division of Readerlink Distribution Services, LLC.
Canterbury Classics is a registered trademark of Readerlink Distribution Services, LLC.

Correspondence concerning the content of this book should be sent to Canterbury Classics,
Editorial Department, at the above address. Author or illustration inquiries should be
addressed to Pyramid, an imprint of Octopus Publishing Group Ltd, Carmelite House, 50
Victoria Embankment, London EC4Y 0DZ.

Canterbury Classics
Publisher: Peter Norton
Associate Publisher: Ana Parker
Publishing/Editorial Team: April Farr, Vicki Jaeger, Kelly Larsen, Stephanie Romero,
Kathryn C. Dalby
Editorial Team: JoAnn Padgett, Melinda Allman
Production Team: Jonathan Lopes, Rusty von Dyl

Pyramid
Publisher: Lucy Pessell
Editor: Sarah Vaughan
Copyeditor: Robert Anderson
Proofreader and Americanizer: Constance Novis
Senior Production Manager: Peter Hunt

Front cover illustration: Ian Miller, *Dunlending* and *Grey Mountain Dwarves*
Back cover illustration: Ian Miller, *A Haradrim warrior riding an Oliphaunt*
Front endpaper illustration: Linda Garland, *Tirion*
Back endpaper illustration: Kip Rasmussen, *Smaug verses Bard the Bowman*

Library of Congress Control Number: 2019944775

ISBN: 978-1-64517-009-9

Printed in China

24 23 22 21 20   3 4 5 6 7

CONTENTS

Mirkwood. In Tolkien's legendarium, woods and forests are places of both beauty and peril.

LIST OF ILLUSTRATIONS

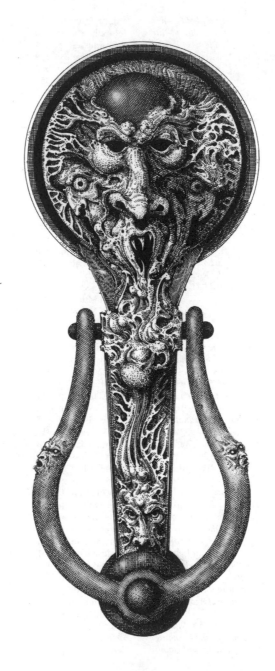

Enter

An Encyclopedia of Tolkien: The History and Mythology That Inspired Tolkien's World has been compiled as an easily accessible compendium for general readers who are interested in the mythological, literary, historical, and philological sources that inspired the author in his creation of Middle-earth and the Undying Lands. Many of these sources relate to Tolkien's scholarly studies and his personal life. Other sources have been specifically acknowledged by the author, himself; while many entries in this dictionary examine world mythologies, histories, and literatures that have themes, motifs, characters, and events in common with Tolkien's original tales. That is, these similarities suggest that elements of J. R. R. Tolkien's cosmos may simply comfortably coexist within the universal archetypal world of mythology and folklore.

Forty years ago, I published *A Tolkien Bestiary*, the first fully illustrated reference book and guide to Middle-earth and the Undying Lands. It was written shortly after the publication of *The Silmarillion* in 1977: the book that first revealed the immense scope of Tolkien's vast mythology and cosmos. Since that time, I have published a dozen books on the works of J. R. R. Tolkien. And the one consistent perspective I have kept throughout these books has been to view Tolkien's tales in this context of the mythologies and literatures of other nations and cultures. It is a perspective that Tolkien himself understood and cherished over his entire life.

For those who may have read any of my subsequent books, such as *The Hobbit Companion* or *Tolkien's Ring* published in the 1990s—or any of my more recent Tolkien reference library series—the approach taken in this compendium will be a familiar one. *An Encyclopedia of Tolkien* is a compilation that draws heavily and directly on the writing and illustrations in these earlier published works. However, it differs in its purpose as it is not a general guide, but is specifically a dictionary of sources. It is organized in an easily accessed single volume of alphabetically listed sources of J. R. R. Tolkien's writing.

This book is intended for those general readers of J. R. R. Tolkien who wish to learn more about the genius behind this awesome body of literature and the origin of some of the author's remarkable ideas. For in his construction of the Middle-earth, Tolkien drew on an enormous range of sources, from the mythological to the historical, the literary to the linguistic, and the personal to geographic. It is hoped that through *An Encyclopedia of Tolkien*, readers may both broaden their appreciation of this extraordinary author, and understand a little more of the sources of his inspiration. In this compendium, readers may discover something of the myths and legends with which Professor Tolkien was intimately acquainted, and about which he often despaired because so few of readers were even vaguely familiar with them.

The focus of this book is an examination of the heroes, villains, creatures, peoples, and geography of Tolkien's world, as well as his archetypal themes and motifs, in order to understand how they compare and relate to the literature, history, and mythology of other nations and cultures.

"I am interested in mythological invention, and the mystery of literary creation," Tolkien once wrote in a letter to a reader. "I was from early days grieved by the poverty of my own beloved country: it had no stories of its own, not of the quality that I sought, and found in legends of other lands. There was Greek, and Celtic, and Romance, Germanic, Scandinavian, and Finnish; but nothing English, save impoverished chap-book stuff."

This was Tolkien's life ambition. So great was this obsession that it could be argued that the undoubted literary merits of Tolkien's epic tale of *The Lord of the Rings* were almost a secondary concern. Important as the novel is, any analysis of Tolkien's life and work makes one aware that his greatest passion and grandest ambitions were focused on the creation of an entire mythological system for the English people. In his own words, we learn: "I had a mind to make a body of more or less connected legend, ranging from the large and cosmogenic, to the level of romantic fairy-story . . . which I could dedicate simply: to England; to my country."

As I have often observed, the enormity of this undertaking is staggering. It would be as if Homer, before writing the *Iliad* and the *Odyssey*, had first to invent the whole of Greek mythology and history. The degree to which he has actually succeeded is remarkable. In large part, Tolkien's invented mythology in the popular imagination has definitely become that of England. Furthermore, it is certainly the most complex and detailed invented world in all literature.

Naturally, Tolkien's world didn't come out of nowhere. It was a composite of all Tolkien was: creative author, philologist, historian, folklorist, mythographer, geographer, philosopher, and artist. It was once written of Dante: "Well nigh all the encyclopedic erudition of the Middle Ages was forged and welded in the white heat of an indomitable will, into the steel-knit structure of the *Divine Comedy*." Similarly, of Tolkien it can be said that a compression of everything he read knew, dreamed, and believed of Western history and culture went into the creation of his world of Middle-earth and the Undying Lands.

To understand the creative process of Tolkien's mind, it is interesting to look into his lecture and essay "On Fairy-Stories." Tolkien suggested the process by which fairy-tales were traditionally created was well encompassed in the homely metaphor of soup-making: "Speaking of the history of stories and especially of fairy-stories we may say that the Pot of Soup, the Cauldron of Story, has always been boiling, and to it have continually been added new bits, dainty and undainty."

Tolkien rather warns us off the task of examining the bones in an attempt to determine the nature of the ox from which the soup is made. "The history of fairy-stories is: probably more complex than the physical history of the human race, and as complex as the history of human language." He warns us that "the intricate web of Story is now beyond all the skill but that of the elves to unravel it." Certainly, the recipe for Tolkien's "Cauldron of Story" was very, very complex. Its bones and bits were drawn from a vast range of histories, myths, tales, folklore and sagas. To this was added the magical ingredient of pure invention.

This book is essentially an alphabetical dictionary or an illustrated index of ingredients of that Pot of Soup in the Cauldron of Story. It is arranged in such a way as to give anyone from the casual diner to the seasoned gourmet a means of dipping into and tracing a specific taste or aroma of this wonderful soup back to its original bones and "bits, dainty and undainty."

Through tracing these sources of inspiration in Tolkien's world—as well as its shared themes and motifs—it is hoped readers may appreciate the archetypal dimension of myth and legend that so enthralled Tolkien throughout his life. The richness of this heritage is evident in his tales and the vast mythological structures of his complex yet minutely detailed imaginary world. Tolkien was deeply committed to the study of the ancient wisdom of the soul as preserved in myth and legend. This was one of the most profound aspects of Tolkien's genius as an author. He combined a natural storyteller's ability and inventiveness with a scholar's capacity to draw on the deep well of myth, legend, literature, language, and history. He breathed life into ancient traditions that but for him, would have remained forever unknown to millions of modern readers.

A DICTIONARY

OF SOURCES

AA

Alfirin. To the Elves, the Alfirin flowers were like the great gold bell of Valinor in miniature.

AEGIR   A Norse nature spirit, or *jötunn*, comparable to the Greco-Roman sea-god Pontus and Tolkien's Ossë, the Maia of the Waves. Aegir was subservient to Njörd, the Norse god of the sea, just as Ossë is to Tolkien's Ulmo, the Lord of Waters. Like Ossë and Pontus, Aegir was known for his wildly shifting moods and his tempestuous nature, and was much feared by mariners.

AEGLOS ("SNOW POINT" OR "ICICLE")

The Elf-forged spear of Gil-galad, the High King of the Noldor of Middle-earth in the Second Age. Aeglos's inspiration was likely Gungnir—meaning "swaying one"—the magical Dwarf-forged spear of Odin, the Norse god. Like Aeglos, Gungnir was a weapon before which "none could stand" and that would always strike its mark. Aeglos is broken when Gil-galad falls in his duel with Sauron at the close of the War of the Last Alliance. Gungnir was broken when Odin carried it into the final battle of Ragnarök.

AENEAS   The mythical prince of the ancient city of Troy and Tolkien's Prince Eärendil the Mariner have parallel lives, both being founders of nations. According to the Roman poet Virgil in his epic poem the *Aeneid* (completed 19 BC), the progenitor of the Romans was Aeneas, the son of the mortal Prince Anchises and the immortal goddess Venus. According to Tolkien, the progenitor of the Númenóreans is Prince Eärendil, the son of the mortal nobleman Tuor and Idril, the immortal Elven princess. Aeneas survived the destruction of the royal city of Troy and then sailed for many years lost in the paths of many enchanted isles, while Eärendil survived the destruction of the royal city of Gondolin and then sailed for many years lost in the paths of the Enchanted Isles. With the help of the goddess Venus, Aeneas traveled to Elysium, the Land of the Blessed, then returned to guide his people into a western sea and their promised land in Italy. Similarly, with the help of Elwing, the Elvish princess, Eärendil travels to Aman, the Blessed Realm, then returns to guide his people into the Western Sea and the promised land of Númenor.

In Italy, descendants of Aeneas, the brothers Romulus and Remus, founded Rome, a city and civilization that was destined to develop into an empire that would conquer and rule the world. In Middle-earth, descendants of Eärendil, the brothers Isildur and Anárion, founded Gondor, a city and civilization that was destined to create an empire that would likewise conquer and rule the world.

A E S I R

One of the two groups of Norse gods (the other being the Vanir) who united to form a single pantheon. In many respects, the Aesir are comparable to the Vanir, one of the two groups of "angelic powers" in Tolkien's legendarium (the other being the Maiar). Although in terms of their hierarchical structure, Tolkien's Valarian pantheon clearly shows the influence of the Greco-Roman gods of Olympus, in appearance and temperament the Valar and Maiar have far more in common with the gods of the Norsemen and other Germanic peoples. The home of the Aesir was Asgard, one of the Nine Worlds of the Norse cosmos, located at one end of Bifrost, the rainbow bridge, and on the highest branch of Yggdrasil, the world tree. Tolkien's Manwë, king of the Valar, is enthroned on Taniquetil, the highest mountain in Arda, while Odin, king of the Aesir, was enthroned in Hildskjalf, the highest hall in Asgard. Among the other Aesir gods were Thor, Frigg, Tyr, Loki, Baldur, Heimdall, Idunn, and Bragi. The Vanir gods, including Freya, Freyr, Njörd, and Nerthus, lived in the nearby world of Vanaheim, on another branch of Yggdrasil.

AGLAROND

Meaning "Caves of Glory" in Sindarin (Grey Elvish), Aglarond is the name given to the spectacular caverns in the White Mountains, close to Helm's Deep. Aglarond, as translated from the common tongue of Westron, is known as the "Glittering Caves." There, in the wake of the War of the Ring, Gimli the Dwarf founds a new colony of Durin's Folk. Tolkien acknowledged that the caves were inspired by the vast real-world caves of Cheddar Gorge in the Mendip Hills of Somerset, in southwestern England. One of the greatest "natural wonders" of Britain, this vast limestone gorge and cave complex is the site of some of the island's earliest Paleolithic human remains. Aglarond and the Cheddar Gorge and Caves both appear to have been formed by underground rivers, and their vast galleries contain deep reflecting pools with remarkable stalactite and stalagmite formations. Tolkien was known to have visited Cheddar Gorge and its caves on at least two occasions: in 1916, while on his honeymoon, and again in 1940.

See also: GIMLI

AINUR

AINUR The "Holy Ones" are the angelic powers serving Tolkien's supreme being, Eru, "The One." The Ainur are comparable to the angels in the service of the one God, the biblical Jehovah or Yahweh, in the Judaeo-Christian tradition. In Tolkien's cosmology, it is the Ainur as a celestial choir who, at the bidding of Eru, sing the world into existence. The contribution of the Judeo-Christian tradition to Tolkien's imaginative writing is profound in its moral implications. However, in most respects, the ancient Judeo-Christian world is very unlike Tolkien's.

As Tolkien informs us, the Ainur, many of whom subsequently enter the created world of Arda, are "beings of the same order of beauty, power, and majesty as the gods of higher mythology." Indeed, those Ainur who enter Arda become known as the Valar and the Maiar, taking physical forms comparable to the gods of ancient Greek, Roman, and Germanic mythology. And although the inhabitants of Tolkien's world do not quite worship these "gods," the beliefs they hold surrounding these angelic powers are much closer to those of the ancient Greeks, Romans, and Germanic peoples than they are to the fierce monotheism of the ancient Israelites.

See also: ANGELS; MAIAR; "MUSIC OF THE AINUR"; VALAR

AKALLABÊTH

AKALLABÊTH "The Downfall of Númenor" is Tolkien's reinvention of the ancient Greek Atlantis legend. Tolkien often mentioned that he had "an Atlantis complex," which took the form of a "terrible recurrent dream of the Great Wave, towering up, and coming in ineluctably over the trees and green fields." He appears to have believed that this was some kind of racial memory of the ancient catastrophe of the sinking of Atlantis, and stated on more than one occasion that he had inherited this dream from his parents

Akallabêth

and had passed it on to his son Michael. In the writing of *Akallabêth*, however, Tolkien found that he had managed to exorcise this disturbing dream. Evidently, the dream did not reoccur after he dramatized the event in his own tale of the catastrophe. The original legend of Atlantis comes from Plato's dialogues, *Timaeus* and *Critias* (both c. 360 BC), which include the story of an island kingdom that some nine thousand years before had been home to the mightiest civilization the world had ever known. Atlantis was an island about the size of Spain in the western sea beyond the Pillars of Heracles. Its power extended over all the nations of Europe and the Mediterranean, but the overwhelming pride of these powerful people brought them into conflict with the immortals. Finally, a great cataclysm in the form of a volcanic eruption and a tidal wave resulted in Atlantis sinking beneath the sea. Tolkien used Plato's legend as an outline for *Akallabêth*. However, Tolkien seems to have been incapable of doing what most authors would have done—writing a straightforward dramatic narrative based on the legend. Typically, he just couldn't help adding little personal touches such as the compilation of three thousand years of detailed history, sociology, geography, linguistics, and genealogy.

See also: ATLANTIS

ALCUIN OF YORK (c. 735–804)

The Christian tutor and adviser to Charlemagne, King of the Franks and Holy Roman Emperor. His role is comparable to that of Gandalf as Aragorn's mentor, counselor, and spiritual guide. Just as the Wizard Gandalf inspired Aragorn's revival of the Reunited Kingdom of Arnor and Gondor, so the English churchman Alcuin was the driving force behind Charlemagne's revival of the Roman Empire. There is a deeper, theological connection between the two figures, however. Alcuin dared to remind Charlemagne that an emperor's authority was only borrowed from God, advising him: "Do not think of yourself as a lord of the world, but as a steward." Alcuin's words may remind us of those of Gandalf to Denethor the Ruling Steward of Gondor: "For I am also a steward. Did you not know?" Both Alcuin the churchman and Gandalf the Wizard had obligations far beyond the rise and fall of the petty kingdoms of mortal humans. Gandalf the Wizard is the embodied form of the immortal Maia Olórin and his allegiance is to the Guardians of Arda, whose authority is only borrowed from Eru Ilúvatar. Ultimately, Gandalf is steward to Eru the One, as Alcuin was steward to his Christian God.
See also: CHARLEMAGNE

ALFHEIM
One of the Nine Worlds of the Norse world and comparable to Tolkien's land of Eldamar in the Undying Lands. As the name Alfheim implies, this was the "home of the elves," or, more specifically, of the light elves. There was a second Norse elf-world called Swartalfheim, "home of the dark elves." These divisions reappear in Tolkien's division of his race of Elves: the Caliquendi, the Light-Elves who came, at least for a while, to the immortal lands of Eldamar ("Elvenhome"), and the Moriquendi, or Dark-Elves, who remained in the mortal lands of Middle-earth.

ALFIRIN
An often white, bell-like flower of Middle-earth known for blooming profusely about the tombs of Men. To the Men of Rohan it is Simbelmynë ("evermind"), while its Elvish name, Alfirin, means "immortal"—

both names suggesting its association with commemoration of the dead. As a flower, Tolkien himself compared it to the anemone, which the ancient Greeks associated with mourning: when the goddess of love Aphrodite wept over the grave of her lover Adonis, her tears turned into anemones.

ALI BABA   In the famous Middle Eastern folktale, Ali Baba is the unassuming hero who discovers that the secret to opening the stone door of the Forty Thieves' treasure cave is uttering the words: "Open Sesame!" The "door in the mountain" theme is a common one in fairy tales and legends, found, for example, not only in "Ali Baba and the Forty Thieves" but also in "Aladdin" and "The Pied Piper of Hamelin." Tolkien, too, drew on the motif. Entry into the treasure cave of the Dwarves in *The Hobbit* is by way of a secret door in the Lonely Mountain of Erebor, and he repeats the motif in *The Lord of the Rings*. When the Fellowship of the Ring arrives at the West Door of Moria, the entrance is sealed shut, though, as Gandalf states: "these doors are probably governed by words." In this case, the West Door of Moria is unlocked and opened by uttering the Elvish word *mellon*, meaning "friend." For Tolkien, however, the motif—and Gandalf's statement—had a deeper, creative meaning. Words were the keys to all of Tolkien's kingdoms of Middle-earth: a world he explored and discovered through language, runes, gnomic script, and riddles. Words unlocked the doors of Tolkien's imagination as a writer.

ANCALAGON THE BLACK   The first and greatest of the vast legion of Winged Fire Drakes that Morgoth releases from the deep dungeons of Angband in the last battle of the War of Wrath at the end of the First Age. The attack of Ancalagon (meaning "rushing jaws") in that last Great Battle has a precedent in the account of the great Norse battle of Ragnarök found in the Old Norse poem *Völuspá* (part of the *Poetic Edda*) where "the flying dragon, glowing serpent" known as Nidhogg (meaning "malice striker") emerges from the underworld, Niflheim. Like Nidhogg, the ravening majesty that is Ancalagon unleashes a terrible withering fire down from the heavens.

In the *Prose Edda*'s account of Ragnarök, we have another dragonlike monster, Jörmungandr, the World-Serpent, who rises up with the giants to do battle with the gods, and bring about the destruction of the Nine Worlds. In this version of Ragnarök, the god Thor appears in his flying chariot and, armed with the thunderbolt hammer Mjölnir, slays Jörmungandr. In Tolkien's Great Battle, the hero Eärendil, appears in his flying ship *Vingilótë* and, armed with a Silmaril, slays Ancalagon.

ANDÚRIL
The reforged ancestral sword of the kings of Arnor whose name means "flame of the west." Originally known as Narsil ("red and white flame"), it is first forged by Telchar, the Dwarf-smith of Nogrod and wielded by King Elendil. The weapon largely has its inspiration in the thirteenth-century Icelandic poem *Völsunga Saga*, where the dynastic sword of the Völsung clan, known as Gram ("wrath"), is forged by the elves

Ancalagon the Black

of Alfheim and first wielded by King Sigmund, until the blade was broken in his duel with Odin, the Lord of Battles. This is comparable to the fate of Narsil, which is wielded by Elendil until the blade is broken in his duel with Sauron, the Dark Lord.

The shards of Narsil are reforged by the Elves of Rivendell for Aragorn, the rightful heir to the kings of Arnor, and renamed Andúril. Its unbreakable blade flickers with a living red flame in sunlight and a white flame in moonlight. Similarly, the Völsung sword Gram is reforged by Regin the Dwarf-smith for Sigurd, the rightful heir to the kings of the Völsungs. Its unbreakable blade is distinguished by the blue flames that play along its razor-sharp edge.

See also: TELCHAR

ANDVARI   In Norse mythology, a dwarf who lives under a waterfall and possesses a magical ring called the Andvarinaut, or "Gift of Andvari." In some respects, Andvari's tale resembles that of Gollum. Both are solitary hoarders of magic rings but lose them through trickery: Andvari is tricked by the god Loki, and Gollum by the Hobbit Bilbo Baggins. Both lust after its return, and both curse ever after all those who take possession of the ring. In the Norse tradition, the ring was also known as "Andvari's loom" because of its power "to weave gold" and was believed to be the ultimate source of the cursed gold of the Nibelung and Völsung treasure hoards. This ring is comparable in its powers to that of the Seven Dwarf Rings of Middle-earth: the ultimate source of the cursed gold of the Seven Dwarf treasure hoards. As Tolkien would also have been aware, these ancient ring legends were the source of the riddling story "Rumpelstiltskin," where the ring is substituted with a spinning wheel that has the power "to spin gold"—a fairy-tale version of "Andvari's loom." In Richard Wagner's opera cycle *Der Ring des Nibelungen* (first performed 1876), Andvari appears as the dwarf Alberich the Nibelung.

ANGBAND ("IRON PRISON")   A subterranean fortress and armory inhabited by Morgoth, the Dark Enemy, and his army of fallen Maiar spirits. In many respects, Angband is comparable to the subterranean fortress and armory of Tartarus or Hell in John Milton's *Paradise Lost* (first edition, 1667), inhabited by the biblical Satan, the Prince of Darkness, and his army of fallen angels. A major difference, however, is that the pits of Angband are created by Morgoth and his allies because of their love of evil and hellish darkness, while Tartarus is created as a place of punishment for Satan and the other fallen angels. Both Angband and Tartarus serve as mighty fortresses and armories out of which lords of darkness launch their wars against the forces of light.

See also: STRONGHOLDS

ANGELS
The mighty spirits who serve the god Jehovah/Yahweh in Judeo-Christian tradition provide some of the inspiration for the Ainur, or "Holy Ones," in Tolkien's cosmology. The Ainur are brought into being as thoughts from the mind of Eru Ilúvatar. Drawing on the ancient classical tradition of the Music of the Spheres (attributed to Pythagoras), Tolkien's creation myth, told in *Ainulindalë*, has these angelic powers form a heavenly choir and sing the cosmos into existence. Thereafter, many of the angelic spirits choose to enter the newly created world of Arda in the form of the Valar and Maiar, supernatural beings of the same order and power as the gods of the Germanic and Greco-Roman pantheons.

See also: RELIGION: CHRISTIANITY

ANGMAR ("IRON HOME")
One of the domains of the Hill-men, lying on the northern borders of Eriador in the foothills of the Misty Mountains. By the year 1300 TA the area is ruled by the Lord of the Nazgûl, who subsequently becomes known as the fearful "Witch-king of Angmar."

In the context of European history, the Hill-men of Angmar most resemble the Basques, the indigenous mountain people of the western Pyrenees bordering modern France and Spain. For centuries the Basques fought against Roman, French, and Spanish incursions into their lands, and

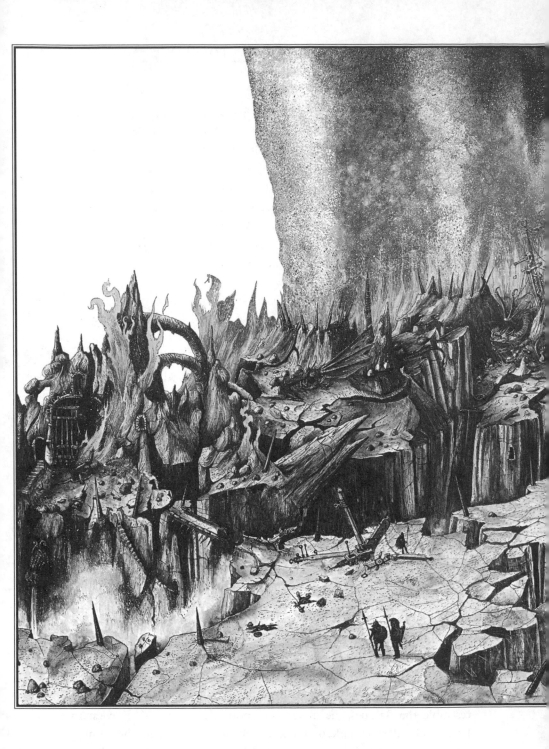

The Destruction of Angband

Aragorn II. The last Chieftain of the Dúnedain of the North after he was crowned King Elessar of the Reunited Kingdom of Gondor and Arnor after the War of the Ring.

constantly rebelled against those powers. The Basques were long resentful of the powerful Roman Empire and its later successor states, just as the Hill-men, too, resent the kings of Arnor. Consequently, the Hill-men were easily corrupted by the Witch-king and persuaded to enter into a disastrous war of attrition. After seven centuries, the Witch-king's long war ended with the Battle of Fornost (1975 TA) and the mutual destruction of both Arnor and Angmar.

ANNATAR
See: PROMETHEUS

ARAGORN Tolkien's archetypal hero and future king of the Reunited Kingdom of Arnor and Gondor. English-language readers of *The Lord of the Rings* frequently register a connection between the legendary King Arthur and Aragorn. What is not often apparent, however, is that twelfth- to fourteenth-century Arthurian romances are often based on fifth-century AD Germanic–Gothic oral epics—epics that now only survive in the myths of their Norse and Icelandic descendants. Tolkien was far more interested in the early Germanic elements of his tales, which link Aragorn with Sigurd the Völsung, the archetypal hero of the Teutonic ring legend.

Although all three heroic warrior kings—Sigurd, Arthur, and Aragorn— are clearly similar, the context out of which each arises—in pagan saga, medieval romance, and modern fantasy—is very different. The creation of the essentially medieval King Arthur and his court of Camelot, with its Christian ethos, naturally resulted in some reshaping of many of the fiercer aspects of the early pagan tradition. Sigurd the Völsung is a wild warrior who would have been out of place at Arthur's polite, courtly Round Table. Curiously, although Tolkien's Aragorn is an essentially a pagan hero, he is often even more upright and ethically driven than the Christian King Arthur.

ARAWN A Celtic otherworld deity and the likely inspiration for Tolkien's Oromë, the Huntsman of the Valar. Arawn provides an imaginative link between the fictional history of the Elves and the mythological world of the ancient Britons. The Welsh knew this god as Arawn the Huntsman, while Oromë (meaning "horn blower") was known to the Sindar (Grey Elves) as Araw the Huntsman. The Welsh Arawn was an immortal huntsman who like Araw/Oromë rode like the wind with horse and hounds through the forests of the mortal world. In the *First Branch of the Mabinogi,* Arawn the Huntsman befriends the mortal Welsh king, Pwyll, who travels into the immortal Otherworld of Annwn. In the mortal lands of Middle-earth, Araw/Oromë the Huntsman befriends three Elven kings (Ingwë, Finwë, and Elwë), who travel to the immortal Undying Lands of Aman.

ARDA The High Elven (Quenya) name for Tolkien's fictional world, encompassing the mortal lands of Middle-earth and the immortal Undying Lands of Aman. Arda, Tolkien insisted, is not another planet, but our world: the planet Earth. As the author himself explained: "The theatre of my tale is this earth, the one in which we now live, but the historical period is imaginary." The connection is made clear in the name: Arda is connected to the Old High German *Erda* and Gothic *airþa*, both of which translate as "Earth."
See also: MIDDLE-EARTH

ARIEN Maia maiden spirit of fire who each day carries the Sun aloft, illuminating Tolkien's world of Arda. She is very much like the Norse goddess Sunna, who was the guardian and fiery personification of the Sun.

In the ages following the destruction of the Trees of Light in Arda, the angelic Arien rises into the air and carries aloft the crystal vessel that contains the last glowing fruit of the Golden Tree of the Valar into the firmament. Similarly, it was the Norse goddess Sunna who drove the chariot of the Sun across the sky each day to light the Nine Worlds. Sunna's brother was Mani, the Norse god and personification of the moon, who in turn is comparable to Tolkien's Maia moon spirit, Tilion of the Silver Bow. Both Tolkien's and Norse mythology reverse the more commonly found gender of the deities of the Sun and Moon. The Greek and Roman deities of the Sun, for example, were respectively the male gods Helios and Sol while the Greek and Roman deities of the Moon were respectively the female goddesses Selene and Luna.

ARMAGEDDON
The location of the prophesied great battle fought between the forces of good and evil at the "end of time" (and by extension the name of the cataclysm itself), as revealed in the Book of Revelation in the New Testament. Tolkien's Great Battle in the War of Wrath at the end of the First Age owes some of its inspiration to the biblical Armageddon. However, instead of an ultimate duel between Tolkien's Eärendil the Mariner and Ancalagon the Black Dragon, we have a duel between the Archangel Michael and the "Red Dragon," as described in the Book of Revelation (12:7–10): "Then war broke out in heaven. Michael and his angels fought against the dragon, and the dragon and his angels fought back. But he was not strong enough, and they lost their place in heaven. The great dragon was hurled down—that ancient serpent called the devil, or Satan, who leads the whole world astray. He was hurled to the earth, and his angels with him." Just as the Red Dragon's downfall marks Satan's defeat, so the Black Dragon's downfall marks the defeat of Morgoth in Middle-earth. The Host of the West, like the Host of Heaven, prevails, and, as with Satan, no mercy or forgiveness is granted: Morgoth the Dark Enemy is cast forever after into the darkness of the Eternal Void.

AR-PHARAZÔN
The twenty-fifth and last king of Númenor. His seduction and downfall through the deceit of Sauron the Ring Lord is comparable to the biblical legend of that other Ring Lord, King Solomon. In the tale of Solomon's Ring (or Seal) found in Jewish tradition, we find a mighty demon, Asmodeus, who resembles Sauron at his most guileful. In the Hebrew story, Asmodeus—as the king of earthly demons—acts as a subtle agent of evil who corrupts the all-powerful but fatally proud King Solomon of Israel. In Sauron the Dark Lord, similarly, we see a subtle agent of evil who corrupts the all-powerful but fatally proud King Ar-Pharazôn of Númenor.

Ar-Pharazôn. The last, too-proud king of Nûmenor.

Just as Sauron surrenders to Ar-Pharazôn and begs to be his trusted royal servant, so the demon Asmodeus, in his guise as a trusted royal servant, becomes Solomon's evil tempter. Solomon is given visions of power and grandeur and begins sacrificing to the gods his various wives, going so far as to build a great temple to the goddess Ashtaroth on the slopes of Mount Moriah. As a consequence, he falls from the grace of Yahweh, the One God of the Israelites. This is comparable to Sauron's temptation of Ar-Pharazôn through visions of conquest and immortality and to the building of a great temple to Morgoth on the slopes of Mount Meneltarma, where sacrifices were made to this evil god. Like Soloman, Ar-Pharazôn falls from the grace of Eru the One. Upon King Solomon's death, it is prophesied, Solomon's kingdom would be divided, his temple and books destroyed, and the demons of disease and war released again upon the world. The fate of Tolkien's Númenor is even more disastrous: earthquakes and tidal waves destroy both nation and people as the island-continent sinks beneath the waters of the Western Sea.

ARTEMIS

As well as goddess of the Moon, Artemis was the Greek goddess of the hunt and the protector of wild animals and wild places. Forest groves, meadows, and deer were sacred to this goddess, whom the Romans equated with the goddess Diana. Tolkien's Nessa the Swift, the Vala sister of Oromë the Huntsman and the spouse of Tulkas the Strong, has some similarities with Artemis. Although Nessa is not a virgin huntress like Artemis, both are "swift as an arrow" with the ability to outrun the deer of the forest. Nessa cultivates all forms of animal and vegetable life in the Woods of Oromë in the Undying Lands. And, like Artemis, she also takes great delight in gatherings with other maids in its glades and meadows (both deities are closely associated with dancing). Another interesting comparison lies in the sibling kinship between Nessa and Oromë and Artemis and Apollo, although Tolkien does not elaborate on this.

ARTHUR   The legendary British king is on many levels similar to Aragorn the Dúnedain, Tolkien's most prominent hero in *The Lord of the Rings*. Aragorn is destined to become Elessar, the king of the Reunited Kingdom of Gondor and Arnor.

The comparison of Arthur and Aragorn demonstrates the power of archetypes, especially in dictating aspects of character in the heroes of legend and myth. If we look at their lives, we see certain identical patterns: Arthur and Aragorn are orphaned sons and rightful heirs to kings slain in battle; both are deprived of their inherited kingdoms and are in danger of assassination. Both are apparently the last of their dynasty, their lineage ending if they were slain; and both are raised secretly in foster homes under the protection of a foreign noble who is a distant relative (Arthur is raised in the castle of Sir Ector and Aragorn in Rivendell in the house of Elrond). During their fostering—in childhood and as youths—each hero achieves feats of strength and skill that mark them for future greatness. Both fall in love with beautiful maidens, but must overcome several seemingly impossible obstacles before they can marry: Arthur to Guinevere and Aragorn to Arwen. And, ultimately, by overcoming these obstacles they win both love and their kingdoms.

See also: *MORTE D'ARTHUR*

ARWEN EVENSTAR   The Elven princess also known as Arwen Undómiel, meaning "evening maid" or "nightingale." Arwen has many links with the fairy-tale heroine Snow White, whose story was first written down by the Brothers Grimm in 1812. Both are raven-haired beauties with luminous white skin. Both have associations with supernaturally powerful queens who possess magic mirrors (although, unlike Snow White's stepmother, Arwen's grandmother Galadriel is a benign figure). And Arwen, like Snow White, has a "Prince Charming" lover: the future king of the Reunited Kingdom of Arnor and Gondor, Aragorn. Tolkien also pointedly links Arwen Evenstar to Varda Elentári, the Valarian "Queen of the Stars" who is also known by the epithet "Fanuilos," meaning "Ever-White."

ASGARD

One of the Nine Worlds of the Norse cosmos, home to the all-powerful and immortal Aesir, ruled by Odin and Frigg, the king and queen of the gods. It has similarities with Tolkien's Valinor, home to the Valar, ruled by Manwë and Varda. Asgard is divided into several regions, each of which has a great hall belonging to one of the gods. The greatest of the halls is Hildskjalf, which contains the high seat of Odin the Allfather. Valinor is similarly divided into several regions, each of which has a great hall belonging to one of the Valar. The greatest stands on Taniquetil, the highest mountain in Arda, where Manwë, Lord of the Winds, is enthroned.

ASMODEUS

The powerful demon in the ancient Hebrew legend of Solomon's Ring. As the king of earthly demons, Asmodeus's role in the seduction of King Solomon is comparable to that of Sauron the Dark Lord in the seduction of Ar-Pharazôn, the twenty-fifth and last king of Númenor. Both Asmodeus and Sauron surrender to powerful human kings, but through guile, flattery, and promises of unfettered earthly power rise from captivity and virtual slavery to become the most trusted of royal advisers. Both subsequently corrupt their masters, leading them to war, false worship, and destruction. Both are aided in their usurping of power by all-powerful magical rings. *See also*: AR-PHARAZÔN

ASTERIA

The Titan goddess of falling stars and night oracles whose name means "of the stars" in Greek. She is comparable to Tolkien's Ilmarë, handmaid of Varda, Lady of the Stars. Ilmarë is among the greatest of the Maiar spirits and her name, which may mean "starlight" in Quenya, appears to have been inspired by Ilmarinen, the Finnic smith-god who appears in the epic *Kalevala*.

ATHELAS

A sweet-smelling herb with healing powers found in Middle-earth, which may have been inspired by basil. In Middle-earth, athelas is also known as kingsfoil or *asëa aranion*, meaning "leaf of kings,"

Athelas. The herbal lore attached to this herb relates to the European tradition of the "healing hands of the king."

in Quenya. The word "basil," too, derives from the Greek for "king," and in German the plant is sometimes known as Königskraut, or "king's herb." In Tolkien's legendarium, the healing powers of the herb are believed to be greatly enhanced when royal hands apply it. In this, Tolkien was drawing on the ancient English and French tradition of "the healing hands of the king," which dates at least to the reign of Edward the Confessor (1042–66). In the War of the Ring, Aragorn's use of athelas to combat the deadly magic of the Black Breath after the Battle of the Pelennor Fields is seen by Gondorians as evidence that the king has returned to Gondor.

ATHENS
The ancient Greek city-state—and its best-known mythical king, Theseus—are imaginatively linked to the city-state of Middle-earth's Gondor. Both the citadel of Gondor and the Acropolis of Athens have comparable traditions of sacred fountains and sacred trees. In Athens, there was the Fountain of Poseidon and the Olive Tree of Athena, while in Gondor there is the Fountain of Minas Tirith and the White Tree of Gondor. Furthermore, the citadel of Gondor is similar in its basic structure to the Acropolis, including the ship-prow ridge that is a feature of both. From the heights of the Acropolis, the Athenians could look down on the Long Walls that linked Athens to its ports at Piraeus and Phalerum on the Aegean Sea, just as, from the heights of citadel, the citizens of Gondor can look down on the Great Wall that links the citadel to its ports on the Anduin River. In the siege of Gondor, toward the close of the War of the Ring, the appearance of black-sailed ships sailing upstream from the port-city of Umbar results in the suicide of Denethor, the Ruling Steward of Gondor. This was undoubtedly inspired by the ancient myth of Theseus, where the appearance of black-sailed ships from Crete results in the suicide of Aegeus, Theseus' father and king of Athens. Both rulers mistake the black sail as signals of death and defeat when in fact their rescuer and heir, respectively, Aragorn and Theseus, command the ships. *See also*: BLACK SAILS

The Downfall of Númenor. The Downfall of Númenor was in large part inspired by Plato's
account of the ancient legend of the rise and fall of the mythical utopian island continent of Atlantis.

ATLANTIS   The legendary island kingdom that inspired Tolkien's tale *Akallabêth*, or "The Downfall of Númenor." This was one very distinct case of Tolkien taking an ancient legend and rewriting it in such a way as to suggest that his tale is the real history on which the ancient myth was based. So that we do not miss the point, Tolkien tells us that the Quenya name for Númenor is Atalantë. Plato's dialogues *Timaeus* and *Critias* are the primary sources for the Atlantis legend. In the *Timaeus*, Critias tells how the Athenian statesman Solon travels to Egypt where he learns the history of Atlantis. According to Plato, Atlantis lay in the ocean beyond the Pillars of Heracles (i.e., in the Atlantic Ocean) and that on "this island of Atlantis there existed a confederation of kings, of great and marvelous power, which held sway over all the island, and over many other islands also and parts of the continent." In Tolkien's retelling of the Atlantis story, the island continent of Númenor is located in the middle of the Western Sea between Middle-earth and the Undying Lands. Like Atlantis, Númenor is a fabulously rich and blessed realm whose kings wield great power and hold sway not only over all the island but, by dint of their fleets of mighty ships, over many parts of Middle-earth as well. The fate of Númenor is all but identical to that of Atlantis, as described by the first-century AD Hellenistic Jewish philosopher Philo, who wrote: ". . . in one day and one night [Atlantis] was overwhelmed by the sea in consequence of an extraordinary earthquake and inundation and suddenly disappeared, becoming sea, not indeed navigable, but full of gulfs and eddies."

AULË   In Tolkien's Valarian god Aulë the Smith, the Maker of Mountains, we have the counterpart of the Greek god Hephaestus (the Roman Vulcan). Both are capable of forging untold wonders from the metals and elements of the Earth. Both are smiths, armorers, and jewelers. Like Hephaestus, Aulë is depicted as a true craftsman and artisan, someone who creates for the joy of making, not for the sake of possession or gaining power and dominion over others.

Aulë is also the maker of Tolkien's race of Dwarves. These in their origins are very like the race of automatons created by Hephaestus, who appeared to be living creatures, but in fact were machines similar to robots designed to help in the smithy with the beating of metal and the working of the forges. In Tolkien, Aulë creates the Dwarves because he is impatient for pupils who can carry out his knowledge and craft. However, they are given true life and independent minds only at the command of Eru Ilúvatar. Among the Norsemen, Aulë's counterpart as the smith to the gods and heroes is Völundr. Among the Anglo-Saxons, he is Wayland.

AVALLÓNË

A port and city on the "Lonely Isle" of Tol Eressëa, originally home to those of the Teleri Elves (the so-called Sea Elves), who came to Aman. Its name is reminiscent of Avalon, the "Isle of Apples," to which the mortally wounded King Arthur is taken to be healed and given immortality. In a letter to a publisher, Tolkien acknowledged that this allusion was deliberately planned so as to give his Hobbit heroes, Bilbo and Frodo Baggins, an "Arthurian ending." That is, like King Arthur, these Hobbit heroes sail off over the Western Sea to Avalon/Avallónë where they too find healing and are given immortality. See also: AVALON

AVALON

The isle to which the mortally wounded King Arthur is taken after the Battle of Camlann. In Tolkien we have its counterpart in Avallónë on Tol Eressëa, the

Aulë the Smith. His spouse is Yavanna the Fruitful.

"Lonely Isle" of the Teleri Sea Elves. Avalon means "Isle of Apples" and is comparable to the classical Garden of the Hesperides where the beautiful daughters of Atlas and Hesperis ("Evening") tend the tree (or whole grove of trees) that bears the golden apples of immortality. A similar story can be found in Norse mythology, where Idunn, the goddess of youth, keeps golden apples that protect the Aesir from the ravages of time. The bittersweet ending of *The Lord of the Rings*—the departure of the Ring-bearers from the Grey Havens—is consciously modeled on the myths and legends surrounding King Arthur's departure to the isle of Avalon. It is an ending that is derived from the Celtic aspects of the Arthurian tradition, rather than the Teutonic ones. After his final battle, the mortally wounded Arthur is carried onto a mysterious boat by a beautiful queen (or sometimes three queens) and taken westward across the water to the faerie land of Avalon, where he is healed and given immortality. This end to Arthur's mortal life is very like the end of Tolkien's novel. However, it is important to point out that this is not the end of Aragorn, the figure most like Arthur in *The Lord of the Rings*. Aragorn dies within the mortal world. The supreme reward of this voyage into the land of immortals is reserved for another. The "wounded king" who sails on the Elf-queen Galadriel's ship across the Western Sea to the Elven towers of Avallónë is Frodo the Ring-bearer, the real hero of *The Lord of the Rings*.

AVARI The "Dark-elves," or Avari, of Middle-earth were very likely inspired by the categorization of the two races of elves in Norse mythology who inhabited two distinct worlds: Alfheim and Swartalfheim. Alfheim was the "Elf home" of the light elves, while Swartalfheim was the home of the dark elves. These divisions are similar to those Tolkien imposed on his own race of Elves: the Calaquendi, or Light-elves, who live for the most part in the immortal lands of Eldamar; and the Moriquendi, or Dark-elves, who live in the mortal lands of Middle-earth.
See also: A L F H E I M

Aulë and Yavanna Look Over Their Creations

B

Bats. Of the many creatures that Melkor the Dark Enemy bred in darkness, the blood-sucking bat was one. Sauron himself changed into a bat when he fled after the fall of Tol-in-Gaurhoth.

BAG END The Hobbit hole (*smial*) and ancestral home of the Baggins family of Hobbiton in the Shire. Bag End was the original name for Tolkien's aunt Jane Neave's Dormston Manor Farm, just a few miles from the author's childhood home in the hamlet of Sarehole in what was then rural Worcestershire. The manor's origins stretch back to Anglo-Saxon times, and it undoubtedly fired Tolkien's imagination in his construction of the fictional world of Middle-earth. However, it was perhaps more than just his childhood memories that Tolkien drew on in his creation of Bag End. "I came from the end of a bag, but no bag went over me," riddles Bilbo Baggins of Bag End in his contest of wits with the Dragon of Erebor. Just like the Hobbit, his creator was fascinated with puns, word games, and riddles, and by literary sleights of hand. Furthermore, there are elements of social satire in the name of Bag End. As the eminent Tolkien scholar Tom Shipley has observed, Bag End is a literal translation of the French *cul de sac*, a term employed by snobbish British real estate agents in the early twentieth century who felt the English term "dead-end road" was just too vulgar. Naturally, Tolkien's very English Baggins family would have no truck with this kind of Frenchified silliness, and so decided upon this suitably authentic local English name of Bag End. As a rule, Tolkien despised the pretensions and snobbery that looked down on all things English. He preferred plain English in language, food, and culture. Calling the Hobbit home of Bilbo Baggins "Bag End" is the epitome of everything that is honest, plain, and thoroughly English. Through the Hobbits of Bag End, Tolkien both extols and gently parodies the Englishman's love of simple home comforts, seen as both delightful and absurd. Overall, the only thing that seems surprising is that he didn't write a parody aphorism along the lines of "The Hobbit's hole is his castle."

BAGGINS The family name of Tolkien's principal Hobbit heroes in *The Hobbit* and *The Lord of the Rings*. It derives from a double source—the English Somerset surname Bagg, meaning "money-bag" or "wealthy," and the term "baggins," meaning "afternoon tea or snack between meals"—and is certainly appropriate for a prosperous and well-fed Hobbit.

Initially, the "original Hobbit," Bilbo Baggins, is presented as a mildly comic, home-loving, rustic, middle-class "gentle-Hobbit." He seems harmless and placid enough, if given to a little irritability, and full of gossip, homespun wisdom, wordy euphemisms, and elaborate family histories. He is largely concerned with domestic comforts, village fetes, dinner parties, flower gardens, vegetable gardens, and grain harvests. However, once recruited by Thorin and his Dwarf Company, the respectable Bilbo Baggins is revealed—much to his own astonishment—to be a highly skilled master burglar.

Tolkien always maintained that his tales were often inspired by names and words, and indeed, in the jargon of the nineteenth- and early twentieth-century criminal underworld there is a cluster of terms around "bag" and "baggage" that link up with one or other of the various highly specialized forms of larceny. Three are especially noteworthy: "to bag" means to capture, to acquire, or to steal; a "baggage man" is the outlaw who carries off the loot or booty; and a "bagman" is the man who collects and distributes money on behalf of others by dishonest means or for dishonest purposes.

It appears, then, that the name Baggins not only helped to create the character of Tolkien's Hobbit hero, but also went a long way toward plotting the adventure his hero embarks on. For, in *The Hobbit*, we discover a Baggins who is hired by Dwarves to bag the Dragon's treasure. He then becomes a baggage man who carries off the loot. However, after the death of the Dragon and because of a dispute after the Battle of Five Armies, the Baggins Hobbit becomes the bagman who collects the whole treasure together and distributes it among the victors.

Along with the Baggins name, further "baggage" is passed on to Bilbo's heir, Frodo Baggins. In the context of the One Ring, there is a link between the name Baggins and another specialized underworld occupation: the bagger or bag thief. This bagger or bag thief has nothing to do with baggage, but was derived from the French *bague*, meaning "ring." A bagger, then, is a thief who specializes in stealing rings by seizing a victim's hand and stripping it of its rings. It appears to have been in common usage in Britain's criminal underworld between about 1890 and 1940.

Consequently, one might speculate that from the beginning the Baggins name contained the seeds of the plot of both *The Hobbit* and *The Lord of the Rings*. For one step beyond Bilbo's skill as a burglar, one might also conclude that—from the perspective of the Ring Lord (or indeed Gollum)—the Baggins baggers of Bag End, Bilbo and his heir, Frodo, are also natural-born Ring thieves.

BALCHOTH
A barbarian horde of Easterlings from Rhovanion which, in 2510 TA, invade Gondor and engage with the Gondorian forces in the critical Battle of the Field of Celebrant. The tide of battle turns against the Balchoth when, unexpectedly, the cavalry of the Éothéod (ancestors of the Horsemen of Rohan) join forces with the Men of Gondor.

This has an historic precedent in the Battle of the Catalaunian Fields in AD 451 when the Roman army formed an alliance with the Visigoths (West Goths) and Lombard cavalry and defeated the barbarian horde of Attila the Hun. This is considered one of the most critical battles in the history of Europe as it turned back what seemed an unstoppable wave of Asiatic conquest of the West. In Middle-earth, in the wake of the Battle of the Field of Celebrant, the Balchoth confederacies rapidly disintegrated, as did the Hunnish confederacies after the Battle of Catalaunian Fields.

BALOR OF THE EVIL EYE
King of a race of deformed Irish giants known as the Formorians. Balor's name derives from the Celtic Baleros, meaning "the deadly one" suggestive of a spirit or god of drought and plague. He was also known as Balor Béimnech, meaning "Balor the Smiter," and Balor Birugderc, meaning "Balor of the Piercing Eye."

One of Balor's eyes was normal, but the other was an evil eye that was so deadly that he opened it only when he was called into battle whereupon its searing glance would wreak terrible destruction on the opposing army. There are obvious affinities with the Eye of Sauron here, which is variously described

Balchoth. One of the many great Easterling peoples who harry and assail Gondor during the Third Age.

as the "Evil Eye," the "Red Eye," the "Lidless Eye," and the "Great Eye." Unlike Balor's Eye, however, it does not serve as a kind of supernatural artillery but has a psychic power and will that could overwhelm and conquer the minds and souls of servants and foes alike. As related in *The Silmarillion,* "the Eye of Sauron the Terrible few could endure." Certainly, Christopher Tolkien concluded that, in the War of the Ring, his "father had come to identify the Eye of Barad-dûr with the mind and will of Sauron."

In all cultures, eyes are believed to have special powers and are said to be windows of the soul. So Tolkien's description of the evil Eye of Sauron gives us considerable insight into the Dark Lord himself: "The Eye was rimmed with fire, but was itself glazed, yellow as a cat's, watchful and intent, and the black slit of its pupil opened on a pit, a window into nothing."

BALROG OF MORIA
A nameless terror known only as "Durin's Bane." For over a thousand years of the Third Age, the menace of the Balrog keeps the Dwarves from their ancient kingdom of Khazad-dûm, named during that time Moria ("black pit"). It is not until Gandalf's encounter with the creature during the Quest of the Ring that its identity is revealed as one of the Balrogs, the monstrous Maiar fire spirits inspired by the fire giants of Muspelheim in Norse mythology. This particular Balrog is a survivor of the War of Wrath in the First Age, having hidden itself for millennia deep beneath the Misty Mountains. It is only by chance, or perhaps fate, that it is awakened by the deep-delving Dwarves of Khazad-dûm.

The monster's tenure in Moria ends with the fateful Battle on the Bridge of Khazad-dûm. This battle between Gandalf the Wizard and the Balrog of Moria actually has a very specific precedent in the Norse mythological battle between the god Freyr and the fire giant Surt on the last day of Ragnarök. Both battles begin with a blast of a battle horn. In Tolkien's tale, Boromir blows the Horn of Gondor, while in the Norse myth the god Heimdall blows the Gjallarhorn, the horn of Asgard. Like the Balrog of Moria who fights Gandalf on the Bridge of Khazad-dûm, Surt, the Lord of Muspelheim, fought Freyr, the god of the sun and rain, on the Rainbow Bridge that links

The Balrog of Moria

Middle-earth to Asgard. Tolkien's Bridge of Khazad-dûm and the Norse Rainbow Bridge both collapse in the conflict and the combatants in both battles topple into the abyss below. Surt and Freyr are entirely destroyed in this battle, while the Balrog and Wizard continue their struggle until the Balrog is slain, though at the cost of Gandalf's bodily form as the Grey Wizard.

BALROGS OF ANGBAND
Known as the Valaraukar or "Cruel Demons" in Quenya, these mighty Maiar fire spirits are among the most terrifying of Morgoth's servants in the War of the Jewels. More commonly known to the Sindar of Beleriand as Balrogs, or "Demons of Might," they take the form of man-shaped giants shrouded in darkness, with manes of fire, eyes that glow like burning coals, and nostrils that breathe flame. Balrogs wield many-thonged whips of fire in battle, in combination with a mace, ax, or flaming sword.

Visually, the Balrogs, while male, are comparable to the demonic Erinyes (Furies) of Greek mythology, female chthonic deities and avenging spirits—called Alecto, Tisiphone, and Megaera—who emerged from the pits of the Underworld to pursue those guilty of crime. Furies were variously described as having snakes for hair, coal-black bodies, bats' wings, and blood-red eyes. They attacked their victims with blazing torches and many-thonged brass-studded whips. There can be little doubt, however, that Tolkien's primary source for the Balrogs was the fire giants of Muspelheim, the mythical Norse "region of fire." The giant inhabitants of Muspelheim were demonic fire spirits who—once released—were as unstoppable as the volcanic lava floes that were so familiar to the Norsemen of Iceland.

There is also a link with Tolkien's Anglo-Saxon studies. Since Joan Turville-Petre's publication of Tolkien's notes on the Old English poem *Exodus*, several scholars have linked this text with his invention of the Balrogs. In these notes, Tolkien took issue with the usual modern translation of the *Exodus*'s "Sigelwara land" as the land of the Ethiopians. Tolkien believed that Sigelwara was a scribal error for sigel-hearwa, the land of "sun-soot," and was instead a reference to Muspelheim. The Sigelwara therefore were the fire giants—in Tolkien's own words, "rather the sons of Músspel . . .

than of Ham [the biblical ancestor of the Ethiopians], the ancestors of the Silhearwan with red-hot eyes that emitted sparks, with faces as black as soot."

Tolkien changed his concept of Balrogs over time, the fire demons becoming fewer, larger, and more powerful. Through multiple drafts, Balrogs dwindled from "a host" of hundreds or even thousands, down to "at most seven," as noted by Tolkien in a curious marginal note. Whatever their number, by the end of the First Age, Tolkien informs us, the Balrogs were entirely destroyed in the War of Wrath "save a few that fled and hid themselves in caverns inaccessible at the roots of the earth."

BARD THE BOWMAN In *The Hobbit*, the slayer of Smaug the Dragon of Mount Erebor, liberator of the Men of Esgaroth and first king of the new kingdom of Dale. Bard is an archetypal dragon-slayer in the tradition of the Greek god Apollo, patron of archers, who slew the great serpent Python, which lived beside a spring at Delphi and terrorized the people of the locality. Just as Bard the Bowman slays Smaug with his bow and arrow, so Apollo the Archer arrow slew Python and liberated the people of Delphi, enabling the god to take possession of its oracle.
See also: DELPHI

BARROW-DOWNS Low hills in Eriador crowned with megaliths, tumuli, and long barrows that are the ancient burial grounds of Men dating back to the First Age of Middle-earth. In the Third Age they become the Great Barrows of the kings of Arnor but in the wake of Arnor's destruction, they are invaded and haunted by evil spirits.

Tolkien took his inspiration for the Barrow-downs from Britain's monumental Neolithic earthworks and later Anglo-Saxon barrow graves, which in later times often became the focus of folktales and legends. The Neolithic long barrows and Bronze Age round barrows of Normanton Down, on a ridge just south of Stonehenge in Wiltshire, southwestern England, is one possible real-world source for Tolkien's Barrow-downs.

Another candidate is an impressive Neolithic site just 20 miles from Oxford, locally known as Wayland's Smithy. Tolkien had visited the site in outings with his family and knew well the many myths relating to Wayland the Smith (the Old Norse Völundr), a Germanic figure who was inspirational in the creation of the Elven Telchar the Smith. Both were master sword smiths who forged weapons with charmed blades like those discovered by the Hobbits in the Barrow-downs.

In 1939, at about the time Tolkien was writing the opening chapters of *The Lord of the Rings*, archeologists made an extraordinary discovery in Suffolk of three Anglo-Saxon long barrow graves at a site called Sutton Hoo. Covering about 16 acres, the site had been occupied for more than three and a half millennia before becoming an Anglo-Saxon burial site. The excavation also revealed the richest treasure trove of Anglo-Saxon artifacts ever found. The discoveries at Sutton Hoo were as revelatory of the Anglo-Saxon world as the discovery of Tutankhamen's tomb was of the ancient Egyptian world.

While Tolkien makes no mention of Sutton Hoo in his letters, it is hard to resist the idea that the Hobbits' imprisonment by a Barrow-wight in one of the barrows and their discovery of ancient swords were in part inspired by the great discoveries at Sutton Hoo. *See also*: BARROW-WIGHTS

BARROW-WIGHTS Evil undead
spirits that animate the bones of entombed Men in the Barrow-downs of Eriador. Early in *The Lord of the Rings*, one of the Barrow-wights briefly imprisons Frodo, Sam, Merry, and Pippin in a barrow until Tom Bombadil frees them.

Barrow-wights. The wraiths and spirits who haunt the graves and tombs of the dead are a fixture of many cultures.

The Barrow-wights are not an original Tolkien creation since they already had a long history, especially in the sagas of the Norsemen. These Norse tales tell of encounters similar to those experienced by the Hobbits in which evil spirits with terrifying luminous eyes and hypnotic voices hold unwary travelers captive. Having paralyzed a victim with its skeletal grip, the wight performed rituals around the body before finally dispatching him using a sword, as a kind of bloody sacrifice.

A belief in haunted tombs and the cursed treasures of the dead is among the oldest of superstitions and also one of the most widespread. Truly bloodcurdling curses (meant as a deterrent to grave robbers) have been discovered written on the walls of Egyptian tombs. Other examples can be found in ancient cultures as different and mutually remote as China and Mexico. The Anglo-Saxons, too, had similar beliefs: after all, it is the disturbance of a barrow grave that leads directly to the death of Beowulf, the greatest hero in Anglo-Saxon literature. It was just Beowulf's bad luck that the guardian of this particular barrow happened to be a fire-breathing dragon.

BATS
See: VAMPIRES

BATTLES   Tolkien's tales of Middle-earth abound in battles—from skirmishes and frays to cataclysmic conflicts of end-of-days proportions—and many have parallels with historic real-world battles as well as with those found in mythology and literature. The Battle of Dagorlad is comparable, in the utter destruction it wreaks and its massive body count, to the Battle of the Somme that Tolkien witnessed in 1916 during World War I. The Battle of the Field of Celebrant (between the invading Balchoth and the Men of Gondor and the Éothéod) has similarities to the Battle of Catalaunian Fields in which the Romans and the Visigoth cavalry allied against the Huns of Attila in AD 451. The Great Battle in the War of Wrath at the end of the First Age was, as Tolkien acknowledged, primarily inspired by the Norse myth of the final battle-to-be, known as Ragnarök. The Battle of Pelennor Fields, in *The Lord of the Rings*, is certainly the most spectacular and richly observed of all Tolkien's battles and consequently has multiple parallels in, and allusions to, history, myth, and literature.

See also: CATALAUNIAN FIELDS; DAGORLAD; PELENNOR FIELDS

Battlefield. The carnage of the battlefield haunted Tolkien's imagination.

BELEGAER

The "Great Sea" that separates the mortal lands of Middle-earth from the immortal lands of Aman. This Western Sea was essentially inspired by the Atlantic Ocean, though as it was known or imagined in the mythology and legends of the ancient Greeks and Celts. The drowned island of Atlantis, the paradisical Fortunate Isles, inhabited by the Greek heroes after their deaths, and the Irish phantom-island of Hy-Brasil were all considered to lie somewhere in the Atlantic. All were inspirations for the islands of Númenor and Tol Eressëa.

BELERIAND

In the First Age, a region in the northwest of Middle-earth that was home to several Elven kingdoms and cities, including Doriath, Gondolin, and Nargothrond. Toward the end of the First Age, during the War of Wrath, Belariand is largely destroyed and lost beneath the waves.

In Tolkien's earliest drafts of *The Silmarillion*, his original name for Beleriand was Broceliand, obviously inspired by Brocéliande, the magical forest in Brittany, which features in many Arthurian tales. Tolkien's conception of Beleriand—and especially the forested region of Doriath—owes a great deal to Brocéliande, which was closely associated with enchantments and perilous quests.

As a drowned land, Beleriand has parallels with the Welsh Cantref y Gwaelod in Cardigan Bay or the Cornish Lyonesse in the waters about the Isles of Scilly, two of the many "lost and drowned kingdoms" that abound in the Celtic legends of Wales, Cornwall, and Brittany.

BEORN

Eponymous chieftain of the Beornings who can take the form of a bear. In human guise, he is a huge, black-bearded man garbed in a coarse wool tunic and armed with a woodsman's ax.

Beorn's appearance in latter half of the *The Hobbit* establishes the fact that we are now firmly in the heroic world of the Anglo-Saxons, for he appears to be something approaching a twin brother of the epic hero Beowulf. With his pride in his strength, his code of honor, his terrible wrath, and his hospitality, Beorn is Beowulf transposed and brought down in scale. Even his home seems a smaller version of Heorot, the mead hall of King Hrothgar in the Anglo-Saxon epic poem.

Indeed, Tolkien gives his character a name that, while it sounds and looks a little different from Beowulf's, ends up having much the same meaning, via one of the author's typically convoluted philological puns. Beorn's name means "man" in Old English. However, in its Norse form, it means "bear." Meanwhile, if we look at the Old English name Beowulf, we discover that it literally means "bee-wolf." What, we may wonder, is a bee-wolf? This is typical of the sort of riddle-names that the Anglo-Saxons liked to construct. "What wolf hunts bees—and steals their honey?" The answer is obvious enough: "bee-wolf" is a kenning for a bear: Beowulf and Beorn, then, both mean "bear." Beorn, moreover, is a keeper of bees and a lover of honey. One might say that Beowulf and Beorn are the same man with different names. Or, in their symbolic guise as bee-wolf and bear, they are the same animal in different skins.

Furthermore, Beorn is a "skin-changer," whose people are the likewise shape-shifting Beornings (the "man-bear" people)—Tolkien's fairy-tale version of the historic berserkers (from *bear-sark*, or "bear-shirt") of the Germanic and Norse peoples. When the berserkers went into battle, they performed rituals and acts of wild frenzy in an attempt to transform into the bears that they believed possessed them. Likewise, in the Battle of Five Armies, Beorn transforms from fierce warrior to enraged Were-bear, a miraculous event that turns the tide of this critical battle.

BEOWULF The most famous epic poem of the Anglo-Saxons, composed as early as the eighth century AD and surviving in manuscript form until the turn of the tenth and eleventh centuries. It was a touchstone for Tolkien's writing both as an academic scholar and as a creative author. Tolkien acknowledged that the circumstances of Bilbo's first encounter with the Dragon of Erebor were—at least subconsciously—inspired by a

Beorn. One of the many characters for which Tolkien took his inspiration from
Anglo-Saxon literature.

passage in *Beowulf*. In a letter to the English newspaper the *Observer* in 1938, Tolkien wrote: "*Beowulf* is among my most valued sources; though it was not consciously present to the mind in the process of writing, in which the episode of the theft arose naturally (and almost inevitably) from the circumstances." While the two tales are not overtly similar, there are strong plot parallels between the dragon episode in *Beowulf* and the slaying of Smaug in *The Hobbit*. Beowulf's dragon wakes when a thief finds his way into the creature's cave and steals a jeweled cup from the treasure hoard. This scenario is duplicated when Bilbo finds his way into Smaug the Dragon's cavern and steals a jeweled cup from the treasure hoard. Both thieves avoid immediate detection of their crime and the danger of the dragons themselves. However, nearby human settlements in the tales suffer terribly from the dragons' wrath. Beyond this specific narrative parallel in *The Hobbit*, the influence of *Beowulf* is evident throughout Tolkien's Middle-earth, in its landscapes, peoples, cultures, and languages, as well as in his use of language itself—the high epic tone of especially the last two books of *The Lord of the Rings* and Tolkien's love of richly alliterative language and kennings.

See also: BEORN; DRAGONS; GOLLUM; ROHIRRIM

BEOWULF: THE MONSTERS AND THE CRITICS
Tolkien's most important and influential analysis of Anglo-Saxon literature, published in 1936. It was the first work by an Anglo-Saxon scholar to look at *Beowulf*'s literary value rather than its historic or linguistic aspects. Tolkien focused on the strong storytelling found in the epic and foregrounded the roles of Grendel and the Dragon, in which "the evil spirits took visible shape." Even earlier than this study, between 1920 and 1926, Tolkien wrote his own rough translation of the epic, entitled *Beowulf: A Translation and Commentary together with a Sellic Spell*. This was posthumously edited by his son Christopher Tolkien, and published in 2017. Tolkien's emphasis on the narrative power of *Beowulf* undoubtedly influenced his own storytelling craft.

BEREN

BEREN One of the greatest heroes of the First Age of Middle-earth, and the character whose story (along with that of Beren's beloved, Lúthien) was most meaningful to Tolkien himself. So great was the author's identification with the hero that he had the names Lúthien and Beren included beneath his wife Edith's and his own on their shared gravestone in Wolvercote Cemetery in Oxford.

Beren Erchamion and Lúthien Tinúviel are the central protagonists in the Quest for the Silmaril, the story of a mortal man's quest for the hand of an immortal Elf-maid. As in many myths, legends, and fairy tales, the hero must prove his worthiness by achieving an impossible task, often set by the heroine's father, who believes that the hero will die in the attempt. Here it is King Thingol who sets Beren the task of retrieving a Silmaril, set into the crown of Morgoth, who dwells in the evil fortress of Angband. To Thingol's horror, Lúthien sets out on the quest alongside her beloved Beren.

As Tolkien freely acknowledged, the subsequent development of the tale was closely patterned on the Greek myth of Orpheus and Eurydice, only with the male and female roles reversed. In the myth, the musician Orpheus attempts to bring Eurydice back from the dead. Making his descent into the underworld, Orpheus plays his harp and sings to make the three-headed hound Cerberus, who guards the gates of hell, fall asleep. Brought before Hades, king of the underworld, Orpheus again plays and sings so beautifully that the god is moved to grant him the life of Eurydice, on condition that he does not look back at her as they make their way back into the land of the living. At the last moment, at the mouth of the tunnel, Orpheus cannot resist looking back at his beloved and she is taken from him and returned to Hades forever.

In Tolkien, it is Lúthien who, when the lovers reach the gates of the underworld-like fortress of Angband, lulls its unsleeping guardian, the gigantic wolf Carcharoth. It is she, too, who lulls Morgoth—the king of this underworld—to sleep (rather than moving him), enabling Beren to prise one of the Silmarils from Morgoth's crown. Like Orpheus and Eurydice, Tolkien's lovers fail at the last hurdle when Carcharoth wakes before the lovers can make their escape. At this point in the narrative, Tolkien departs from the Greek tale and introduces an allusion to the Norse legend of Fenrir, the Great Wolf of Midgard, who bites off the hand of the god Tyr when the gods bind him. Carcharoth, too, bites off Beren's hand and swallows both the hand and the Silmaril he is holding. It is from this episode that Beren gains the epithet Erchamion, meaning "One Handed."

To underscore the connection between the Greek myth and his tale, Tolkien duplicates the descent into the underworld motif by having Lúthien pursue Beren's soul after his death. This time, in the House of the Dead in the Undying Lands, Lúthien exactly repeats Orpheus' journey by singing to Mandos, the Doomsman of the Valar (a figure comparable to the Greek Hades), and winning from him a second life for her lover. Unlike Orpheus and Eurydice, however, Lúthien and Beren are allowed to live out their newly won mortal lives quietly. Thus, in the Quest for the Silmaril, Tolkien not only reversed the roles of Orpheus and Eurydice, but also overturned that story's tragic end. In so doing, for a time at least, Tolkien allowed love to conquer death.

BERSERKERS The frenzied bear-cult warriors found in Icelandic, Norse, and Germanic cultures whose name derives from *bear-sark*, meaning "bear-shirt." The berserkers inspired Tolkien's depiction of the Were-bear Beorn in *The Hobbit*.

In their "holy battle rage," the historical berserkers felt themselves to be possessed by the spirits of enraged bears. As Odin's holy warriors, wearing only bearskins, they sometimes charged into battle unarmed, but in such a rage that they tore the enemy limb from limb with their bare hands and teeth. Such states, however, were essentially in imitation of what was the core miracle of the bear cult: the incarnate transformation of man into bear. Once again, Tolkien uses a name to inspire his imagination. Beorn's name in Norse means "bear," and in *The Hobbit* we soon discover that Beorn is a "skin-changer" with the power of transformation from man to beast and beast to man. It is a supernatural power that eventually makes Beorn a critical factor in the outcome of the Battle of the Five Armies.

BIFROST (THE RAINBOW BRIDGE)

In Norse mythology the bridge that links Asgard, the immortal world of the gods, to Midgard, the mortal world of human. In the great final battle of Ragnarök, it is there that Surt, the fire giant of Muspelheim, takes up his sword of flame and duels with Freyr, the god of sun and rain. The battle seems to be the inspiration for the Battle on the Bridge of Khazad-dûm between Gandalf the Grey and the Balrog of Moria in *The Lord of the Rings*.

See also: BALROG OF MORIA

BILBO BAGGINS

The first and original Hobbit created by Tolkien, the comic antihero of the eponymous *The Hobbit* who goes off on a journey into a heroic world. It is a world where the commonplace collides with the heroic, where the corresponding values clash to entertaining effect. In Bilbo Baggins, we have a character with whose everyday sensibilities the reader may identify, while vicariously having an adventure in a heroic world.

As Tolkien often observed, "names often generate a story"; they also nearly always contributed and suggested something of the nature or character of the person, place, or thing named. (We look at the influence of the character's family name in the entry "Baggins.") Another aspect of Bilbo Baggins's character may be revealed by an analysis of his first name. The word "bilbo" entered into the English language in the late sixteenth century as the name for a short but deadly piercing sword of the kind once made in the northern Spanish port-city of Bilbao, from whence the name.

This is an excellent description of Bilbo's sword, the charmed Elf knife called Sting. Found in a Troll hoard, Bilbo's "Bilbo" can pierce through armor or animal hide that would break any other sword. In *The Hobbit*, however, it is our hero's sharp wit rather than his sharp sword that gives Bilbo the edge. In his bids to escape Orcs, Elves, Gollum, or the Dragon, Bilbo's well-honed wits allow him to solve riddles, trick villains, and generally get himself out of sticky situations.

When we put the two names together as Bilbo Baggins, we have two aspects of our hero's character and to some degree the character of Hobbits in general. On the face of it, the name Baggins suggests a harmless, well-to-do, contented character (though with criminal undertones!), while the name Bilbo suggests an individual who is sharp, intelligent, and even a little dangerous.

BLACK GATE

Morannon ("Black Gate" in Sindarin Elvish) is the great fortified iron gate in the stone rampart that bars the way into Mordor at the pass of Cirith Gorgor. There is a possible inspiration for the Morannon in the legendary Gates of Alexander, built by Alexander the Great in the Caucasus to keep out the barbarians of the north. However, the Morannon, which keeps out the civilized forces of Gondor and its allies, inverts this idea.

The Black Gate is the site of the terrible battle that closes the War of the Ring and sees the final overthrow of Sauron the Ring Lord and all his minions. In medieval German romance, this battle has a precedent in the famous battle between Dietrich von Bern and the forces of Janibas the Necromancer, who shares characteristics with both Sauron the Necromancer and the Witch-king of Angmar. Janibas appears in the form of a phantom Black Rider but commands massive armies of giants, evil men, monsters, and demons by the power of a sorcerer's black tablet. This is comparable to the power and fate of Sauron's One Ring in the Battle of the Black Gate. The ultimate contest comes when Janibas's forces are about to overwhelm those of Dietrich's at the gates to the mountain kingdom of Jeruspunt. In that moment the Black Tablet (like the One Ring) is destroyed and the mountains split and shatter and come thundering down in massive avalanches that bury the whole evil host of giants, demons, and undead phantoms forever.

BLACK NÚMENÓREANS

Descendants of the King's Men—supporters of Ar-Pharazôn, last king of the lost island-continent of Númenor—and sworn enemies of the Númenórean Men of Gondor and Arnor. After their settlement in the Númenórean colonies of Middle-earth, the Black Númenóreans—long corrupted by Sauron—continued to worship Morgoth and to flourish even after the downfall of Númenor. Their main center of power was the city, port, fortress, and empire of Umbar.

The portrayal of the Black Númenóreans of Umbar has clear similarities with the Punic inhabitants of the city, port, fortress, and empire of Carthage in North Africa. The Carthaginians had a rich, sophisticated culture, but

Black Númenórean

their image in posterity has been largely formed by accounts written by their main rivals for dominance in the western Mediterranean, the Romans, who eventually destroyed Carthage in 146 BC. For the Romans, the Carthaginians were the barbarian "other," whose practices —the worship of demonic gods and, most notoriously, the institution of child sacrifice—contrasted with and validated their own civilized values.

Similarly, in Tolkien's works we typically see the Black Númenóreans through the eyes of the civilized Gondorians: they are lawless, being little better than pirates; they are worshippers of the Lord of the Dark, Morgoth/Melkor (whose name recalls that of Moloch, who is often identified with the Carthaginian chief god Baal Hammon); and they practice human sacrifice to Morgoth using fire, just as the Carthaginians were said to have burned children alive as an offering to Baal.

BLACK RIDERS

Name given to the Nazgûl when Sauron sends them out on horseback to track down the Ring and its keeper, "Baggins." They are the first truly evil entities to appear in *The Lord of the Rings*, in the green and pleasant Hobbit land of the Shire. The identity of these cloaked and hooded horsemen is not immediately revealed, but eventually they are proved to be the Ringwraiths. It is only later, through the eyes of the Ring-bearer Frodo Baggins, that the reader is given a glance of the Nazgûl as they appear to the Necromancer and those who inhabit the wraith-world. After slipping the One Ring on his finger, the Hobbit is suddenly able to see in the phantom shapes of the Ringwraiths their terrible white faces, gray hair, long gray robes, and "helms of silver."

In some ways, the Black Riders are not unlike the phantom horsemen in the English poet John Keats's ballad "La Belle Dame Sans Merci" (1819): a ghostly host of men seduced and enslaved by the "beautiful lady without mercy" of the title, and described as "Pale kings and princes, too, / Pale warriors, death-pale were they all." The "palely loitering" kings and sorcerers who make up the Nazgûl have been similarly seduced, though not by the charms of a beautiful enchantress, but by Sauron and their overweening desire for power and a near-eternal life.

See also: HORSEMEN OF THE APOCALYPSE

BLACK SAILS

At a critical moment during the Battle of Pelennor Fields in the siege of Gondor, black sails appear upon the Anduin River. It is an episode that mirrors the climax of the ancient myth of the Greek hero Theseus. In the Greek tale, the hero is revealed as the heir to the throne of Athens. His father, King Atreus, welcomes him back despite prophecies of regicide and patricide. When Theseus discovers that Athens must pay an annual tribute to the Minoans of seven youths and seven maidens as sacrificial victims, he decides to end this bloody payment. Theseus sets out in a black-sailed tribute ship to Crete where, along with 13 other young Athenians, he is to be sacrificed to the monstrous Minotaur in the palace of King Minos. With the help of Ariadne, the Minoan princess, he is able to slay the Minotaur, save his companions, and flee Crete.

On leaving Athens, Theseus promised his father that if he slays the Minotaur and releases his people from bondage, he would change the sails to white for his return voyage as a signal of victory. In the rush of his triumph, however, Theseus forgets his promise. Tragically, his father, the old king, sees the tribute ship returning with its great black sail still set. Believing his son Theseus to be dead, and his nation still enslaved, the old king throws himself from the high lookout prow of the Acropolis onto the rocks far below.

In *The Lord of the Rings*, Denethor, the Ruling Steward of Gondor, sees a mighty fleet of the black-sailed ships of the Corsairs of Umbar sailing up the Anduin River at a critical moment in the Battle of the Pelennor Fields. Believing that his son Faramir is dying of a poison wound, and that all his forces upon the battlefield are being overwhelmed and slaughtered, the Steward assumes that the black-sailed ships, and the reinforcements they carry, would make the defense of Gondor impossible. Mad with despair, Denethor commits suicide. However, like Theseus' father, the Steward of Gondor is tragically mistaken.

In reality, Aragorn has been victorious: he has captured the black-sailed ships of the Corsairs, using them to transport fighting men from the coastal fiefs of Gondor and bring them to the Battle of the Pelennor Fields. It proves to be a decisive blow and turning point in the battle and the war. Just as Athens is freed from the threat of the tyrant Minos and Theseus succeeds his father as king, so Gondor is freed from the threat of the Witch-king, and Aragorn is restored as king.

Black Riders. The imagery of the Black Riders draws on popular representations of the figure of Death in Christian Europe.

BOROMIR   Son and heir of Denethor II, Ruling Steward of Gondor. As a member of the Fellowship of the Ring, he survives many perils until the party reaches the foot of Amon Hen near the Rauros Falls. There, his desire to seize the One Ring from Frodo Baggins overcomes him. Although Boromir immediately repents, his actions result in the breaking and scattering of the Fellowship. Boromir sets off to look for Merry and Pippin and finds them surrounded by Orcs. He rescues them, but soon after an even bigger party of Orcs ambushes them. He fights valiantly to save them, but dies overwhelmed by the arrows of his enemies.

Tolkien's account of Boromir's heroic death is redolent of *La Chanson de Roland*. This, the best known of the medieval chansons de geste (songs of heroic deeds), is about Charlemagne's most famous paladin, Roland, who makes his heroic last stand in the Roncevaux Pass in the Pyrenees while under attack from the Saracens. Ambushed and vastly outnumbered, Roland fights valiantly on until his sword breaks, and he is overwhelmed by the infidel hordes. As he dies, Roland blows his olifant (ivory hunting horn) to warn Charlemagne of the proximity of his foes. As Charlemagne hastens toward the pass, the Saracens flee, but the king is too late to save his liegeman.

Roland's last stand is comparable to that of Boromir, Gondor's greatest warrior, on the cliff pass above the Ramos Falls. Ambushed by a troop of Orcs and heavily armed Uruks, Boromir blows the Great Horn of Gondor. Aragorn, like Charlemagne, rushes to the site of the battle. The Dúnadan is too late to help Boromir, but is able to hear him utter a few last words of confession and to offer him hope and consolation. What marks out both scenes is a sense of ultimate victory despite the defeat of death.

"BRAVE LITTLE TAILOR, THE"

A German fairy tale collected by the Brothers Grimm, but found in many versions. The story tells of how a poor young man, alone and armed only with his wits, is able to overcome all obstacles and slay powerful but slow-witted giants or trolls. In *The Hobbit* the three Trolls encountered by Bilbo Baggins and Thorin and Company are very like the Grimm Brothers' trolls.

Although immensely stupid by human and hobbit standards, these Trolls—Bert, Tom, and William Huggins—are capable of understanding and speaking Westron (though they have very poor grammar!). This makes them geniuses among the Trolls of Middle-earth, and almost smart enough to put an end to the Hobbit's adventure. In the Grimm version of the tale, the Tailor hides from sight and throws a stone at each of the dim-witted trolls, who then accuse one another of the deed. This results in a fight that ends with the death of all the trolls. This scenario is largely repeated in *The Hobbit*. Here, however, it is the Wizard Gandalf who throws the stones that keep the Trolls quarreling until the Sun rises and they are turned to stone. As an aside, Tolkien as narrator adds: "Trolls, as you probably know, must be underground before dawn." Here he is alluding to a folk belief likely dating back long before the twelfth century when it was first recorded in the Icelandic poem "Alvíssmál" in the *Poetic Edda*. In *The Hobbit*, it is through this particular episode that Gandalf provides Bilbo Baggins with his first lesson in using his wits to outsmart larger and more powerful foes. As is typical in such fairy tales, the reward is a treasure hoard and the acquisition of weapons that prove essential in the adventures ahead. In this instance, there are three Elven blades: one lethal sword each for Gandalf and Thorin, and one dagger that serves well enough as a Hobbit's sword.

BRÍSINGAMEN   A jeweled necklace or torc in Norse legend whose theft results in an endless war between two kings. The name is sometimes translated as the "shining necklace" or "the necklace of the Brisings [dwarfs]." In *The Hobbit*, the Elven-king of the Woodland Realm alludes to the theft of the Nauglamír, or "Necklace of the Dwarves," that resulted in a 6,000-year feud between the Grey Elves of Doriath and the Dwarves of Belegost. Little more about the necklace's history was known until the publication of *The Silmarillion*. There the king of Doriath, Thingol, commissions the Dwarves to reforge the necklace (originally a gift from the Dwarves to Finrod Felagund but which has passed into the king's hands via Húrin) and set within it one of the three Silmarils. The Dwarves treacherously murder Thingol and take the necklace for themselves. This terrible deed eventually results in the destruction of all the Elf and Dwarf kingdoms of Beleriand in the First Age.

The Norse legend as retold in a fourteenth-century Christian version by Jon Thordson and Magnus Throhalson was similarly disastrous and far more scandalous. Freya, the goddess of love and war, offered to pay for the "priceless" Brísingamen by bedding each of its four dwarf owners: Alfrigg, Dvalin, Berling, and Grerr. Loki, the god of mischief, steals the necklace and eventually it comes into the possession of Freya's spouse, Odin, the bloodthirsty god of battles. The price of the necklace's return was for Freya to establish a constant state of war between two kings whose armies would battle from dawn until dusk, and then the next day those slain would rise up and slaughter one another again. Both Brísingamen and Nauglamir are imitative of the far more ancient and well-known legend of the Necklace of Harmonia in Greek mythology. This is the tale of a beautiful and magical jeweled necklace forged by the crippled Hephaestus, the smith of the gods, as an act of vengeance against his wife, Aphrodite, the goddess of love, for her adulterous affair with Ares, the god of war. The result of their affair was Harmonia who married Cadmus to become queen of Thebes. At the wedding feast Hephaestus gifted this jeweled necklace to the young queen. Like Tolkien's Nauglamir and Brísingamen, the Greek necklace magically enhanced the beauty of any who wore it, but also like those other necklaces, it carried a terrible curse. And just as Tolkien and the Norse necklaces brought death and disaster, so the cursed necklace foredoomed Harmonia, and visited tragedy upon the royal House of Thebes (and indeed upon their descendants), until its ultimate destruction in a murderous and all-consuming fire.

BROCÉLIANDE   A forest in Brittany that is the setting for a number of Celtic and Arthurian legends. In Tolkien's earliest drafts of *The Silmarillion*, the original name for the region of Beleriand—the setting of his tales of the First Age—is Brocéliand. Located in the northwest of Middle-earth and home to the Sindar (the Grey Elves), Beleriand is ruled for many ages by King Thingol and his queen, Melian the Maia. At the heart of Thingol's kingdom are the enchanted forests of Doriath and its citadel, Menegroth, the "Thousand Caves." While there are clear similarities between the two forest realms, there are important differences, too. The chief, perhaps, is that while Doriath is a place of safety, protected by the "Girdle of Melian," Brocéliande is somewhat less benign

in nature. The most famous story of Brocéliande is that of the enchantress Vivien, the Lady of the Lake, who comes upon the wizard Merlin asleep beneath a thorn tree. There the enchantress imprisons the magician in a "tower of air" from which he can never emerge. There is a superficial resemblance here with Thingol's first meeting with Melian in the woods of Nan Elmoth and her subsequent enchantment of his realm, but in Tolkien's tale the motive is love.

BROWNIES
Originally a dialect name for rural household spirits in Scotland and northern England that became a common term in the folklore of farmers and farm laborers throughout Britain by the nineteenth century. These sprites were a diminutive, hairy, elusive race, and mostly friendly toward humans.

There are many characteristics common to brownies and Hobbits: both are about three feet tall with curly brown hair and brownish skin and are dressed largely in brown and earthy colors that blend in to the landscape. Both races are usually shy and secretive, capable of vanishing quickly and quietly from sight. Both are usually benevolent and helpful to humans, although occasionally of a humorous and mischievous disposition. There even appear to be different breeds of both races that prefer different types of landscape.

However, Tolkien's Hobbits are more strongly linked in other ways to the later invaders of Britain, the Anglo-Saxons, and their descendants, the English. What Tolkien gives us in his tea-drinking, pipe-smoking, middle-class, home-and-garden-oriented Hobbits is a distinctively Victorian English transmutation of the rough and anything-but-middle-class Brownies. In 1865, Juliana Horatio Ewing, the popular children's author much admired by Rudyard Kipling and Edith Nesbit, published her novel *The Brownies*. It was a story about helpful sprites that inspired Lord Baden-Powell—creator of the Boy Scouts—to adopt the name for this youngest level (ages 7 to 10) of girls in the Girl Guide movement.

BRYNHILD
In the late thirteenth-century Icelandic *Völsunga Saga*, a Valkyrie (or battle maiden) who defies Odin and is subsequently pierced with a sleep-thorn and imprisoned in a ring of fire as punishment. She is awakened

by Sigurd the Dragon-slayer, with whom she falls in love. In the medieval German epic *Nibelungenlied*, she becomes Brunhild ("armored warrior maid"), the warrior-queen of Iceland, who falls for the Sigurd's medieval German equivalent, Siegfried. Brynhild/Brunhild is in some respects the model for Tolkien's heroic character Éowyn, the shield maiden of Rohan who, with the aid of the Hobbit Meriadoc Brandybuck, slays the Witch-king in the Battle of Pelennor Fields. However, in the stories told about her, Brynhild/Brunhild always retains something dark and elemental. Éowyn, by contrast, is shown as resolutely good. Just as there are elements of Brynhild/Brunhild to be found in Éowyn, so there are comparisons to be drawn between Sigurd/Siegfried and Aragorn. It is Brynhild/Brunhild's hopeless love for Sigurd/Siegfried that Tolkien draws on for Éowyn's own unrequited feelings for Aragorn. Siegfried is betrothed to another queen, Kriemheld, in the same way that Aragorn is betrothed to Arwen Evenstar. And just as the warrior queen Brunhild puts her martial life behind her as the wife of King Gunnar, so too is Éowyn, the shield maiden, pacified through her marriage to Faramir, the Steward of Gondor.

BURGLARS

In the everyday world, society shuns burglars, but in the world of fairy tale, the burglar is a hero whose skill, wit, and bravery are celebrated and whose deeds result in the enrichment of himself, his family, and/or people. This is typical of many fairy-tale plots, such as "Jack and the Beanstalk," and of many myths where the hero travels to another realm and steals treasure, magical weapons, or even the secret of making fire. Bilbo the Burglar is more or less how Gandalf introduces Bilbo Baggins to the Dwarves of Thorin and Company at the beginning of Quest of Lonely Mountain. On the surface, this seemed an unlikely role, but there is always something different and contrary in Bilbo's nature. He is a typical Hobbit full of practical common sense, but is also sharp-witted and very un-Hobbitish in his curiosity about the wider world. He has been chosen, Tolkien explains, as the "lucky number fourteen" to avoid the unlucky number of the thirteen adventurers who make up Thorin and Company. Nevertheless, most obviously, Bilbo has been chosen for the job of master burglar for his stealth, as Hobbits possess a natural ability to move quietly and unnoticed by larger folk.

As usual, too, there is some wordplay behind the choice. Bilbo Baggins is a burgher who becomes a burglar. Tom Shipley in his *Road to Middle-earth* (1982) explores this idea in the chapter "The Bourgeois Burglar." A burgher, he observes, was a freeman of a burgh or borough (or, in this case, a burrow), which certainly applies to Bilbo Baggins. Even more, its derivative, bourgeois, describes a person with humdrum middle-class ideas. The Germanic root word *Burg* means "mound, fort, stockaded house." A burger is one who owns a house. A burglar is one who plunders a house. So, we have the everyday humdrum middle-class burgher entering a fairy-tale world and being transformed into his opposite—a burglar!

BYZANTINE EMPIRE Name given to the Eastern Roman Empire, which had its capital at Constantinople. Founded on the site of the Greek colony of Byzantium by Emperor Constantine I as the "New Rome" in AD 330, it survived the sacking of Rome in AD 476 and the collapse of the Western Roman Empire by almost a thousand years. In some respects, its history is comparable to the fictional history of Middle-earth's South-kingdom of Gondor with its capital first at Osgiliath and later Minas Anor (Minas Tirith). Gondor survived the destruction of the last remnant of the North-kingdom, Arthedain, in 1974 TA by a thousand years (at the time of the War of the Ring). On the other hand, while Gondor certainly has its own dark periods—notably the Kin-strife— the Byzantine Empire is notorious for its bloody and convoluted history of brutal palace murders, revolts, and all-out civil war.

C

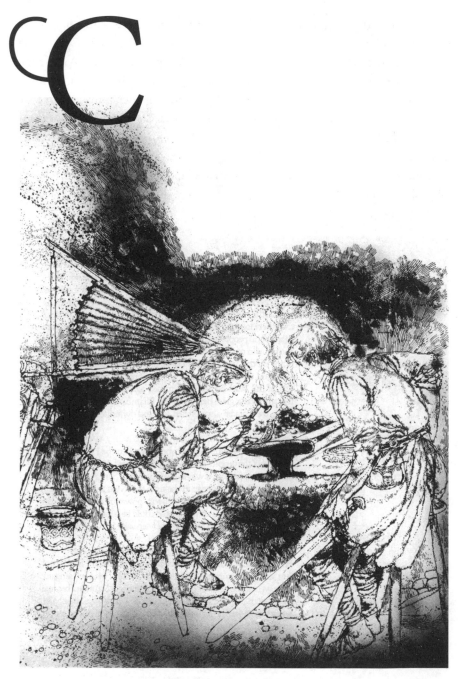

Celebrimbor Forges the Three Rings for Elves

CAMLANN The site of the last battle of the Arthurian age according to Welsh tradition as recorded by the twelfth-century cleric Geoffrey of Monmouth in his pseudo-historical *Historia regum Britanniae* (*History of the Kings of Britain*; c. 1136). Such end-of-times battles fulfill a requirement common to epic poetry and romance whereby a golden age of heroes and heroines ends in cataclysm. In many respects, Camlann provided the template for the end of Tolkien's Second Age in the last battle of the Last Alliance of Elves and Men where Gil-galad, the High King of the Noldor, takes part in a mutually fatal duel with Sauron, the Dark Lord of Mordor. This final alliance of warrior Elves and Men cannot fail to remind us of the alliance of the Knights of the Round Table in the Battle of Camlann, where a similar fatal duel is fought between Arthur, the high king of the Britons, and Mordred, the lord of an evil alliance of barbarian Picts, Scots, and Saxons.

CARCHAROTH ("RED MAW") The greatest Wolf to appear in Middle-earth. Sired by Draugluin, the Father of Werewolves, and reared on living flesh by the hand of Morgoth, Carcharoth is the unsleeping guardian at the gates of the subterranean kingdom of Angband. Carcharoth is comparable to guardians of the gates in other mythological underworlds, such as the Norse Garm, the gigantic hound guardian of Helheim, and the Greek Cerberus, the monstrous three-headed hound that was the unsleeping guardian at the gates of Hades.

As Tolkien acknowledged, he patterned his Quest for the Silmaril on the Greek myth of Orpheus and Eurydice, only with the roles of the lovers reversed. In Tolkien's quest, it is the Elf-maid Lúthien who enchants Carcharoth in order to enter Angband's underworld, while in the Greek tale it is the male musician Orpheus who enchants Cerberus in order to enter Hades. However, like the lovers Orpheus and Eurydice, Beren and Lúthien fail at the last hurdle to escape the underworld unscathed.

By the power of Lúthien's enchantment, the lovers seize the Silmaril, but tragically Carcharoth wakes before the lovers can make their escape. Then, as in the Norse legend of Fenrir, the Father of Wolves that bites off the hand

Carcharoth. Guardian of Angband.

of the god Tyr, Carcharoth bites off Beren's hand and swallows both the hand and the Silmaril in its grip. Only after a great hunt does Carcharoth finally meet his fate in the jaws of Huan, the Wolf Hound of the Valar, and the Silmaril is recovered.

CARTHAGE   An ancient city on the coast of North Africa, close to present-day Tunis, and capital of the mighty Punic Empire. From the third century BC, it was Rome's great rival in the contest over control of the Mediterranean. Carthage's mighty war fleets were the terror of the seas, and its powerful allies and mercenary armies—supported by war-elephants— were a terror over all the coastal lands. This is exactly comparable to Gondor's great rival, Umbar, in Near Harad, in a contest over control of the vast Bay of Belfalas. Just as Umbar was originally a colony of the mighty sea power of Númenor for a thousand years, so Carthage was believed to be a colony of the mighty sea power of Phoenicia for a thousand years. In the wake of the destruction of the island nation of Númenor, Umbar became an independent and powerful maritime rival to Gondor. This has a parallel in the rise of Carthage as an independent and powerful maritime rival to Rome in the wake of the destruction of the Phoenician island city-state of Tyre. In the Third Age, after centuries of rivalry, the Ship Kings of Gondor engaged in the century-long wars (933–1050 TA) on sea and land that resulted in the eventual conquest and subjugation of Umbar and its Southron Empire. Historically, this is similar to the Rome's century-long Punic Wars (256–146 BC) on sea and land, which resulted in the eventual conquest and subjugation of Carthage and its North African Empire. The Black Númenórean rulers of Umbar were slain or scattered, and the city and port served as Gondor's southern fortress controlling its vast Haradrim territories. It was a fate comparable to that suffered by the Carthaginians who were slain or sold into slavery, and by Carthage, which subsequently served as Rome's southern fortress controlling its vast North African territories. Tolkien's chronologies inform us that, after five centuries, Umbar slipped from Gondor's grasp. In 1448 TA Gondor rebelled and lords among the Haradrim captured Umbar. These new lords became known as the Corsairs of Umbar and their mighty pirate fleets once again became a terror of the seas that harassed and attacked Gondor and its allies. Similarly, we learn that after seven centuries, Carthage slipped from Rome's grasp. In AD 439, the Vandals (who had been former allies of Rome) rebelled and captured Carthage. With the native Berbers, they ruled North Africa and the Mediterranean, and with their mighty pirate fleets became a terror of the seas that harassed and attacked Rome and its allies.

The Corsairs' fleets were ultimately destroyed by Aragorn II (the future King Elessar of Gondor) in his quest to win control of the seas and reunite the North and South Kingdoms of Gondor and Arnor. Suffering a similar fate, the historic Vandal fleets of Carthage were ultimately destroyed by the Eastern Roman emperor, Justinian the Great (ruled AD 527–65), in his quest to win control of the seas and reunite the Eastern and Western Empires of Rome.

CASTOR AND POLYDEUCES In Greek
mythology, twin half-brothers and sons of the mortal woman Leda. Known as the Dioscuri ("Divine Twins"), Castor was the mortal son of Tyndareus, king of Sparta, while Polydeuces (or Pollux to the Romans) was the immortal son of Zeus, king of the gods. When Castor was slain in battle, Polydeuces suffered such terrible grief that Zeus took pity on him and transformed and

reunited the brothers as the stellar constellation Gemini, the Heavenly Twins. In Tolkien's world, Castor and Polydeuces have their counterparts in the twin brothers Elros and Elrond, though both are the sons of a mortal man, Eärendil the Mariner, and an immortal Elven maid, Elwing the White. Because of their mixed blood, each is allowed to choose their race and fate: the mortal world of Men or the immortal world of Elves. Elrond chooses to be immortal and eventually becomes the Elf Lord of Imladris on Middle-earth, while his brother, Elros, chooses to be mortal (although he is granted a lifespan of five centuries) and becomes the founding king of the Númenóreans. While Tolkien's twins are not reunited and placed among the stars, there is a star connection in the figure of the twin's father, Eärendil the Mariner. In *The Silmarillion*, we learn that Eärendil binds the shining Silmaril to his brow and forever rides his flying ship *Vigilot* through the firmament, where in the form of the Morning Star (the brightest "star"—the planet Venus) he guides all sailors and travelers.

See also: PEREDHIL

CATALAUNIAN FIELDS The site in present-day northeastern France of the one of the most critical battles in the history of Europe. In the Battle of the Catalaunian Fields in AD 451, the Roman army formed an alliance with the Visigoths and Lombard cavalry to defeat the barbarian horde of Attila the Hun (reigned AD 434–53). This victory was credited with turning back what was considered to be an unstoppable wave of Asiatic conquest of Europe. This historic battle is comparable to Tolkien's critical Battle of the Field of Celebrant in 2050 TA when Gondor's army engaged in battle with an invading Easterling barbarian horde known as the Balchoth. Only the unexpected appearance of the Éothéod cavalry (forebears of the Horsemen of Rohan) turned the tide of battle in the Gondorians' favor. In the wake of the Battle of the Field of Celebrant, the Easterling and Balchoth confederacies rapidly disintegrated, much as the Hunnish confederacies did after the Battle of the Catalaunian Fields. The Huns' defeat at the Catalaunian Fields, combined with the sudden and unexpected death of Attila, resulted in a chaotic dispute over succession that brought about the collapse and dissolution of the Hunnic Empire. The sixth-

century AD historian Jordanes, in his *Roma*—one of Tolkien's primary sources on Rome and the Goths—describes how the allies of the Hunnic Confederacy self-destructed at the Battle of Nedao in AD 454: "And so the bravest nations tore themselves to pieces. For then, I think, must have occurred a most remarkable spectacle, where one might see the Goths fighting with pikes, the Gepidae raging with the sword, the Rugi breaking off the spears in their own wounds, the Suavi fighting on foot, the Huns with bows, the Alani drawing up a battle-line of heavy-armed and the Heruli of light-armed warriors." It is easy to see how such vivid historic records might have inspired Tolkien in his own accounts of Easterling wars.

CELEBRIMBOR ("SILVER-FIST") A Noldor
prince, the son of Curufin and grandson of Fëanor, the creator of the Silmarils. In the Second Age he becomes the Lord of the Gwaith-i-Mírdain, the Elven-smiths of Eregion, who under the influence of Annatar (Sauron the Ring Lord in disguise) forge the Rings of Power. Celebrimbor mistrusts Annatar and creates the Three Rings of the Elves, which remain uncorrupted by Sauron's influence. The history and fate of Elves and Men in the Second and Third Ages are in large part determined by the struggle over the possession of the Rings of Power forged in Eregion and—above all—of the One Ring that is secretly forged by Sauron in the fires of Mount Doom. The Rings of Power and especially the One Ring are comparable to the ring of the Norse god Odin, known as Draupnir, meaning "the dripper." This was a golden ring that had the power to drip eight other rings of equal size every nine days. Its possession by Odin was emblematic of his dominion over the Nine Worlds. This scenario seems to be fairly suggestive of Celebrimbor's "Nine Rings of Mortal Men" that Sauron used to buy the allegiance of the Men of Middle-earth and ultimately entrap their souls. Sauron was less successful with the Seven Rings of the Dwarves, and failed altogether to gain influence over the Three Rings of the Elves. However, the rings resulted in the disastrous War of the Elves and Sauron (1693–1701 SA) that ended with the slaying of Celebrimbor and the destruction of Eregion.

CELTIC MYTHOLOGY One of the most important

sources of inspiration in Tolkien's creation of his Elves of Middle-earth and the Undying Lands. In general terms, it is quite easy to see how Tolkien largely aligned the traditions of the older Celtic peoples of the British Isles with his Elves, while the invading Romans, Anglo-Saxons, and Norse have the characteristics of his Men. The two most storied kindreds in Tolkien's legendarium—the Sindar (Grey Elves) and the Noldor (Deep Elves)—are inspired by the mythologies of Wales and Ireland, respectively.

When we learn that the most important source of Welsh Celtic lore was preserved in the fourteenth-century *Red Book of Hergest*, we realize that Tolkien was making a small scholarly joke when he named his own source of Elf-lore the *Red Book of Westmarch*. The *Red Book of Hergest* is a manuscript that includes the most important compendium of Welsh legends, *The Mabinogion* (compiled in the twelfth to thirteenth centuries). That collection contains many stories of magic rings. In *Owain, or the Lady of the Fountain*, the Lady of the Fountain gives a ring of invisibility to the hero Owain; in *Geraint and Enid*, Dame Lyonesse gives the hero Gareth a magic ring that will not allow him to be wounded, and in *Peredur, Son of Efrawg*, Peredur goes on a quest for a gold ring during which he slays the Black Serpent of the Barrows and wins a stone of invisibility and a gold-making stone.

It is important to understand that, before Tolkien, the term "elf" was very loose, most often associated with pixies, flower-fairies, gnomes, dwarfs, and goblins and considered to be of diminutive and inconsequential nature. Tolkien's Elves are not a race of pixies. They are a powerful, full-blooded people who closely resemble the pre-human Irish race of immortals called the Tuatha Dé Danann. Like the Tuatha Dé Danann, Tolkien's Elves are taller and stronger than mortals, are incapable of suffering sickness, are possessed of more than human beauty, and are filled with greater wisdom in all things. They possess talismans, jewels, and weapons that humans might consider magical in their powers. They ride supernatural horses and understand the languages of animals. They love song, poetry, and music, all of which they compose and perform perfectly.

See also: ARAWN; DAGDA, THE; OLWYN; TUATHA DÉ DANANN; WHITE LADIES

CERBERUS The monstrous three-headed hound of hell in Greek mythology, the (usually) unsleeping guardian at the gates of the underground realm of Hades, god of the dead. In Middle-earth, Tolkien provides a comparable monster in Carcharoth, meaning "red maw," a (usually) unsleeping guardian wolf at the gates of the Angband, the underworld realm of Morgoth the Dark Enemy. Considered the greatest of his race, Carcharoth is comparable to other hellhounds found in mythology, such as the Norse Garm.

CERES The Roman goddess of agriculture. It is from her association with grain crops that we derive the word "cereal." In ancient times, the Roman cult of the goddess was associated with that of Demeter, the Greek goddess of the harvest. In the Norse pantheon she is comparable with Sif of the Golden Hair, another harvest goddess. In Tolkien's world she is closest to Yavanna Kementári, who is the conceiver and guardian of all things that grow, including the grains of the harvest. The Vala's name Yavanna means "giver of fruits," and her epithet Kementari literally translates as "queen of the Earth." In mythology Ceres/Demeter is known as the mother of Proserpine/Persephone, a goddess associated with the spring and flowers. Yavanna, meanwhile, has a younger sister named Vána the Ever-Young, at whose passing flowers blossom about her feet.

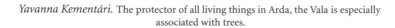

Yavanna Kementári. The protector of all living things in Arda, the Vala is especially associated with trees.

CHARLEMAGNE (AD 742–814) The warrior
king of the Franks who became the first Holy Roman Emperor (reigned
AD 800–814). Tolkien often pointed out the parallel between his hero Aragorn
and the historic Charlemagne and their tasks of reconstructing lost or ruined
empires (the Reunited Kingdom of the Dúnedain and the Roman Empire,
respectively). Both Aragorn and Charlemagne fought many battles that resulted
in the expulsion of invaders and the formation of military and civil alliances
that brought about eras of peace and prosperity. Once their foes were defeated,
both Aragorn and Charlemagne quickly reestablished the ancient common laws,
rebuilt the ancient roads, and reestablished trade routes and postal systems. Both
inspired a golden age of culture, art, and literature.

Geographically, Tolkien saw in the Reunited Kingdom an expanse of lands
akin to the expanse of Charlemagne's Empire and roughly equivalent to the
European landmass. Indeed, in a letter Tolkien remarked: "The progress of the
tale ends in what is . . . like the reestablishment of an effective Holy Roman
Empire with its seat in Rome." Charlemagne was crowned the first Holy Roman
Emperor while Aragorn, under the name Elessar Telcondar, is crowned high king
of the Reunited Kingdom of Arnor and Gondor.

Furthermore, both Charlemagne and Aragorn were credited with a
charismatic power to heal and command. It is noteworthy that Aragorn is able
to add authenticity to his claim as the true heir to the Dúnedain Kingdom by
virtue of the "healing hands," and is marked apart by his Elvish knowledge of the
healing properties of plants and herbs. After the Siege of Gondor, Aragorn uses
the herb *athelas* to bring Éowyn, shield maiden of Rohan, and others back from
the deathlike trance induced by the poisonous Black Breath of the Witch-king.
In Carolingian legends, Charlemagne was reputed to have been able to cure those
struck down by the plague, the "Black Death," by using the plant known as sow
thistle. In both cases, these plants worked their magical cures only if administered
by the healing hands of the king. This is acknowledged in the folklore of Middle-
earth, where the common name for *athelas* is "kingsfoil."
See also: ATHELAS

CHEDDAR GORGE
A limestone gorge in the Mendip Hills in Somerset, southwestern England, famous for its intricate, spectacular caves. Tolkien acknowledged that the gorge and cave complex was the real-world inspiration for Helm's Deep in Rohan, together with the Glittering Caves of Aglarond where Gimli founds a new Dwarf colony after the end of the War of the Ring.

See also: AGLAROND; HELM'S DEEP

CLOTHO
In Greek mythology, one of the Morae, or Fates (the others being Lachesis and Atropos). To the Romans, Clotho was Nona the Spinner and one of the Parcae (the others being Decima and Morta), while to the Norsemen she was Urd, one of the Norns (the others being Verdandi and Skuld). All three sisters were conceived as the weavers of human destiny or fate. In Tolkien's world, Clotho has a counterpart in the Valarian, Vairë the Weaver, who dwells in the Halls of Mandos and weaves the unfolding story of the world into the tapestries that hang upon its walls.

COOPER, JAMES FENIMORE (1789–1851)
American writer of historical romances. Like many middle-class children who grew up in the Victorian and Edwardian age, Tolkien read Cooper's novels with enthusiasm—stories about "Red Indians" were a childhood passion, he admitted. The inspiration of such novels as *The Last of the Mohicans* (1826) and *The Pathfinder* (1840), portraying adventurous journeys through the wilderness of America, have left their trace on Tolkien's descriptions of the journeys of *The Fellowship of the Ring* through the wildernesses of Middle-earth, on foot and by boat. Cooper's "romantic" hero in the *Leatherstocking Tales*, the scout Nathaniel Bumppo, has some similarities with the Aragorn in his role as a Ranger of the North.

The Corsairs of Umbar. Pirates of the southern port-city of Umbar whose kings fell under the
evil power of Sauron and made constant war on Gondor. Corsair ships had both oars and distinctive
black sails.

CORSAIRS OF UMBAR, THE

People of the port-city of Umbar, originally of Númenórean but increasingly of Haradrim blood, who use their naval power to ravage the coasts of Gondor through much of the Third Age right up until the time of the War of the Ring. The Corsairs (a term used to describe pirates and privateers in European history) are comparable with the ancient Carthaginians who were famous for their innovative seafaring skills and who used their domination of the Mediterranean to harry the Roman Empire.

CRACK OF DOOM

A phrase or expression that long before Tolkien's time had become something of a cliché. It first appears in literature in William Shakespeare's tragedy *Macbeth* (1606), in the scene (Act IV, scene i) where Macbeth is shown prophetic visions of the murdered Banquo's royal descendants by the witches: "What, will the line stretch out to th' crack of doom?" The word "doom" itself comes from the Old English *dom* meaning "judgment," and in origin the crack of doom is a biblical allusion to the sound that heralds the Last Judgment when God will weigh up the fates of all souls.

Tolkien took some delight in rehabilitating worn-out words and phrases, giving them new life, and reawakening the power innate within them. Consequently, Tolkien makes the "Cracks of Doom" into an actual place within Mount Doom, the massive volcanic mountain in Mordor that serves as Sauron the Ring Lord's smithy in the forging of the One Ring of Power. And, ultimately, it proves to be the place of final reckoning in the story of Middle-earth.

See also: *MACBETH*

Crows. The Men of Middle-earth call them birds of ill-omen, believing them to be allied with dark powers.

ÞD

Durin the Deathless

DAGDA, THE

In Irish mythology, the great king of the Tuatha Dé Danann, a race of immortals who crossed a western sea and settled in Ireland. The history of this people closely resembles that of the Noldor (Deep Elves), a race of immortals who cross the Western Sea (though in the contrary direction!) and settle in Middle-earth.

The Dagda's personal history is also comparable to that of Fingolfin, the High King of the Noldor. In Ireland, the Dagda led his people to victory in the Second Battle of Magh Tuireadh against an army of Fomorians, a monstrous race of underworld demons. In Beleriand, Fingolfin leads his people to victory in the Dagor Aglare—the Glorious Battle—against an army of underworld demons known as Orcs, Trolls, and Balrogs. The Dagda's victory over the Fomorian legions gave the Tuatha Dé Danann an age of relative peace during which the king's sons and those of his chieftains established fiefdoms over much of Ireland. In like manner, Fingolfin's victory over Morgoth's legions gives the Noldor nearly four centuries of relative peace. During that time Fingolfin's sons and those of his brothers, Fëanor and Finarfin, establish a dozen Noldor fiefdoms in northern Beleriand as a bulwark against their foes.

DAGOR DAGORATH

See: RAGNARÖK

DAGORLAD ("BATTLE PLAIN")

The site, on the vast open plain in southeastern Rhovanion, near Mordor, of the greatest battle of Tolkien's Second Age wherein "All living things were divided in that day, and some of every kind, even of beasts and birds." Tolkien's Battle of Dagorlad (3434 SA) is the single greatest battle in the War of the Last Alliance, fought between the forces of Gil-galad and Elendil on the one hand and the Orc army of Sauron on the other. Perhaps more than any other battle in the history of Middle-earth the Battle of Dagorlad was informed by the author's own experience in the First World War and, specifically, as a soldier in the disastrous, semi-suicidal Battle of the Somme (July 1 to November 18, 1916).

In that terrible conflict, Tolkien witnessed the near-total obliteration of the French landscape whose fields and woods were transformed into a blood-soaked wasteland littered with rotting corpses. It was a futile battle in which the armies fought for months, resulting in over a million casualties. There are powerful reminiscences of this in Tolkien's Battle of Dagorlad, which sees the greatest assemblage of combatants since the War of Wrath in the First Age, and which results in over a million casualties. The area, through which Frodo and Samwise pass in *The Lord of the Rings*, subsequently becomes a contaminated bogland where, even many centuries later, the faces of the slain can still be seen in the vile waters.

DARK ELVES
The Norse myths tell of the realms of the light elves and dark elves—Alfheim ("elf-home") and Swartalfheim ("dark elf-home")—although surviving Norse literature does not provide an explanation for this division. There is a similar division in Tolkien, between the Dark-Elves (Moriquendi) and the Light-Elves (Caliquendi). The writer, however, provided a (relatively) clear explanation for the categorization. The Caliquendi were those who were in favor of accepting the offer of the Valar to migrate to Valinor and the Moriquendi those who refused to embark on the Great Migration. Those who actually completed the journey were the Light-Elves, or Eldar; those who remained were the Dark-Elves, or Avari—meaning the "Unwilling." The Dark-Elves were considered to be far lesser beings than the Light-Elves, and even sinister, in that they seemed prepared to tolerate the evil works of Morgoth.

DÉAGOL
The Stoorish Hobbit who first discovers the lost One Ring of Sauron in the shallows of the Anduin River. Corrupted by his own desire to possess the Ring, Déagol's cousin Sméagol murders him and becomes the cursed and exiled ghoul known as Gollum. This scenario recalls the biblical story of Cain and Abel (Genesis 4:11–16), where the

firstborn of Adam and Eve murders his brother (seemingly out of jealousy) and is condemned to a life of exile and wandering.

Déagol's name literally means "secret." This is doubly appropriate as the cursed Sméagol (meaning "burrowing and worming in") always insists on his legitimate ownership of the Ring, and his darkest secret is that he acquired it only by murdering his kinsman Déagol. Guilt and fear that someone might discover his secret and take the Ring away from him so terrifies the miserable Sméagol that he hides himself away by "burrowing and worming in" beneath the roots of the Misty Mountains.

DELPHI   In ancient Greece, one of the most important sanctuaries of the god Apollo, situated on the slopes of Mount Parnassus. Its oracle was famous throughout the ancient classical world, consulted by kings and lords well into late antiquity. The name Delphi seems to come from the same root as the Greek word *delphys*, meaning "womb" or "cleft" in Greek. Beneath the Sanctuary of Apollo was a cleft or fissure in the sacred mountain from which rose vapors that induced a prophetic trance in Apollo's priestess and oracle, the Pythia.

In some respects, Middle-earth's Rivendell is comparable with Delphi, which shares its mountainous location as well as its associations with wisdom. There may even be references to Delphi's name. Rivendell's Westron name, Karningul, meaning "cleft valley," is repeated in its Sindarin name Imladris, which means "deep cleft dale" because it is in a hidden rock cleft at the foot of a pass to the Misty Mountains. This is an Elvish allusion to Calacirya ("cleft of light"), a mountain pass in Aman through which the Light of the Trees of Valinor lit Eldamar. Light, we should remember, was closely associated with Apollo.

Both Imladris and Delphi were "sanctuaries" that were consulted before any great adventure or campaign of war. Rivendell not only houses a vast library of Elvish lore, but is the home of the immortal Elrond Half-elven, who is something of an oracle as a living witness to some six thousand years of history. There is a more explicit analogy, too. In *The Lord of the Rings* the Ringwraiths attempt an attack on Rivendell, but are repelled when the Bruinen River rises in a mighty flood that sweeps the demonic horsemen away. This is comparable to a historical attack made on the sacred sanctuary of Delphi during the Persian Wars

(499–449 BC). Just as the Ford of Bruinen is protected by the power of Elrond's Ring, Delphi was thought to be under the protection of Apollo.

As recorded by the Herodotus in Book 8 of *The Histories*, the Persian King Xerxes, upon invading Greece in 480 BC, sent a division of his army to march on the unfortified sanctuary of Delphi. As they drew near, however, "thunderbolts fell on them from the sky, and two pinnacles of rock torn from Parnassus, came crashing and rumbling down among them, killing a large number" and causing the Persians to flee. This attempted violation of the sacred sanctuary of Delphi was followed by a series of astonishing defeats in battle, and an end to war for Xerxes that was nearly as disastrous as the end of the War of the Ring is for Sauron.

DEMETER
The Greek goddess of the harvest who has her counterpart in Tolkien's Yavanna Kementári, queen of the Earth, who planted the first seeds of "all things that grow" on Arda.
See also: CERES; YAVANNA

DEMONS
In numerous myths and tales from around the world demons have much in common with Tolkien's Orcs as hideous, vicious underlings programmed to do the bidding of evil masters. The numerous demons mentioned in the Old Testament, like the Orcs, preferred to live in isolated, unclean places such as deserts and ruins and were greatly feared, especially at night. Like Orcs, demons were prone to acts of violence, mayhem, rage, gluttony, and greed. However, biblical demons are unlike Orcs in that they were most often invisible and were considered the unseen cause of physical ailments, plagues, and mental illnesses.
See also: BALROGS OF ANGBAND; DAGDA, THE; FURIES

Orcs. The evil underling race and soldiers of Morgoth and Sauron. They are a stunted,
black-skinned, yellow-fanged, and crimson-eyed race of cannibal warriors whose only skills
lie in murder and war.

DIANA
In Roman mythology, a goddess associated with wild animals and woodlands. Groves, meadows, and deer were especially sacred to this goddess, whose personality and worship later became closely aligned with that of the Greek goddess Artemis. In Tolkien's legendarium, Diana/Artemis most closely resembles the Vala Nessa the Swift, who was also associated with deer and dancing, though there are important differences.

See also: ARTEMIS; NESSA

DIETRICH VON BERN
One of the greatest heroes of medieval German romance. The legends concerning him were loosely based on a real historical figure, Theodoric the Great (AD 454–526), king of the Ostrogoths and later the conqueror and king of Italy. In the fictional cycle of tales featuring Dietrich, his rise to power is not unlike that of Tolkien's Aragorn. Indeed, the tale of the hero's war with Janibas the Necromancer has striking parallels with Aragorn's war with Sauron the Ring Lord and his servants the Ringwraiths. Dietrich's foe, Janibas, shares traits with both Sauron and the Witch-king, leader of the Ringwraiths: he is depicted as a powerful wizard who reveals himself in the form of a phantom black rider on a phantom steed and commands massive armies of giants, evil men, monsters, demons, and hellhounds in a mountainous stronghold in the Alps. Janibas, moreover, commands his forces by means of a magical Iron Tablet, which has comparable powers to those of the One Ring. The eventual destruction of the Iron Tablet causes the glaciers of the mountain passes to split and shatter and come thundering down in massive avalanches that bury Janibas's entire evil host forever. The sorcerer's cataclysmic end is reminiscent of the fate of Sauron the Ring Lord and his legions at the Black Gate in the wake of the destruction of the One Ring in the fires of Mount Doom.

DIOSCURI, THE
See: CASTOR AND POLYDEUCES

DORIATH A forest realm in Beleriand, which becomes known as the "Hidden Realm" after the Maia Melian, wife of King Thingol, casts a girdle of enchantment about it to protect the Sindar (Grey Elves) from the ravages of the War of the Jewels. Doriath means "Fenced Land," in reference to the "Girdle of Melian," a spell that prevents all from entering save those given leave by Thingol.

In Tolkien's earliest drafts of *The Silmarillion*, his original name for Beleriand was Broceliand, a name clearly derived from the legendary forest of Brocéliande in Brittany that often features in medieval Arthurian romances. Tolkien's Beleriand—and most specifically the enchanted forest of Doriath—was to a considerable degree modeled on Brocéliande: a vast forest with magical fountains, glittering grottoes, and hidden palaces, and the haunt of powerful enchantresses such as Vivien or Nimue, the Lady of the Lake, and King Arthur's sister, Morgan le Faye.

The enchantments of Brocéliande, however, were somewhat less benign in nature than those of Doriath. Brocéliande was a place of temptations and entrapment for many of Arthur's knights and, most famously, even for the great wizard Merlin, who is ensnared and imprisoned there by Vivien. By contrast, the enchantments of Doriath are entirely defensive in nature and succeed in keeping the Grey Elves of the "Hidden Kingdom" safe. In Doriath and Menegroth, its city, there is peace and the Sindar prosper while much of Beleriand suffers destruction.

Ultimately, Doriath does not survive into the Second Age. Menegroth is sacked and King Thingol is treacherously murdered by the Dwarves of Belegost over a dispute about the possession of a Silmaril. Melian abandons the kingdom, and, without the protection of her enchantment, Doriath is no longer protected against invasion by Orcs, Balrogs, and Dragons. Total ruin ultimately comes in the wake of the War of Wrath when almost all of Beleriand is broken apart and swallowed up by the Western Sea. Like the Welsh Cantref y Gwaelod in Cardigan Bay or the Cornish Lyonesse near the Isles of Scilly, Doriath and Beleriand may be numbered among those "lost and drowned kingdoms" that abound in the legends of the Celtic fringes of the British Isles.

DRAGONS Winged, lizardlike, and often fire-breathing beasts found in myths and legends around the world. As the Argentinian author Jorge Luis Borges once explained, dragons are a great mystery: "We are as ignorant of the meaning of the dragon as we are of the meaning of the universe, but there is something in the dragon's image that appeals to the human imagination, and so we find the dragon in quite distant places and times. It is, so to speak, a necessary monster." There is no doubt that Tolkien would have agreed with Borges. Indeed, the appeal of this "necessary monster" was embedded so early and deep in Tolkien's mind that, by the age of seven, "a green great dragon" appeared in his very first original fictional composition. In his landmark lecture and essay "On Fairy-Stories" (lecture 1939; published 1947), Tolkien proudly proclaims this childhood obsession: "I desired dragons with a profound desire. Of course, I in my timid body did not wish to have them in the neighbourhood . . . but the world that contained even the imagination of Fáfnir [a dragon in Norse mythology] was richer and more beautiful, at whatever the cost of peril."

That childhood obsession eventually inspired his creation of Glaurung, the Father of Dragons, and Ancalagon

Dragons. The most terrible monsters of Middle-earth. Some slithered like snakes, others walked on clawed feet, and still others fly with lizard wings. Some fight with tooth and claw—the greatest breathed flames.

the Black in *The Silmarillion* and Smaug the Golden in *The Hobbit*, who terrorize the inhabitants of Middle-earth during, respectively, the First and Third Ages. Glaurung was certainly directly inspired by Fáfnir the Dragon slain by Sigurd, the hero of the *Völsunga Saga*. Ancalagon owes his origin in part to the Norse poem *Völuspá*'s account of Ragnarök where a flying dragon, glowing serpent known as Nidhogg (meaning "malice striker"), appears in that final battle.

After the near-obliteration of the Dragons of Middle-earth at the end of the First Age in the last Great Battle of the War of Wrath, it is not until the twentieth century of the Third Age that the histories of Middle-earth speak again of dragons. These monsters are akin to the dragons found in the Middle High German heroic epics of *Wolfdietrich* and *Ortnit*. Like the dragons of the mountains of Lombardy who appear in these thirteenth-century tales, the monsters who make their presence known in the Grey Mountains of Middle-earth in the Third Age are Cold-drakes: a somewhat less formidable breed of dragon than either the Fire-drakes

or the Winged Fire-drakes of the First Age. The mightiest of the Cold-drakes of the Grey Mountains is Scatha the Worm, who slaughters Dwarves and Men and takes possession of a great treasure hoard until he is slain by Fram, the fifth Lord of the Éothéod, in c. 2000 TA.

Tolkien was one who searched for "dragons, real dragons, essential both to the machinery and the ideas of a poem or tale." He found it in his last Dragon tale of Middle-earth, *The Hobbit*, which features one of his most beguiling creations, Smaug the Golden Dragon of Erebor. For his tale, Tolkien took his inspiration from a fatal encounter with a dragon in the Anglo-Saxon poem *Beowulf*. In that Old English poem, a thief enters the dragon's lair and steals a gold cup. In Tolkien's tale, the thief is the titular Hobbit, Bilbo Baggins. And, in both tales, the theft of a gold cup awakens a sleeping dragon, who then emerges from his lair to lay waste to a nearby kingdom. *The Hobbit* is essentially the *Beowulf* dragon story told from the thief's point of view. In the creation of Smaug the Golden, however, we see the perfect fairy-tale dragon: a villain of great charm, intelligence, and fatal vanity; a flying, fire-breathing beast whose terrible wrath and vengeance somehow still wins our admiration. And so it is that, betrayed by his own vanity, Smaug the Smug is outwitted by a humble Hobbit—and then ultimately slain by the courageous Bard the Bowman.

DRAUGLUIN The Father of Werewolves—sire of all those "creatures that walk in wolf-shape" upon Middle-earth. His name in Sindarin means "Blue Wolf," in reference to the color of his coat. Draugluin was bred by Morgoth or else was a corrupted Maia. He haunts the dungeons within the fortress of Tol-in-Gaurhoth ("Isle of Werewolves") in Beleriand and plays a key role in the Quest for the Silmaril, where he is slain by Huan, the Hound of the Valar.

As a "hellhound" guardian, Draugluin shares many similarities with Carcharoth, whom he sires, and hence with other hellhounds such as Cerberus in Greek mythology and Garm in Norse mythology. As a demonic spirit, his creation may owe something to the darker aspects of both Odin and Zeus, who were both associated with wolves and werewolves.

Draugluin. The Father of Werewolves.

DRAUPNIR   In Norse mythology, the great gold ring of Odin, the king of the gods and ruler of the Nine Worlds. Draupnir means "the dripper": this magical golden ring had the power to drip eight new rings of equal size every nine days. Its possession by Odin was not only emblematic of his dominion of the Nine Worlds but also consolidated his power by giving him a source of almost infinite wealth. This scenario seems to be fairly suggestive of Tolkien's "Nine Rings of Mortal Men" that Sauron uses to buy the allegiance of the Men of Middle-earth and ultimately to entrap their souls. In Tolkien's tale, all the skill of Celebrimbor, the greatest Elven-smith of Middle-earth, goes into the forging of the Rings of Power. Likewise, it takes all the knowledge and skill of Sauron the Dark Lord—who as a Maia learned his craft from the Vala Aulë the Smith—to forge the One Ring that strives to command all the others. In Norse myth, it was by means of all the knowledge and skill of Sindri and Brok—the greatest smiths (usually considered dwarfs) in the Norse Nine Worlds—to forge Draupnir, the ring of the king of the gods.

DRÚEDAIN
See: WOSES

DULLAHAN   In Irish legend, the "Dark Man" is a terrifying demonic, headless horseman. Like Tolkien's Witch-king of Angmar, the Dullahan is one variation in a tradition of archetypal phantom horsemen who personify death. By some accounts, each time the Dullahan halts his ride, a death occurs. In other versions, as the Dullahan horseman passes, he calls out a name and whoever is named is seized by death. It is the Dullahan who is perhaps addressed in the great Irish poet W. B. Yeats's famous gravestone epitaph: "Cast a cold eye / On life, on death, / Horseman, pass by!" In Tolkien, the Witch-king appears before the gates of Gondor as the archetypal "Black Rider." Defiantly, he flings back his hood to reveal "a kingly crown; yet upon no head visible was it set." And to Gandalf this headless horseman

declares: "This is my hour. Do you not know Death when you see it?"
See also: A R A W N ;   W I L D   H U N T

DÚNEDAIN ("MEN OF THE WEST")

The Númenóreans in exile who survive the downfall of their Atlantis-like island-continent of Númenor and found the South- and North-kingdoms of Gondor and Arnor in Middle-earth at the end of the Second Age. Tolkien's tales at the end of the Second Age and throughout the three millennia of the Third Age are concerned primarily with the fate of these two kingdoms—only briefly united under High King Isildur—until their final (re)unification under Aragorn.

Tolkien's account of the rise and fall of the Dúnedain kingdoms of Middle-earth owes much to his detailed knowledge of the history of the Roman Empire. Tolkien certainly encouraged this comparison. To begin with, he created a landmass for the Dúnedain kingdoms that was roughly equivalent to that of France, Germany, Italy, Spain, Greece, Britain, and Ireland combined. Also, in an interview with a journalist in the 1950s, he spoke of the action of the story taking place "in the north-west of Middle-earth, equivalent in latitude to the coastlines of Europe and the north shore of the Mediterranean."

Importantly, too, there are some broad similarities between the historical fate of the Roman Empire and the Dúnedain kingdoms. The division of the Roman Empire into Western and Eastern parts and its eventual resurrection in the form of the Holy Roman Empire mirror the fate of the Númenórean empire in Middle-earth. Thus, it is reasonably easy to equate the disastrous military history of Arnor and its collapse with the similarly disastrous military history and collapse of the Western Roman Empire. We may even equate the successor kingdoms of Arthedain, Cardolan, and Rhudaur with the early medieval kingdoms that rose out of the ruins of the empire. Meanwhile, the long-enduring South-kingdom of Gondor has certain similarities with the Byzantine Empire, as the Eastern Roman Empire came to be called.

By the end of the Third Age, after three millennia of conflict, Tolkien presents the reader with a remarkable Dúnedain hero, Aragorn—comparable to the historic Charlemagne—who is also the legitimate heir to the double crown of the Dúnedain kingdoms. In so doing, Tolkien implicitly draws an analogy to what he called "the re-establishment of an effective Holy Roman Empire."

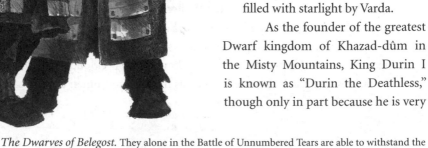

DURIN THE DEATHLESS

The first king of the Longbeards, one of the seven kindreds of Dwarves. The Longbeards—with whom Tolkien's histories of the Dwarves of Middle-earth are largely concerned—are more commonly known as Durin's Folk in honor of their first king.

The name Durin (or Durinn) is first recorded in the Icelandic *Prose Edda*, in the *Dvergatal*, or "Dwarf's Roll." The name translates as "The Sleeper" or "Sleepy" and is the key to Tolkien's inspiration in his creation story of the "Seven Fathers of the Dwarves," otherwise known as the "Seven Sleepers." In *The Silmarillion* the first Dwarves are shaped by Aulë the Smith but, on the command of Eru, are kept sleeping "under stone" until awakened when the dark skies are filled with starlight by Varda.

As the founder of the greatest Dwarf kingdom of Khazad-dûm in the Misty Mountains, King Durin I is known as "Durin the Deathless," though only in part because he is very

The Dwarves of Belegost. They alone in the Battle of Unnumbered Tears are able to withstand the blaze of dragon-fire because on their helms they wear flameproof masks of steel.

long-lived. Tolkien's Dwarves have a messianic belief—not unlike real-world beliefs about spiritual leaders—that each king who carries the name Durin is actually a reincarnation of the original Father of the Longbeards. It is an article of faith among the Longbeards that this mysterious cycle spanning many ages will end only with the seventh and final incarnation, Durin VII, who will appear at some undisclosed time in Middle-earth's future ages.

Despite wars and conflicts over the millennia, Durin's Folk prospered well until the year 1980 of the Third Age of the Sun when the Dwarves of Khazad-dûm, by chance or fate, delved too deep in their mines and awoke a monstrous demon of fire. This is an ancient Maia fire spirit known as a Balrog or Valaraukar, meaning "demon of might." The source of Tolkien's inspiration for this monster is the Norse fire giant Surt who was the Lord of Muspelheim, the evil volcanic underworld domain of fire. In Middle-earth, this Balrog with his flaming sword and "scourges of fire" slew King Durin VI and drove Durin's folk from Khazad-dûm.

This disaster marked the beginning of the diaspora of Durin's Folk. Driven from their ancient kingdom—renamed Moria, meaning "Black Chasm"—the Longbeards were constantly on the move, exiles in search of a safe new realm. But in the Third Age the terrors that lurked in the scattered realms of Durin's Folk also endanger the kingdoms of the Dúnedain. The Balrog in Moria, Orcs in the Misty Mountains, and Dragons in the Grey Mountains and Erebor not only threatened the Dwarves of Durin's Folk, but all the Free Peoples of Middle-earth. And so, in the Dúnedain of Arnor and Gondor, Durin's Dwarves became natural allies in the War of the Ring as recounted in Tolkien's *The Lord of the Rings*.

DVERGATAL (OR THE "DWARF'S ROLL")
A list of the names of mythological dwarfs found in the Icelandic twelfth-century text known as the *Prose Edda* on which Tolkien drew for many of his Dwarvish names. All the Dwarves in *The Hobbit* appear in this list: Thorin, Dwalin, Balin, Kili, Fili, Bifur, Bofur, Bombur, Dori, Nori, Ori, Óin, and Glóin. Other names of dwarfs which Tolkien also found in the *Dvergatal*, and which he used later, include: Thráin, Thrór, Dáin, and Náin. The *Dvergatal*,

Dwarf Kingdom of Belegost. "Belegost" is Elvish for "mighty fortress." In Khuzdul, the language of the Dwarves, it is called Gabligathol, or Mickleburg.

however, was not only a fruitful source of names but also an inspiration for Tolkien in creating the characters and backgrounds of his Dwarves.

Not surprisingly, the name of the leader of the Tolkien's Company of adventurers, Thorin, means "Bold." However, Tolkien also gave him another dwarf-name from the *Dvergatal*: Eikinskjaldi, meaning "he of the Oakenshield." This name provoked Tolkien into inventing a complex piece of background history in which, during a battle in the Goblin Wars, Thorin breaks his sword but fights on by picking up an oak bough, which he uses as both club and shield. Another story-inspiring name is that of Thorin's father, Thráin, meaning "stubborn," who is slain while stubbornly resisting Dragon invasions of his realm. Thorin's only sister and, interestingly, the only named female dwarf in Tolkien's works, is named Dis, which simply means "Sister." Unlike most of the male Dwarves—whose names mean or reflect a personal attribute—Dis, the "Sister" is solely identified by her family position in relation to Thorin. Thorin's heir, Dáin II, known as Ironfoot, proves true to his warrior name ("deadly") when he and several hundred Dwarves come to Thorin's aid in the Battle of Five Armies. The names of other members of the Thorin's Company were instrumental in Tolkien's shaping of their characters. Bombur, meaning "Bulging," is certainly the fattest of the Dwarves, and Nori, meaning "Peewee," is the smallest; Balin, meaning "Burning One," is fiery in battle, but warm with his friends; Ori, meaning "Furious," fights furiously before he is slain in Moria; and Glóin, meaning "Glowing One," wins glory and riches. There seems little doubt, then, that the *Dvergatal* was a rich inspiration for Tolkien and the means by which he "discovered" the characters of his Dwarves.

Dwarves

DVERGATAL

FROM *THE POETIC EDDA*, VOLUME I, LAYS OF THE GODS, VOLUSPO

10. There was Motsognir | the mightiest made
Of all the dwarfs, | and Durin next;
Many a likeness | of men they made,
The dwarfs in the earth, | as Durin said.

11. Nyi and Nithi, | Northri and Suthri,
Austri and Vestri, | Althjof, Dvalin,
Nar and Nain, | Niping, Dain,
Bifur, Bofur, | Bombur, Nori,
An and Onar, | Ai, Mjothvitnir.

12. Vigg and Gandalf | Vindalf, Thrain,
Thekk and Thorin, | Thror, Vit and Lit,
Nyr and Nyrath,—| now have I told—
Regin and Rathsvith—| the list aright.

13. Fili, Kili, | Fundin, Nali,
Heptifili, | Hannar, Sviur,
Frar, Hornbori, | Fraeg and Loni,
Aurvang, Jari, | Eikinskjaldi.

14. The race of the dwarfs | in Dvalin's throng
Down to Lofar | the list must I tell;
The rocks they left, | and through wet lands
They sought a home | in the fields of sand.

15. There were Draupnir | and Dolgthrasir,
Hor, Haugspori, | Hlevang, Gloin,
Dori, Ori, | Duf, Andvari,
Skirfir, Virfir, | Skafith, Ai.

16. Alf and Yngvi, | Eikinskjaldi,
Fjalar and Frosti, | Fith and Ginnar;
So for all time | shall the tale be known,
The list of all | the forbears of Lofar.

DWARFS   The dwarfs of the fairy tales and mythologies of the Norse and other Germanic peoples were the primary source for Tolkien's creation of his own race of "Dwarves." Keen to distinguish this race from the latter-day use of the term "dwarf" to describe humans of diminutive stature, and to connect them instead with the bearded, stocky, cavern-dwelling beings of Germanic mythology, Tolkien began his attempt by recognizing a proper plural term. He came up with "Dwarves," all the while acknowledging that, from a linguistic perspective, it would be more correct to call them "Dwarrows."

By exploring Germanic mythology and traditional fairy tales, Tolkien also attempted to discover more about this race and their connection with mines, the hoarding of treasure, the forging of supernatural weapons, and the creation of magical jewelry and gifts. All of these aspects, to a greater or lesser degree, contributed to Tolkien's reinvention of Dwarves for his tales of Middle-earth.

DWARVES   Tolkien's doughty race of Dwarves in Middle-earth was inspired by Norse and other Germanic tales of a powerful but stunted subterranean race that lived within mountain kingdoms: masters of fire and forge, makers of weapons and jewels, guardians of treasures, and bestowers of magical gifts. Dissatisfied with the portrayal of dwarfs in popular fairy tales as diminutive, rather comic creatures, Tolkien set out to create a race that was altogether more ambivalent, at times even sinister.

The reader's initial impression of the Dwarves of Thorin and Company in *The Hobbit* is largely consistent with the dwarfs of the mildly comic fairy-tale variety. Even within the course of that book, however, the Dwarves seem to "grow in stature" and take on more heroic attributes. It is in *The Silmarillion*, though, that they most fully reveal their true nature as a dark and brooding race with the fatalistic character of the dwarf-smiths of Norse mythology. Indeed, Tolkien's Dwarves are comparable—in all but size—to the Norsemen of Scandinavia: a proud race of warriors, craftsmen, and traders. Stoic and stubborn, both Dwarves and Norsemen are alike in their admiration of strength and bravery, in their sense of honor and loyalty, and in their love of gold and treasure. They are all but identical in their skill in the wielding and forging of weapons, in their stubborn pride, and their determination to avenge perceived injustice.

However brave and fearless Tolkien's Dwarves are on their own ground (underground), they are mistrustful, dismissive, and fearful of all that they do not know. Unlike the Norsemen, they hate the open sea, deep forests, and wide plains. They would rather burn a boat than sail in it, cut down a tree than climb it, and carry a horse than ride it. Dwarves only find security in the deep roots of mountains and joy in the working of gold and precious metals, the forging of steel, the carving of stone, and the setting of gems.

Ultimately, however, we find that Tolkien remains largely consistent with ancient folk tradition: his Dwarves are the genies of the mountains, just as Hobbits are the genies of tilled soil and farmlands, and Ents are the genies of the forests. Through his research, Tolkien felt that he was able to understand fully the true nature and character of this secretive, stunted, mountain-dwelling race.

The Eagles of Manwë. The Eagles numbered among the most ancient and wisest of races: they were made before the Stars were rekindled and the Elves awoke.

EAGLES OF MANWË

Emissaries of Manwë, the king of the Valar, whose mansions are perched upon Taniquetil, the tallest mountain in the world. In the First Age, the Lord of Eagles is Thorondor whose wings measure 30 fathoms (180 ft.) and whose strength and power prove even greater than that of the mighty Dragons of Morgoth in that era-ending War of Wrath.

The Eagles of Manwë of Tolkienian mythology are consistent with the eagle emissaries of the Greek Zeus (and the Roman Jupiter) as the king of gods whose mansion stood on Mount Olympus, considered by the Greeks the tallest mountain in their world. Throughout Indo-European mythology, where the king of the gods is usually also a mountain and storm god, the eagle is typically found as one of his principal attributes or emblems. This also applied to the earthly rulers of most Eurasian empires. The *aquila* (eagle) was from early on associated with Roman imperial rule, carried as a standard by the Roman legions. And, subsequently, the Imperial Eagle was adopted by the Russian Czar, the German and Austro-Hungarian Kaisers, and the self-created emperor, Napoleon.

The Great Eagles of the Third Age are not a match in size to those of the First, but are nonetheless awesome birds capable of easily swooping down and carrying Men, Elves, and Dwarves aloft in their grip. The intervention of the Giant Eagles in Tolkien's narratives is always crucial and climactic: they arrive at times of desperate need as, for example, in the Battle of the Five Armies in *The Hobbit*. They frequently appear when rescue can be achieved only by the power of flight, as in the rescue of Gandalf from Saruman's tower of Orthanc, and Frodo and Sam from Mount Doom.

In this way, the Eagles seem to serve as vehicles of destiny, as *dei ex machina* who, when all seems lost, appear almost out of nowhere to save the day. They are part of a long tradition of eagle-emissaries in myth and literature, leading from the birds of the Greek god Zeus to the vassals of Manwë, the Lord of the Winds of Arda.

EÄRENDIL THE MARINER

A Half-elven, son of Tuor and Idril, husband of Ewing, and father of Elrond and Elros, whose ultimate destiny is to carry one of the Silmarils through the sky as the Morning Star. He is one of Tolkien's earliest original literary creations, born out of his philological studies.

One might say that Middle-earth all began with a star. In 1913, while still a student at Oxford, Tolkien discovered a bright star in the text of an Old English (Anglo-Saxon) mystical poem known as the *Christ II* (*Ascension*), written by the ninth-century AD churchman Cynewulf: "Hail, Eärendel, brightest of angels, / Above the middle-earth sent unto men." The young scholar deduced that Eärendel must refer to the Morning Star—the planet Venus as it appears in the dawn sky—shining above the land of men midway between heaven and hell, otherwise known as "Middle-

Eärendil the Mariner. Círdan the Shipwright builds the ship *Vingilótë* in which Eärendil will sail through the Shadowy Seas and eventually through the sky.

earth." In Eärendil, "brightest of angels," Tolkien believed that he had discovered an original Old English myth, which also survived in an Icelandic fairy tale about the hero Orentil, who, in Norse mythology was identified with the Morning Star. Over the following year, Tolkien set himself the task of imaginatively reconstructing what he considered the "true" myth of Eärendil—the end result of which was a poem entitled "The Voyage of Eärendil."

Modest as the poem is (it remained unpublished until after Tolkien's death), it seems to have been the spark that ignited Tolkien's imaginative journey in the creation of Middle-earth. For, although his poem and tale had its genesis in the lines of another poem from another time, as Humphrey Carpenter explains in his biography of the author, Tolkien had created in Eärendil something uniquely his own—and more besides. As Carpenter put it: "It was in fact the beginning of Tolkien's own mythology."

Ultimately, the poem would evolve into one of the key stories of *The Silmarillion*, which tells of an emissary of the Elves and Edain of Beleriand, who, with a

Easterlings. Easterlings are a westward-migrating barbarian nation on the eastern borders of Gondor—comparable to the historic Germanic tribes that threatened the eastern borders of the Roman Empire.

Silmaril bound to his brow, sails to the Undying Lands and successfully pleads for help against the enemy, Morgoth. Both Tolkien's Eärendil poem and its Anglo-Saxon inspiration are echoed in the narrative of *The Lord of the Rings*: Bilbo composes (with Aragorn's help) a "Song of Eärendil" in Rivendell after the safe arrival of the Fellowship. And later, in Shelob's Lair, when Frodo wields the star-glass, which contains the light of Eärendil's Silmaril, he exclaims: "Aiya Eärendil Elenion Ancalima!" ("Hail, Eärendil, brightest of stars!"), in a near-direct quotation of Cynewulf's poem and Tolkien's inspiration.

EASTERLINGS Men living in the east of Middle-earth, beyond Mordor and the Sea of Rhun, who from the First Age onward were largely allied with Morgoth and, after his downfall, his successor, Sauron. Easterlings is a translation of the Quenya *Romenildi*, meaning "East Men."

The east in Tolkien's writing is both a geographic reality in Middle-earth and an evocation of the history of the European subcontinent, which, in Late Antiquity (third–sixth centuries AD) in particular, saw wave after wave of nomadic peoples, such as the Huns, migrating from the east.

Throughout the history of Tolkien's world, Easterlings in Middle-earth are a constant threat to the kingdoms of the West, just as the Huns and others were a threat to the already crumbling Roman Empire.

In the First Age, the term "Easterling" was applied to Men who came to Beleriand long after the Edain. They were initially known to the Elves as the Swarthy Men on account of their dark hair and skin. One of the great Easterling chieftains is Ulfang the Black, who on his arrival swears allegiance to the Elves of Beleriand, even though he is secretly in league with Morgoth. His betrayal of the Elves in the middle of the Battle of Unnumbered Tears leads to the single most disastrous defeat in the history of Beleriand. This has similarities to the historic betrayal by the Germanic general Arminius (18/17 BC–AD 21), who swore allegiance to Rome but was secretly in league with other German tribes. In the Battle of Teutoburg Forest in AD 9, Arminius and his allies destroyed three Roman legions in what became known as the Varian Disaster, perhaps the single most costly defeat in Roman history.

As barbarian hordes in the service of Sauron the Necromancer, who for centuries menaced Gondor's eastern borders and territories, the role of the Easterlings in the annals of the Third Age is much greater.

In this they are comparable to the Roman Empire's Germanic barbarian hordes in the service of the Odin the Necromancer, who for centuries menaced the empire's eastern borders.

Gondor's century of Wainrider invasions (1851–1944 TA), which result in the loss of its eastern territories, owes something to real-world historic accounts of the century-long Roman conflict with the Ostrogoths (East Goths). The Wainriders of Rhûn are a nomadic confederacy of people that travels as an army and nation in vast caravans of wains (wagons) and war chariots. This is certainly comparable to the nomadic Ostrogoths (East Goths), whom one ancient historian described as "an entire nation on the move in great wains."

Later, in 2050 TA, another massive invading Easterling horde known as the Balchoth almost routed the forces of Gondor in the critical Battle of the Field of Celebrant, but the tide is turned by the unexpected intervention of the cavalry of the Éothéod. This has a historical precedent in the Battle of the Catalaunian Fields in AD 451 when the Roman army formed an alliance with the Visigoths (West Goths) and the Lombard cavalry and defeated the massive barbarian horde of Attila the Hun.

EDAIN
The heroic first Men in the east of Middle-earth who migrate westward into the Elf kingdoms of Beleriand during the early Years of the Sun and aid the Elves in their struggle against Morgoth.

Just as the earlier journey of the Elves during the Years of the Trees was inspired by tales relating to the historic westward migration of Celtic peoples, so the journey of Men was inspired by the historic westward migration of the Teutonic (Germanic) peoples. And just as the immortal Elves can be aligned with the myths and folk traditions of the Celts, so Tolkien's mortal Men may be equally aligned with the myths and folk traditions of the Germans, Norsemen, and Anglo-Saxons. The contrast extends to the linguistic field, too. While the dominant language of the Elves of Beleriand is Sindarin, modeled on the Celtic language of Welsh, the dominant Mannish language

Wainriders. The Wainriders are a formidable Easterling people who are comparable to the nomadic Ostrogoths who invaded the Roman Empire.

of the Edain is Taliska, modeled on Gothic, a now-extinct East Germanic language of deep fascination to Tolkien.

When the Edain enter Beleriand early in the fourth century of the First Age, Tolkien portrays them as a wild and proud tribal people who have endured terrible trials in their westward migration. Their suffering and brief lifespan draw the pity of the Elves, and yet they quickly reveal a primitive nobility and innate sense of honor that brings them close in spirit to the mortal heroes of Germanic and Norse mythology.

The Edain are comprised of three houses, or dynastic clans, each named after a founding ancestor: the House of Bëor, the House of Haleth, and the House of Marach (or Hador). We find similar dynastic clans in Norse and Germanic legend and protohistory, such as the Völsungs (to which Sigurd/Siegfried belongs) and the semilegendary House of Munsö. In their bravery, strong code of honor, and fierce pride, many of the prominent figures in the stories of the Edain—such as Beren, Huor, and Tuor—also bear a strong resemblance to the heroes of the Norse and Germanic sagas.

Elanor. A fair winter flower of Lothlórien.

EGYPT Ancient Egypt and its long history were influential in Tolkien's depiction and characterization of the Númenóreans. This is not by chance, as the story of Atlantis itself—the clear, primary inspiration for Tolkien's island continent of Númenor—was, according to Plato, first revealed in ancient Egyptian texts.

In a letter, Tolkien explicitly compared the two peoples: "The Númenóreans of Gondor were proud, peculiar, and archaic, and I think are best pictured in (say) Egyptian terms. In many ways they resemble 'Egyptians'—the love of, and power to construct, the gigantic and massive. And their great interest in ancestry and in tombs. (But not of course in 'theology': in which respect they were Hebraic and even more puritan . . .)."

Curiously enough, in another of his letters, Tolkien compares the struggle of the North- and South-kingdoms of the Dúnedain toward unity with the efforts of the Egyptian pharaohs to unite Upper and Lower Egypt at the end of the fourth millennium BC. This comparison was made explicit in the author's conception of the double crown of his Reunited Kingdom, for which he made a sketch. In the same letter, Tolkien noted: "I think the crown of Gondor (the South Kingdom) was very tall, like that of Egypt, but with wings attached, not set straight back but at an angle. The North Kingdom had only a diadem—Cf. the difference between the North and South kingdoms of Egypt."

EIR THE MERCIFUL The Norse goddess of healing and one of the handmaidens of Frigg, queen of the gods. Eir, "the best of physicians," lives in the woodlands of Lyfjaberg ("hill of healing") and heals and protects the other gods and goddesses. She has a direct counterpart in Tolkien's world in Estë the Gentle, the Vala who has the power to heal all hurts and soothe weariness. Estë lives on a wooded island on the lake of Lórellin in Valinor that provides rest and repose to the Valar and the Elves of Eldamar.

ELANOR A flower of Arda characterized by yellow, star-shaped flowers, hence its name, which means "sun-star" in Sindarin. According to one of Tolkien's letters, it was inspired by the real-world flower the pimpernel.

ELDAMAR The land of the Eldar, or Light-Elves, in the Undying Lands. Eldamar, meaning "Elven home," was the land of the Elves from the three kindreds of the Vanyar, Noldor, and Teleri people east of Valinor and west of the Great Sea. Eldamar was undoubtedly inspired by Alfheim, one of the Nine Worlds of the Norse cosmology and, as the name Alfheim ("elf-home") implies, the homeland of the elves or, more specifically, the Light-Elves. An inspiration, likewise, were the related Elfhame (or Elphame) of Scottish folklore and the Faerie (or Fairyland) of English folklore. Both of these "otherworlds," though largely benevolent, are shot through with a vein of peril for mortals that is not entirely absent from Tolkien's conception of Eldamar. In *The Hobbit*, indeed, the Hobbitish name for Eldamar, or perhaps Valinor, is Faerie.

ELDAR (SINGULAR: ELDA) Originally the name for all Elves, but in time applied only to the West Elves who answered the summons of the Valar and who took part in the great migration from the east of the mortal lands of Middle-earth into the west and hence, with some exceptions, to Valinor. Eldar comes from the Quenya root word *elda* meaning "of the stars," as the Elves were first awakened upon Middle-earth by the light of the stars set ablaze by Varda Elentári, queen of the Heavens. Tolkien noted but dismissed as accidental the similarity between the word Eldar—the Firstborn of the Children of Ilúvitar—and English word "elder." *See also*: E L V E S

ELENDIL THE TALL The last Lord of Andúnië, who sails with his people into exile in seven ships and so survived the destruction and downfall of the Atlantis-like island-continent of Númenor. In the *Aeneid* (completed 19 BC) the ancient Roman poet Virgil wrote of how Aeneas, the last Trojan prince, survives the downfall of Troy and sails west to Italy where his descendants Romulus and Remus will eventually found the great city of

Rome. Similarly, Tolkien's histories tell of how Elendil, the last Númenórean prince, sails east to Middle-earth, where he and his sons, Isildur and Anárion, found the mighty Númenórean kingdoms-in-exile: the North-kingdom of Arnor and the South-kingdom of Gondor.

ELESSAR   Formal title assumed by Aragorn II, the Chieftain of the Dunedain upon his coronation in the wake of the War of the Ring. Elessar means "Elfstone," after the green jewel set into an eagle-shaped silver brooch, given to Aragorn by Galadriel when the Fellowship of the Ring departs from Lothlórien. Galadriel proclaims: "In this hour take the name that was foretold for you, Elessar, the Elfstone of the house of Elendil!"

Tolkien himself noted that Aragorn's assumption of the title of Elessar, king of the Reunited Kingdom of the Dúnedain, is comparable to that of the historic figure of Charlemagne's assumption of the title of the Holy Roman Emperor after his part in the reunification of the scattered provinces of the ancient Roman Empire. Both Aragorn and Charlemagne fight many battles that result in the expulsion of invaders and the formation of military and civil alliances that bring about eras of peace and prosperity.

ELROND   Half-Elven Son of Eärendil the Mariner and Elwing the White, and twin brother of Elrond. He is first introduced to readers of *The Hobbit* as the Master of the "Last Homely House East of the Sea," in Rivendell, the 4,000-year-old refuge of wisdom and great learning for all Elves and Men of goodwill. It was not until the publication of *The Silmarillion* that Elrond's early history as one of the Peredhil ("Half-elven") was fully revealed, shown as choosing the fate and immortality of the Elves.

At Rivendell, Elrond serves as a kind of oracle, providing the ancient lore and wisdom essential for the progress of questing heroes, and setting them off in a fresh direction. Just as Bilbo Baggins finds refuge and guidance from Elrond Half-elven in *The Hobbit*, a generation later Frodo Baggins finds healing, rest, and guidance during his own quest to destroy the ring.

A figure like this commonly appears in quest stories, such as the hermits and wizards often met by the Arthurian knights, especially during the Quest of the Holy Grail.

For the psychoanalyst Carl Jung (1875–1961), the Wise Old Man, or senex, is one of the archetypes of the human psyche and a stock character of storytelling. It should be noted, however, that Elrond, although some six and a half thousand years old at the time of the War of the Ring, is shown as ageless.

See also: DELPHI

ELROS Son of Eärendil the Mariner and Elwing the White, twin brother of Elrond, and the founder and first king of Númenor. Because they are Peredhil (Half-elven), the twins are allowed to choose their race and fate, Elrond choosing to be immortal and Elros to be mortal, though gifted with a lifespan of five centuries. The brothers have a counterpart in the Greek myth of the twin brothers Castor and Polydeuces, known as the Dioscuri ("divine twins"), one of whom was mortal and one immortal.

Elros's long lifespan (he was already 90 when he began to rule in Númenor)—and that of the other kings and queens of the island-continent—may make us think of figures in the Old Testament such as Methuselah, who lived to be 969 years of age. Before the biblical Flood, humans had a much greater lifespan than after the cataclysm. Similarly, before the fall of Númenor and its loss beneath the waves, all Númenóreans enjoyed a long life (around 300 years) and those of the Line of Elros an even longer one. After the Downfall, their lifespan dwindled considerably.

ELVES In Tolkien's world, elves were in large part inspired by the author's wish to give precise definition to a multitude of lost traditions and mythologies relating to supernatural beings known as "Elfs" which, in the passage of history, had been reduced to little more than the pixies, flower-fairies, sprites, and gnomes of English folklore and Victorian children's stories. Tolkien came

Opposite: Journey of the Elves

to the rescue of these long-lost traditions and revived them again in the pages of literature. In the writing of *The Silmarillion*, Tolkien gave life and context to the millennia-long histories of over 40 races, nations, kindreds, and city-states of Elves.

Tolkien began his "rescue" of the Elves by clarifying matters linguistically, just as he had done with his Dwarves: "Elfs" became "Elves" and "Elfin" became "Elven." Tolkien wished to define the "Elf" as a distinct and singularly important race. The word "elf "means white, related to the *alba* and Greek *alphos* (both meaning white), and also retains an association with "swan." It is through this tracking back to the roots of language that Tolkien's Elves gradually reemerged from the ancient legends of Britain, originally known as Albion (a name possibly related to the Indo-Euopean root *albho*, or white), which Tolkien implies could be literally translated as "Elf-land."

We know that Tolkien also looked to Norse mythology for the history of his Elves. In Norse mythology, there are references to both the light elfs of Alfheim ("elf home") and the rather sinister dark elfs of the subterranean Svartalfheim ("black elf home"). Tolkien took this somewhat mysterious division and used it to create the first great event in the history of his Elves: the "Sundering of the Elves" after their

awakening by Cuiviénen, between the Calaquendi ("Light-Elves") who made the journey to Eldamar (meaning "elven home") and the Moriquendi ("Dark-Elves") who refused the journey and remained under the starlight in the east of Middle-earth, never seeing the divine Trees of Light in the Undying Lands.

Above all, it should be stressed that Tolkien's Elves are not a race of pixies. They are a powerful, full-blooded people who closely resemble the prehuman Irish race of immortals called the Tuatha Dé Danann. Like the Tuatha Dé Danann, Tolkien's Elves are taller and stronger than mortals, are incapable of suffering sickness, are possessed of more-than-human beauty, and are filled with greater wisdom in all things. Tolkien took the sketchy myths and legends of the Tuatha Dé Danann and created a vast civilization, history, and genealogy for his Elves. He gave them a rich family of languages and a vast cultural inheritance that, for all that it was rooted in real traditions, required all his genius and imagination to truly flourish.

Elves Listening to a Minstrel. Music plays an important role in the culture of the Elves, especially the Teleri.

ELWË

See: THINGOL

ELWING ("STAR-SPRAY") THE WHITE

The daughter of Dior and Nimloth, granddaughter of Beren and Lúthien, wife of Eärendil, and the inheritor of the Silmaril. While by birth she is Half-elven, she ultimately chooses the fate of the Elves.

The story of Elwing's love for her husband takes some of its inspiration from Richard Wagner's opera *Der fliegende Holländer* (*The Flying Dutchman*; 1847), in which the Dutchman of the title is doomed to sail the oceans forever unless he can find the love of a true woman. The heroine, Senta, the daughter of a sea captain, falls instantly in love with the Dutchman when her father brings him home after a voyage (under the terms of his curse he is allowed to set foot on land once in every seven years). When the Dutchman sets sail again, Senta leaps into the sea, and so lifts the curse on his soul. The opera ends with the reunited couple's ascent into heaven.

The motif of the leap into the sea features prominently in Tolkien's tale of Eärendil and Elwing. While her husband wanders lost at sea, Elwing find herself at the mercy of the sons of Fëanor. Rather than be captured, she duplicates Senta's final act by leaping to a seemingly certain death from a high cliff into the sea. However, unlike Senta, Elwing is transformed into a seabird and in this form flies to Eärendil, carrying the Silmaril, the holy jewel of living light in her beak. Paralleling the Dutchman and Senta's ascent to heaven, Eärendil, with the Silmaril bound to his brow lighting the way, succeeds at last in steering his ship to the shores of the Undying Lands.

There may be a further connection between Elwing the White, with her strong maritime associations, and the Greek myth of Ino, a Theban princess who leaps into the sea and is transformed into the sea goddess Leucothea ("white goddess"). In Homer's *Odyssey* she rescues the shipwrecked Odysseus, just as Elwing rescues her husband from his hopeless sea wanderings.

ENGLISH MYTHOLOGY

ENGLISH MYTHOLOGY The mythology of the Anglo-Saxon peoples, as Tolkien saw it, survived only in a single surviving epic, *Beowulf*, a handful of Old English poems (such as *The Wanderer*), and a scattering of folktales. As he once wrote in a letter to a reader: "I was from early days grieved by the poverty of my own beloved country: it had no stories of its own, not of the quality that I sought and found in legends of other lands. There was Greek and Celtic, and Romance, Germanic, Scandinavian, and Finnish; but nothing English, save impoverished chap-book stuff." It was Tolkien's wish to find a means of "rediscovering" that lost mythology through his imaginative writing. So great was his obsession that it could be argued that the literary merits of Tolkien's *The Lord of the Rings* and other related works were almost of secondary concern to him (although they are undoubtedly present). Important as the novel is, any analysis of Tolkien's life and work makes one aware that his greatest passion and grandest ambition were focused on the creation of an entire mythological system for the English people. "I had in mind the large and cosmogenic, to the level of romantic fairy-story . . . which I could dedicate simply: to England, to my country."

ENTS Treelike beings and "Shepherds of Trees" of Middle-earth, and among Tolkien's most original creations. Once asked about the origin of his Ents, Tolkien wrote: "I should say that Ents are composed of philology, literature, and life. They owe their name to the *eald enta geweorc* of Anglo-Saxon." The Anglo-Saxon reference is to a fragment of the hauntingly beautiful Old English poem *The Wanderer*. The word *enta* there is usually translated "giant," so that the phrase means "old work of giants," and relates to the prehistoric stone ruins of Britain, then considered to be the work of an ancient race of giants. Out of such simple philological origins, Tolkien created beings of great and beguiling complexity—generally slow and gentle in their thoughts, words, and deeds but capable of swift and elemental violence when roused, as in their overthrow of Isengard.

To find beings of myth and legend that correspond directly to the Ents, Tolkien had only to look back into English folklore, in which the Green Man plays a such a key and distinctive part. Green Man stories and carvings are common in Tolkien's beloved West Midlands as well as in the Welsh Marches just beyond. The Green Man was in origin a Celtic nature spirit and tree god who represented the victory of the powers of growth over the powers of ice and frost. Essentially benevolent, he could also be powerful and destructive, just like the Ents and the even more belligerent Huorn tree spirits.

The March of the Ents—one of the most powerfully imagined events in *The Lord of the Rings*—also has a more personal inspiration. The creation of the Ents, Tolkien once explained, "is due, I think, to my bitter disappointment and disgust from schooldays with the shabby use made in Shakespeare of the coming of 'Great Birnam Wood to high Dunsinane Hill': I longed to devise a setting in which the trees might really march to war." The reference here is to the play *Macbeth* (1606) where the English army advances on Macbeth's fortress of Dunsinane by shielding themselves with tree branches, thereby fulfilling a prophecy about the usurper-king's downfall.

Tolkien believed that Shakespeare had trivialized and misinterpreted an ancient and authentic myth, providing a cheap, simplistic interpretation of the prophecy of this march of a wood against a hill. Thus, in *The Lord of the Rings* he devised a situation in which the Ents, the spirits of the forest and personifications of growth and renewal, march against their foes, the Orcs, the spirits of the mountain and personifications of winter and death.

EÖNWË THE HERALD OF VALAR

The greatest of the Maiar and the standard-bearer of Manwë, king of the Valar. He bears some resemblance to the Greco-Roman god Hermes/ Mercury in his guise as herald and messenger to Zeus/Jupiter, king of the gods. However, because of the more martial quality of his character, Eönwë (whose strength in battle rivals that of even the Valar) has a greater affinity with the Norse god Heimdall, the herald of the gods, who will blow his horn to announce Ragnarök, the last great battle between the gods and giants. It is Eönwë, too, who blows his horn to announce the Great Battle in the War of Wrath, in which the host of the Valar, Maiar, and Eldar destroy the host of Morgoth, the Dark Enemy of the World, marking the end of the First Age.

Marching Ents

ÉOTHÉOD   A group of Northmen who settle in the Vales of the Anduin in the twentieth century of the Third Age and who are the ancestors of the Rohirrim. A strong and fair-haired race of horsemen and men-at-arms, in 2050 TA they unexpectedly come to the aid of the Men of Gondor. Led by Eorl the Young, the Éothéod cavalry turn the tide of war in the critical Battle of the Field of Celebrant in favor of Gondor, resulting in the rout of the Balchoth, a barbarian horde of invading Easterlings.

Culturally, the Éothéod take much of their inspiration from the Anglo-Saxons in that they live in small villages rather than towns; have a strong oral tradition of heroic song, rather than books; and have a high regard for horses and horsemanship. The horse is central to the lives of the Éothéod, meaning "horse-people," as it was to the Anglo-Saxons, although among the latter, mounted warfare was probably confined to the elite, with horses reserved primarily for transportation. *See also*: CATALAUNIAN FIELDS; ROHIRRIM; MERCIA

ÉOWYN   Noblewoman of Rohan, sister of Éomer and niece of King Théoden. In *The Lord of the Rings* she disguises herself as a young cavalryman, rides to Gondor, and takes part in the Battle of Pelennor Fields, slaying the Witch-king of Morgul. Éowyn belongs to the ancient Germanic tradition of the shield-maiden (Old Norse: *skjaldmaer*), warrior women found widely in the world of epic romance and saga, most notably the semidivine figures of the Valkyries. Whether shield-maidens existed in reality is much debated.

Éowyn owes most to the twin figures of Brynhild and Brunhild, found in the Norse *Völsunga Saga* and the German *Nibelungenlied*, respectively. In the *Völsunga Saga*, Brynhild is a Valkyrie, a beautiful battle maiden who defies Odin and was subsequently pierced with a sleep-thorn and imprisoned in a ring of fire. Like Sleeping Beauty, she is awakened from sleep by Sigurd the Dragon-slayer, with whom she falls in love. In the *Nibelungenlied*, Brunhild ("armored warrior maid") is the warrior-queen of Iceland, who falls for Sigurd's medieval German equivalent, Siegfried.

Éomer and Aragorn Ride to the Lands of the East

Tolkien's conception of Éowyn, however, might be said to be somewhat Christianized. In Éowyn's combination of patriotism and goodness we cannot help being reminded of the historic Joan of Arc (c. 1412–31), the "Maid of Orleans," who led the forces of the French against the English in a phase of the Hundred Years War. It is also somewhat romanticized, since her donning of a male disguise to assert her personality and achieve her goals in a male world makes us think of any number of Shakespearean heroines, such as Rosalind in *As You Like It* (1599).

See also: BRYNHILD

ERU ("THE ONE")

The creator-god of Tolkien's world of Arda, known to the Elves as Ilúvatar ("Allfather"). He was certainly in part inspired by the Judeo-Christian creator-god, Yahweh/Jehovah, although there are important differences in conception.

In the beginning, Tolkien tells us his cosmogony (creation myth), Eru's "thoughts" took the form of entities known as the Ainur, or "Holy Ones," vastly powerful spirits that are comparable to the Judeo-Christian angels and archangels. He then commands the Ainur to sing in a celestial choir, thereby revealing his vision of "what was, and is, and is to come." Eru creates and wakens first the Elves and then Men (just as Yahweh/Jehovah creates Adam). And, like the God of the Bible, Eru is conceived of as making decisive interventions in world history, such as the destruction of the fleet of King Ar-Pharazôn and the reembodiment of Gandalf after his death in Moria.

In most other respects, however, the early Judeo-Christian world is very unlike Tolkien's world. Tolkien purposely created a world that is without formal religion, and Eru is far from being the vengeful, jealous deity of the Old Testament (it is Melkor/Morgoth who perhaps takes on these aspects). And, although the inhabitants of Tolkien's world do not quite worship "gods," their beliefs are shown as more closely resembling the pantheism of the pagan Teutons, Celts, and Greeks.

ESTË THE GENTLE One of the seven queens of the Valar, who has the power to heal all hurts and relieve weariness. She dwells with her spouse, Irmo (also known as Lórien), the master of visions and dreams, in the Gardens of Lórien on a wooded island in the lake of Lórellin in Valinor. In Norse mythology Eir the Merciful is a comparable goddess of healing, as is the Greek goddess of healing, Hygieia, from whose name, meaning "health," we get the word "hygiene." Of Estë (meaning "rest") we are told, "Grey is her raiment; and rest is her gift."

EURYDICE In Greek mythology the wife of Orpheus, the poet and musician who descends into the underworld after her death and attempts to bring her back to the world of the living through the enchantment of music and song. This famous legend of a lover's attempt to defeat death was acknowledged by Tolkien as his inspiration for his tale of Beren and Lúthien, though in Tolkien's adaptation the male and female roles are reversed and the Eurydice figure is given a far more important and heroic role in the tale. For more on Tolkien's tale— one of the most significant in the history of Middle-earth and personally for the author—and its inspiration, *see* BEREN; LÚTHIEN.

EVIL EYE A widespread superstition throughout human history, recorded in ancient Greek and Roman texts as well as many religious scriptures, from the Koran to the Bible, by which an individual, often a sorcerer, has the power to injure or harm by means of a simple, but baleful, glance. Attempts to ward off the power of the evil eye have resulted in the creation of talismans featuring a staring eye, which is supposed to reflect back the malicious gaze on the evildoer. Such talismans are found painted on the prows of boats and ships, on houses and vehicles, and are worn as beads and jewels in a multitude of cultures from the Mediterranean to the Indian Ocean.

In all cultures, eyes are believed to have special powers and are said to be windows onto the soul. So Tolkien's description of the evil Eye of Sauron gives

Eye of Sauron

us considerable insight into the Dark Lord himself: "The Eye was rimmed with fire, but was itself glazed, yellow as a cat's, watchful and intent, and the black slit of its pupil opened on a pit, a window into nothing." That last descriptive phrase, "a window into nothing," reveals Tolkien's Catholic and Augustinian moral view that evil is essentially the absence of good, and that ultimately evil in itself is a soul-destroying nothingness.

EYE OF SAURON

The most common visible manifestation of the spirit of the Dark Lord of Mordor in the Third Age. In *The Lord of the Rings*, the fiery "Eye of Sauron" is variously described as the "Red Eye," the "Evil Eye," the "Lidless Eye," and the "Great Eye." Tolkien developed this malign manifestation in part out of the tradition of the Evil Eye and imbued it with such a hallucinatory, elemental quality that it has the power to disturb and even terrify the reader.

It is difficult to determine whether the spirit of Sauron, after his defeat at the end of the Second Age, was ever able to regain an actual material form—a disembodiment, perhaps, that makes his malign power seem all the greater. Late in the last century of the Third Age, we are given one fearful encounter describing the Dark Lord's four-fingered "Black Hand," but whether this is a phantom shape or the actual material form of the Dark Lord is open to debate. Nonetheless we have it on the authority of Tolkien's son and executor, Christopher Tolkien, that in the War of the Ring it is the Eye that was the Dark Lord's primary manifestation: "father had come to identify the Eye of Barad-dûr with the mind and will of Sauron."

There is one important mythological source for the Eye. More generally, Odin in his guise as necromancer was the mythological figure who most obviously informed the identity of Sauron the Necromancer and, not coincidentally, was also known as the One-Eyed God. In the Norse canon, Odin sacrificed one of his eyes in exchange for one deep draft from Mirmir's Well, the "Well of Secret Knowledge." Thereafter, Odin—like Sauron— was able to consult with and command wraiths, phantoms, and spirits of the dead.

F

Fëanor. The greatest of the Eldar whose pride brings disaster on his kinsmen.

FÁFNIR   In Norse mythology the great dragon slain by Sigurd, originally a dwarf prince who transformed himself in order to protect his stolen treasure hoard. His story is told in the Old Norse *Völsunga Saga*. In the opera cycle *Ring der Nibelungen* (1848–74) by Richard Wagner, Fáfnir is portrayed originally as a giant.

Fáfnir was Tolkien's primary source of inspiration when he began to cast about for a dragon appropriate to the setting of Angband, Morgoth the Enemy's fortress. Tolkien required a creature that was brutal, murderous, and filled with low cunning. He wanted a creature that wallowed in the pleasures of torture of mind, body, and spirit. Tolkien knew exactly what he wanted and where to find it: the embodiment of something akin to the most evil of all monsters created by the collective imagination of the Germanic and Norse peoples. Few would disagree with Tolkien when it came to his choice: (and his inspiration for Glaurung the Father of Dragons): Fáfnir, the "Prince of All Dragons," and the spectacularly patricidal, fratricidal, genocidal, and deeply unpleasant usurper of the cursed golden treasure of Andvari.

Tolkien acknowledged that he had first encountered Fáfnir as a child, in Andrew Lang's *The Red Fairy Book* (1890). This included "The Story of Sigurd," a condensed version of William Morris and Eiríkur Magnússon's translation of the Old Norse *Völsunga Saga*. It was a tale that would fuel his imagination for the rest of his life. This early enthusiasm not only led to his study of Norse and Germanic literature and language—the focus of his life as a scholar—but also inspired his first serious attempt, at 22 years of age, as the creator of his own original stories. Those early compositions—drafted long before a glimmer of a Hobbit or a Ring Lord entered his mind—resulted in Tolkien's creation of his own full-blooded, fire-breathing monster.

In Tolkien's great Dragon of the First Age, Glaurung, we find a match in evil with Fáfnir. For, beyond dragon-fire and serpent-strength, Glaurung has more subtle powers: the keenest eyesight, the greatest sense of hearing and smell. He is a serpent of great cunning and cleverness, but his intelligence—like that of his entire race in Norse and Germanic legend—has the flaws of vanity, gluttony, greed, and deceit. The life and death of Glaurung the Deceiver is the tale of a powerful and original character that is central to *The Silmarillion*. While very much inspired by the *Völsunga Saga*, in many ways Tolkien's portrayal and characterization of this father of Dragons is much more nuanced and complex than his ancient model. And yet, in the end, Glaurung and Fáfnir suffer almost identical deaths. For just as Tolkien's hero Túrin Turambar plunges his sword Gurthang into Glaurung's soft underbelly in the slaying of the "Father of Dragons," so Sigurd the Völsung plunges his sword Gram into Fáfnir's soft underbelly in the slaying of the "Prince of All Dragons."

FALL OF ARTHUR, THE Tolkien's unfinished long poem about the death of King Arthur, largely written in the early 1930s, and edited and posthumously published by his son, Christopher, in 2013. Although Tolkien employed Arthurian motifs throughout his creative writing about Middle-earth and the Undying Lands, he did not care for the largely French-inspired courtly elements of Arthurian romance, as found, for example, in Thomas Malory's *Morte d'Arthur* (1485). Consequently, his own *Fall of Arthur* is an alliterative poem of nearly a thousand verses in the style and meter of the Old English *Beowulf* in which Arthur is a British military leader fighting a dark shadowy army of invaders out of the east led by the evil, dark knight Mordred. "The endless East in anger woke, / and black thunder born in dungeons / under mountains of menace moved above them." These lines could be directly transferred to Tolkien's Middle-earth to perfectly describe the dark forces of Mordor. It is tempting to link, too, the forces of Mordor led by the Nazgûl with Tolkien's description of Mordred's "wan horsemen wild in windy clouds" who appear as almost spectral warriors "shadow-helmed to war, shapes disastrous."

FALLOHIDE The least numerous and the most unconventional of the three kindreds of Hobbit, in origin woodland-dwelling and thus most friendly with the Elves. Usually the tallest and slimmest of their race, they are commonly fair-skinned, fair-haired, and most likely to go on adventures. Almost any display of individuality or ambition exhibited by a normally conventional Hobbit is usually attributed to a distant Fallohide bloodline.

The name Fallohide provides some of the inspiration for the character Tolkien gives to this kindred. *Falo* is an Old High German word meaning "pale yellow" (as in the color of a fallow deer), and "hide," of course, is a skin or pelt, and so together is descriptive of the outward appearance of the Fallohides. *Fallow*, meanwhile, is also Old English for "newly plowed land," and *hide* is an Old English measure of land sufficient for a household (about one hundred acres). This second derivation suggests the characteristics shared by all Hobbits: a love of newly tilled land and an uncanny ability to hide away in the landscape, so as to appear almost invisible to Men. Furthermore, one cannot help but think that there is yet another layer of wordplay with "Follow and Hide" as a Hobbitish version of the game of Hide and Seek. Typically fair-haired Fallohide family names are Fairbairn, Goold, and Goldworthy, while their unconventional, independent nature and their intelligence are suggested by such names as Headstrong and Boffin.

FARAMIR The second son of Denethor II, the last Ruling Steward of Gondor, and the Captain of the Rangers of Ithilien. Somewhat overshadowed by Boromir, his bold and ambitious brother, Faramir is depicted as humbler but more thoughtful, and just as steadfast in his defense of his homeland. Farimir is the character in *The Lord of the Rings* with whom the writer was most empathetic (though he could not claim his bravery), and so we may think of him as in some sense a self-portrait and certainly as a cypher for the author's outlook. Tolkien's personal perspective on heroism can be deduced from this quiet hero's eloquent statement: "I do not love the bright sword for its sharpness, not the arrow for its swiftness, nor the warrior for his glory. I love only for that which they defend."

FASTITOCALON In Hobbit lore, a vast Turtle-fish that Men believe is an island in the seas. Men build their camps on its back, but when they light their fires, the beast dives beneath the sea drowning all and sundry. A poem about the Fastitocalon is included in Tolkien's *The Adventures of Tom Bombadil* (1968) and is based on medieval legends of the

The Fall of Gondolin. The destruction of the Elven city of Gondolin in 511 FA recalls the fall of Troy in Greek mythology—a city likewise famous for its massive walls.

aspidochelone—a giant whale or sea turtle that sailors often mistook for an island and made landfall on its back. An Old English poem about the creature called "The Whal" provided Tolkien with his direct source.

FËANOR

The eldest son of Finwë, the High King of the Noldor Elves of Beleriand and creator of the Silmarils. Called Curufinwë at birth, he is later renamed Fëanor, meaning "Spirit of Fire." He is considered the greatest of all the Eldar in gifts of the mind, body, and spirit.

To some degree, Fëanor is comparable to the supernatural smith Ilmarinen in the Finnish epic the *Kalevala*. In that tale Ilmarinen forges the artifact known as the Sampo that could bring great wealth and good fortune to its possessor. In *The Silmarillion* Fëanor, likewise, creates three Elven gemstones filled with the light of the Trees of the Valar. Both artifacts excite greed and envy. See the entries on the Sampo and Silmarils for more on the connections between these

Fastitocalon. It is likely that this story from Hobbit lore—that Men built their camps on its back but when they lit their fires, the beast dived beneath the sea—is in fact an allegory of the Downfall of Númenóreans, as told in the *Akallabêth*.

magical artifacts. It is possible to draw parallels between Fëanor and other consummate craftsmen in the world's mythologies. The Greek craftsman-hero Daedalus, whose name means "cunningly wrought," also created artifacts that ultimately bring death and grief, most famously the wax wings that lead to his son Icarus's death when he flies too close to the sun. Ultimately, all such stories are warnings about the dangers of human—or indeed Elven—hubris.

FENRIR In Norse mythology the monstrous wolf that will slay Odin, the king of the gods, in the battle of Ragnarök, which brings an end to the world. He is the son of Loki, the trickster god, and is himself father of Sköll and Hati Hróthvitnisson, the two wolves that pursue the sun and the moon. In one of the best-known Norse myths concerning Fenrir, the gods, knowing the trouble he is destined to cause, attempt to bind him. The tasks proves impossible until Tyr, the brave god of war and law, sacrifices his right hand by placing it in the jaws of the wolf as a pledge of the gods' supposed good faith.

In Tolkien's legendarium we have a comparable monster in Carcharoth, meaning "red maw," the mightiest Wolf on Middle-earth. Sired by Draugluin, the Father of Werewolves, Carcharoth is the unsleeping guardian at the gates of the dark, subterranean kingdom of Angband. It is in that role of guardian of the gates in the Quest for the Silmaril that Carcharoth bites off the hand of Beren Erchamion (meaning "one-handed") in an episode redolent of the "Binding of the Wolf" myth.

FIELD OF CELEBRANT The site of one of the most critical battles in the history of Gondor. In 2050 TA in the Battle of the Field of Celebrant, the forces of Gondor were about to be overrun by barbarian Easterling invaders known as the Balchoth. At a critical moment, the tide of battle was turned by the sudden appearance of the Éothéod cavalry of Eorl the Young that crushed and destroyed the Easterling forces, driving them back to their own lands.

The Battle of the Field of Celebrant has a historic precedence in AD 451, when the Visigoth cavalry carried out a dramatic rescue of the Roman Empire in the Battle of the Catalaunian Fields. This proved to be one of the most critical battles in European history, as the invader was Attila the Hun (c. AD 406–53), leader of the most formidable barbarian force the Romans had ever faced.

After the Battle of the Catalaunian Fields and the retreat of the invading Huns, as reward for their military service, the Visigoths became the main inheritors of the lands devastated by the barbarian wars and plagues. Similarly, after the Battle of the Field of Celebrant and the retreat of the Balchoth, as reward for their military service the Éothéod became the main inheritors of the lands devastated by those same factors. This was the fief of Gondor previously called Calenardhon, which now became known as Rohan, "Land of the Horse Lords." In these lands, the Horse Lords of Rohan were able to live as free men under their own kings and laws, though always in alliance with Gondor.

The leader of the Visigoths in the Battle of the Catalaunian Fields was King Theodoric I (c. AD 390–451). His service inspired Tolkien's account not only of the Battle of the Field of Celebrant led by Eorl, the first king of Rohan, but also the cavalry charge in the Battle of Pelennor Fields led by Théoden, the seventeenth king of Rohan, a thousand years later. Not only were the kings' names almost identical but also their victories came at the cost of their own lives, with both kings crushed beneath their fallen steeds.

FINNISH LANGUAGE AND LITERATURE

While an undergraduate at Oxford, Tolkien discovered a Finnish grammar, which fascinated him: "It was like discovering a complete wine-cellar filled with bottles of an amazing wine of a kind and flavour never tasted before. It quite intoxicated me." It was a fascination that proved to be influential in the invention of his High Elvish language, Quenya, though only a few words can be shown to be directly derived from Finnish.

Soon after his discovery of the Finnish grammar, Tolkien read the *Kalevala*, a collection of Finnish tales and poems put together by the philologist Elias Lönnrot

(1802–84), which became the national epic of Finland. It revealed a mythology that would be hugely influential on the composition of *The Silmarillion*. Many years later, in a letter to the poet W. H. Auden, Tolkien acknowledged the importance of the *Kalevala* in his creative life: ". . . the beginning of the legendarium . . . was in an attempt to reorganize some of the *Kalevala*, especially the tale of Kullervo the hapless, into a form of my own." The tale of Kullervo the hapless, one of the key figures in the epic, eventually appeared in Tolkien's writing in the tragic figure of Túrin Turambar (ironically meaning "Turin the Master of Doom"). Other characters and themes of the *Kalevala* may be discovered in Tolkien's *The Silmarillion*. To some degree, Fëanor the Elven-smith who forges the Silmarils is comparable to the supernatural smith Ilmarinen who forges the mysterious, magical artifact known as the Sampo.

The degree of Tolkien's engagement with Finnish literature became fully apparent in 2015 with the publication of his own 1914 prose version of *The Story of Kullervo*, edited by Verlyn Flieger and illustrated by Alan Lee.

See also: QUENYA

FINWË   The first King of the Noldor who undertakes the Great Journey out of the wilderness of the eastern mortal lands of Middle-earth and leads his people across the sea to the promised land of Eldamar, the immortal "Elven-home" in the Undying Lands of Aman. There, after the death of his first wife, Miriel (who willingly chooses to die after giving birth to Fëanor) he decides to remarry. This decision has disastrous consequences, as Melkor is able to exploit Fëanor's feelings of enmity toward his half-brothers.

Like Ingwë, king of the Vanyar, he is something of a Moses figure. However, in other ways Finwë is like the biblical Adam. In some Jewish traditions the first man has two wives, first Lilith and then Eve, and it is Adam's fateful choice, when tempted by Eve in the Garden of Eden, that dooms humankind to sin. Finwë becomes the first victim in the War of the Jewels, as he is slain by Melkor/Morgoth, the Dark Enemy, before the gates of the Noldor fortress of Formenos where the Silmarils are hidden.

FLYING DUTCHMAN

The name of a ghost ship that can never make port and is doomed to sail the oceans forever. Sightings of this phantom ship, glowing with a spectral light, were made starting in the eighteenth century. In 1843, this legend became the focus of Richard Wagner's early opera *Der fliegende Holländer*, in which the curse that kept the *Flying Dutchman* and its captain forever at sea is ultimately lifted by the love of a virtuous maiden.

Tolkien's tale of another lonely mariner, Eärendil, takes some of its inspiration from the legend. However, he entirely inverts the story by making his mariner not cursed and aimless but blessed and purposeful. Eärendil, in his wanderings on his ship *Vingilótë* through an endless maze of shadowy seas and enchanted isles, is acting as emissary of the Elves and Edain of Beleriand.

The comparison tightens, however, in the motif of the leaping lover. In Wagner's opera, the heroine Senta, in an act of self-sacrifice and love, throws herself from a cliff into the sea, and so lifts the curse on the soul of the captain of the *Flying Dutchman*. In Tolkien's tale, Eärendil's wife, Elwing the White, also leaps to a seemingly certain death from a high cliff into the sea. However, unlike Senta, Elwing is transformed into a seabird. In this form, she seeks out Eärendil, carrying the Silmaril, the holy jewel of living light, in her beak.

Flies of Mordor. These gray, black, and brown blood-sucking insects are marked, as Orcs are marked, with a red eye-shape upon their backs.

FOUR-FARTHING STONE

See: THREE-FARTHING STONE

FREYA/FREJA   One of the preeminent goddesses in Norse mythology, Freya is the goddess of love and war and sister of Freyr. She may be in origin identical with another goddess, Frigg, wife of Odin, and queen of both the Aer and Vanir gods. As a fertility goddess, she has something in common with Tolkien's Yavanna Kementári, whose character, however, is far removed from the often scandalous tales associated with Freya. Curiously enough, one of Freya's typically adulterous adventures, involving the acquisition of the Brísingamen, the "Necklace of the Dwarves," was undoubtedly the inspiration for Tolkien's somewhat less salacious (although equally disastrous) tale of the Nauglamír, the "Necklace of the Dwarves."

FREYR   The Norse god of the sun and rain. Like his sister Freya, the goddess of love and war, Freyr is one of the Vanir, a tribe of fertility gods who united with the Aesir gods of war to form a single pantheon under Odin. Just as his sister Freya's name means "the Lady," so Freyr's name means "the Lord." Tolkien observed that this golden-haired god was also known as "Yngvi-freyr" or "Ingwe-the-Lord" of the Vanir and imaginatively linked this god to his own golden-haired lord Ingwe of the Vanyar, the High Elven King of Eldamar.

Tolkien was also inspired by Freyr's heroic last stand during Ragnarök, the last battle in the war of the gods and the giants. Standing on Bifrost—the Rainbow Bridge between Middle-earth and Asgard—Freyr fights Surt the Fire Giant the Lord of Muspelheim who is armed with a great sword of flame. This duel is mirrored in Tolkien's Battle on the Bridge of Khazad-dûm between Gandalf the Wizard and the Balrog of Moria with his fiery sword and whips of flame. Surt and Freya are entirely destroyed in their last battle, while the Balrog and Wizard continue their struggle until the Balrog is slain, but at the cost of life of Gandalf in his bodily form as the Grey Wizard.

FRIGG   In Norse mythology, a goddess of wisdom and foresight, and the wife of Odin. She is commonly identified with Freya, and there is a certain overlap in the stories told about the two goddesses. Her position in the Norse pantheon makes her comparable with Tolkien's Queen Varda Elentári, the "Lady of the Stars," who is spouse of Manwë, the king of the Valar. However, while Frigg can seem a rather shadowy goddess, best known for the tale in which she attempts to make her doomed son Baldr invulnerable, Varda is one of the most characterful figures in Tolkien's pantheon.

FRODA   The name of several legendary Danish kings and the source for the name of Tolkien's Hobbit hero Frodo Baggins. In the Old English epic of *Beowulf* there is Froda, the powerful king of the Heathobards, who attempts to make peace between the Danes and Bards. Likewise, the medieval Icelandic poet and historian Snorri Sturluson (1179–1241) recorded that another King Froda was a contemporary of the Roman Emperor Augustus and that his reign was conspicuous for peacefulness. In Icelandic texts, indeed, we find the expression *Frotha-frith*, meaning "Frotha's peace," referring to just such a golden age of peace and wealth.

All this is in tune with Frodo's compassion and attempts to avoid bloodshed in all his adventures. After the carnage of the war, Frodo the Wise becomes a respected counselor and peacemaker throughout Middle-earth. Certainly, within the Shire, Hobbits experience the equivalent of the Norse legend of *Frotha-frith* with Frodo's Peace, the year after the Battle of Bywater, in the time of the First Blossoming of the Golden Tree of Hobbiton. The war-ravaged Shire is transformed and filled with Elvish enchantment. In that year, many children born to Hobbits are golden-haired and beautiful, and everything prospers in the Shire. This is the Great Year of Plenty that marks the beginning of a golden age of the Shire, the Age of Peace and Wealth.

FRODO BAGGINS   The cousin, adopted "nephew," and heir to Tolkien's original Hobbit, Bilbo Baggins of Bag End. Tolkien's

Frodo and the Barrow-wight

acknowledgment that "names always generate a story in my mind" reveals a great deal about Hobbits in general, and Bilbo and Frodo Baggins in particular. In Frodo's case there is a linguistic chain of logic: Frodo's name in the original Hobbitish is Froda, and, as Tolkien knew well enough, *fród* in Old English meant "wise"; while its Norse equivalent *Frothi* was a name meaning "wise one." Frodo, as well as being peace-loving, is depicted throughout *The Lord of the Rings* as thoughtful and measured, contrasting with the "half-wise" Sam Gamgee and the foolish Peregrin Took. At the end of the book he is celebrated as "Frodo the Wise" and "Frodo the Peacemaker."

Deeper historical and mythical associations also contributed to the character and the destiny of the Ring-bearer. In Old English literature and Scandinavian mythology, the name Frodo (or Froda, Frothi, Frotha) is often connected with figures associated with peace.

FURIES
In Greco-Roman mythology, the female chthonic deities who avenge crimes. Perhaps the best-known myth associated with the Furies—or the Erinyes—concerns the Greek hero Orestes who, after murdering his mother, Clytemnestra, is ruthlessly pursued by the goddesses. So great was the fear of their wrath that the Furies were often spoken of as the Eumenides (ironically meaning "the kindly ones"). These terrible avengers were variously described as having snakes for hair, coal-black bodies, bats' wings, and blood-red eyes; they attacked their victims with blazing torches and many-thonged brass-studded whips.

In some respects, the Furies are comparable to Morgoth's servants the terrifying Valaraukar ("cruel demons"), better known under their Sindarin name the Balrogs ("demons of might"). These spirits upon Middle-earth took the form of man-shaped giants shrouded in darkness with manes of fire, eyes that glowed like burning coals, and nostrils that breathed flame. Balrogs wielded many-thonged whips of fire in combination with a mace or flaming sword.

Falls of Rauros. Rauros means "roaring foam" and describes the most spectacular waterfalls of Middle-earth. After Boromir's death, Aragorn and his companions lay his body in a funeral boat, which passes over the Falls before continuing down the Great River.

Galadriel and Her Mirror

GALADRIEL
A Noldor noblewoman, only daughter of Finarfin, and, in *The Lord of the Rings*, the ruler of the enchanted Elven realm of Lothlórien, "the land of blossoms dreaming." In that hidden wooded land, robed in white and golden-haired, she commands great powers of enchantment and prophecy.

In ancient Welsh mythology we find forest and water nymphs who closely resemble Galadriel, the guardians of sacred fountains, wells, and grottoes hidden in deep forest vales. Like Tolkien's "Lady of Light," White Ladies have eyes like stars and bodies that shimmer with light, betokening their close affinity with the starlit night. To reach their realms it is commonly necessary to pass through or across water that was—as is said when the Fellowship cross over a river into Lothlórien—"like crossing a bridge in time." These White Ladies often lived in realms "outside of time" in crystal palaces beneath water or floating in air, all glowing with silver and golden light.

In Arthurian tradition, Vivien, the Lady of the Lake and perhaps in origin a Celtic White Lady herself, rises dressed in white from her palace beneath the lake to present the sword and scabbard of Excalibur to the rightful king. Vivien also raises Lancelot du Lac before sending him into the world with the arms of war. We might see a similar figure in Greek mythology, the sea nymph Thetis, mother of Achilles, the greatest hero of the Trojan War, who gifts her son with his armor.

Across cultures and times we find water and forest deities who give protection, prophecies, inspiration, invisibility, and strength to their protégés. Galadriel, too, belongs to this tradition, presiding over a realm of dreams and desires, visions and illusions, and gifts and blessings.

GAMGEE
Surname of Samwise Gamgee, the constant loyal companion of the Ring-bearer Frodo Baggins in the great Quest of the Ring. Samwise Gamgee is the son of the Bag-End gardener, Hamfast Gamgee.

Father and son's working-class family name Gamgee is both descriptive and playful. The original Hobbitish name is Galpsi, an abbreviated form of Galbasi, meaning from the village of Galabas (Galpsi), a name derived from *galab*, meaning "game," "jest," or "joke," and *bas*, meaning "village" (in Old English, *wich*). So we have "Game Village," which translates into English as Gamwich (pronounced Gammidge), becomes Gammidgy, and ends up as Gamgee.

In Samwise Gamgee we have the perfect foil to his master, Frodo Baggins. Simple, down-to-earth Sam Gamgee is both game for any challenge and, despite terrible hardships, always willing to attempt a jest or joke to keep everyone's spirits up during the Quest of the Ring.

GANDALF THE GREY
One of the Istari (order of Wizards)—Maiar sent to Middle-earth in about 1,000 TA to aid in the struggle against Sauron. Known to various peoples as Mithrandir, Tharkûn, and Incánus, in Valinor he is Olórin, of the people of Manwë. He is one of the central figures in both *The Hobbit* and *The Lord of the Rings*.

Gandalf has multiple sources of inspiration in the mythologies of many nations. He is akin to Merlin of the Britons, Odin of the Norsemen, Wotan of the Germans, Mercury of the Romans, Hermes of the Greeks, and Thoth of the Egyptians. All are linked with magic, sorcery, arcane knowledge, and secret doctrine. Most obviously, in appearance, Gandalf, like Merlin, Odin, and Wotan, takes on the form of a wandering old man in a gray cloak carrying a staff. Gandalf is comparable to these figures in his powers and deeds, like Merlin or Hermes, for example, serving as a guide to the hero and helping him to win against impossible odds by using his supernatural powers.

In *The Hobbit*, however, Gandalf appears largely as a standard fairy-tale character: a rather comic, eccentric magician in the company of a band of Dwarves. (He even has something of the character of an absent-minded history professor about him, of which Tolkien would have had firsthand experience.) Like his fairy-tale counterparts, Gandalf also fulfills the traditional role of mentor, adviser, and tour guide for the hero and in so doing moves the plot rapidly forward. Wizards usually provide a narrative that comprises a reluctant hero, secret maps, translations of ancient documents, supernatural weapons (and how to use them), some monsters (and how to kill them), location of treasure (and how to steal it), and an escape plan (negotiable).

Galadhrim. Within the forest of Lothlórien is the concealed Elven kingdom of the Galadhrim, the "tree people." They are mostly Silvan Elves, but their lords are Sindar and Noldor nobles.

Gandalf the White

Gandalf the Grey certainly fits into this tradition. It is Gandalf who brings the Dwarves and the Hobbit Bilbo Baggins together at the start of the story and sets them on their quest. It is his injection of adventure and magic into the mundane world of the Hobbits that transforms Bilbo Baggins's world. It is Gandalf who leads the band of outlaw adventurers in the form of Thorin and Company to Bilbo's door. It is just this combination of the everyday and the epic that makes *The Hobbit* so compelling. Grand adventures with Dragons, Trolls, Elves, and treasure are combined with the afternoon teas, toasted English muffins, pints of ale, and smoke-ring-blowing contests.

In *The Hobbit*, then, Gandalf is an amusing and reassuring presence, something like a fairy godfather. In the opening chapter of *The Lord of the Rings*, he seems to reprise the role, appearing much like an odd but much-loved uncle who always amuses everyone with his amateur magic tricks. Gandalf's subsequent transformation into a grave and formidable figure is something of a surprise. As the book continues, the force of his personality and ethical purpose increases tenfold as he is revealed as a powerful archetypal wizard. His later transformation into Gandalf the White is even more shocking. In this, Tolkien seems to be making the point that behind all fairy-tale magicians are the powerful archetypes from myth and epic. *See also*: ODIN

GANDALF THE WHITE

The powerful reincarnation of the wizard Gandalf the Grey after his battle with the Balrog of Moria in *The Lord of the Rings*. In this startling transformation, Gandalf fully reveals his status as one of Istari, the order of Wizards who in origin are among the immortal angelic powers known as the Maiar. Sent to Middle-earth at the end of the first millennium of the Third Age, the Istari, as emissaries of the Valar, serve as advisers to the rulers of the mortal lands.

Gandalf's name derives from the Old Icelandic *Dvergatal*, "Roll of the Dwarves," where it appears as Gandalfr. The two Old Norse elements of Gandalfr are either *gand*, or *gandr*, and *alf(r)*. *Alf(r)* means either "elf" or "white." If the first element is *gand*, it suggests magical power, while, if it is *gandr*, it means an object used by sorcerers, such as an enchanted staff.

As to the direct translation of the name Gandalf, then, there are three fairly solid alternatives: "elf wizard," "white staff," and "white sorcerer." All three translations are admirably suitable names for a wizard. However, Tolkien would likely argue that each translated aspect of this particular Wizard has other definitions hidden within, and we can see how the implications of both layers of meaning played a considerable part in shaping the fate of the character. The translation "elf wizard" is appropriate because Gandalf is the Wizard most closely associated with the Elves of Middle-earth and the Undying Lands. "White staff" is an apt name as the staff is the primary symbol by which a wizard is known. The translation of Gandalf as "white wizard," meanwhile, is initially confusing, as his Grey Elven name is Mithrandir, meaning "gray wanderer" (echoed in his common epithet, "the Grey"), and may seem to make the name a more suitable one for Saruman the White.

However, this conflict in meaning appears to be a foreshadowing of a twist in plot in which Gandalf the Grey is transformed into Gandalf the White.

Beyond these relatively straightforward translations of the name, we may contemplate an alternative one for the first element in Gandalf's name: *gand*, meaning "astral traveling." After falling with the Balrog from the Bridge of Moria, the Wizard's salvation and resurrection seem to come about through a form of astral traveling. As Gandalf the White, the Wizard offers no explanation for his resurrection, but simply states: "I strayed out of thought and time." A better definition of "astral traveling" could not, perhaps, be imagined.

As an astral traveler, Gandalf is comparable to the Norse god Odin who, in his shamanic wizard form, traveled between the world of men and the worlds of spirits, and even into the land of the dead. Certainly, Tolkien had this in mind when he gave Gandalf's horse the name Shadowfax meaning "silver-gray." Shadowfax has a direct counterpart in Norse myth in Grani, Sigurd's horse in the *Völsunga Saga*. Shadowfax, moreover, is the offspring of the supernatural horse Nahar, the Valarian steed of Oromë the Hunter, while Grani is the offspring of the supernatural eight-legged horse Sleipnir on which Odin rode down through the Nine Worlds.

GARM In Norse mythology the gigantic dog or wolf that is the guardian at the gates of Helheim, the realm of the dead. This bloody and ferocious monster will be chained at the entrance to Gnipahellir, his kennel-cave, until Ragnarök, when his chains will be broken and he will join in that final battle with the giants against the gods. Garm will attack Tyr the One-handed, god of war, and engage in a battle that will end in their mutual destruction.

In Tolkien's world we have a comparable monster in the gigantic Carcharoth, meaning "red maw," the greatest wolf of the First Age and the unsleeping guardian at the gates of Morgoth's underworld realm of Angband. In the Quest for the Silmaril, Carcharoth bites off hand of the hero, Beren (henceforth, like Tyr, known as the One-handed). Both Garm and Carcharoth are comparable to the ancient Greek Cerberus, the unsleeping three-headed hellhound that guards the underworld gates of Hades.

GESER KHAGAN

In the mythology of Central Asia and northeastern South Asia, a warrior, magician, smith, and king who rules the greatest mountain kingdom in the East. The story of this culture's hero is recorded in poetry and prose across Asia, together forming a loose epic cycle. Although there is no definitive version, it is reputed to be the longest oral epic in existence with well over a million recorded verses in multiple languages and dialects.

Geser is a warrior-king who is both a smith and a magician. To such a hero, all things are possible. He assumes many forms, creates invulnerable weapons, conjures up phantom armies, and creates wealth and prosperity for his people. In Asian myth and history, the ancient connection between alchemy or metallurgy and the power of kings and heroes is often made explicit (the connection is also present but obscured in European ring quest epics like the *Völsunga Saga* and the *Nibelungenlied*). Tradition insists, for instance, that the great historic Mongol conqueror Genghis Khan was descended from a family of smiths, as was the legendary Tartar hero Kok Chan.

The multiskilled hero Geser becomes king of his lands by virtue of many feats of heroism and magic. His confirmation as king comes when the supernatural guardians of the kingdom allow him entry into a crystal mountain where the treasures of the kingdom are kept. The most important of these is the emblematic throne of the realm. On this rests a huge gold mandala ring, at the center of which is a crystal vessel from where the shining "waters of immortality" flow. His archenemy, the evil Kurkar, has a similar ring or talisman that must be kept safe and by whose power he rules his kingdom.

There is no indication that Tolkien knew or was inspired by the tales of Geser and Kurkar, but both *The Lord of the Rings* and the stories of Geser share an ancient and widespread archetypal theme of kings as magician-smiths and ring lords. Sauron the Ring Lord shares many characteristics with both Geser and Kurkar. Like Geser, Sauron is both a supernaturally gifted smith capable of creating unmatched wonders in his forge, and a magician capable of terrifying acts of sorcery. Both have mountain strongholds, and both must keep safe the golden rings by whose powers they rule their kingdoms.

At this point, the comparison between Geser and Sauron largely ceases. Sauron the Dark Lord is much more closely akin to the malevolent Kurkar. Kurkar's iron talisman, too, is much more like Sauron's One Ring because both are inherently

Warrior-king. There is an ancient and widespread archetypal theme of warrior kings as magician-smiths and ring lords.

evil, and the sorcerers' lives depend on the survival of the rings. Kurkar's iron ring also shares the One Ring's characteristic of being almost indestructible. Normal fires do not even cause the metal to redden, and both require supernatural fires of volcanic intensity to melt them down.

GHOST WITCH

In the mythology of the Mi'kmaq, indigenous First Nations people, a terrifying wraithlike entity, properly known as a *skadegamutc*. The Mi'kmaq ghost witch arises out of a widespread tradition in which an evil spirit inhabits the dead body of a black sorcerer. Although Tolkien was unlikely to have known of this particular myth, the ghost witch bears some resemblance to his Nazgûl, who used the Rings of Power to establish themselves as mighty kings and sorcerers. Like the Nazgûl, ghost witches avoid daylight and emerge by night to track down and murder their prey. They have the power to paralyze with terror or enthrall with a glance of the eye or the sound of their voice. Also like the Nazgûl, as shown in the attack on the Hobbits on Weathertop in *The Lord of the Rings*, they appear to be repelled by fire.

GIGANTOMACHY

The war between the Olympian gods led by Zeus (the Roman Jupiter) and the giants. Like the Titanomachy—the primordial war between the Olympians and the Titans—before it, it is comparable to the first battles on Tolkien's Arda between the Valar and Morgoth and the rebel Maiar. An epic on the battle has been lost (if it ever existed), but accounts or allusions can be found in, among other places, the works of the Greek poet Pindar and the Roman poet Ovid's *Metamorphoses*. In the latter we find extraordinary descriptions of the giants' attempt to seize "the throne of Heaven" by piling "mountain on mountain to the lofty stars" that may well remind us of Tolkien's descriptions of the rending and splitting of mountains that takes place during Arda's primordial cosmic wars.

GIL-GALAD

Elven nobleman, son of Fingon, and high king of the Noldor—and indeed the Eldar—through the Second Age. At the end of that age he leads the Elves in the Last Alliance of Elves and Men and, with Elendil, duels with Sauron, resulting in both Sauron's and his own death.

Gil-galad's story was in part informed by the legends relating to the downfall of Arthur and the knights of the Round Table. Even his name, meaning "Star of Radiance," cannot help but conjure up the most perfect knight of the Round Table, Sir Galahad, even if the characters meet very different—even inverted—fates. While Galahad achieves the Holy Grail and ascends into Heaven, Gil-galad is burned by the heat of Sauron's hand and passes to the Halls of Mandos.

The Last Battle of the Arthurian Age at Camlann and the Last Battle of the Alliance of Elves and Men at Dagorlad both result in the downfall of the dark forces—of Arthur's enemy, Mordred, and Middle-earth's enemy Sauron. However, in both realms, this victory of the righteous and good comes at the cost of the lives of their kings and the loss of alliances that can never be recovered. The end of the knights of the Round Table and the descent of Arthur's kingdom into chaos is echoed in the end of the Alliance of Elves and Men, with the retreat of the Elves to hidden kingdoms and the slow decline of the kingdoms of Arnor and Gondor over the millennia to come.

Also, in Arthur's world and in Tolkien's Middle-earth, both wars ultimately come down to one final duel. King Arthur slays and is slain by the forever-damned Mordred, while Sauron slays both Gil-galad and Elendil, but is finally overthrown when the One Ring is cut from his hand.

GIMLI The only Dwarf in the Fellowship of the Ring in *The Lord of the Rings*. His father, Glóin, is one of the thirteen Dwarves in the Company of Thorin Oakenshield in the Quest of Erebor in *The Hobbit*. After the Battle of Hornburg, Gimli is forced to take refuge and defend the redoubt in the caverns of Helm's Deep, and thereby discovers the Glittering Caves of Aglarond. These, he believes, are the greatest interlocking network of caverns and grottos in all of Middle-earth, a discovery that could make it a potential paradise for Dwarves. Here, once again, Tolkien's precise use of language is worth noting. In this case, it is in the relationship between the word "glittering" and the name Gimli.

All of Tolkien's Dwarves' names— except for one—were taken from the *Dvergatal*, an Old Norse list of dwarf names. That one is Gimli, which is mentioned in a very different Norse text, an ancient poem entitled *Völuspá*, or *Sybil's Prophecy*, the first poem of the *Poetic Edda*. However, Gimli in this instance is not the name of a dwarf or man but rather a place. Gimli actually means, "glittering," and is the name given to the Norse paradise: a great golden-roofed hall and kingdom that will appear after the great battle of Ragnarök as a new Valhalla.

It seems that, just as Gimli will be revealed in the wake of Ragnarök as a glittering paradise for the Norse people, so in the wake of the War of the Ring, Gimli reveals a new paradise for Dwarves by colonizing the Glittering Caves of Aglarond.

GJALLARHORN

In Norse mythology, the horn of Heimdall, the vigilant watchman of the gods of Asgard. It was foretold that the final battle of Ragnarök between the gods and the giant would begin when Heimdall sounded the Gjallarhorn ("resounding horn") as Loki and the *jötnar* stormed Bifrost, the Rainbow Bridge.

Heimdall's horn has two key parallels in Tolkien. First, there is Valaróma, the hunting horn of Oromë, the Huntsman of the Valar, whose terrifying sound (like lightning striking clouds), resounds as the Vala pursues the servants of Morgoth. And second there is the Horn of Gondor blown by Boromir before the battle on the Bridge of Khazad-dûm and just before his own death near Parth Galen, two crucial moments in *The Lord of the Rings*.

GLAURUNG, THE FATHER OF DRAGONS

The first and greatest of the Urulóki, or fire-breathing Dragons, of Middle-earth. This mighty serpent is depicted as being of massive size and strength, and protected by scales of impenetrable iron. His fangs and claws are rapier-sharp, and his great tail can crush the shield-wall of any army. An original creation and villain, Glaurung was—like all of Tolkien's creatures—nonetheless deeply rooted in ancient literature and language.

As his principal inspiration for Glaurung, Tolkien looked to the dragon Fáfnir, the "Prince of All Dragons" in Norse myth and legend, where he guards a mighty treasure horde and is ultimately slain by the hero Sigurd. Glaurung, however, is perhaps an even more malevolent figure than Fáfnir, because beyond dragon-fire and serpent-strength, Glaurung is cunning (though his intelligence—like all of his species in Norse and Germanic legends—is tempered by the flaws of vanity, gluttony, and greed).

The life and death of Glaurung is one of the central tales of *The Silmarillion*, a tale very much inspired by the *Völsunga Saga*. In Tolkien's tale, the Dragon-slayer is Túrin Turambar, who shares many of the characteristics and adventures of Sigurd, the Norse hero of the Icelandic saga. The hero's guile and battle tactics are certainly comparable. For just as Túrin plunges his sword Gurthang into Glaurung's soft underbelly in the slaying of the "Father of Dragons," so Sigurd plunges his sword Gram into Fáfnir's soft underbelly in the slaying of the "Prince of All Dragons."

GNOMES
In European folklore a stunted race of beings that dwell under the earth and are associated with its mineral riches. They seem to have been originally invented by the Swiss alchemist Paracelsus (1493/4–1541), who described them as measuring "two span" (18 in.) in height and capable of moving through solid earth as easily as humans move through air. He derived their name from the Latin *genomos*, which in turn was probably a transliteration of a Greek word meaning "earth-dweller." Over time, gnomes became associated with the much older Germanic dwarfs and by the twentieth century were reduced to the status of garden ornaments throughout Europe and North America.

However, just as Tolkien rehabilitated fairy-tale dwarfs and reinvented them as his Dwarves of Middle-earth, in early versions of *The Silmarillion* Tolkien attempted to rehabilitate these *Gartenzwerge* (German "garden dwarfs") by reinventing them as his Second Kindred of Elves. In Tolkien's original drafts, this powerful kindred of Elves was to be called the Gnomes, a name that Tolkien derived from the Greek *gnosis*, meaning "knowledge." In the end, the difficulty of overcoming popular conceptions of gnomes as tubby garden fixtures probably proved too much of an obstacle, and Tolkien settled on the name Noldor instead.

However, so as to keep to his original intention of associating the Second

Glaurung at the Fifth Battle

Kindred with knowledge, he derived the new name from his invented Elvish language Quenya, where *noldo* means "knowledge." Some of the gnomes' association with the earth and minerals also survives in the Noldor: on settling in the immortal land of Eldamar, they become apprentices to Aulë the Smith. From him they learn all the secrets of the treasures to be found in the deep earth, and become the greatest craftsmen of the Elves in the shaping of jewels and forging of metals. For this knowledge and skill, the Noldor—once related to the humble garden gnome—become the "Wise Elves" and "Deep Elves" of Tolkien's epic tale *The Silmarillion*.

GOBLINS   In European folklore, grotesque, devil-like creatures akin to imps and kobolds, usually but not always malevolent, or at least mischievous. In Tolkien's legendarium, they appear in *The Hobbit*, as the Goblins and as the Great Goblin of Goblin-town, used as a synonym for the evil race of Orcs.

Tolkien's *The Hobbit* and its Goblins owe a debt of inspiration to the Scottish writer George MacDonald (1824–1905) and his 1872 novel *The Princess and the Goblin*, as Tolkien explicitly acknowledged in a letter. Even without this admission, we have some clear textual evidence: a little MacDonald song, included in his novel, begins: "Once there was a Goblin / Living in a hole . . .". This is very close to Tolkien's opening line in *The Hobbit*: "In a hole in the ground there lived a hobbit." However, while both Goblins and Hobbits are hole-dwellers, they are quite different in their nature.

In *The Hobbit* the narrator warns the reader that the Misty Mountains are made perilous by hordes of "goblins, hobgoblins, and orcs of the worst description." Each of these names is a synonym for the other, or very nearly, as Tolkien himself explained in the preface to his novel: "Orc is not an English word. It occurs in one or two places [in *The Hobbit*] but is usually translated goblin (or hobgoblin for the larger kinds)." Orcs, of course, in Middle-earth, are the evil foot soldiers of the Dark Lords Morgoth and Sauron. However, the publishing history of Tolkien novels ensured that readers would first encounter them under the Goblin name.

The Hobbit was written decades after most of *The Silmarillion* was conceived, but with his young audience in mind Tolkien needed to somewhat mute the evil nature of his cannibalistic Orcs, adopting instead the rather more mischievous comic nature of the fairy-tale goblins found in MacDonald's work. However, readers who progress from *The Hobbit* to the high romance of *The Lord of the Rings* and the heroic age of *The Silmarillion* soon discover that Tolkien no longer portrays Goblins simply as comic grotesques, but as the seriously irredeemably evil race of Middle-earth in thrall to the Dark Lord.

In his letter mentioning the influence of George MacDonald, Tolkien speaks of his borrowing from "the Goblin tradition," so one must also acknowledge the international nature of these creatures. His Goblins share many aspects with Germanic, Nordic, and British traditions, with kobolds, bogies, knockers, bugbears, red caps, demons, imps, sprites, and gremlins, as well as with beings from the folk traditions of Asia, such as the Malayan Toyol or Cambodian Cohen Kroh, evil, twisted spirits animating the bodies of murdered children or fetuses.

GOLDBERRY

In *The Lord of the Rings*, Goldberry is the wife of Tom Bombadil and the "River-woman's daughter." While the text is not explicit about her origin, she is perhaps the entity in Tolkien's world who comes closest to being a Greek Naiad, or water nymph, a *genius loci* (spirit of the place) of the River Withywindle.

See also: NYMPHS

GOLLUM

Originally known as Sméagol, a Hobbit who, under the influence of the One Ring, becomes a murderous ghoul and cannibal that shuns the light and finds grim solace in dark caverns and dank pools. He plays a key role in both *The Hobbit* and *The Lord of the Rings*, where he appears as a foil and even alter ego of the main protagonists, Bilbo and Frodo Baggins, respectively. There is some inconsistency in his portrayal across the two books: in *The Hobbit* he is shown as some sort of murderous, cannibalistic Goblin feared even by other Goblins, while in *The Lord of the Rings* Tolkien reveals Gollum to be an ancestral Stoorish Hobbit long

Goblins. In *The Hobbit*, the foul race of Orcs are most often called by the more familar
name of Goblins.

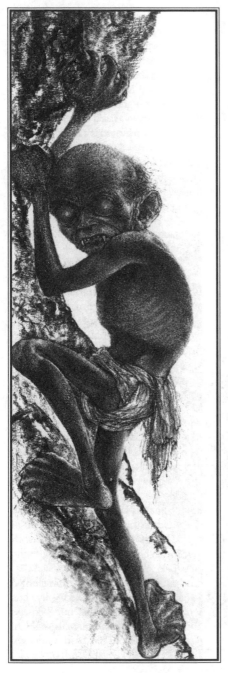

Gollum

banished from his people and corrupted by the One Ring.

The evolution of the character Sméagol and his alter ego Gollum draws on a considerable body of mythology related to ring legends. In the Icelandic *Völsunga Saga*, the most famous ring legend in Norse mythology, Fáfnir, the son of the dwarf king (also called "Magician-King") Hreidmar, murders his own father because of his desire to possess a cursed ring and its treasure. This is comparable to Sméagol's murder of his cousin Déagol because of his desire to possess the One Ring. Retreating, like Sméagol, to a mountain cave, Fáfnir broods over his ring and eventually transforms into a monstrous dragon. Similarly, Sméagol, who through the power of the One Ring extends his life over many centuries, transforms into a ghoul twisted in mind and body, ultimately emerging as the cannibalistic Gollum brooding over his "precious." The Icelandic narrative poem *Völundarkvitha*, part of the *Poetic Edda*, reveals a similar ghoul, Sote the Outlaw. Sote steals a cursed ring, but he so fears it may be taken from him, he has himself buried alive with it, and sleeplessly guards it with his weapons drawn.

Gollum's name cannot but remind us of the Golem of Jewish folklore, a creature created out of clay and of a similar ambivalent nature. The Modern Hebrew word *golem* means "dumb" and popularly is applied to someone who serves another under certain conditions, but is just as likely to turn against him if given the chance—a description that perfectly describes the relationship between Gollum and Frodo in *The Lord of the Rings*. In Gollum, this characteristic might be called pathological, so that in Sméagol–Gollum we have a classic case of a split personality, of the kind portrayed in Robert Louis Stevenson's *The Strange Case of Dr. Jekyll and Mr. Hyde* or Charles Dickens's *The Mystery of Edwin Drood*.
See also: J E K Y L L   A N D   H Y D E

G O N D O R   The greatest realm of Men in the west of the Middle-earth, founded at the end of the Second Age by the Númenórean exiles Isildur and Anárion as the South-kingdom of the Dúnedain. Increasingly during the Third Age the realms—first under its kings and later under the Ruling Stewards—provide a bulwark against the growing power of Sauron and Mordor and Easterling and Southron hordes. Its capital lies first at Osgiliath and later Minas Tirith.

In elaborating the history of his fictional kingdom, Tolkien drew extensively on his knowledge of ancient history. We thus find echoes of events and characters from the history of not only the Roman Empire—Gondor's most obvious analogy—but also to the Western and Eastern Roman (Byzantine) Empires that succeeded to it after its division.

Thus, many of the wars of Gondor on its southern borders, especially with the Corsairs of Umbar, have a parallel in Rome's long rivalry with the city-state of Carthage both on sea and land. Like Umbar, Carthage in North Africa commanded mighty fleets of warships, and allied itself with mercenary armies supported by war elephants and cavalries. Similarly, one of the most devastating incursions into Gondor, by a confederacy of Easterlings known as the Wainriders of Rhûn, in 1851 TA, echoes the Visigoths' defeat of the Romans at Adrianople in AD 378. The Western Roman Empire, too, had to endure centuries of warfare with invading barbarians on its eastern borders. Likewise, the South-kingdom of the Dúnedain has to endure centuries of warfare from similar barbarian invasions from the east.

The ascension of King Elessar at the end of the War of the Ring marks the restoration of the kingdom of Gondor and a new, more prosperous age in its history. Here there is an analogy with the creation of the Holy Roman Empire—a restoration of the old Western Roman Empire—under the rule of Charlemagne.

GOTHS An East Germanic people who, in the first few centuries AD, dominated a vast area of Central and Eastern Europe, often threatening the integrity of the Roman Empire especially during the Gothic Wars (AD 259–544).

Both historically and linguistically, the Goths fascinated Tolkien from an early age. His study of Joseph Wright's *Grammar of the Gothic Language* (1910) was a critical event in his intellectual life. In Gothic, Tolkien observed the first recorded language of the Germanic people and the first recorded language spoken by the progenitors of the English people. Tolkien believed that through his study of the language, and the surviving fragments of Gothic texts, he would gain new insights into this elusive people.

The Goths were partly Tolkien's inspiration for the Éothéod (meaning "horse people"), the Rhovanion ancestors the Riders of Rohan and Lords of the Mark. Both peoples were migrants from the north of their respective continents, and both had legendary dragon-slaying forebears. The Éothéod claimed Fram, son of Frumgar, as slayer of Scatha the Worm, the Cold-drake of the Grey Mountains, while the Goths claimed their culture hero Wolfdietrich as slayer of the Cold-drakes of the Tyrolean Mountains.

From time to time, too, the Goths allied themselves with the Roman Empire, most notably at the Battle of the Catalaunian Fields (AD 451) where Gothic cavalry staged a dramatic rescue of the beleaguered Roman troops. A comparable event occurs in the history of Gondor, where the Éothéod cavalry of Eorl the Young arrives at a critical moment in the Battle of the Field of Celebrant.

GRAM ("WRATH")

In Norse mythology the dynastic sword of the Völsungs forged by the elves of Alfheim. The sword is wielded by King Sigmund until the blade is broken in a duel with Odin, the Lord of Battles. Reforged, it later comes into the possession of Sigmund's son, Siegfried.

Gram and its history are comparable to Narsil, the dynastic sword of the kings of Arnor and Gondor, and its history. Meaning "red and white flame," Narsil is originally forged by the Dwarf-smith Telchar in Nogrod in the First Age. Passing into the possession of the Númenórean kings, it is eventually wielded by King Elendil until the blade is broken in his duel with Sauron the Dark Lord at the end of the Second Age. The shards of Narsil are saved, and three millennia later the sword is reforged by the Elves of Rivendell for Aragorn, the rightful heir to the kings of Arnor and Gondor. Renamed Andúril, meaning "flame of the west," its blade flickers with a living red flame in sunlight and a white flame in moonlight.

Similarly, the Völsung sword Gram is reforged by the dwarf-smith Regin for Sigurd, the rightful heir to the kings of the Völsungs. Its blade is distinguished by the blue flames that play along its razor edges. In the Norse *Völsunga Saga*, Sigurd uses Gram to slay the monstrous dragon Fáfnir.

In the *Nibelungenlied*, Sigurd is transformed into the German hero Siegfried and the Dwarf-reforged sword used in the slaying of the dragon is called Balmung. In Richard Wagner's *Siegfried* (1876), the third opera (or "music-drama") of *Der Ring des Nibelungen*, the dwarf-reforged sword in Siegfried's hands is known as Nothung. However, in the second opera of the Ring Cycle, *The Valkyrie*, Act One, near the end of Scene Three, in Siegmund's hands it is also referred to as "Nothung," when Siegmund hauls the sword out of the tree.

GREAT BATTLE

In the War of Wrath the great final battle between the forces of Morgoth the Dark Enemy and the Valarian Host of the West that brings an end to the First Age. While the Valar and Elves are ultimately victorious, the near-cosmic violence of the battle results in the shattering of the Iron Mountains and the sinking of almost all of the land of Beleriand.

Tolkien freely acknowledged that the Great Battle "owes, I suppose, more to the Norse vision of Ragnarök than to anything else." Certainly, there are a great number of similarities in these doomsday battles. Just as the final battle of Ragnarök will begin with the sounding of the Horn of Heimdall the Watchman of the Gods, Tolkien's Great Battle of the War of Wrath begins with the blast of the Horn of Eönwë, the Herald of the Valar. Gothmog, Lord of Balrogs, bears a flaming sword into the Great Battle, as does Surt, Lord of the Fire Giants, in the Norse legend. And in both battles, all the legions of good and evil—all creatures, spirits, demons, and dragons—meet in one final terrible conflict.

Another likely source of inspiration, though less widely acknowledged, is to be found in the biblical Armageddon, a prophetic vision of the great battle fought between the forces of good and evil at the "end of time," as revealed in the Book of Revelation. There, in the duel between the Archangel Michael and the "Red Dragon," we find one possible source for the climatic duel between the Eärendil the Mariner and Ancalagon the Black Dragon: "Then war broke out in heaven. Michael and his angels fought against the dragon, and the dragon and his angels fought back. But he was not strong enough, and they lost their place in heaven. The great dragon was hurled down—that ancient serpent called the devil, or Satan, who leads the whole world astray. He was hurled to the earth, and his angels with him."

Just as the Red Dragon's downfall marks Satan's defeat, so Ancalagon the Black Dragon's downfall marks the defeat of Morgoth in Middle-earth. The Host of the West, like the Host of Heaven, prevails, and Morgoth the Dark Enemy is cast forever after into the darkness of the Eternal Void.

GRECO-ROMAN MYTHOLOGY The collected body of myths originally told by the ancient Greeks but which were also taken over and elaborated on by the ancient Romans; also known as classical mythology. It was a staple element of the humanist education of Europeans starting from the Renaissance and onward, mostly transmitted through the great

works of Greek and Roman literature, including Homer's *Iliad* and *Odyssey* and, above all, Ovid's *Metamorphoses.*

Greco-Roman mythology inevitably had a considerable influence on Tolkien's imagination in the creation of Middle-earth: "I was brought up in the Classics," he wrote in a letter to his friend Father Robert Murray, "and first discovered the sensation of literary pleasure in Homer." From a young age, Tolkien learned to read both classical and Homeric Greek as well as Latin, and his grounding in Greco-Roman literature remained strong and helped in the shaping of his imaginary world.

This was particularly true in Tolkien's creation of the Valar and Maiar, the "gods" and "demigods" of Tolkien's world, many of whom have counterparts (or close counterparts) in the classical gods, demigods, and heroes. As with the classical gods, Tolkien had a hierarchy of "angelic powers," with a pantheon of supreme beings, the Valar (like the Olympians) and then a host of lesser beings, the Maiar (the various lesser gods, demigods, and divine heroes). It is noteworthy that while there were twelve Olympian gods and goddesses, the Valar number fourteen.

GRENDEL   The hulking monster of the Anglo-Saxon epic poem *Beowulf* may be discovered in a scaled-down version in Tolkien's *The Hobbit.* For as Tolkien acknowledged, the plot of *The Hobbit* was largely inspired by *Beowulf*, and quite clearly Gollum was a miniature version of the monster Grendel. By some evil power, the ogre Grendel was granted supernatural strength and protection from attack by the weapons of his enemies. The monster came by night and murdered scores of warriors as they slept. It then broke their bones and consumed their flesh "like a wolf might eat a rabbit." Grendel was even feared by the walking corpses and blood-sucking man-beasts that haunted the foul serpent-infested mire that he had made his home.

Although a diminished version of Grendel, Gollum was no less a terror to his less celebrated victims, such as the Goblins (the fairy-tale name for Tolkien's demonic Orcs) and the Hobbit Bilbo Baggins. For, just as some unknown power gave Grendel enormous physical strength and long life, so the evil power of the Ring lengthened Gollum's miserable life for centuries and seemingly enhanced the power of his wraithlike hands, giving them murderous power to strangle his prey.

Both monsters are subhuman grotesques in appearance and habit. Gollum lived in the dank pools of dark caverns, where he became thin and hairless, a murderer and a cannibal. His eyes became bulbous, his feet webbed, and his teeth grew long and sharp through living off raw, unclean meat.

The monster Grendel had a similar damned existence. He seems to have had little or no human speech and his nocturnal life was largely occupied with stalking prey, murder, and cannibalism. Daylight hours seem to have been spent sleeping in a murky cave at the bottom of a filthy pool in the middle of a haunted wetland, not unlike the Dead Marshes of Middle-earth. Surrounded by his treasure and trophy weapons stolen from murdered men, the creature lived only to feed on human flesh. He was finally put out of his miserable existence when, in hand-to-hand combat with Beowulf, the hero rips the monster's arm from his torso. Mortally wounded Grendel crawls off to die in the grotto at the bottom of his haunted pool.

In the Gollum's final struggle with Frodo the Hobbit, we have a version of Beowulf locked in mortal combat with the monster Grendel, albeit with slightly more diminutive—though equally determined—combatants. In Tolkien's Middle-earth, the fate of the world is determined by the least of its champions, and the struggle for the fate of the World is more a personal struggle over the fate of one's soul. Even so, everything seems to have gone wrong. The Hobbit is doubly defeated: morally by the power of the Ring and physically by the power of Gollum. As the power of Beowulf's superhuman grip allows the hero to tear Grendel's arm from his shoulder socket, so the power of Gollum's supernatural grip (and his Orkish fangs) enables the antihero to sever the Hobbit's finger and claim the One Ring that encircles it. Yet upon Middle-earth, the victory of evil often leads to its own defeat. So it proved with Gollum's victory as he falls into the volcano fissure of the Cracks of Doom. Gollum ends up a reluctant martyr whose evil intent resulted in the greatest good.

GREY ELVES In Tolkien's legendarium, a twilight Elvish people who, in the First Age, dwell in Beleriand, principally in the forest kingdom of Doriath, where they are ruled by king Thingol and his wife, the Maia

Melian. They are of Telerin descent and are usually known by their Quenya name, the Sindar ("Grey People"). In his creation of races and realms of the Elves, Tolkien was to some degree guided by the Norse cosmology of the light elves of Alfheim and the dark elves of Swartalfheim. Similarly, in Tolkien's world, we have the Caliquendi, or Light-elves, of Eldamar and the Moriquendi, or Dark-elves, of Middle-earth. In the Grey Elves, however, he created a category between the Light-elves of the west and Dark-elves of the east: the "Elves of the Twilight" of Beleriand. While the Grey Elves had embarked on the Great Journey to Valinor with the rest of the Teleri, under the leadership of Elwë, they abandoned the trek in Beleriand after the disappearance of Elwë in the forest of Doriath, where he had fallen under the spell of Melian. Later, with Elwë's reemergence as Thingol, he gathered together those of the Teleri who had tarried and founded the forest kingdom of Doriath, protected by the enchantments of Melian.

In European folklore the association of elves with forests and woodlands, as well as with the mysterious, gray hours around twilight, is an old one. In Germanic folklore there are the *Moosleute* ("moss people"), an elven folk associated with the great forests that once covered much of Europe and considered by humans as both dangerous and potentially beneficial (the Men of Beleriand have similar beliefs about the Grey Elves and the enchantments of Doriath). The sylvan association continued into early modern times, as we see in the fairies of William Shakespeare's *A Midsummer Night's Dream* (1595–6). There, in Oberon and Titania (the king and queen of the fairies), we may see a buried inspiration for King Thingol and Queen Melian.

GUNGNIR ("SWAYING ONE") The dwarf-forged spear of the Norse god Odin. This appears to have inspired Tolkien's Aeglos ("icicle"), the name of the Elf-forged spear of Gil-galad, the high king of the Noldor in the Second Age.

Like Aeglos, Gungnir is a weapon that, when wielded, "none could withstand," and, when thrown, always strikes its mark. Aeglos is broken when Gil-galad falls in his duel with Sauron the Dark Lord in the last battle of the War of the Last

Alliance. Gungnir will be broken when Odin carries it into the last battle of Ragnarök in the war of the gods and giants.

GURTHANG ("IRON DEATH")

In Tolkien's legendarium the sword wielded by Túrin Turambar in the slaying of Glaurung the Father of Dragons. Also known as the Black Sword of Brethil, the blade is originally forged by Eöl the Dark Elf and given the name Anglachel, meaning "flaming iron." The black blade glows with a "pale fire" and is so hard that it can slice through iron. Reforged by Túrin Turambar and the Elven-smiths of Nargothrond, the sword is renamed Gurthang.

The sword has a direct counterpart in Norse mythology in Gram ("wrath"), the blade reforged by the dwarf Regin for the Norse hero Sigurd, who wields it in the slaying of Fáfnir, "Prince of All Dragons." However, there is also a darker comparison to be made with the sword of the Finnish hero Kullervo the hapless. Kullervo and Túrin Turambar each discover that they have unwittingly committed incest with a long-lost sister and commit suicide by falling on their own sword. In the *Kalevala*, Kullervo requests of his sentient sword that it drink his blood and take his life. This is duplicated in Tolkien's *The Children of Hurin* when the doomed Túrin Turambar talks to Gurthang before throwing himself on its black blade.

GWAITH-I-MIRDAIN
See: CELEBRIMBOR; RINGS OF POWER

GYGES' RING

In ancient Greek legend a magical ring possessed by the king of Lydia, Gyges, in fact a historical figure (reigned c. 687–c. 652 BC) and founder of the Mermnad dynasty of Lydia. The legend of his rise to power from shepherd to king was recorded by both Plato in *The Republic* and Herodotus in *The Histories.*

According to these accounts, after an earthquake opened a hidden cave, the young shepherd entered it and discovered a tomb and a magic ring that could make the wearer invisible. Armed with this ring of invisibility, Gyges managed to enter the Lydian royal palace, seduce the queen and, with her aid, slay the king, and become king in his place. Plato used the legend of Gyges' Ring in a debate about the nature of humanity. One of the debaters argues that possession of such a ring would turn every human into a monster, unfettered by the laws of society: "No man would keep his hands off what was not his own when he could safely take what he liked out of the market or go into houses and lie with anyone at his pleasure, or kill or release from prison whom he would, and in all respects be like a god among men." Socrates, however, counters this by arguing that a truly just man would not be tempted to give way to his baser instincts.

As Tolkien once explained, in *The Hobbit*, Bilbo's discovery of his own ring of invisibility serves essentially as a device quite commonly found in the plots of many legends and fairy tales, useful—as in the case of Gyges—in transforming the everyday individual into an extraordinary hero (or villain). We can also find many echoes of Plato's dialogue in *The Lord of the Rings*, where many of characters are tested by the corruption offered by the Ring. Sauron has long ago given in to the desire to be a "god among men," while the truly just, like Bilbo and Frodo, are able to stay true to their principles, showing their innate goodness.

A Haradrim warrior riding an Oliphaunt

HADES
In Greek mythology the name of both the god of the dead and the underworld over which he ruled. He was known to the Romans as Pluto. This Greco-Roman deity is akin to Tolkien's Mandos, the Doomsman of the Valar, whose actual name was Namo, but who is most often known by the name of his underworld domain, Mandos the Hall of the Slain. Both were stern and dreaded rulers of the dead, and enforcers of fate.

According to one Greek myth, the three sons of Cronos divided the realms of the Earth between them: Hades was ruler of the dead; Zeus (the Roman Jupiter) ruler of the living who breathed the air; while Poseidon (the Roman Neptune) was ruler of all the life of the seas. This order was mirrored in the character and domain of each of the three greatest Valar: Mandos, lord of the underworld; Manwë, lord of the skies; and Ulmo, lord of the seas.

HARAD, THE
The vast territories to the south of Gondor. A land of desert, grasslands, and jungles and of blistering heat, it has strong associations with the real-world Africa. Its peoples are the Haradrim.

HARFOOT
The smallest in stature and most typical of the three strains of Hobbits: the standard-issue diminutive, brown-skinned, curly-haired, hairy-footed, hole-dwelling Hobbit. The other two Hobbit breeds are the Fallohide and Stoor. Together, these three races were meant to link the history of the Hobbits with that of the Germanic settlers of Britain: the Saxons, the Angles, and the Jutes. The Harfoots were most likely to trade with Dwarves, while the Fallohides were most likely to consort with Elves, and the Stoors with Men.

Harfoot is in fact a English surname derived from the Old English *haer-fot* (hare-foot), meaning "fast runner" or "nimble as a hare." The best-known historic individual to bear this name was Harold Harefoot, who became Harold I (reigned 1035–40), one of the last Saxon kings. The association of Hobbits with hares not only implies nimbleness, but also keen sight and

hearing, as well as oversized feet. Also there is the implied pun on "hair-foot," referring to the Hobbits' distinctively furry feet. Together all these allusions provide a succinct description of this Hobbit kind: a small, nimble creature with large, hairy feet. Typical Harfoot surnames are: Brown, Brownlock, Sandheaver, Tunnelly, Burrows, Gardner, Hayward, and Roper.

HEIMDALL In

Norse mythology the herald of the gods and the vigilant watchman who dwells in a fortress called Himinbjörg ("heaven's castle") on Bifrost, the Rainbow Bridge between Asgard and Midgard. He watches and listens, and he holds ready the Gjallarhorn ("resounding horn"), which he blows when intruders attempt to enter Asgard. It is foretold that in the final battle of Ragnarök, the gods will know their doom is at hand when Heimdall sounds the Gjallarhorn to signal the storming of the Rainbow Bridge by the *jötnar*. In that battle, Heimdall will engage in a fatal duel with the evil god Loki, the commander of the *jötnar*, which

Dunlending. The tall, dark-haired people of Dunland who made a pact with the Wizard Saruman and joined his Orc legions.

will cause the bridge to collapse and both shall perish in their fall as all the world burns and sinks into chaos.

In Tolkien's world, we have something of a comparable figure in Eönwë, the herald of the Valar, who blows his horn to announce the Great Battle in the War of Wrath that brings an end to the First Age when the Host of the Valar, Maiar, and Eldar destroy the Host of Morgoth, the Dark Enemy of the World. Tolkien also wrote several unfinished drafts concerning Dagor Dagorak, or the "Last Battle and the Day of Doom," which his son and literary heir, Christopher Tolkien, has suggested is akin to Arda's version of Ragnarök. In one of these drafts, it is Eönwë who once again blows his horn and then engages in a fatal battle with the evil Morgoth the Dark Lord.

Heimdall's signaling of the battle on Bifrost by blowing the Horn of Asgard is also echoed in the War of the Ring when Boromir signals the battle on the Bridge of Khazad-dûm by blowing the Horn of Gondor.

HELM'S DIKE
A mile-long earthen wall and trench that is an outlying defense of the Hornburg, a great Gondorian and later Rohirric fortress in the northeastern White Mountains. The dike is named after Helm Hammerhand, ninth king of Rohan. Some two and a half centuries before the Battle of Hornburg in the War of the Ring, King Helm defended the Hornburg during the long siege of the Rohan–Dunlending wars. Rohirric legends told of the night-stalking Helm descending from the dike like a mighty Snow Troll and slaying his foes with his bare hands.

Helm's Dike was likely inspired by the much longer earthen wall and trench system known as Offa's Dyke. Named after Offa, the powerful eighth-century AD Anglo-Saxon king of Mercia, Offa's Dyke (known as Clawdd Offa in Welsh) ran— and for the most part still runs as a footpath—over 170 miles along the border between Mercia and the Welsh kingdom of Powys, or what today is essentially the border between England and Wales. Mercia was, for Tolkien, the celebrated homeland of the English (Anglo-Saxons) and these Mercians of the Welsh Marshes were directly linked in Tolkien's mind to the Riders of the Mark (the Rohirrim). Thus, we discover, the centuries-long wars between the fair-haired Anglo-Saxons of Mercia and the dark-haired Celts of Wales are mirrored in the centuries-long wars between the fair-haired Rohirrim of the Mark and the dark-haired Dunlendings of Dunland.

HENGIST AND HORSA Legendary fifth-century

AD chieftains and founders of the first Angle, Saxon, and Jute kingdoms in Britain. Fictional Hobbits and historic Anglo-Saxons were linked in Tolkien's mind as the progenitors of their people. As he often stated, Hobbits were meant to be quintessentially English, so logic dictated that the history of Hobbits and the Anglo-Saxons should have much in common. Consequently, Tolkien records his "discovery" of both their origins in the distant mists of time beyond a massive eastern range of mountains: the Alps in the case of the Anglo-Saxons and the Misty Mountains in the case of the Hobbits. Eventually, both races make mountain crossings and settle for centuries in wedge-shaped delta regions called the Angle. Wars and invasions force both peoples to make water crossings and establish new homelands: the English Shires for the Anglo-Saxons and the Shire for the Hobbits. Not so coincidentally, the names of the Anglo-Saxon and Hobbit chieftains and founders are linked by Old English words for "horse": the historic Hengist meaning "stallion" and Horsa meaning "horse"; and the fictional Marcho meaning "horse" and Blanco meaning "white horse."

HEOROT (HEROT) THE MEAD HALL

In the Anglo-Saxon epic poem *Beowulf*, "the foremost of halls under heaven" and the seat of power of the Danish king Hrothgar. As Beowulf approaches the kingdom of Hrothgar, the hero catches sight of Heorot's roof gables covered with hammered gold, which glistens and glints in the sunlight. This is very like the scene in *The Lord of the Rings* where Gandalf approaches the kingdom of Théoden of Rohan, and catches sight of the great royal hall of Meduseld's roof gables covered with hammered gold glistening in the sunlight.

The name Meduseld is in fact the ancient Anglo-Saxon word for "mead hall": a hall where mead-drinking feasts were held to celebrate enthronements, victories, and other events. Both Tolkien's Meduseld and Hrothgar's Heorot have

Helm Hammerhand. Helm froze to death in a night raid against the Dunlendings.

divine models: Meduseld in the Great Hall of Oromë, the Horseman of the Valar, in Valinor; Heorot in Valhalla, the Great Hall of Odin.

HEPHAESTUS THE SMITH Greek god of

blacksmiths, metalworkers, and artificers, known to the Romans as Vulcan. Hephaestus most closely resembles Tolkien's Aulë the Smith and Maker of Mountains. Both are proud, strong-willed, and secretive artisans, though Aulë does not share Hephaestus' most distinctive physical trait, his lameness, nor the slightly comic role the god often plays in Greek myth. Hephaestus' wife is Aphrodite, the beautiful goddess of love, while Aulë's spouse is Yavanna, whose character is more closely allied with the Greek goddess of the harvest, Demeter.

HERACLES In Greek mythology, the greatest of the heroes, son

of Zeus and Alcmene, famous for his Twelve Labors, a series of "impossible" tasks, especially the killing of various monsters, undertaken in the service of King Eurystheus to expunge his guilt for the murder of his (Heracles') wife and children.

The most direct comparison in Tolkien's world is Tulkas, the strongman and champion of the Valar, whose binding of Melkor may recall Heracles' chaining of the hell-hound Cerberus. However, another close figure is Beren, the greatest hero of the First Age, who, in the service of King Thingol, also sets out to perform an "impossible task" —the retrieval of a Silmaril. However, in this case the task is performed in order to win the hand of the king's daughter, Lúthien. Eventually, Beren must descend into the "underworld" of Angband, Morgoth's fortress, to fulfill his task, encountering the hellhound Carcharoth, just as in the Twelfth Labor, Heracles descends into Hades to retrieve the three-headed hellhound Cerberus. *See also*: TULKAS

HERCULES
See: HERACLES

HERMES In Greek mythology the herald and messenger of Zeus, the king of the Olympian gods. He was known to the Romans as Mercury. He shares some aspects of his nature with Tolkien's Eönwë, the herald and messenger of Manwë, the king of the Valar. However, Hermes is a far more complex figure, as well as being higher in status (the Greek god is one of the twelve Olympians; Eönwë is among the Maiar, even if he is one of the most powerful, even their "leader").

Hermes is a psychopomp—the conveyer of souls to the underworld—and is also the god of commerce, roads, merchants, travelers, thieves, magicians, and alchemists. Indeed, in some of these aspects Hermes has more in common with Odin, the king of the gods in Norse mythology, and, in his association with traveling and magic, with the Istari or Wizards of Middle-earth.

HLIDSKJALF The tallest tower in Asgard where Odin in his role as *Valdr vagnbrautar* ("ruler of heaven") is enthroned and watches over all Nine Worlds of the Norse cosmos. Hlidskjalf has a close comparison in Tolkien's Ilmarin, the marble watchtower of Manwë, the king of the Valar, from which he and his spouse, Varda, can survey all of Arda.

HOBBITON Hobbit village and ancestral home of the Baggins family of Bag End, located almost at the center (or midland) of the Shire, not too far away from the Three-Farthing Stone.

The fictional Hobbiton was inspired by Tolkien's childhood memories of the then-rural Worcestershire village of Sarehole, four miles from industrial Birmingham in the West Midlands. With his mother and his brother, from the age of four to eight (between 1896 and 1900) he lived at 5 Gracewell Road in the village. The green, pleasant farmland, fields, and the woods of Sarehole with its nearby water-driven mill, were deeply imprinted on Tolkien's imagination and resurfaced in his creation of Hobbiton, which likewise has a water-driven mill, as we can see in the foreground of the lovely painting he made of *The Hill: Hobbiton-across-the-Water* (1937) as an illustration for *The Hobbit*.

In 1968 Tolkien made a contribution toward the restoration of Sarehole's eighteenth-century mill, and in 2002 a blue commemorative plaque was placed on it, funded by the Tolkien Society and the Birmingham Civic Society.

HOBBITS
Small, hairy-footed race of Middle-earth, living for the most part in the Shire, a number of whom play a central, heroic role in the events leading up to and during the War of the Ring. Hobbits were

Hobbits with Tom Bombadil

first introduced to the world with the 1937 publication of Tolkien's novel *The Hobbit*. This rapidly established itself as a children's classic, and its first sentence became arguably one of the best-known opening lines in the history of literature: "In a hole in the ground there lived a hobbit." Curiously, we actually know exactly where and how the first Hobbit made its appearance in his creator's mind. On a warm summer afternoon in 1930, Tolkien was sitting at his desk in his study at 20 Northmoor Road in the suburbs of Oxford. He was engaged in the "everlasting weariness" of marking school certificate papers, when "on a blank leaf [he] scrawled 'In a hole in the ground there lived a hobbit'." Tolkien "did not [. . .] know why."

Tolkien was a professor of Anglo-Saxon and a philologist. He had worked as a scholar on the *Oxford English Dictionary* and knew the English language (and a multitude of other languages) to its very roots. Words—the look and feel of them as well as their origins—inspired him. Of that moment when the word "hobbit" first came to him, he commented: "Names always generate a story in my mind. Eventually I thought I'd better find out what hobbits were like. But that was only a beginning." Indeed, "only a beginning" is a profound understatement.

Tolkien really did start with the word "Hobbit." It became a kind of riddle that needed solving. He decided that he must begin by inventing a philological origin for the word as a worn-down form of an original invented word, *holbytla* (which is actually an Anglo-Saxon or Old English construct), meaning "hole builder." The opening line of the novel-to-be, therefore, was an obscure lexicographical joke and a weird piece of circular thinking: "In a hole in the ground there lived a hole builder."

This is an unusual way to develop a character and write a novel, but it was clearly an essential part of Tolkien's creative process. Nearly all aspects of Hobbit life and adventure seem to evolve from their given names, which themselves dictate the direction of the story, as witnessed above all in the stories of Tolkien's greatest Hobbit heroes, Bilbo and Frodo Baggins.

HOLY GRAIL
In medieval Christian legend, the chalice or a platter used by Christ at the Last Supper, credited with miraculous powers, and

a key motif in Arthurian romance, most notably in Chretien de Troyes's *Perceval, le conte du Graal* (c. 1190) and Wolfram von Eschenbach's *Parzifal* (early 1200s), where it is a gemstone. The Quest of the Holy Grail, in which Arthur's knights become enmeshed, brings about many deaths and, indirectly, the fall of Arthur and his kingdom. In the many stories surrounding it, the Grail becomes an elusive and enigmatic symbol whose exact meaning scholars have much debated.

Tolkien drew a comparison between the Holy Grail and the Sampo, a similarly mysterious artifact that plays a key role in the Finnish national epic, the *Kavalla*. For Tolkien, both Grail and Sampo are at once artifacts and allegories—both real and abstract—and considered the quintessence of creative power, capable of provoking both good and evil, especially among the less than pure.

Tolkien intended the Silmarils to be objects of similarly intense but obscure symbolism, focal points of the inexorable pattern of fate. The Holy Grail, the Sampo, and the Silmarils all serve as a reminder that the mystery of ultimate destiny and purpose is something that cannot be penetrated. However, all three generate an ardent yearning to find, hold, and possess them, which leads to much shedding of blood. The paradox of the Silmarils specifically is that they, like the Grail, shine with a divine light, but to those who pursue them they bring about a descent into darkness and tragedy.

In the end, only Tolkien's angelic hero Eärendil proves pure enough to keep hold of a Silmaril. In this respect, Eärendil resembles Sir Galahad (or, in earlier versions, Percival), the only knight perfect enough to succeed in the Quest of the Holy Grail, and who at the moment of his quest's fulfilment ascends, like Eärendil, into heaven.

HOLY ROMAN EMPIRE Term used to describe
the imperial territories of Western and Central Europe ruled by Charlemagne (emperor AD 800–814) and his successors, set up as a revived, Christianized form of the ancient Roman Western Empire. The empire lasted from the coronation of Charlemagne (the usual starting point accepted by historians) to its dissolution in 1806. The empire was Tolkien's historical model for the fictional re-establishment of the Reunited Kingdom of Gondor and Arnor, with King Elessar (Aragorn) playing a role parallel to that of Charlemagne.

Beren Holding a Silmaril. The elusive Silmarils have a Grail-like mystery and sacredness.

HORN OF GONDOR
The thousand-year-old silver-tipped hunting horn in the keeping of the Ruling Stewards of Gondor. Originally the possession of the Ruling Stewards' ancestor, Vorondil the Hunter. The horn is that of one of the gigantic wild white oxen called the Kine of Araw which Tolkien modeled on the historic aurochs, the now-extinct wild white ox hunted by the ancient Germans, who also turned their horns into silver-tipped hunting horns. Araw is another name for the Valarian huntsman Oromë (meaning "hornblower"), who in turn was undoubtedly inspired by the Welsh god Arawn the Huntsman. The horn is modeled on a number of mythological or legendary horns, most notably the horn of the Norse god, Heimdall, known as Gjallarhorn, and the oliphant horn of the Frankish hero Roland in the medieval *La Chanson de Roland*.
See also: KINE OF ARAW

HORSEMEN OF THE APOCALYPSE
Four horsemen in the biblical Book of Revelation (6:1–8), harbingers of an age of destruction and catastrophe. Each horseman was thought to symbolize a scourge: Pestilence, War, Famine, and Death. Although four Horsemen of the Apocalypse are described, their terrifying collective impact is comparable to the nine mounted Ringwraiths, or Nazgûl, of Middle-earth, who are the ghastly servants of Sauron the Ring Lord. One traditional Christian reading of the Four Horsemen saw in them a prophecy of the eventual decline and fall of the Roman Empire. And in the nine Ringwraiths, too, we see a foreshadowing of the Pestilence, War, Famine, and Death that threaten to come down upon the inhabitants on the kingdom of Gondor and the other lands of Middle-earth.

HORSES
The horse plays a large part in the stories of Middle-earth—as steeds for warriors, as a means of transportation, and as beasts of burden. While the Rohirrim are the supreme "horse people," horses are used by almost every other people in the legendarium, though Dwarves show a strong aversion to horses. The

Nazgûl

Mearas. The "horse princes" of Rohan. These white and silver-gray horses are the strongest and fastest of the Third Age. Most famous is Shadowfax, the steed of Gandalf the White during the War of the Ring.

predominance of the horse reflects preindustrial societies generally, and Anglo-Saxon culture more specifically. It should be remembered that in Tolkien's lifetime the horse was still widely used for transportation and agriculture as well as in war. *See also*: BLACK RIDERS; SHADOWFAX

HÚRIN THE STEADFAST
Father of Túrin Turambar the Dragon-slayer in the First Age. In good part, Tolkien's tale of Húrin was inspired by the tale of Sigmund, the father of Sigurd the Dragon-slayer in the *Völsunga Saga*, the Norse epic, described by the nineteenth-century designer and poet William Morris as "the great story of the North, which should be to all our race what the tale of Troy was to the Greeks."

Tolkien's tale and the Norse saga both begin with the deeds of the fathers. Both Húrin and Sigmund survive the near-extermination of their dynastic houses. In the Dagor Nírnaeth Arnoediad (Battle of Unnumbered Tears), Húrin is the last man standing in the Edain rearguard and, by single-handedly slaying 70 trolls, saves the retreating Noldor army from certain annihilation. With equal courage, Sigmund slaughters scores of his foes in acts of bloody revenge for the murder of his entire clan, including his eight brothers. However, both are eventually defeated: Húrin when his war axe withers in the heat of battle and Sigmund when his dynastic sword breaks in one last fatal duel. Among the Elves and Men of Beleriand, Húrin the Steadfast is celebrated as "the mightiest warrior of mortal men" but, like the Norse hero Sigmund, he becomes even more renowned as the father of a dragon-slayer.

HYGIEIA
In Greek and Roman mythology, one of the four daughters of Aesclepius, the Greek god of medicine. She was the goddess of health and, although she was quite widely worshipped, she is close to being a personification. In cult statues she was depicted as a young woman of tender expression.

Hygieia has something of a counterpart in Tolkien's Estë the Gentle, one of the seven queens of the Valar. Estë, meaning "rest," dwells in the Gardens of Lórien and possesses the power to heal all hurts and soothe weariness.

I J

Isildur. The oldest son of Elendil and, with his brother Anárion, coruler of Gondor.

ILMARĒ ("STARLIGHT") Handmaid of Varda, the

Valarian queen of the Stars, and numbered among the greatest of the Maiar. Although her name, Tolkien assures us, is derived from his invented Elvish language of Quenya, it appears to have its origin in the Finno-Ugric root word *ilma*, meaning "sky" and closely resembles Ilmarinen, the name of both an ancient Finnish sky god and Ilmarinen, the maker of the Sampo, in the *Kalevala*. Ilmarē also appears to bear some resemblance to Asteria, meaning "of the stars," the Greek Titan goddess of falling stars and night oracles.

ILMARIN Great mansion of Manwë Súlimo and Varda Elentári,

the king and queen of the Valar on the summit of Taniquetil, the tallest mountain on Arda. It is comparable to the palace of the Greek gods Zeus (the Roman Jupiter) and Hera (the Roman Juno), the king and queen of the gods on the summit of Mount Olympus, as well as to the hall or tower of Hlidskjalf, seat of the Norse king of the gods Odin. Ilmarin in Quenya translates as "mansion of the high air," although like Ilmarē it seems to be related to the Fino-Urgic root word *ilma*, meaning "sky" and suggesting "stars." From their thrones in Ilmarin, Manwë and Varda "could look out across the Earth," just as Odin enthroned in Hlidskjalf could see out over all the Nine Worlds.

ILMARINEN THE SMITH The "Eternal Hammerer"

and supreme artificer and inventor in the Finnish epic *Kalevala* who, among his many accomplishments, forges the mysterious artifact known as the Sampo. He seems originally to have been an ancient Finnish sky god who later took on the characteristics of other Indo-European smith-gods, such as Hephaestus and Vulcan. In the *Kalevala*, Ilmarinen is shown as capable of creating practically anything that can be worked from copper, brass, iron, silver, or gold. The Sampo is variously described, but in the epic is depicted as a kind of magic mill that can perpetually produce salt, grain, and gold and thus is a source of phenomenal wealth and good fortune. Ilmarinen creates the Sampo in order to win the Maiden of Pohjola.

Early in adult life, Tolkien was deeply influenced by the strange, poetic stories of the *Kalevala*, and in some respects, Ilmarinen inspired the figure of Fëanor in *The Silmarillion*, the greatest of all the Elves in gifts of mind, body, and spirit. Fëanor, too, is a great smith and the creator of extraordinary artifacts—the Silmarils, three Elven gemstones filled with the sacred living light of the Trees of the Valar. Both characters are shown to combine their supreme artisanship with hubris, although the consequences of Fëanor's pride and arrogance are much graver. Ilmarinen, having created the Sampo, rushes to claim his promised bride, but she refuses him. Fëanor's pride leads to the Kinslaying of the Teleri Elves. *See also*: SAMPO; SILMARILS

ILÚVATAR ("ALLFATHER")
See: ERU THE ONE

IMLADRIS
See: RIVENDALE

INGWË
One of the first Elves and king of the First Kindred of the Elves, known as the Vanyar or "Fair Elves." In the history of the Elves he plays an equivalent role to the biblical Moses. Just as Moses in the Old Testament was chosen by God to lead the Hebrews out of Egypt to their Promised Land, so Ingwë is chosen by the Valar to lead the Elves in what became known as the Great Journey out of Middle-earth to their promised land of Eldamar. Tolkien provided the philological sources of the name Ingwë as well as that of the Vanyar when writing about a Norse/Anglo-Saxon warrior named Ingeld, who appears in the epic *Beowulf* as the son of Froda, king of the Heathobards. Tolkien argued that behind this hero was a

"god the Angles called Ing." Among the Norse, this god was known as Freyr ("the Lord"), though his true or older name was Yngvi. Freyr was one of the Vanir, a race of fertility and corn gods, a name that seems to have also inspired the name of the Vanyar.

Tolkien's Elven High King Ingwë eventually leads his people to the Undying Lands. On the Hill of Túna in Eldamar, Ingwë raises the white towers and crystals stairs of the city of Tirion, and rules there for a time as High King of the Eldar. In time, however, he departs with the greater part of the Vanyar to finally settle on the slopes of Mount Taniquetil, close to the halls of Manwë Súlimo, king of the Valar.

IRISH MYTHOLOGY While Tolkien's Middle-earth was born out of a desire to create a mythology specifically "of England," the myths and legends of Ireland played an important role in shaping aspects of the legendarium. Irish mythology has survived in an extremely rich number of medieval Irish tales, poems, and pseudo-chronicles, such as the *Lebor Gabála Érenn* (The Book of the Taking of Ireland).

The extent and nature of such influence has been much debated, but there are incontrovertibly Irish elements in many of the stories, especially as related to the character and history of the Noldor Elves, who share much in common with the early prehuman inhabitants of Ireland known as the Tuatha Dé Danann. Irish stories of the paradise-like Tír na nÓg, the "land of the young," clearly also had some influence on the creation of Valinor, the Undying Lands, and some scholars have detected the influence of the Irish story of the mist-shrouded island of Hy Brasil, which could only be glimpsed from the west coast of Ireland once in every seven years, on Tolkien's statement that keen-eyed Númenórean sailors could sometimes catch a glimpse of Tol Eressëa.

There are many other hints and connections which, however, can only remain supposition. While many such motifs are part of a wider Celtic or even Indo-European body of myth and legend, it is impossible to imagine that Tolkien remained unaffected, let alone ignorant, of such a powerful, poetic tradition. *See also*: DAGDA, THE; DULLAHAN; SIDHE; TUATHA DÉ DANANN

Saruman the White

ISTARI The order of five wizards, in origin mighty Maiar spirits, who appear in Middle-earth in the Third Age as emissaries of the Valar. Only three of the Istari figure prominently in the Tolkien's tales, each named for the color of his raiment: Saruman the White; Gandalf the Grey; and Radagast the Brown. Tolkien tells us the names of the two others, Alatar and Pallando (together known as the Blue Wizards for their sea-blue cloaks) but that, since they wandered into the far east of Middle-earth, nothing is known of their doings. The meaning of their name (Quenya for "wise ones") may remind us of the biblical Three Wise Men (the Magi), who set out on a journey to visit the infant Jesus.

Tolkien's portrayal of the Istari, and most especially Gandalf, has much in common with the wizards of folktales where they traditionally appear as solitary wanderers wearing a broad-brimmed hat and a long traveler's cape, and bearing a long staff. They are conjurers, tellers of tales, and repositories of wisdom, often appearing out of the blue, all characteristics that might equally apply to Gandalf, as he is depicted in *The Hobbit* and the early part of *The Lord of the Rings*, especially through the eyes of Hobbits.

The Istari, however, also have more specific origins in figures from the world's mythologies. Certainly, Gandalf and Saruman, at least, have much in common with Merlin of the Britons, Odin of the Norsemen, Wotan of the ancient Germans, Mercury of the Romans, Hermes of the Greeks, and Thoth of the Egyptians. All are linked with magic, sorcery, arcane knowledge, and secret doctrine. Most obviously, Merlin, Odin, and Wotan commonly took the form of a wandering old man in a traveler's cloak and carrying a staff. And typically—for good or for ill—these disguised deities served as a guide to kings and rulers and often aided them against impossible odds by using their supernatural powers.

See also: GANDALF THE GREY; RADAGAST; SARUMAN

JANIBAS THE NECROMANCER
A phantom sorcerer and one of the greatest foes of Dietrich von Berne, the legendary hero of several medieval German romances. The tale of Janibas's war with Dietrich is redolent of Aragorn's war with Sauron the Ring Lord and his servants. His and his army's cataclysmic end is likewise comparable to the fate of Sauron the Ring Lord and his legions at the Black Gate.
See also: DIETRICH VON BERNE

JEHOVAH (YAHWEH)
The Judeo–Christian god and inspiration for Tolkien's Eru the One (or Illuvatar the Allfather), the creator of Arda.
See also: ERU THE ONE

JEKYLL AND HYDE
The two characters or aspects of the protagonist in the Scottish writer Robert Louis Stevenson's influential

Isengard. Saruman's fortress and the black tower of Orthanc falls to the army of Ents and Huorns.

gothic novella *The Strange Case of Dr. Jekyll and Mr. Hyde* (1886). One is Dr. Henry Jekyll, who is mild-mannered and conforming. The other is Mr. Hyde, who is cruel and murderous. In the popular imagination, Stevenson's character has become the classic example of the psychological condition loosely known as split personality and properly known as dissociative identity disorder (DID). Tolkien undoubtedly knew of Stevenson's tale and may have had it in mind when he developed the character of Sméagol–Gollum in *The Lord of the Rings.* Certainly, in Tolkien's portrayal of Sméagol–Gollum, and the struggle between his "good" and "evil" selves, we have a rival popular character displaying something similar to the disorder. When Sméagol is in control, he has pale eyes and refers to himself as "I." Gollum, however, is a green-eyed creature that refers to itself as "we," amalgamating itself with his prized possession and other "self," the Ring. DID can often be traced to childhood trauma, and the young Sméagol's murder of his cousin Déagol, out of his lust to possess the Ring, seems to serve this function.

The agonizing struggles of Jekyll/Hyde and Sméagol/Gollum have different outcomes. While Dr. Jekyll eventually decides to commit suicide rather than allow Mr. Hyde to gain the upper hand, Sméagol–Gollum ultimately succumbs to his lust for possession of the Ring and plunges into the fires of the cracks of Mount Doom, to gain possession of the One Ring. An incipient case of split personality is also shown in Bilbo Baggins, although his innate goodness—shown, for example, in the pity he feels for Gollum, as Gandalf remarks—wins through and saves him, allowing him to willingly give up the One Ring.

JORDANES East Roman historian and author of sixth-century AD, who wrote *Romana* and *Getica* (both dated to around AD 551). Jordanes was one of Tolkien's primary sources on the military encounters between the Romans and Goths, which seem to have inspired his history of the Gondorians and the Balchoth, a confederacy of Easterlings.

JÖRMUNGANDR The World Serpent of Norse mythology: it surrounds the world of Midgard, grasping its own tail in its mouth, and is an example of a widely found motif, the *ourobos*. One of the children of Loki and a giantess, Jörmungandr is an archenemy of the god Thor, with whom it has a series of encounters, most famously when Thor catches the serpent while out on a fishing trip.

The day when Jörmungandr releases its tail will be the signal for the terrible last battle of Ragnarök to begin. In the *Prose Edda*'s account of Ragnarök, Thor appears in his flying chariot armed with his thunderbolt hammer Mjölnir and slays Jörmungandr, though at the cost of his own life.

In Tolkien's story we have a similar Great Battle in the War of Wrath that brings an end to the First Age. Here the hero Eärendil the Mariner appears in his flying ship *Vingilótë* armed with the Silmaril and slays Ancalagon the Black, the great fire-breathing serpent of Angband. Fortunately, Eärendil survives.

Jörmungandr

JÖTNAR (SINGULAR: JÖTUUN) In Norse

mythology the stone and frost "giants" who inhabit the dark, cold mountainous realm known as Jötunheim, or "*jötuun*-home." In Norse myths and legends they are shown as forever at war with the gods of Asgard, though liaisons between the two "races" or entities are not uncommon, and a few gods, such as the hunting goddess Skadi, are even said to be *jötnar*. While it is usual to translate the word *jötuun* as "giant," in fact the meaning seems to be much less clear: their primary association, however, is always with the mountains and earth. Only in later Scandinavian folktales do they come closer to the purely malevolent beings known as trolls—powerful if dull-witted.

In Tolkien's many epic tales in *The Silmarillion* armies of Trolls are often allied with Orcs, Balrogs, Dragons, and other evil forces in cataclysmic battles with the Elves and the Valarian gods. These Trolls appear to be much closer in spirit to the Norse legends of *jötnar*, who are similarly allied with fire giants, serpents, and various other monsters in cataclysmic battles with the Norse gods of Asgard. By contrast, the Trolls that Bilbo and Thorin and Company encounter in *The Hobbit* seem to be directly inspired by the dull-witted trolls of folklore.

JÖTUNHEIM One of the Nine Worlds of Norse cosmology and

home to the *jötnar*, the stone "giants," who constantly threaten the neighboring worlds of Asgard and Midgard. Jötunheim is portrayed as dark and cold, as opposed to another of the worlds, Muspelheim, the region of volcanic fire that is the land of the terrible fire giants, which so vividly inspired Tolkien's terrifying Balrogs. It might be argued that Mordor, a land of mountain and fire, is an imaginative amalgamation of these two Norse worlds.

JUDEO-CHRISTIAN MYTHOLOGY

The world of the Old Testament, its conception of the divine, and various Hebrew and Christian stories had a profound if paradoxical influence on Tolkien's imaginative writing. The influence is at its clearest in the *Ainulindalë*, the story of the creation of Arda with which *The Silmarillion* opens. As in Genesis, Tolkien conceives of creation as having a primal cause in the form of a single entity: the biblical creator-god Yahweh/Jehovah has his direct counterpart in Eru the One. Similarly, in Tolkien's creation story we find entities known as the Ainur, "Holy Ones," vastly powerful spirits who are comparable to the Judeo-Christian angels and archangels.

Once the Ainur spirits enter Arda as the Valar, Tolkien's conception of these angelic spirits changes dramatically, so that they strongly resemble the early pagan gods of Olympus and Asgard, often having direct counterparts. On the other hand, the great conflict that unfolds through *The Silmarillion* between Eru and the Valar, on one side, and Melkor/Morgoth, on the other, owes much to the war between God and the rebel Angel, Lucifer/Satan, as perhaps most famously portrayed in literature in John Milton's epic poem *Paradise Lost* (1667/1674). Such "wars in heaven" can also be found in many of the mythologies of the Near East, as in the Titanomachy (the struggle between the Olympian gods and Titans for supremacy) in Greek mythology.

See also: ANGELS; ERU THE ONE; LUCIFER; *PARADISE LOST*

JUPITER   The Roman king of the gods—and Greek counterpart Zeus—was in good part Tolkien's inspiration for Manwë, the King of the Valar. Manwë rules from his throne on top of Taniquetil, the tallest mountain in the world. The eagle is sacred to Manwë, who is a fierce, bearded god of storms. Jupiter rules from his throne and temple on the top of Olympus, the tallest mountain in the world. The eagle is also sacred to Jupiter, who is a fierce, bearded god of storms. And just as Manwë rules over and commands the Valarian Powers of Arda, so Jupiter rules over and commands the Roman gods and goddesses.

K

Ungoliant

KALEVALA The national epic of Finland, compiled by the philologist Elias Lönnrot (1802–84) from Finnish oral folklore and mythology and published in its first version 1835. A second version—the version known today—was published in 1849 and consisted of over 22,000 verses divided into 50 songs. It was translated into English in 1888 and again in 1907.

Tolkien first read the *Kalevala* as a student at Oxford University, and it profoundly influenced his imaginative writings, especially as found in *The Silmarillion*. This Tolkien freely admitted. In 1955, he wrote to his friend the poet W. H. Auden, "the beginning of the legendarium [. . .] was in an attempt to reorganize some of the *Kalevala*, especially the tale of Kullervo the hapless, into a form of my own." In 1914 Tolkien had even begun to write his own version of Kullervo's story, though he never finished it.

The tale of Kullervo the Hapless eventually appeared in *The Silmarillion* in the tragic story of Túrin Turambar. In Túrin we have the first of Middle-earth's heroic Dragon-slayers, whose fate duplicates the tragic course of Kullervo's life and eventual suicide, when it is revealed that has unwittingly married and slept with his long-lost sister. Other characters and themes of the *Kalevala* may also be discovered in Tolkien's *The Silmarillion*. To some degree, Fëanor, the Elven-smith who forges the Silmarils, is comparable to the supernatural smith Ilmarinen in the *Kalevala* who forges the mysterious artifact known as the Sampo. Likewise the Orpheus-like figure of Väinämöinen seems to have influenced the depiction of Tom Bombadil in his love of song and deep connection to the Earth.

KALI Hindu goddess whose name means "she who is black" or "she who is death." She is associated with both destruction and creation and, though terrible in form, is ultimately benevolent, a destroyer of evil. However, as the eight-limbed "devi of death," Kali comes close to the horror conjured up by Tolkien's Ungoliant, a primordial eight-limbed evil spirit that takes on the shape of a gigantic spider and weaves a web of darkness and horror from a substance that Tolkien calls the "Unlight of Ungoliant." His tale of this murderous, cannibalistic monster is a depiction of the self-defeating nature of evil: ultimately, Ungoliant is destined to self-devouring annihilation and a return to the nothingness of "non-being."

KHAZAD-DÛM ("DWARROWDELF")

The greatest and grandest of all the mansions and mines of the Dwarves in Middle-earth. Founded by Durin the Deathless, the first of the Seven Fathers of the Dwarves in the Ages of Stars, Khazad-dûm in the Misty Mountains encompasses the greatest mines in Middle-earth, famous for their rich seams of mithril, the "silver steel" that is worth ten times its weight in gold.

We can only speculate about the inspirations for this magnificent Dwarvish kingdom. We know for sure that the great three peaks above Khazad-dûm were inspired by a walking vacation in the Alps as a young man. The origins of the mines beneath are more doubtful. There are many legends of lost mines around the world, most notably King Solomon's Mines, which supplied the biblical king with his fabulous wealth. On the more realistic side of things, Tolkien grew up not far from the Black Country in the Midlands, home to hundreds of coal pits (though coal is hardly comparable to the precious and beautiful mithril).

Whatever its origins, Khazad-dûm thrives until the year 1980 of the Third Age when the Dwarves delve too deep in search of mithril and an entombed Balrog is released within the halls of the Dwarves. So terrible was the Balrog's strength and wrath that the Dwarves were driven from their kingdom. Thereafter, the abandoned realm is known by its Elvish name of Moria, the "Black Pit."

KHUZDUL

Tolkien's language of the Dwarves, supposedly devised for them by Aulë, the Smith of the Valar. As the Dwarves seldom spoke the language to others, only a few names, words, and phrases survive. Two of the most memorable are the battle cries of the Dwarves, terrifying no doubt to their enemies: "Baruk Khazâd!" "Khazâd ai-mênu!" These translate to "Axes of the Dwarves!" and "The Dwarves are upon you!" There seems to have been less secrecy in speaking the Khuzdul names of some places as with Khazad-dûm and the mountains above it: Zirakzigil ("Silverspike"), Barazinbar ("Redhorn"), and Bundushathûr ("Cloudyhead").

Tolkien appears to have developed Khuzdul during the early 1930s, before the publication of *The Hobbit*, and acknowledged that it was based

Khazad-dûm

on Semitic languages (a family of languages, including Hebrew and Arabic, originally spoken in the Middle East): "their words are Semitic obviously, constructed to be Semitic." Khuzdul was, more specifically, rooted in Hebrew, in its word structure, phonology, and morphology. Although careful to argue that there were no anti-Semitic implications in the comparison, Tolkien noted some similarities in the speech of Dwarves and Jews as both were "at once natives and aliens in their habitations, speaking the languages of the country, but with an accent due to their own private tongue . . ."

The secrecy of Khuzdul extended to the Dwarves' personal names, which they kept a closely guarded secret. All the Dwarf names revealed to others were not true names, but "outer names," which amounted to nicknames or titles in Westron, or other Mannish languages. In this we may find an echo of the

Kraken. Tolkien's Watcher-in-the-Water inhabits a foul dark pool near the West-gate of Moria. Its inspiration, the Norse Kraken, dwells off the coasts of Norway and Greenland.

fairy tale of *Rumpelstiltskin*, collected by the Brothers Grimm, in which an imp asks the heroine to guess his secret name.

KINE OF ARAW

Tolkien's version of the historic auroch (*Bos primigenius*), the now-extinct wild white ox of Eurasia, hunted by the ancient Germans and valued for its horns. In the stories told in Middle-earth they are reputed to be descended from the cattle of the Vala Oromë, known as Araw in Sindarin. Kine is an archaic English plural of "cow."

Aurochs are depicted in prehistoric cave paintings and are the archetypal wild bulls found in the literature and mythology of Sumeria, Assyria, Egypt, India, and Greece. They were known to the Romans as *uri*, described by Julius Caesar in *The Gallic Wars*: "[The *uri*] are a little below elephants in size and of the appearance, color, and shape of a bull. Their strength and speed are extraordinary, and they spare neither man nor wild beasts." The horns, he continues, among the people of Gaul, "are much sought after and, having been edged with silver at their mouths, they are used for drinking vessels at great feasts." As Tolkien was well aware, aurochs also appear in the German epic *Nibelungenlied*, where the hero Siegfried hunts and kills them. Silver-tipped hunting horns made from auroch horns are still to be found in many German museums and private collections.

The ancestor of the Ruling Stewards, Vorondil, is depicted as hunting the Kine of Araw in the wildernesses of Rhûn and fashioning a silver-tipped hunting horn out of one of the beasts' horns. This Great Horn becomes an heirloom of the Stewards and is eventually inherited by Boromir.

KULLERVO THE HAPLESS

A tragic hero whose tale is told in the Finnish national epic the *Kalevala*, a book read and studied by Tolkien while he was at Exeter College, Oxford. The portrayal of the foredoomed Kullervo was the inspiration for Tolkien's own fictional tragic figure of Túrin Turambar.

KURKAR, THE KING OF HOR   In Eastern
mythology a sorcerer-smith comparable to Sauron the Ring Lord who dwells in a mountain-kingdom akin to that of Mordor. Like Sauron, this sorcerer's power over his hellish kingdom is reliant on the supernatural power of a ring. Kurkar's ring is a massive iron mandala ring that we are told contains the "life" or "soul" of Kurkar and all his ancestors, and which cannot be melted by any known means. So long as it is kept safe in his mountain stronghold, Kurkar believes his power and his life are safe.

The One Ring, too, in some sense is bound up with Sauron's being and it too seems indestructible, remaining unchanged in color and cool to the touch even after being thrown into a fire. Kurkar, the Ring Lord, gathers demons and human allies around him in the mountain kingdom of Hor, just as Sauron the Ring Lord gathers Orcs and human allies around him in the mountain kingdom of Mordor. However, unlike Sauron, Kurkar is ultimately destroyed, not by Hobbits, but by another magician king, Geser.

While he is still a child, Geser's parents are slain by Kurkar, the king of Hor. With his inherited powers of sorcery, the orphaned Geser becomes an extraordinary smith. He forges an unbreakable sword from celestial (meteoric) iron and prepares himself for his ultimate duel with his great enemy, the king of Hor. However, he knows that Kurkar cannot be slain until the huge iron mandala ring itself is destroyed. Geser summons his supernatural brothers and a multitude of spirits to a huge volcanic forge where they strike the iron mandala with hammer blows that sound like thunder.

The destruction of Kurkar's iron ring of Hor in Geser's volcanic forge-room causes a cataclysm in which "the three worlds shook" and ultimately brings an end to the kingdom of Hor and its ruler. This is matched by the climax of *The Lord of the Rings*, when the destruction of Sauron's One Ring in Mount Doom's volcanic forge-room causes a comparable cataclysm in which "the earth shook, the plain heaved and cracked, and [. . .] the skies burst into thunder seared with lightning."

Túrin approaches the Pools of Ivrin

L

Arwen Evenstar. Arwen lives in Lothlórien and Rivendell for nearly three thousand years.
Her beauty is said to resemble that of Lúthien, Elven princess of Doriath.

LAKE-TOWN

A small settlement of Men on the Long Lake in Rhovanion. Also known as Esgaroth, its wooden buildings stand on wooden pillars sunk into the mud of the lake. Tolkien may have taken some of his his inspiration for Lake-Town from the crannogs—artificial islands—of prehistoric Britain and elsewhere in Europe, such as those found at Glastonbury. However, Esgaroth, with its busy trade, more immediately suggests a kind of proto-Venice.

LANGOBARDS

One of the many powerful Germanic tribes who lived on the eastern European borderlands of the Roman Empire. These warrior people swept into northern Italy in the late sixth century AD where they settled and gave their name to the region today called Lombardy. Described by Latin historians as the supreme horsemen of the German peoples, the Langobards were one of Tolkien's models for his own Northmen, the Éothéod, and their heirs, the Rohirrim—the Horsemen of Rohan. On the other hand, Tolkien also associated the Langobards with his Dwarves: the name "Langobards" translates directly into English as "Longbeards," the same name Tolkien gave to the Dwarves of Durin's Line.

The Middle High German epic *Ortnit*, dating to around the end of the twelfth century, tells the story of a king of Lambarten (Lombardy), Ortnit, whose kingdom is terrorized by dragons, just as the kingdom of the Longbeard Dwarf Dáin I is terrorized by the Cold-drakes of the Grey Mountains. Ortnit is eventually killed when he is crushed to death by a dragon. This finds a parallel in Dáin's own death, when he is slain by a Cold-drake despite his formidable strength and his own Dwarf-forged Dragon-proof armor.

LAST ALLIANCE OF ELVES AND MEN

The alliance formed by the Elves and Men toward the end of the Second Age in response to the military rise of Sauron. The two key events are the Battle of Dagorlad (3434 SA) and the Siege of Barad-dûr (3434–41 SA).

Master of Esgaroth. The ruler of the Lake Men, Northmen who had been traders upon the Long
Lake and the Running River.

Such climatic final battles in which a golden age of heroes ends in cataclysm are a stock feature of epic poetry and heroic romance. The great age of the Greek heroes comes to an end in the long, bitter war between the Greeks and Trojans beneath the walls of Troy, while in the Norse *Völsunga Saga* and the German epic *Nibelungenlied*, similar final conflicts end tragically with the extinction of the entire Völsung and Nibelung dynasties. In Arthurian legend, the Battle of Camlann brings an end to Arthur's reign and the knights of the Round Table. In some instances, as in Tolkien's Battle of Dagorlad and the Arthurian Battle of Camlann, there is a clear distinction between the good and evil sides.

Often in such stories the cosmic struggle boils down to a duel between the leaders, as in that between Arthur and Mordred. Similarly, in the Siege of Barad-dûr, Tolkien stages a duel between Gil-galad, high king of the Noldor, and Elendil, high king of the Númenóreans-in-exile, on the one side, and Sauron, the Dark Lord, on the other. All parties are destroyed, if only temporarily in the case of Sauron.

The dark forces of both Mordred and Sauron are annihilated, but the cost to the victors is so great that what follows is centuries of chaos and warfare. In Britain, King Arthur and the greater part of the knights of the Round Table are slain. In Middle-earth, the greater part of the allied forces of Elves and Men are slain. In both instances, a golden, heroic age comes to a close, and a new, less noble age begins.

LEGOLAS

The sole representative of the Elves in the Fellowship of the Ring. Legolas is the only son of the Elven-king of the Woodland Realm in Mirkwood, one of Bilbo's antagonists in *The Hobbit*. In *The Lord of the Rings*, Tolkien reveals the Elven-king's name as Thranduil, meaning "vigorous spring," so it is appropriate that Legolas's name means "green leaf" suggesting his own vigor and youthfulness. In *The Lord of the Rings*, Legolas displays the many remarkable qualities of his race: superior eyesight and hearing, lightness of foot, ability to track, and strength and skill in archery.

Legolas

It is perhaps noteworthy that these are characteristic gifts and skills in the portrayals of the Native American peoples ("Indians") found in the popular fiction of Tolkien's childhood reading. Tom Shippey in his *Road to Middle-earth* (1982) noted that Tolkien himself acknowledged "an early devotion to Red Indians, bows and arrows and forests" inspired by his early reading of the historical romances of the American writer James Fenimore Cooper (1789–1851). And, among many examples, Shippey specifically suggests that "the journey of the Fellowship from Lórien to Tol Brandir, with its canoes and portages, often recalls *The Last of the Mohicans*," Cooper's novel of 1826.

As an archer-hero, Legolas is reminiscent of numerous mythological figures, from Heracles, whose skill in archery enables him to kill the Stymphalian birds, to the Hindu god Rama, who is usually depicted with a bow and arrow, and even the forest-dwelling outlaw of English folklore, Robin Hood.

LINDON The Sindar and Noldor Elven kingdom of the westernmost lands of Middle-earth after the First Age. Founded by Gil-galad in the first year of the Second Age, it is divided into Forlindon ("North Lindon") and Harlindon ("South Lindon") by the Gulf of Lune and the mouth of the River Lhûn, where stands its capital, the port-city of Mithlond, the Grey Havens.

Tolkien frequently pointed out that the Shire of the Hobbits is geographically analogous to the shires of the English Midlands on the edge of the Welsh Marches. Extending this comparison, we can see how the geography of Lindon broadly recalls that of Wales and Cornwall, two Celtic lands severed by that distinctive wedge of the Bristol Channel and the River Severn. The Grey Havens may suggest the Pembrokeshire port of Milford Haven, mentioned in William Shakespeare's *Cymbeline* as "blessed Milford."

There are further connections between Lindon and Wales. Welsh choirs are renowned throughout the world, while Lindon is the "land of song" or, more precisely, "land of sacred song." Linguistically, too, Tolkien wrote of how Sindarin, the language of the Elves of Lindor, was created to resemble the Welsh language.

LOKI A Norse god who in the last great battle of Ragnarök will command the rebellious giants against the gods of Asgard. He is the father of several monstrous beings including the wolf Fenrir and the world serpent Jörmungandr. An example of a trickster god, and a shape-shifter, he is the embodiment of discord and chaos.

Loki is comparable to Tolkien's Dark Lord, Morgoth, commander of the rebel Maiar spirits against the Valar "gods" of Arda in the last Great Battle of the War of Wrath. Morgoth is also a shape-shifter, master deceiver, and creator of discord (marring the Music of the Ainur even at the beginning of creation) and breeds monstrous beings, including Orcs and Werewolves. Both Loki and Morgoth, after millennia of conflict, bring ruin to their worlds and obliteration to themselves.

The Two Lamps. Illuin and Ormal are great lamps set up by the Valar at the northern and southern ends of Arda to illuminate the world during the Spring of Arda. They are eventually destroyed by Melkor.

LONGSHANKS   A nickname that one of the Men of Bree uses to insult Strider, the Ranger of the North, in *The Lord of the Rings*. Strider, of course, is later revealed to be Aragorn II, the Chieftain of the Dúnedain and the future King Elessar Telcondar (meaning "Elfstone Strider"). Both the names, Longshanks and Strider, undoubtedly refer to the Ranger's height and his remarkable speed in traversing across vast tracts of Middle-earth (one of the Riders of Rohan addresses him by the rather more flattering name of "Wingfoot"). In the apparently insulting nickname of Longshanks, we find an allusion to real history that hints at Aragorn's royal heritage. As Tolkien was well aware, Longshanks was the nickname given to Edward I, king of England, who ruled from 1272 to 1307. Edward Longshanks was a tall and physically intimidating warrior king who reestablished royal authority and the rule of law in England. Although ruthless in establishing his authority over the Welsh and the Scots, Longshanks was one of the most formidable and effective of all medieval English kings.

Edward was also an enthusiast for Arthurian legend and seems to have made several great round tables (perhaps including the extant medieval table today in the city of Winchester, in Hampshire, England), so there may be another link between Aragorn's nickname and his own Arthur-like role.

LÓRIEN   In Tolkien's legendarium, both the name of a garden isle in Valinor belonging to Irmo, the Vala Master of Dreams and Visions, and a name for Irmo himself. The name may mean "dreamland." In Middle-earth, Lórien is also a name for the Elven domain of Lothlórien. The isle has parallels in mythological paradises (a word ultimately derived from an Old Persian word for a walled garden), notably to Avalon. The mother of Fëanor, Míriel, is taken there to be healed, just as Arthur is taken to Avalon to be healed after his death.

The figure of Lórien/Irmo, meanwhile, most closely resembles the Greek Morpheus (the Roman Somnus), the god of dreams and visions from whom the word for the drug "morphine" is derived. The Greek word *morph*

Lúthien dances before Morgoth

means "form," and Morpheus was thus the deity who shaped and formed dreams. Like Lórien, Morpheus blessed the dreamer with healing rest and prophetic visions.

LOTHLÓRIEN

The fairest Elf-kingdom remaining on Middle-earth at the time of the War of the Ring, the domain of Galadriel and Celeborn. The name means "the land of blossoms dreaming." Lothlórien is also known as Lórien (perhaps meaning "dreamland"), and Laurelindórenan ("the valley of the singing gold"). The domain echoes both Doriath, the domain of Thingol and Melian in Beleriand, and the Garden of Lórien in Valinor, whose trees Melian once tended.

Lothlórien is largely inspired by the ancient Celtic tradition of enchanted forests ruled by "white ladies." This enchanted forest of golden-leaved, silver-barked *mallorn* trees is protected by the power of the white-clad Galadriel, the possessor of Nenya, the White Ring of Adamant and Water. Using the power of the ring, Galadriel is able to keep her domain out of time, in a state of perpetual spring, immune to death and decay—a trope that allies it to many mythological paradises.

Such Celtic otherworlds were considered both potentially perilous and places of rest and healing. This ambiguity can be glimpsed in some views of Lothlórien in *The Lord of the Rings*, where the people of Gondor and Rohan are depicted as deeply suspicious of it and its ruler. Of the Golden Wood Boromir remarks, "few come out who once go in; and of that few none have escaped unscathed." Aragorn reproves this judgment, replacing "unscathed" with "unchanged." For the Fellowship of the Ring, it provides a place not only of rest and healing but also transformation, as we see in the Dwarf Gimli's change of heart in relation to the Elves.

LUCIFER

In Greco-Roman mythology the personification or god of the planet Venus in its guise as the Morning Star, and in Christian tradition the name given to the fallen angel Satan before his fall in the story of the War in Heaven found in the New Testament Book of Revelation (12:7–9). The name "Lucifer" is the Latin for "light bringer." In Tolkien it can be connected to two figures: the Dark Lord Melkor/Morgoth, and Eärendil, who carries a Silmaril, the Morning Star, through the sky. Though very diverse, the two figures were ultimately allies.

Because of the "wayward" movements of the planet Venus in the sky, many ancient mythologies have stories connecting the Morning Star with figures who strive for God's seat in heaven and who are punished by being thrown down into the underworld. Perhaps the best-known myth that seems to echo such tales is that of the Greek youth Phaeton ("shining one"), who tricks his father Helios, the sun god, into lending him his sun chariot. When Phaeton proves unable to control the horses and so threatens to destroy the Earth, Zeus strikes him with a thunderbolt and he falls to his death down through the sky.

There seems to be a reference to the falling Morning Star in the Old Testament, in Isaiah (14:12), where a ruler is taunted in the following way: "How you have fallen from heaven, morning star, son of the dawn! You have been cast down to the earth, you who once laid low the nations! You said in your heart, 'I will ascend to the heavens; I will raise my throne above the stars of God; I will sit enthroned on the mount of assembly, on the utmost heights of Mount Zaphon. I will ascend above the tops of the clouds; I will make myself like the Most High.' But you are brought down to the realm of the dead, to the depths of the pit."

In some older English translations of this passage, "Morning Star" was rendered as Lucifer, and the passage and the name thus became associated with various references in the New Testament to Satan and his fall: in Revelation (12:7–9) and in Luke (10:18): "I saw Satan fall like lightning from heaven." From a conflation of these scattered biblical sources, Lucifer became a major figure in the Christian imagination, identified with the Devil and extensively found in art and literature, perhaps most notably in Milton's Christian epic *Paradise Lost* (1667–74). It is certainly Milton's proud, defiant Lucifer who most clearly inspired Tolkien's own fallen Ainur, Melkor/Melkoth, who similarly strives to godlike power and freedom.

Curiously, as the "bringer of light" and light bearer, the name Lucifer was also an epithet given to Jesus, who in the New Testament is associated with "the day star" (2 Peter 1:19). Tolkien's most Christlike figure is Eärendil, who brings salvation to the Elves and Men of Middle-earth, and who, as Mandos prophesies,

Lúthien finds Beren

will be the ultimate vanquisher of Morgoth at the end of time. Tolkien derived Eärendil's name from what seems to have been the Anglo-Saxon name for the Morning Star, and in his own mythology Eärendil, another light bearer, carries a Silmaril as the Morning Star through the sky on his ship *Vingilótë*. In Eärendil, then, it seems that Tolkien redeems the original Lucifer, restoring him to his prelapsarian place as a star of the heavens.

LÚTHIEN ("MAIDEN OF TWILIGHT")

Daughter of Thingol, the high king of the Grey Elves and his queen, Melian the Maia, considered the most beautiful child of any race and the fairest singer within the spheres of the world, around whom nightingales gathered.

Lúthien, like Galadriel, is another embodiment of the "lady in white" of Celtic legend, though here there seems to be a direct inspiration in the figure of Olwyn, whose eyes, like Lúthien's, shine with light and whose skin is also as white as snow. Both figures are closely associated with flowers: Lúthien with the white star-shaped flower *niphredil* and Olwyn with the white trefoil or clover.

In terms of her and her lover Beren's story, as Tolkien freely admitted, his inspiration lies in the Greek myth of Orpheus and Eurydice. However, it is not the Greek oak nymph Eurydice, who is her counterpart here, but Orpheus, whose musical powers and descent into the underworld she shares. There may also be a buried connection between Lúthien and Persephone, the Greek goddess of the spring, who makes an annual descent into Hades.

Tolkien's tale of star-crossed lovers was his perhaps his most personal, inspired by his own love for his wife, Edith Bratt. This is certainly confirmed by the couple's gravestone, on which is engraved "John Ronald Reuel Tolkien (1892–1973)—Beren" and "Edith Bratt Tolkien (1889–1971)—Lúthien." In a letter to his son Christopher, Tolkien wrote: "I never called Edith *Lúthien*—but she was the source of the story that in time became the chief part of *The Silmarillion*."

See also: WHITE LADIES

LYCANTHROPY

The belief in werewolves, or lycanthropes—humans, who because of a curse or a bite from another werewolf, can shape-shift into a wolf, especially during night of a full moon.

The transformation of humans into animals has been a part of every shamanistic culture. And ancient wolf cults, evidence for which is found widely, likely rose out of the initiation rites of young warriors possessed by the spirits of wolves. The Greek myth of Lycaon, who was turned into a wolf by Zeus for the crime of either child sacrifice or cannibalism, was in origin probably related to such rites, but already suggests the evil associations of werewolves. In medieval folklore and onward, werewolves became closely associated with both witches and vampires.

Elements of these traditions find their way into Tolkien's world in the figure of Draugluin, the Father of Werewolves, who is bred by Morgoth seemingly from the spirit of a corrupted Maia. He is the sire of all the Werewolves of Middle-earth, the servant of the Gorthaur "The Cruel" (the necromancer Sauron), and is closely associated with Thuringwethil, the vampire messenger of Morgoth.
See also: VAMPIRES

Werewolves of Middle-earth

M

Melian, Thingol, and Lúthien

MACBETH Tragedy by William Shakespeare, probably first performed in 1606, and a play that Tolkien loved to hate. However, curiously enough it was a notable source of inspiration for *The Lord of the Rings*. For, although Tolkien profoundly disliked the play, he was fascinated by the historic and mythic story on which it was based. In fact, he went even further and tended to voice his dismissal of drama as a form of literature at all. In his lecture and essay "On Fairy-Stories," Tolkien stated that, more than any other form of literature, fantasy needs a "willing suspension of disbelief" to survive. In dramatized fantasy (such as the witches scenes in *Macbeth*) Tolkien found "disbelief had not so much to be suspended as hanged, drawn and quartered."

However peculiar Tolkien's dislike of Shakespeare and *Macbeth*, it proved to be a very fruitful hatred. The March of the Ents was, as Tolkien explained, "due, I think, to my bitter disappointment and disgust from schooldays with the shabby use made in Shakespeare of the coming of 'Great Birnam wood to high Dunsinane hill': I longed to devise a setting in which the trees might really march to war." Tolkien felt Shakespeare had trivialized and misinterpreted an authentic myth, providing a cheap, simplistic interpretation of the prophecy of this march of a wood upon a hill. And so Tolkien gives us the "true story" behind the prophecy in *Macbeth* in the epic March of the Ents on Isengard.

Tolkien went further still, challenging Shakespeare's portrayal of Macbeth himself in his own evil Lord of the Ringwraiths—the Witch-king of Angmar—who sells his mortal soul to Sauron for a Ring of Power and the illusion of earthly dominion. So that none will mistake the comparison, or Tolkien's challenge to Shakespeare, the life of the Witch-king is protected by a prophecy that is almost identical to the final one that safeguards Macbeth. In the play the witches prophesy that the murderous Scottish king should "laugh to scorn / The power of man, for none of woman born / Shall harm Macbeth." Tolkien's prophecy about the Witch-king—"not by the hand of man will he fall"—is certainly comparable to *Macbeth*'s prophecy that is circumvented when at the end of the play he is killed by Macduff, who "was from his mother's womb / Untimely ripp'd."

The prophecy concerning the Witch-king's fate also proves to be simultaneously true and false. In the Battle of Pelennor Fields, the Witch-king falls "not by the hand of man" but by the hand of the shield-maiden Éowyn of Rohan and her Hobbit squire, Meriadoc Brandybuck. In this, Tolkien once again "improves" upon Shakespeare's unsatisfactory fulfilment of the prophecy about Macbeth. And, certainly, one must acknowledge that the Witch-king's death at the hand of a Hobbit and a woman disguised as a warrior is rather more satisfying than Shakespeare's rather quibbling solution that someone born by caesarean section is not, strictly speaking, "of woman born."

MAIAR (SINGULAR: MAIA) The lesser angelic powers who descend from the Timeless Halls into Tolkien's world of Arda as servants of the more powerful Valar. The Maiar sometimes have counterparts among the gods, spirits, heroes, and nymphs of Greek and Norse mythology. The charts on pages 450 and 451 list the principal Maiar in Tolkien's legendarium, and their possible inspirations. The resemblances are not always clear-cut. Thus Eönwë, the herald of Manwë, king of the Valar, is comparable to the Greek Hermes, the herald of the Zeus, but has little of the multifaceted, not to say mercurial, nature of Hermes who, among many other roles also guided the dead to the underworld.

MASTER OF NON-BEING An entity in Eastern Painted Scrolls that resembles Tolkien's Morgoth the Black Foe of the World. Few cultures have really grasped the concept of nonexistence, as have Indian and Eastern religions. Indeed, in this huge Eastern "Master of Non-Being" we have an entity comparable in form and ambition to that of the mighty Morgoth: a massive scorched black demon described as a "Black Man, as tall as a spear . . . the Master of Non-Existence, of instability, of murder and destruction." And just as Morgoth the Black Foe—armed with a spear and in alliance with the great spider Ungoliant—extinguished the sacred Trees of Light in the Undying Lands, so the terrible Eastern Master "made the sun and the moon die and assigned demons to the planets and harmed the stars."

Meduseld. It is to the Golden Hall of Meduseld and King Théoden that four of the Fellowship of the Ring come, as emissaries of the Dúnedain, to call the Rohirrim to arms in the War of the Ring.

MEDUSELD   The "Golden Hall" of the king of Rohan. When Gandalf rides toward the royal city of Edoras, Tolkien describes the distant sight of the gold roof of the Golden Hall of Meduseld glinting in the sunlight. The name Meduseld is Anglo-Saxon for "mead hall," and the description of the hall is almost identical to that of Herot, the Golden Hall of King Hrothgar in *Beowulf*. As Beowulf approaches the kingdom of Hrothgar, the poet catches sight of Herot's roof gables covered with hammered gold that glistens and glints in the light of the sun. Both of these great halls have even greater divine models. Meduseld has its divine model in Valinor in the Great Hall of Oromë the Horseman, and Herot's Hall has the Great Hall of Valhalla as its divine model. This was the "Hall of Slain Heroes," roofed with golden shields. It was the mead hall and heaven of fallen warriors, created for them in Asgard by Odin.

MELIAN   Maia of Yavanna who early in the First Age falls in love with and becomes the wife and queen to Thingol, Sindar king of Doriath. Her love of wood and forest and the song of nightingales allies her with countless nymphs and nature spirits of mythology, while her powers as an enchantress recall the powerful female figures in Arthurian legend such as Vivien and Morgan le Fay, though without their darker aspects. Her first meeting with Thingol specifically resembles the story of how Vivien comes upon Merlin asleep beneath a thorn tree and imprisons the magician in a "tower of air" from which he can never emerge. However, while Vivien acts out of malice, Melian's enchantment of Thingol is entirely benevolent, born out of mutual love.

MELKOR   In Tolkien's creation story *Ainulindalë* the most powerful, inventive, and magnificent of the angelic powers known as the Ainur but who, out of his desire to create on his account and in his own way, is corrupted and becomes Morgoth, the first Dark Lord of Middle-earth.

In Tolkien's legendarium, he most resembles the rebel archangel Lucifer of Christian tradition, especially as depicted in John Milton's *Paradise Lost*. Just as the proud Lucifer questions the ways of God, so Melkor asks why the Ainur cannot be allowed to compose their own music and bring forth life and worlds of their own. Both Tolkien's Melkor and Milton's Lucifer are, in one light, heroic in their steadfast "courage never to submit or yield"; however, in truth both rebel angels are primarily motivated by overweening pride and envy.

Setting himself up against the Valar, Melkor builds his fortress of Utumno in the Iron Mountains in the northern wastes of Middle-earth, and digs the foundations of his armory and dungeon of Angband. Thereafter, Melkor wages five great wars against the Valar. These wars before the rising of the first Moon and Sun and the arrival of Men within the spheres of the world are comparable to the cosmological myths of the ancient Greeks, in which the unruly Titans of the Earth rise up to fight the gods. Ultimately the titanic forces of the Earth are conquered and forced underground, just as Melkor's forces are defeated in those primeval wars with the Valar.

MENEGROTH
See: DORIATH; STRONGHOLDS

MERCIA   Anglo-Saxon kingdom that through the sixth to ninth centuries rose to become the most powerful in Britain. This was the heartland of England Tolkien believed was for centuries the homeland of his mother's Mercian ancestors. The name Mercia derives from "Mearc" or "Mark," the Anglo-Saxon name for the borderland between the Celtic tribes of Wales and Anglo-Saxons of England.

This real-world history is comparable to the fictional history of Tolkien's Middle-earth where Rohan is a borderland between the Dunlendings and

Melian and Thingol meet in Nan Elmoth. The story of the enchantment of Thingol by Melian recalls the enchantment of Merlin by Vivien.

Rohan's allies in Gondor. In calling the Rohirrim cavalrymen the "Riders of the Mark," Tolkien clearly linked his fictional Rohan to his beloved and historic Mercia. For, not only was Mercia a buffer region, but its greatest and most powerful ruler—the eighth-century King Offa—built the massive earthen wall and trench that runs over 170 miles and marks the border between England and Wales. So it seems likely that in King Offa of Mercia as the legendary builder and defender of Offa's Dyke, Tolkien found inspiration for his fictional King Helm Hammerhand of Rohan, the legendary builder and defender of Helm's Dike.

In his *JRR Tolkien: A Biography*, Humphrey Carpenter notes that, during the time he was writing *The Lord of the Rings*, Tolkien took his family on a vacation outing to White Horse Hill, less than 20 miles from Oxford, on the borders of Mercia and Wessex. This is the site of the famous prehistoric image of the gigantic White Horse cut into the chalk beneath the green turf and topsoil on the hill. This White Horse undoubtedly inspired Tolkien's image of a white horse on a green field, carried on the banners of the kings of Rohan and the Riders of the Mark.

MERCURY
The Roman counterpart to the Greek god Hermes, the herald of Zeus (the Roman Jupiter) and the god of messengers, merchants, pilgrims, alchemists, and magicians. As protector of travelers, the appearance of Mercury/Hermes as a bearded wanderer in a slouch hat and traveler's cape and carrying a staff helped provide some of Tolkien's inspiration for his Istari Wizards, and most specifically Gandalf the Grey.

Another link of Mercury to Gandalf is the Wizard's Elvish name Mithrandir, meaning "Grey Pilgrim" or "Grey Wanderer." It may be supposed that when the ancients decided to assign gods and their influences to the planets, the god Mercury must have been one of their more obvious candidates. After all, the word "planet" comes from the Greek for "wanderer." (As most stars are "fixed" in the sky, the most obvious quality of a planet is its ability to wander through the night sky, hence the use of this word for this particular meaning.) The planet Mercury is observably a silver-gray "wanderer" traveling at phenomenal speed across the night sky, visiting each god or planet, as paths cross. There could be no clearer case for matching the mercurial nature of both the planet and the god.

MERIADOC ("MERRY") BRANDYBUCK

Hobbit member of the Fellowship of the Ring and heir to the Master of Buckland. For his part in the slaying of the Witch-king he became known as Meriadoc the Magnificent.

Meriadoc has a suitably prophetic name for his role as the courageous (if diminutive) squire to the king of Rohan. In origin, Meriadoc is an ancient Celtic name for the historical founder of the Celtic kingdom of Brittany, as well as the name of one of the knights in King Arthur's court. However, as Tolkien informs us, the names Meriadoc and Merry are translations of the original Hobbitish *Kalimac* and *Kali*, meaning, "jolly." Merry, moreover, derives from the Old English *myrige*, meaning "pleasant," though, in a curious etymological twist, this appears to originate in the Prehistoric German *murgjaz*, meaning "short."

Meriadoc Brandybuck
and Peregrin Took

Menegroth. "The Thousand Caves," the city fortress of the Grey-elves of Doriath in Beleriand.

Merlin. As archetypal wizard and counselor to King Arthur, Merlin is an important source for the character of Gandalf.

MERLIN
In Arthurian romance the greatest of all wizards, and the mentor, adviser, and chief strategist to King Arthur. Merlin is immortal, but has mortal emotions and empathy. He is an enchanter who communes with spirits of woods, mountains, and lakes, and has tested his powers in duels with other wizards and enchantresses.

In his role as Arthur's mentor, we can see a clear analogy with Tolkien's Gandalf as the mentor for Aragorn II, the future king of the Reunited Kingdom of the Dúnedain. Merlin and Gandalf are both travelers of great learning, with long white beards and who carry a staff and wear broad-brimmed hats and long robes. They are both nonhuman beings. Both are counselors for future kings in peace and war, yet they have no interest in worldly power themselves.

Merlin's imprisonment by Vivien in the forest of Brocéliande also has an echo in the enchantment of Thingol by Melian in the forest of Nan Elmoth, in Beleriand.

MICHAEL, ARCHANGEL
In the New Testament Book of Revelation, the dragon-slayer in that prophetic vision of Armageddon: the great battle at the "end of time" fought between the forces of good and evil. In many of its aspects, Tolkien's Great Battle in the War of Wrath at the end of the First Age appears to owe some of its inspiration to the biblical Armageddon. However, unlike the duel described in the book of Revelation, there is no duel between Tolkien's Eärendil the Mariner and Ancalagon the Black Dragon. Archangel Michael and the "Red Dragon" is described in Revelation (12:7–9) as such: "Then war broke out in heaven. Michael and his angels fought against the dragon, and the dragon and his angels fought back. But he was not strong enough, and they lost their place in heaven. The great dragon was hurled down—that ancient serpent called the devil, or Satan, who leads the whole world astray. He was hurled to the Earth, and his angels with him." And so, just as the Red Dragon's downfall marked Satan's defeat, so the Black Dragon's downfall marks the defeat of Morgoth in Middle-earth.

MIDDLE-EARTH The main continent in Tolkien's legendarium, the northwestern regions of which provide the main setting for his epic tales. It is perhaps the most richly imagined land in fantasy fiction, meticulously detailed in terms of its geography, wildlife, peoples, cultures, and, of course, histories.

That said, Tolkien always insisted that Middle-earth is our real world— the planet Earth in another incarnation. He acknowledges in several of his letters of the 1950s that the name often confused his readers: "Many reviewers seem to assume that Middle-earth is another planet!" He found this a perplexing conclusion because in his own mind he had not the least doubt about its locality: "Middle-earth is not an imaginary world. The name is the modern form of *midden-erd* > *middel-erd*, an ancient name for the *oikoumene*, the abiding place of Men, the objectively real world, in use specifically opposed to imaginary worlds (as Fairyland) or unseen worlds (as Heaven or Hell)." A decade later, Tolkien famously even gave a journalist an *exact* geographic location: "the action of the story takes place in North-west of Middle-earth, equivalent in latitude to the coastline of Europe and the north shore of the Mediterranean . . ."

The confusion that arises about Middle-earth can be attributed, however, not so much to a *spatial* issue, but a *temporal* one: a question not so much of *where* Middle-earth is, but *when*. "The theatre of my tale is this earth," Tolkien explained in one letter, "the one in which we now live, but the historical period is imaginary."

For an explanation, one must look to the chronicles of *The Silmarillion*. Tolkien's world begins with the command of Eru the One and a Great Music out of which comes forth a Vision like a globed light in the Void. This Vision becomes manifest in the creation of a flat Earth within spheres of air and light. It is a world inhabited by godlike spirits known as Valar and Maiar as well as newborn races including the Elves, Dwarves, and Ents. We are 30,000 years into this history, however, before the human race actually appears in what Tolkien calls the First Age of Middle-earth. Another 3,900 years pass before the cataclysmic destruction of the Atlantis-like civilization of Númenor during Middle-earth's Second Age, which results in this mythical world's transformation into the globed world we know today.

All in all, it takes some 37,000 years of chronicled history before the events described in *The Lord of the Rings* during the Third Age actually begin. And even after the War of the Ring in Middle-earth's Fourth Age, we are assured that many millennia will have to pass before Tolkien's archetypal world evolves into the real material world of recorded human history.

Tolkien himself estimated that his own time was some 6,000 years after Middle-earth's Third Age. Working backward from our own system of time, this would place the creation of Middle-earth and the Undying Lands at 41,000 BC while the War of the Ring appears to have taken place sometime between 4,000 and 5,000 BC in our historiographical system.

This is the real trick of Tolkien's Middle-earth: an imaginary time in the real world's age of myth that had a parallel existence and evolution just before the beginning of the human race's historic time. Tolkien's Middle-earth is meant to be something akin to what the ancient Greek philosopher Plato saw as the ideal world of archetypes: the world of ideas behind all civilizations and nations of the world.

MIDGARD "Middle-earth"—one of the nine worlds in ancient Norse and Germanic mythology. It is the world inhabited by humans, as opposed to those other worlds inhabited by gods, dwarfs, elves, and other entities. Midgard was conceived as vast and flat, encircled by an ocean that is home to Jörmungandr, the Midgard Serpent, a monster that was so huge it ringed the entire world by grasping its own tail.

In his legendarium, Tolkien somewhat confusingly uses the name Arda to refer to the Earth which, as originally created, is also flat and encircled by a mighty ocean, just like the Norse Midgard. Middle-earth is only a part of Arda, a continental landmass in the middle of Arda. What he insisted upon, though, was that Middle-earth and its neighboring landmasses belonged to *this* Earth, "the one in which we now live," though "the historical period is imaginary." That is, Middle-earth exists in an archetypal age of myth, legends, and dreams that was in good part inspired by the Midgard that existed in myths, legends, and dreams of the Norsemen.

MIGRATION OF THE HOBBITS

The migration of the Hobbits across Middle-Earth to their last and permanent home in the Shire. Tolkien purposely patterned the migration to match up with the migration of the historic Anglo-Saxon peoples.

The origins of both Hobbits and Anglo-Saxons are lost in the mists of time somewhere beyond a distant and massive eastern range of mountains. The ancestors of both the Hobbits and the Anglo-Saxons migrated across these mountains and eventually settled in fertile river-delta regions. Eventually war and invaders forced the Hobbits to leave their second homeland, known as the Angle—a wedge of land between the Loudwater and Hoarwell rivers in Eriador—and migrate across the Brandywine River into what eventually became known as the Shire of Middle-earth.

Similarly, war and invaders forced the Anglo-Saxons to leave their second homeland known as die Angel—a wedge-shaped land between the Schlei River and Flensburg Fjord—and migrate across the English Channel into what eventually became known as the shires of England. Furthermore, there were three races or tribes of Hobbits, the Fallohides, Stoors, and Harfoots, which are directly comparable to the three peoples of the Anglo-Saxons (the Saxons, Angles, and Jutes).

Finally, we find the Hobbit founders of the Shire were the brothers Marcho (meaning "horse") and Blanco (meaning "white horse"), while the Anglo-Saxon founders of England were the brothers Hengist (meaning "stallion") and Horsa (meaning "horse").

MINAS TIRITH

The "Tower of the Guard" is the greatest surviving city and fortress of Gondor at the time of the War of the Ring. Originally known as Minas Anor, the "Tower of the Setting Sun," it is a citadel built on a hill with seven levels, seven concentric walls, and seven gates, each facing a different direction. It is mostly made out of white stone, except for the lowest wall, which is made of the same impervious black stone as Orthanc.

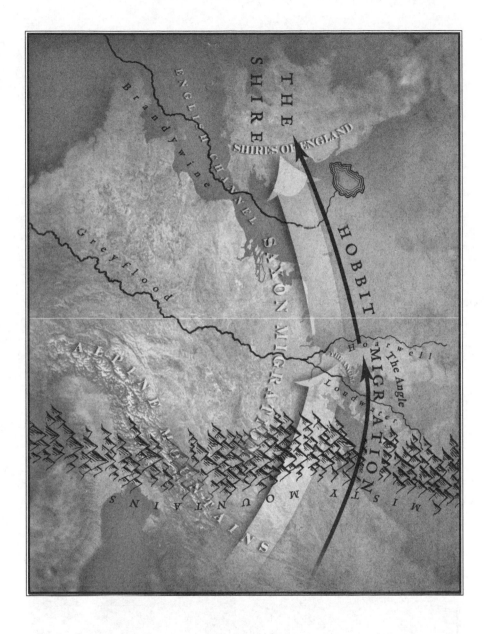

The Migration of the Hobbits

Minas Tirith. A seven-walled citadel much like Campanella's City of the Sun.

The Gondorian capital is comparable to the imaginary City of the Sun, a utopia devised in 1602 by the Renaissance friar and philosopher Tommaso Campanella (1568–1639): "The greater part of the city is built upon a high hill, which rises from an extensive plain, but several of its circles extend for some distance beyond the base of the hill, which is of such a size that the diameter of the city is upward of two miles, so that its circumference becomes about seven. [. . .] It is divided into seven rings or huge circles named from the seven planets . . . " The City of the Sun, however, has only four principal gates, positioned at the compass points in the lowest wall—an arrangement that Tolkien considerably refined upon at Minas Tirith.

Both Minas Tirith and the City of the Sun look back to ancient mythological traditions: the ancient Sumerians believed that there were seven walls and seven gates to both heaven and hell, and the biblical paradise of Eden was surrounded by seven walls entered through seven gates. There are connections, too, with the ancient tradition of the Music of the Spheres and the divine order of the universe—a tradition that fascinated Tolkien deeply.

See also: STRONGHOLDS

MIRKWOOD   A great forest in Rhovanion to the east of the Misty Mountain, home in the Third Age to Elves, Dwarves, and Men, and, for a time, Sauron, the Necromancer of Dol Guldur.

This ancient Anglo-Saxon composite word conveys the lurking superstitious dread of primeval forests. In Germanic and Norse epic poetry, the dark forest is ever present and is even sometimes specifically given the name "Mirkwood."

In the *Völsunga Saga*, Sigurd the Dragon-slayer enters Mirkwood and stops to mourn the loss of the "Glittering Heath," now ruined by the corruption of Fáfnir the dragon. The atavistic dread of the forest survives in many of the fairy tales of the Brothers Grimm, including "Little Red Riding Hood" and "Hansel and Gretel" and can be found, too, in Arthurian legend, where the forest represents a place of danger and dark magic but also transformation, the wild antithesis of the civilized court.

This theme of wilderness contaminated by evil is evident in Tolkien's own spider-infested Mirkwood. But it is also in Mirkwood that Bilbo Baggins twice saves the beleaguered Company of Dwarves and really proves his mettle, becoming the true hero of his own tale.

MISTY MOUNTAINS The greatest and highest mountains in the northwest of Middle-earth, also known as the Hithaeglir, or "misty peaks," in Sindarin. Nearly 1,000 miles long, this massive mountain range runs from the Witch-kingdom of Angmar and the Orc-hold of Gundabad in the far north to the fortress of Isengard and the Gap of Rohan in the south. The Misty Mountains were inspired by Tolkien's walking tour of the Swiss Alps in the summer of 1911 at the age of 19 with 11 companions, including his brother Hilary and his aunt Jane Neave.

The Misty Mountains form a near-impenetrable mountain wall that separates the lands of Eriador from the Vale of Anduin in Rhovanion. There are only three possible passages through that mountain barrier: the High Pass, the Redhorn Pass, and the Dwarf tunnels of Moria. One of the peaks above Moria is called Celebril the White, or the Silvertine in the Westron common tongue. Tolkien clearly confirmed the source of its inspiration in a letter to his son Michael in which he describes the breathtaking panoramic views of the Silberhorn Mountain in the Swiss Alps as "the Silvertine of my dreams." Furthermore, the Elvish name for the Redhorn Mountain and Pass is Caradhas ("red spike or horn"), also similarly inspired by another real-world mountain encountered on that same fateful summer walking tour. In a later note Tolkien observes: "Caradhras seems to have been a great mountain tapering upwards like the Matterhorn."

In a notable example of life imitating art, the Misty Mountains entered into the real world or, more precisely, the real-life solar system. The International Astronomical Union, the international body of scientists responsible for naming stars and geographic features of planets and lunar bodies, voted to name all of the mountains of Saturn's moon Titan after the mountains of Tolkien's world. In 2012 they named a Titanian mountain range the "Misty Montes" after Tolkien's Misty Mountains.

MORDOR

The terrible mountain kingdom of Sauron the Dark Lord throughout the Second and Third Ages. Within this realm Sauron forges the One Ring in the volcanic fires of Mount Doom and gathers vast armies of Orcs, Trolls, Uruks, Southrons, and Easterlings, all in his mission to dominate and enslave the kingdoms of the Elves and Men of Middle-earth.

Tolkien likely derived the name for this evil kingdom from the Anglo-Saxon *morðor*, meaning "murder" or "mortal sin." This seems an appropriate name for an evil kingdom created as an engine for slaughter. However, in Tolkien's own invented languages Mordor means "Black Land" in the Sindarin Grey Elven tongue and "Land of Shadow" in the Quenya language of the Eldar.

Tolkien's Mordor may have partly inspired by his experience of the heavily industrialized coal-mining and iron-smelting region of the West Midlands—just to the west of his childhood Birmingham home— known as the Black Country. This was the furnace room of the Industrial Revolution where days were made black with coal smoke and nights were made hellishly red with the flames of blast furnaces. In 2014 the Wolverhampton Art Gallery made a convincing bid for the Black Country being an inspiration for Sauron's kingdom through an exhibition entitled "The Making of Mordor."

Since Tolkien explained that his map of Middle-earth is essentially an overlay of the real-world map of Europe (though in an imaginary archetypal time), there have been many attempts at determining just where Mordor's might be located in the real world. Among the suggestions are the mountainous regions of the Balkans or even Transylvania, famous as the home of Count Dracula. However, reading Tolkien's directions, a much more likely real-world location for Mordor would be in present-day Turkey, to the south of the Black Sea.

The Destruction of Mordor

MORDRED   In Arthurian legend the nephew—or even son—
of King Arthur, and his opponent and slayer in the Battle of Camlann. This
Arthurian villain made his first appearance in the twelfth century and soon
after became synonymous with treason and evil. In Dante's *Inferno*, Mordred is
to be discovered in the lowest circle of Hell, the domain of traitors: "[Mordred]
who, at one blow, had chest and shadow / shattered by Arthur's hand."

Although Tolkien employed Arthurian motifs throughout his writing, he did
not care for the largely French-inspired courtly elements of medieval Arthurian
romance. Consequently, his own unfinished *Fall of Arthur*—largely written in
the early 1930s and posthumously published in 2013—is an alliterative poem
of nearly a thousand stanzas in the style and meter of the Old English poem
Beowulf. Its focus is Arthur as a British military leader fighting a dark shadowy
army of invaders out of the east led by his nemesis, the evil knight Mordred.

In the *Fall of Arthur*, Tolkien describes Mordred's dark forces: "The endless
East in anger woke, / and black thunder born in dungeons / under mountains
of menace moved above them." These lines could be directly transferred to
Tolkien's Middle-earth, where they are used to describe the dark forces of
Mordor. It is tempting, moreover, to link the forces of Mordor led by the
Nazgûl with Tolkien's description of Mordred's "wan horsemen wild in windy
clouds," who appear as almost spectral warriors "shadow-helmed to war,
shapes disastrous."

In *The Lord of the Rings* and the War of the Last Alliance, the name of the
high king of the Elves, Gil-galad (meaning "Star of Radiance"), cannot help
but conjure up Galahad and the knights of the Round Table. However, most
obviously, in Mordred, the Dark Knight, we have the Arthurian villain who is
most akin to Sauron the Dark Lord. Consequently, it is ironic that the name
Mordred, which one might assume appropriately had its origin in the homonym
"More-dread," is actually derived from the Latin meaning "moderate." However,
in terms of Tolkien's nomenclature, Mordred would be a perfect villain's name.
Just as Morgoth in Sindarin means "Black Enemy," Moria means "Black Chasm,"
Morgul means "Black Sorcery," and Mordor (rhyming with "murder") means
"Black Land." So, the Middle-earth name Mordred would suggest something
akin to his actual Arthurian epithet of "Black Knight."

Morgoth, the Dark Enemy

MORGOTH BAUGLIR

The name given to Melkor, the greatest of the Powers of Arda, after he sinks the world into darkness with the destruction of the Trees of Light in Valinor. Morgoth means "dark enemy" and Bauglir means "tyrant or oppressor" in the Sindar Elvish tongue. In Morgoth, Tolkien tells us, "we have the power of evil visibly incarnate." This warrior king is like a great tower, iron-crowned, with black armor and a shield black, vast, and blank. He wields the mace called Grond, the Hammer of the Underworld, which he uses to strike down his foes with the force of a thunderbolt.

Aspects of Morgoth's dreadful nature can also be found in the tales of the ancient Goths, Germans, Anglo-Saxons, and Norsemen, where similar demonic entities may be found in conflict with pagan gods. Morgoth can be compared in Norse myth to the evil Loki who, at Ragnarök, will lead the giants in a final, world-ending battle against the gods. Loki, the trickster and transformer, was the embodiment of discord and chaos, and he also fathered the monsters that will join him at Ragnarök: Jörmungandr, the World Serpent; Hel, the goddess of the Underworld; and Fenrir the Wolf who will devour the sun and the moon.

Remarkably, other aspects of Morgoth are also comparable to the darkest aspects of Loki's greatest foe, Odin, the king of the Norse gods. Odin is most often assumed to be comparable to Tolkien's Manwë, the king of the Valar. However, Odin also had a terrifying amoral aspect to his worship linked to the requirement of human sacrifice. Linguistically, as well his Elvish name Mor-Goth (meaning "Dark Enemy"), this is suggestive of the dark Germanic (Gothic) "Black-Goth," the god whom Tolkien called "Odin the Goth, the Necromancer, Glutter of Crows, God of the Hanged."

MORIA
See: KHAZAD-DÛM

MORTE D'ARTHUR Sir Thomas Malory's fifteenth-century account of the life of King Arthur and the exploits of his knights of the Round Table. Malory's descriptions of Arthurian battles were authentically informed by his real-life experience as a soldier-knight in that bloody and brutal national disaster known as the Wars of the Roses (1455–87). In Malory's account of the last Battle of Camlann, the final duel that ends with the death of King Arthur and Mordred the Dark Knight, spells an end to a utopian age of Camelot and its ideal chivalric alliance of the knights of Round Table.

Curiously, Tolkien's description of fictional battles upon Middle-earth were authentically informed by the author's own real life experience as a soldier in the First World War, and specifically in the disastrous and bloody Battle of the Somme. In Tolkien's account of the last Battle of Dagorlad, the final duel that ends with the death of Gil-galad and Sauron the Dark Lord spells an end to the age and its utopian ideal of a chivalric alliance of the "knights" of Middle-earth.

MÛMAKIL (OR MÛMAK) The massive elephant-like animals used in battle by the Haradrim, known to the Hobbits as Oliphaunts. The Mûmakil were in large part inspired by historic accounts of the use of war elephants in the Punic Wars (264–146 BC) between Rome and Carthage. The specific employment of Mûmakil by the Southrons in the Battle of Pelennor Fields may have been inspired by accounts of the historic Battle of Zama in 202 BC when the Roman army led by Scipio Africanus defeated the Carthaginian army of Hannibal with its division of war elephants.

However, Tolkien's descriptions of the Mûmakil appear to have been rather larger and more formidable beasts than the elephants recruited by the Carthaginians. Tolkien was certainly influenced by the discovery of bones and paleolithic cave drawings of the extinct species of elephant first identified as mammoths by Georges Cuvier in 1796. Tolkien makes a clear reference to mammot—or their less hairy cousins the mastodons—in one of his annotations: "The Mûmak of Harad was indeed a beast of vast bulk, and the like of him does not walk now in Middle-earth; his kin that live still in latter days are but memories of his girth and majesty."

"MUSIC OF THE AINUR"
The *Ainulindalë* is Tolkien's account of creation, imagined as a multilogue of voices in an angelic choir that evolves into a mighty operatic conflict of opposing themes of harmony and discord. The singing of the Ainur is both generative and prophetic, creating Arda as well as mapping out its destiny. It is a music filled with great beauty and sadness that foretells the fate of all that is to come into existence in the wake of the creation of the world.

Ultimately, in Tolkien's cosmos, music is the organizing principle behind all creation. But as original as Tolkien's "Music of the Ainur" is as a creation story, its conception is entirely consistent with another historic ancient theme known as the "Music of the Spheres." This is perhaps the oldest and most sustained theme in European intellectual life: a belief in a metaphysical musico-mathematical system attributed to the ancient Greek mystic Pythagoras and the philosopher Plato, which was central to art and science for over 2,000 years.

The "Music of the Spheres" was a sublimely harmonious system of a cosmos guided by a Supreme Intelligence that was preordained and eternal. It is a system that (despite allowing the existence of free will) presupposes all that is, was, and will be was encoded within a celestial music. And although belief in this system has faded since the Enlightenment and the advancements of science, even during Tolkien's lifetime—and since—this grand theme has inspired composers and artists as an expression of celestial harmony and a sense of order in the universe.

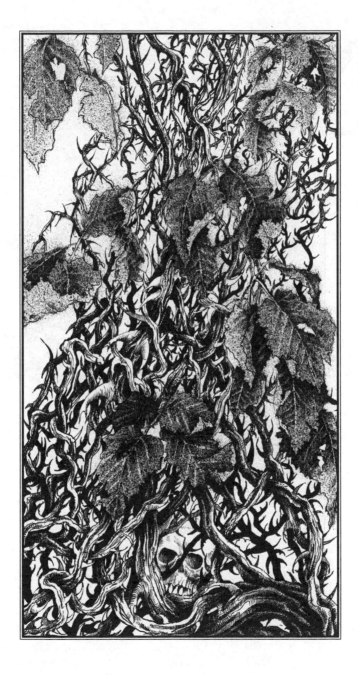

The Brambles of Mordor. The Brambles of Mordor have foot-long thorns, as barbed and dangerous as the daggers of Orcs. They sprawl over the land like the coils of barbed wire.

N

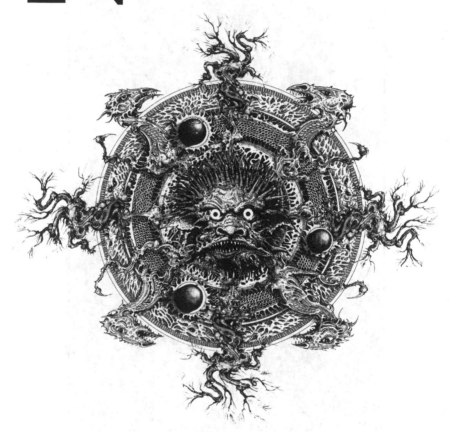

Nidhogg

NARGOTHROND
See: MENEGROTH

NARSIL ("RED AND WHITE FLAME")

The ancestral sword of the kings of Arnor, forged by Telchar the Dwarf-smith of Nogrod in the First Age. The weapon largely owes its inspiration to the dynastic sword of the Völsungs, Gram, in the Norse *Völsunga Saga*.

NAUGLAMÍR
A fabulous necklace created by the Dwarves of Ered Luin in the First Age and later refashioned by Thingol, king of Doriath, so that it holds the Silmaril of Lúthien and Beren. It is first mentioned in *The Hobbit* where the Elven-king of the Woodland Realm suggests that lust for its possession was the motive for a six-thousand-year feud between the Elves and the Dwarves. More of its tragic history emerges in *The Silmarillion*, where we learn that the necklace causes not only war and strife between Elves and Dwarves but also Elves and Elves, in the Second and Third Kinslayings.

In this tale, Tolkien was chiefly inspired by the Norse legend of the Brísingamen, the necklace of the Brising Dwarfs, and its theft, which resulted in endless strife and war. There may be a secondary inspiration in Greek mythology, in the cursed Necklace of Harmonia, wife of Cadmos, founder and king of Thebes. Possession of the necklace brings misfortune to all who possess it, and it is entangled in the various civil wars that plague the ancient Greek city.

NAZGÛL
The name in the Black Speech of the Orcs for the Ringwraiths, the terrible phantom nine Black Riders who are the greatest servants of Sauron the Ring Lord through much of the Second and Third

Hell-hawks. The winged steeds of their riders, the Nazgûl.

Ages. The Nazgûl were once kings and sorcerers, but Sauron corrupted them using the power of the Nine Rings of Mortal Men.

In his creation of the malignant and terrifying Ringwraiths, Tolkien taps into rich lodes of mythology and legend. The wraith is a phantom or specter, either a manifestation of a living being or the ghost of a dead person. In English, "wraith" is a relatively recent word, first noted around 1513, but the notion it conveys is of vastly greater antiquity than the English language. For humans, the primal mysteries are birth and death, and of the two, death is much harder to comprehend. Fear of the dead is a powerful force in all cultures, based on the belief that if the dead were to return, it almost invariably results in evil and disaster.

The Nazgûl have immense powers over the mind and will of their foes, but they themselves are Sauron's slaves in their every action, and they barely exist except as terrifying phantoms, acting as lethal extensions of the Ring Lord's eternal lust for power and his desire to enslave all life. The Nine Rings of Mortal Men give the Nazgûl the power to preserve their "undead" forms as terrifying wraiths for thousands of years. Certain aspects of Tolkien's Nazgûl are shared with the zombie, a mindless reanimated corpse set in motion by a sorcerer. However, in the Nazgûl, Tolkien created beings far more potent and malevolent. Not only are they possessed by the will of Sauron, but even before they were seduced as the Dark Lord's thralls these were sorcerers and king of great power among the Easterlings of Rhûn, the Southrons of Harad, and the mighty Men of Númenor.

We should not overlook the fact that the Nazgûl are nine in number. It is a mystic number in both white and black magic of many nations, from the proverbial nine lives of the cat to Pythagorean numerology in which nine is assigned as the number of the tyrant. In Norse mythology, nine is by far the most significant number, from the Nine Worlds of its cosmology to the nine nights Odin the Hanged God suffered on the World Tree. The greatest Viking religious ceremonies at Uppsala lasted nine days on every ninth year. Nine is the last of the series of single numbers, and, as such, in Norse mythology and others, it is seen as symbolizing both death and rebirth. And, in Tolkien's world, the Nine Rings are Sauron's payment for the purchase of those nine eternally damned souls who become the nine Nazgûl.

See also: P T E R O S A U R S

N E C R O M A N C Y The practice of summoning the spirits of the dead as an apparition or even resurrection of the body for a variety of purposes, including divination, prophecy, obtaining forbidden knowledge, or using the deceased in an act of vengeance or terror. The word is derived from the Greek *nekromanteia,* meaning "divination by means of the dead body."

Necromancers were known in ancient times among the Assyrians, Babylonians, Egyptians, Greeks, and Romans. However, the Christian and Hebrew faiths both condemned the practice: The Book of Deuteronomy specifically decries necromancy as an evil act of a wizard or a witch and as "an abomination unto the Lord."

In Tolkien's world the mysterious Necromancer of Dol Guldur is an evil spirit that in the eleventh century of the Third Age begins to spread a terrible shadow over the southern regions of Greenwood the Great. It is something rather more than a coincidence that Tolkien's Necromancer is eventually revealed to be Sauron the Ring Lord whose name is a Quenya word meaning "abomination."

There is a close association between necromancy and magical rings in both the real world and Middle-earth. In the nineteenth century, the Scottish historical novelist Sir Walter Scott wrote in his *Demonology and Witchcraft* that he knew of many cases of necromancers who claimed to use rings to imprison and compel spirits. The sorcerous use of rings was particularly frequent in medieval Europe. In 1431, one of the many serious charges brought against Joan of Arc was the use of magic rings to enchant and command spirits.

Another case recorded by Joaliun of Cambray in 1545 related the story of a child in thrall to a crystal ring in which he "could see all that the demons within him demanded of him." The demons of the ring so tormented him that in a fit of despair the child smashed the evil crystal ring and finally broke its spell.

Witch-king of Angmar. As his name suggests, the Witch-king of Angmar is another of the "dark lords" of Middle-earth who practices necromancy.

Túrin faces Glaurung on the Bridge of Nargothrond. Nargothrond is the largest kingdom of the Noldor Elves, modeled on the Thousand Caves of Menegroth. The vast complexes of this fortress–palace are expanded by the Noldor and the Dwarves of the Blue Mountains.

NEPTUNE   The Roman god of the sea. For his connections with Tolkien's Vala Ulmo, *see* that entry, U L M O , and P O S E I D O N .

NESSA   One of Tolkien's Valar, wife of Tulkas the Strong (the Valarian Heracles) and the sister of Oromë the Huntsman (the Valarian Orion the Hunter). She is most akin to the forest nymphs (dryads) of the Greco-Roman world, but among the Greek goddesses she most resembles Artemis (equated by the Romans with Diana), a deity associated with wildernesses and wild animals, most especially deer. Although Nessa is not a huntress like Artemis, both are "swift as an arrow" with the ability to outrun deer. Like Artemis, too, Nessa is also associated with dancing, liking nothing better than to dance on the evergreen lawns of Valimar.

NIBELUNGENLIED *(THE SONG OF THE NIBELUNGS)*   The national epic of the German people, written by an anonymous poet around 1200 for performance at the Austrian court. The epic combines elements of myth with a real historical event. This was the catastrophic annihilation of the once-powerful German people, known as the Burgundians, in AD 436 by the Hun legions of Attila acting as mercenary agents for the Roman Emperor. The epic's significance for the German people has been compared to that of the *Iliad* for the Greeks.

The *Nibelungenlied* is a tale of two halves. In the first part Siegfried, in order to win the hand of the Burgundian Princess Kriemhild, successfully helps Kriemhild's brother, Gunther, king of the Burgundians, to woo the Icelandic warrior-queen Brunhild. Back in Gunther's court, Brunhild develops a jealous rivalry with Kriemhild, which eventually results in Siegfried's murder during a hunting expedition. In the second part, Kriemhild, now the wife of the king of the Huns, zealously plots her revenge. She invites her brother, sister-in-law, and the Burgundian vassals to her husband's court. When a feud re-erupts, the resulting bloodbath ends with the death of all the main characters.

While Tolkien took inspiration from the primitive world of Germanic mythology generally, the world he creates in *The Lord of the Rings* has a closer affinity with the world of the medieval German knight Siegfried of the *Nibelungenlied*, than with that of his mythological counterpart, the heroic warrior Sigurd of the *Völsunga Saga*. In the *Völsunga Saga* gods and dragons mix comfortably with mortal heroes, while in the courtly world of the *Nibelungenlied* pagan gods and fantastic dragons have no real place. Siegfried's early exploit of dragon-slaying takes place *offstage*, as it were, before the beginning of the story. It is an event only talked about and appears as more of an ancestral rumor than a real event. The dragon appearing on the medieval battlefield in the *Nibelungenlied* would be as incongruous as the god Odin turning up as a guest at Siegfried's marriage ceremony in Worms cathedral.

This is equally true of Aragorn and the courtly kingdom of Gondor in *The Lord of the Rings*. Such events as the slaying of dragons also take place *offstage*: either in the fairy-tale world of *The Hobbit*, or the genuinely mythic world of *The Silmarillion*. As with the *Nibelungenlied*, it could equally be said that Smaug the Dragon appearing on a battlefield in *The Lord of the Rings* would be as incongruous as the Valarian god Manwë turning up as a guest at Aragorn's marriage ceremony in Gondor.

In the *Nibelungenlied*, a ring is the key to the epic's tragic plot. Once part of the Nibelung treasure horde, at the time of the beginning of the story it is worn by Brunhild. Siegfried (in the guise of her husband, Gunther) takes it from her after wrestling her into submission and rapes her on her and Gunther's wedding night. He gives the ring to his wife, Kriemhild, who later uses it as evidence to Brunhild that she has been deceived and that she is little better than Siegfried's concubine. This humiliating revelation unleashes the subsequent tragedy.

The malevolent One Ring, too, unleashes tragic events, such as the death of Isildur while crossing the Anduin, or the temptation and death of Boromir. Just as the Nibelung ring ultimately seals the fate of all in the *Nibelungenlied*, just as surely does the One Ring seal the fate of all in *The Lord of the Rings*.

Interesting, too, is the Nibelung ring's association with invisibility. To deceive and overcome Brunhild, Siegfried makes much use of the Tarnkappe, the cloak of invisibility he won by wrestling with the dwarf Alberich. In Tolkien's works, the motifs of the ring and the cloak of invisibility are amalgamated: once worn, the One Ring causes the wearer to become invisible. Like Siegfried, Bilbo Baggins uses the power of invisibility to deceive and outmaneuver his enemies.

NIDHOGG A "flying dragon, glowing serpent" described in the Norse text known as *Völuspá*. Meaning "malice striker," Nidhogg is the terrifying winged, fire-breathing monster that emerged from the dark underworld of Niflheim described in one account of the disastrous Battle of Ragnarök, which brought an end to the Nine Worlds of the Norsemen. Nidhogg's ravening majesty in Ragnarök appears to result in similar disastrous consequence to that of Tolkien's Ancalagon the Black (the Winged Fire-drake), which loosed such terrible withering fire down from the heavens in the Great Battle of the War of Wrath. In the *Prose Edda* account of Ragnarök, we have Jörmungandr the World Serpent, another dragonlike monster. Jörmungandr rose up with the giants to do battle against the gods and bring about the destruction of the World. In this version of Ragnarök, the god Thor (associated with thunder) appeared in his flying chariot. Armed with Mjölnir, his hammer, Thor slew Jörmungandr. In Tolkien's Great Battle, the hero Eärendil appeared in *Vingilötë*, his flying ship and, armed with the Silmaril, slew Ancalagon.

NIENNA In Tolkien's pantheon of Valar, the sister of Lórien and Mandos, known as "The Weeper." She lives alone in the west of Valinor where her mansions look out over the sea and the Walls of Night. Her chief concern is mourning, and her tears have the power to heal and fill others with hope and the spirit to endure. She is comparable to the Norse Hlín the Shelterer, the goddess of mourning, grief, and consolation, as well as to the Greek Penthos (and the Roman Luctus), the personification of grief and lamentation. Nienna, also named Lady of Mercy, has a powerful counterpart in the Virgin Mary, as Queen of Heaven and Our Lady of Sorrows, respectively.

NJORD Norse god of the sea and seafaring. He is comparable to Tolkien's Ulmo, the Lord of Waters, whose rise from the deep is announced by the sounding of the Ulumúri, his great conch-shell horn. Ulmo's close association

Noldor Elves

with Middle-earth, and his friendliness toward its peoples, may reflect Njord's popularity among the seafaring Nordic peoples.

NOLDOR The Second Kindred of Elves who undertake the Great Journey over the wilds of Middle-earth, led by their lord Finwë, and eventually cross the Western Sea to the immortal land of Eldamar ("Elven-home"). In the High Elvish language of Quenya, Noldor means "knowledge." However, we know that these Elves were originally to be called Gnomes (and indeed were still thus called in early editions of *The Hobbit*). Tolkien derived the term, not from the creatures of folklore, but from the Greek word *gnosis*, also meaning "knowledge."

The Noldor are accordingly the "intellectuals" among the Elves, associated with arcane knowledge, as well as the greatest craftsmen. As jewel- and metalsmiths and pupils of Aulë the Smith, the Valarian equivalent to the Greek smith god Hephaestus (Vulcan), the Noldor vie in skill with the Dwarves. Their characteristic brilliance and hubris are encapsulated in the figure of Fëanor, who has some connections with Greek craftsman heroes, such as Daedalus and Prometheus.

NORSE MYTHOLOGY The myths and legends of the Norse people found in a rich body of medieval texts, principally such Old Norse poems as the *Poetic Edda* and the *Prose Edda*, and such Icelandic sagas as the *Völsunga Saga*.

These myths and legends provided a deep and enduring source of inspiration for Tolkien in all of his creative works. The influence can be traced not only in specific motifs (e.g., the multiple "worlds" as in Midgard/Middle-earth, Agard/Valinor), characters (e.g., Sigurd/Túrin Turambar), races (e.g., dwarfs/Dwarves), monsters (e.g., dragons), and artifacts (e.g., swords, rings, hunting horns) but in the ethic of stoic fatalism and stubborn code of personal honor shared by most of Tolkien's heroes and, in *The Silmarillion* especially, a wild and dark sense of doom.

The influence is at its clearest, as with Greco-Roman mythology, in Tolkien's pantheon of "gods" and "goddesses," as can be seen in the chart on page 450. There are important differences between figures that superficially appear to be "counterparts," and, in some cases, the differences are very wide indeed as in the respective rulers of the underworld. Hel, a frightening goddess whose subjects are those who died of sickness and disease, is a very different figure to Mandos the Doomsman, the stern but benign Lord of the Halls of Awaiting, who is rather more closely aligned with the Greek Hades. Likewise, there is no counterpart in Tolkien for the important goddess Freya, as goddess of love, sexuality, and fertility; Frey, fertility god; Thor, the thunder god; or Týr, god of war.

Odin is the most complex of the Norse gods and as such had an especially wide-ranging influence on Tolkien. Aspects of his ambivalent character can be found in figures as diverse as Manwë, Morgoth, Gandalf, and Saruman.

NORSEMEN Germanic people of Scandinavia of the early Middle Ages, famous as seafarers and settlers, known as Vikings ("pirates"), and feared during their great age of conquest from the late eighth century to the middle of the eleventh. Their language (Old Norse), literature, and mythology were Tolkien's richest source of inspiration for his legendarium.

Most specifically, as a race or people, the Norse, in all but their skill in seafaring, provided the historic model for Tolkien's Dwarves of Middle-earth. Both are proud races of warriors, craftsmen, and traders, stoic and stubborn, admiring of strength and bravery, and greedy for gold and treasure.

NORTHMEN OF RHOVANION Inhabitants of the region to the east of the Misty Mountains, and, according to Tolkien, a "better and nobler sort of Men" who were kin to the Edain of the First Age. They are shown as largely uncorrupted and, in the Third Age, remain "in a simple 'Homeric' state of patriarchal and tribal life." Rather than being

Sunrise on Númenor

Númenórean king

archaic Greek in character, as Tolkien seems to suggest here, they are in fact very like those men celebrated in the early Anglo-Saxon epic poetry the author so dearly loved.

The Northmen of Rhovanion, or "Wilderland" as this vast region is more often called in the pages of Tolkien's fiction, are essentially the heroic forebears of Beowulf who made their home for millennia in Europe's trackless forests, mountains, and river vales. Rhovanion was intended to resemble what the ancient Romans called Germania, the great northern forest of Europe. Tolkien also gives them a wild eastern frontier comparable to the Russian steppes. Just as the Roman Empire and their sometime Germanic allies faced wave after wave of Hun, Tartar, and Mongol invaders, so the Dúnedain of Gondor and their Northmen allies faced the recurring attacks of Easterling, Balchoth, and Variag invaders.

In the Northmen of Rhovanion we see something of the German tribes at their earliest stages of migration. They are a noble people who do not greatly diminish the forest or plow up the plains, and have only a few large, substantial towns and villages (such as Esgaroth and Dale). Among the many peoples dwelling in Rhovanion were those later known as the Beornings and Woodmen of Mirkwood, as well as the Bardings and the Men of Dale. However, one other people Tolkien "discovered" in the Vales of Anduin became a particular favorite. These fictional people are called the Éothéod, linked in Tolkien's mind to the historic Germanic nation of horsemen known as the Goths.

NÚMENOR

The large island in the Western Sea gifted to the Men of Beleriand by the Valar as reward for their part in the wars against Morgoth in the First Age. Ruled by a dynasty of kings descended from Elros, son of Eärendil, it flourishes for much of the Second Age but is ultimately destroyed, sinking back beneath the waves. In Númenor, we see a great civilization corrupted by power and pride slowly evolve into a tyranny that threatens the peace of the world and finally self-destructs.

Númenor is the most obvious example of the influence of the legends of the ancient Greeks on Tolkien's fiction. His tale *Akallabêth* ("The Downfall

of Númenor") is Tolkien's reinvention of the ancient legend of Atlantis, related by the Greek philosopher Plato in his dialogues *Timaeus* and *Critias*. Atlantis, another island set in a western sea (in this instance the Atlantic), is portrayed as a lost utopian civilization that the gods eventually destroy because of the pride and folly of its people.

Like the myth of Atlantis, Númenor is a cautionary tale of the rise and fall of empires, a common trope since classical times. Not even the greatest civilizations last because pride and power ultimately corrupt. Every rise to power is inevitably followed by a fall and subsequent self-destruction. This is often due to the tragic flaw the Greeks called hubris, a combination of excessive pride, overconfidence, and contempt for the gods. The fall of Tolkien's Númenor is exactly of this kind. The last king, Ar-Pharazôn, in

Goldberry. Goldberry is the nymph-like daughter of the River-woman and the spouse of Tom Bombadil.

his contempt for the Valar and desire for immortality, leads a fleet against Aman, prompting Eru the One to cause the Change of the World: Arda is turned from being flat into a globe, and Númenor sinks beneath the waves. The event is also somewhat akin to the biblical second Fall of Man in the Great Flood.

There may have been a more contemporary allusion to Tolkien's history of Númenor. Christopher Tolkien suggests that his father's portrait of the decline of Númenor into a militaristic tyranny with imperial ambitions was an implicit comment on Nazism.

NYMPHS
In Greco-Roman mythology immortal nature spirits often associated with natural features of the landscape, such as a spring, grove of trees, or the sea. They were often categorized. For example, Naiads were water nymphs, Dryads were wood nymphs, and Nereids were sea nymphs. They were usually thought of as young beautiful women, most often benevolent, and the object of local cults. However, in mythology they could also show a more dangerous side, as when Naiads take the youth Hylas down into a pond as their companion.

In Tolkien's world the influence of the Greek nymphs in their kindly aspect is most obviously seen in the figure of Goldberry, the "River-woman's daughter," but also more widely and loosely in Valar such as Nessa, Maiar such as Uinen, and Elves such as Lúthien.

O

Young Orc Fighting a Scorpion

OATHBREAKERS, THE Wraiths of pre-Númenórean

Men of the White Mountains who haunt the Paths of the Dead. Also known as the Dead Men of Dunharrow, these legions of ghostly warriors are the spirits of Men who swore allegiance to Isildur, king of the Dúnedain, at the time of the Alliance of Elves and Men, but who broke that oath and betrayed him to Sauron. Thereafter all the warriors of the Men of the White Mountains were cursed and known as the Oathbreakers: tormented terrible wraiths that haunted the labyrinthine mountain paths of Dwimorberg.

Tolkien's Oathbreakers were in good part inspired by the many Norse and Germanic myths and real-life histories relating to broken oaths of fealty between warrior and lord, or oaths of alliance between king and king. For the peoples of northern Europe (as elsewhere), such oaths were legally binding. Oaths sworn upon weapons or oath rings were considered sacred trusts, and violation of those oaths had both real world and spiritual consequences. There was a belief that false oaths—sworn upon a sword—animated that sword, which became like an avenging entity that thirsted for blood and could be appeased only by the offender falling upon it. In Norse and German society, murder and manslaughter were not considered illegal offenses so long as they were carried out "honestly" and in the open, with the opponent given fair warning and the ability to defend himself. However, oath breaking was the most heinous of crimes, as it threatened the entire social order and hierarchy. This was especially true if the oath was broken for cowardly reasons, such as refusing the call to arms in the midst of battle, as was the case of the Men of White Mountains.

In the real-world honor code of these warrior societies, once an oath was broken, the offender would be banished and become an outlaw cast out of society. As an outlaw, he was beyond any lord or king's protection. He could be hunted down and, if caught, could legally be hanged: the most shameful of deaths that made entry into the afterworld Valhalla impossible. Like the Dead Men of Dunharrow, in Norse and Icelandic myths and sagas, oathbreakers are frequently trapped in a terrible limbo world, at least until some means of restitution might be discovered.

In Tolkien's tale, the curse is only lifted from the Oathbreakers after more than three millennia, when Isildur's Heir appears at last in the Paths

The Dead Men of Dunharrow

of the Dead. Aragorn, son of Arathorn—the rightful heir and king of the Dúnedain—summons the Dead to fulfil the oath they broke long ago. This Shadow Host manifests itself in a mighty battalion of ghostly warriors that, at Aragorn's command, drive the Corsairs of Umbar from their fleet. Thus the souls of the Sleepless Dead are at last redeemed as the great pale army fade like a mist into the wind.

O D I N   In Norse culture, the king of the gods, Odin is one of the most complex and ambivalent figures in any mythology and perhaps one of the single most important sources of inspiration for Tolkien in the creation of some of his leading protagonists. Through Odin's many and diverse manifestations (as a god associated with battle, death, kingship, sorcery, poetry, and healing) we can trace his influence in such contrasting pivotal characters as Manwë, king of the Valar, and Gandalf the Grey, on the one hand, and Melkor/Morgoth and Saruman the White, on the other.

The beneficent, most godlike aspects of Odin come to the fore in Manwë, king of the Valar. He, like the Norse god, surveys the world from a high seat, sends out birds as his messengers or "eyes" (though Odin's birds are the ravens Huginn and Munnin, as against Manwë's Great Eagles), and has associations with poetry. In *The Book of Lost Tales* the Valar are described as having a "splendour of posey and sing beyond compare." Appropriately enough, one of the Maiar belonging to Manwë, Gandalf, also has characteristics similar to Odin's. Like the Norse God, he appears as a gray-cloaked, bearded wanderer, and has many names ("Many are my names in many countries . . ."). He also has the habit of turning up unexpectedly, and—on his journey from Isengard to Minas Tirith—rides a horse, Shadowfax, of wondrous powers and possibly divine origin, much like Odin's steed Sleipnir.

The darker, necromantic aspects of Odin's persona most obviously emerge in Sauron, aspects that clearly fascinated Tolkien who in his essay "On Fairy-Tales" wrote of "Odin the Goth, the Necromancer, Glutter of Crows, God of the Hanged." Odin, the sorcerer king, rules the Nine Worlds of the Norse universe through possession of the magical power of a Draupnir ("Dripper"), a gold ring that drips eight more gold rings every nine days, a possession that, quite literally, makes Odin

Orcs Debate. Violence, rather than reason, is the usual tool of an Orc who wishes to win an argument.

a "Lord of the Rings." One possible source for the "Eye of Sauron"—the form in which Sauron almost exclusively manifests in *The Lord of the Rings*—lies in Odin's own single eye, the other having been sacrificed in exchange for one deep draft from Mímir's "Well of Secret Knowledge." Thereafter, Odin (like Sauron) was able to consult and command wraiths, phantoms, and spirits of the dead.

In Saruman the White, who ultimately becomes an echo of Sauron, there are also echoes of the necromancer god Odin. Saruman's use of the *palantír*, in the tower of Orthanc to view distant places, recalls not only Odin's high seat Hlidskjalf, but also Odin's grim use of the severed head of Mímir to find out the secret knowledge of the Nine Worlds.

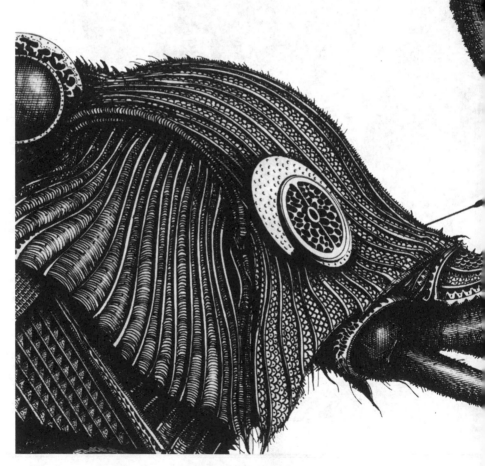

Oliphaunt. Into the Hobbit lands of the Shire creep many legends about the mysterious lands that lie far in the south of Middle-earth. Most fascinating to the Hobbits are the tales of giant Oliphaunts: tusked war beasts with huge pounding feet.

OLWË The younger brother of Elwë, the king of the Teleri in Aman, and the founder of the port cities of Avallónë and, later, Alqualondë, the "Haven of Swans." For his possible associations with the Avalon of Arthurian legend, *see* **AVALLÓNË**.

OLWYN The eponymous heroine in the medieval Welsh legend *Culhwch and Olwen* (one of the tales collected in *The Mabinogion*). She is considered the most beautiful woman of her age. Her eyes shine with light; her skin is also as white as snow. Olwyn's name means "she of the white track," a name she carns because four white trefoils spring up on the forest floor with every step she takes. She appears to be the very embodiment of the enchanting "lady in white" so often found in Celtic legend.

In Middle-earth, Olwyn appears to have partly inspired one of Tolkien's greatest heroines, Lúthien Tinúviel, meaning "maiden of twilight," the daughter of Elu Thingol, the high king of the Grey Elves, and his queen, Melian the Maia. Like Olwyn, she is dark-haired with snow-white skin, and is considered the most beautiful child of any race. Olwyn's "white track" of trefoils finds an echo in the *niphredil*, a white star-shaped flower that first blooms on Middle-earth in celebration of Lúthien's birth and which later grew on her burial mound. Furthermore, the winning of Olwyn's hand required her suitor, Culhwch, to undertake the near-impossible quest of the "Thirteen Treasures of Britain." This is certainly comparable to the near-impossible Quest for the Silmaril, as the price for Lúthien's hand was acquiring one of the three Silmarils in the Iron Crown of Morgoth, the Dark Enemy.

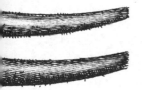

OLYMPUS The home of the gods of ancient Greece where Zeus, king of the gods, is enthroned and holds court. Olympus is both a real mountain and a mythological place. At nearly 10,000 feet, it was the tallest mountain in the Greek world and an obvious inspiration for Tolkien's

Taniquetil, the highest mountain in Arda where Manwë, the king of the Valar and Maiar, is enthroned and holds court.

"ON FAIRY-STORIES" An essay on "fairy stories" first published in 1947 but which in origin was a lecture given in honor of the Scottish folklorist Andrew Lang (1844–1912) in 1938.

In the essay Tolkien attempts to define the fairy tale as different from other kinds of fantastic literary creations such as travelers' tales (*Gulliver's Travels*), Gothic novels (*Frankenstein*), and science fiction (many of the novels of H. G. Wells). A good fairy tale, he argues, creates a serious, consistent "otherworld" (which he called Faerie) that is "true" on its own terms. Such an otherworld offers the reader not only escapism and possible moral insights into the real world (both worthy goals in themselves) but also, and more importantly, a glimpse of joy. Pivotal to this feeling of joy is Tolkien's concept of the "eucatastrophe," or happy ending: "In such stories, when the sudden turn comes, we get a piercing glimpse of joy, and heart's desire, that for a moment passes outside the frame, rends indeed the very web of story, and lets a gleam come through."

Tolkien's essay is a key moment in the evolution of his life as a writer and in the creation of Middle-earth, offering a justification of the genre of fantasy writing of which he, along with his friend and fellow Inkling C. S. Lewis, was a pioneer. *The Lord of the Rings* (1954–5) is in many ways the embodiment of the ideas he set out in "On Fairy-Stories."
See also: RELIGION: CHRISTIANITY

ONE RING, THE
See: RINGS OF POWER

ORC The evil, goblinlike soldiers of the Dark Lords Morgoth and Sauron in Middle-earth. Tolkien's Orcs originate in the early First Age when

Oromë finds the Lords of the Elves

Orc

Melkor captures many of the newly awakened race of Elves, then takes them down into his fortress dungeons of Utumno (and later Angband). There, he tortures and transforms them into a race of slaves and soldiers who are as loathsome as the Elves are fair. The Orcs are hideous, stunted, and muscular with yellow fangs, blackened faces, and red slits for eyes.

Tolkien's Orcs appear, like so many of his races, to have multiple sources of inspiration. In *Beowulf*, mention is made of *orcneas* (ironically in juxtaposition with *ylfe*—elves) as being among the "evil broods." The word perhaps suggests "walking corpses," like living dead, or zombies, the component word *orc* perhaps deriving from the Latin word *Orcus*, an Etruscan and Roman god of the underworld and for the underworld itself. However, in a letter, Tolkien wrote that he himself doubted this derivation. The word "orc" also appears in sixteenth-century English to mean a devouring monster, while the man-eating ogres of fairy tales are another, related breed.

So much for the etymological inspirations. The concept and nature of Orcs, as demonic underlings programmed to do the bidding of their evil masters, has resonance with numerous myths and tales from around the world. Such demons are prominent, for example, in the Old Testament where demons are considered innumerable (and often invisible), preferring to live in isolated, unclean places such as deserts and ruins, and greatly to be feared, especially at night. In all of Tolkien's descriptions of Orcs, they, too, create a sense of vast anonymous numbers and are likened to innumerable swarms or devastating black waves. They come pouring out of caverns with impersonal, insectlike inexorability and are often compared by the author to flies or ants.

Further comparisons with a large number of mythological and legendary monsters can be made, from goblins (indeed, the name more often used for them in *The Hobbit*) to kobolds to the golem.

OROMË The huntsman of the Valar who loves to ride his white horse, Nahar, through the forests of Middle-earth as he hunts down the evil creatures of Melkor/Morgoth. Oromë's name means "horn-blower," and the sound of his horn, Valaróma, is a terror to all servants of darkness. The Sindarin name for Oromë is Araw.

It is fairly certain that Tolkien's inspiration for Oromë was Arawn the Huntsman of Welsh mythology, the ruler of Annwn, an otherworld of youth and pleasure. Like Araw/Oromë, Arawn rides like the wind with his horn and hounds through the forests of the mortal world. In one Welsh legend, found in *The Mabinogion*, Arawn causes Pwyll, lord of Dyfed, to leave his own realm and dwell in Annwn for a time. Tolkien's Oromë befriends three Elven kings at Cuiviénen and acts as their guide to the immortal Undying Lands of Aman.

O R P H E U S   In Greek mythology, the hero-cum-musician who can charm all living things, and even stones, with his singing and lyre-playing. The key myth associated with him is his descent into Hades to rescue his dead wife Eurydice, and his ultimate tragic failure.

Tolkien himself acknowledged that the ancient Greek love story of Orpheus and Eurydice provided the framework for his love story of Beren and Lúthien Tinúviel in *The Silmarillion*. Both Tolkien's tale and the Greek myth concern a descent into the underworld and the power of love and music in the face of death.

In Tolkien's adaptation, however, the male and female roles are reversed. In the Greek myth, Orpheus plays his lyre and sings to make the hellhound Cerberus fall asleep before the gates of Hades. Once within them, he again sings such beautiful songs that Hades weeps and grants him the life of Eurydice, on the condition that as the husband and wife make their way out of the underworld he does not look at his wife. In Tolkien's version, it is Lúthien who sings and makes the wolf-guardian Carcharoth fall asleep before the gates of Morgoth's dark subterranean fortress, and who, once within, yet again sings such beautiful songs that the entranced Morgoth falls into a slumber, enabling Beren to cut one of the Silmarils from his iron crown.

Orpheus fails in his quest at the last moment. Leading Eurydice up to the world of the living, he is unable to resist turning back to look at her and she is instantly returned to Hades. Beren and Lúthien's fate is not quite so tragic. Just as they are about to escape Angband, Beren is attacked by the now wide-awake

Carcharoth. The wolf-guardian bites off Beren's hand holding the Silmaril. The prize at the last moment is lost, though Beren is later healed on the lovers' return to Doriath.

OSSË   Maia spirit of the sea who serves the Vala Ulmo, Lord of Waters. Tolkien's Ossë bears some resemblance to Aegir in Norse mythology, a *jötunn* associated with the ocean, as well as to other minor sea deities in Greco-Roman mythology, such as Proteus and Glaucos. Ossë, like Aegir, is subject to wildly shifting moods and is portrayed as overly fond of whipping up storms and squalls. However, he is also friendly toward the Elves, especially the Teleri.

OXFORD   City in southern England, home to the English-speaking world's oldest university, where Tolkien was at first an undergraduate student (1911–15) and then a professor of Anglo-Saxon/English literature at two of the colleges (1925–59). For Tolkien, who fought in one world war and lived through another, Oxford was a refuge of learning and wisdom in the middle of a world gone mad with the slaughter of conflagration.

Tolkien once described the northwest of Middle-earth as being geographically equivalent to Europe and that his Elven refuge of Rivendell was "taken (as intended) to be at about the latitude of Oxford." However, it is quite apparent that Rivendell was not just "on the latitude of Oxford"—it was an analogue for Oxford itself. Rivendell was the Elven refuge of Elrond Half-elven and his people. Considered the "Last Homely House East of the Sea," for 4,000 years Rivendell (or Imladris in Sindarin) was a refuge of wisdom and great learning for all Elves and Men of goodwill. In Rivendell, the common tongue was Westron, while the true scholar's choice was the ancient Elvish languages of Sindarin and Quenya. In Oxford, the common tongue was English, while the true scholar's choice was the ancient languages of Latin and Greek. Master Elrond's use of language may be somewhat archaic, but not excessively so for someone who is essentially a 6,000-year-old living version of the Ashmolean Institute and Bodleian library combined.

PPQQ

The cavalry charge of the Rohirrim at the Battle of Pelennor Fields

PARADISE LOST

Epic verse narrative by the English poet John Milton (1608–74) about the Old Testament "war in heaven" in which Lucifer/Satan leads an army of rebel angels against God, only to be defeated and hurled down into hell. While there are many aspects of Tolkien's world that differ greatly from Milton's great Christian epic, it influenced Tolkien—especially in his *Ainulindalë* and *Valaquenta*—not only in terms of its grand narrative themes but also in sublime ("Miltonic") literary style.

In Tolkien, it is Melkor/Morgoth who rebels against Eru Ilúvatar in the Timeless Halls. Just as Lucifer questions the ways of God, so Melkor asks why the Ainur (the angelic spirits serving Eru, who sing the world into being) could not be allowed to compose their own music and bring forth life and worlds of their own. This is the nub of Melkor's complaint: he wishes to have freedom over his spirit and his own creations, just as Lucifer proclaims his desire to create things of his own in a manner equal to God.

Both Tolkien's Melkor and Milton's Lucifer seem heroic in their steadfast "courage never to submit or yield." However, in truth, both rebel angels are primarily motivated by overweening pride and envy. It is worth noting how in *Paradise Lost* Satan's minions "Towards him they bend / With awful reverence prone; and as a God / Extol him equal to the highest in Heav'n." It is a description that is comparable to Melkor enthroned in his subterranean halls, and reveals the true motive of both antagonists: to become God the Creator themselves.

As Tolkien explains, Melkor's fall is a moral one: "From splendour he fell through arrogance to contempt for all things [. . .] He began with the desire for Light, but when he could not possess it for himself alone, he descended through fire and wrath into a great burning, down into Darkness." And so, Melkor—like Lucifer—brings corruption into the world. All evil in Tolkien's world has its beginning in Melkor, although in his beginnings, like Lucifer, Melkor is not evil.

PATHS OF THE DEAD

A terrifying underworld passage under the Dwimorberg in the White Mountains, haunted by the Dead Men of Dunharrow, Men cursed by Isildur after they failed to come to Gondor's aid in the War of the Last Alliance. During the War of the Ring, Aragorn, out of need, is forced to take the passage and allows the Shadow Host to finally fulfill their oath.

In his famous cross-cultural study of religion and mythology *The Golden Bough* (1890–1915), the Scottish anthropologist James George Frazer (1854–1941) argues that rites of passage—such as a "descent into the underworld," however this is defined—are found widely across the world as a necessary stage in the ascent to kingship. Frazer's ideas were highly influential for much of the twentieth century and are discernible in the story of Aragorn, who, before he comes to Minas Tirith to be acknowledged as king of Gondor, must pass through a form of the underworld.

When Aragorn emerges, it is as the king of the Dead Men of Dunharrow, in command of a terrifying army of undead warriors against the Corsairs of Umbar. Like Jesus in the New Testament (for Frazer, an example of the "sacred king"), Aragorn has descended into "hell" to free the "imprisoned spirits" of the sinful dead.

PELENNOR FIELDS The site, beneath the walls of Minas
Tirith, of the most richly described conflict in the annals of Middle-earth, and the most dramatic (if not the final) battle of the War of the Ring. It took place on March 15, 3019 TA.

In his unfolding of the battle, Tolkien draws on many aspects of real-world military history, ranging over some 1,500 years of European warfare. To begin with, many of Gondor's opponents in the battle seem to have inspirations in the enemies of ancient Rome or Byzantium: The Mûmakil (Oliphaunts) are tamed and mounted by Haradrim. These creatures evoke the elephants ridden by Carthaginians at the Battle of Zama, fought between the forces of Hannibal and the Roman troops led by Scipio, in 202 BC. The fierce Variags of Khand appear to have been inspired by the Varangians of Rus' who, in the ninth to eleventh century, launched a series of attacks on Byzantium. The Easterlings of Rhûn are likely inspired by the twelfth- and thirteenth-century Seljuk Turks of the Sultanate of Rûm in Anatolia, who harried and seized key Byzantine ports and other territories.

On the Gondorians' own side we have the Rohirrim, whose cavalry charge is solidly based on a historical Gothic cavalry action in support of the Romans at the Battle of Châlons in AD 451. When all seems lost for Gondor, the tide is turned by the appearance of the black-sailed ships of the Corsairs, carrying reinforcements from Gondor's coastal settlements, under the command of Aragorn.

PEREDHIL ("HALF-ELVEN"; SINGULAR: PEREDHEL)
Term used to describe the offspring of Elves and Men, and encompassing, among others, Eärendil and Elwing, their twin sons, Elros and Elrond, as well as Elrond's own offspring, notably Arwen. Most of the Peredhil are granted the choice of deciding which race—the immortal Elves or mortal Men—they wished to belong.

There may be a parallel in Greek mythology where many of the heroes are described as the children of immortal gods or nymphs and of humans. Thus Perseus is the son of Zeus, king of the gods, and the mortal Danaë, and Heracles is the son of Zeus and the mortal Alcmene. Occasionally, such offspring undergo apotheosis, as most notably in the case of Heracles, who, after his mortal death, rises to join Zeus on Mount Olympus. The Greek Dioscuri (the twins Castor and Polydeuces, one mortal, the other immortal) also provide a partial parallel with Elros and Elrond.
See also: CASTOR AND POLYDEUCES

PEREGRIN ("PIPPIN") TOOK
The youngest Hobbit member of the Fellowship of the Ring who, after his adventures in the War of the Ring, becomes Peregrin I, 32nd Thain of the Shire.

His given name, Peregrin, ultimately derives from the Latin *pelegrinus*, meaning "one from abroad," and is related to the Old French *pelegrin*, meaning "wanderer," the Middle English *peleguin*, meaning "traveler," and in the modern English word "pilgrim." This seems quite an appropriate

Pipeweed

name for an individual engaged in a ring quest who travels far abroad. There may very well be a buried etymological joke in Tolkien's choice of name for this Hobbit hero. The peregrine falcon (*Falco peregrinus*, the "pilgrim falcon") is so named because falconers took it into captivity during its migration, fully grown, rather than as a chick from its nest. The Old French name for the peregrine is *hobet*.

Furthermore, as Tolkien would certainly have known, Peregrin's nickname, Pippin, carries some real-world historic and royal baggage: Pippin III (reigned AD 751–68) was the name of a king of the Franks, the founder of the Carolingian dynasty, and the father of Charlemagne. To the French, he is known as Pépin le Bref, with "brief" usually taken to refer to his short stature, an appropriate enough name for Tolkien's Hobbit hero.

PERSEPHONE

In Greek mythology the goddess of spring, daughter of Demeter and Zeus, called Proserpine by the Romans. In her most important myth, Persephone is abducted by Hades, god of the underworld and of the dead, and is forced to spend the winter months at his side to emerge each year in spring.

Persephone is comparable to Tolkien's Valarian power, the beautiful Vána, the Ever Young, and the younger sister of the Demeter-like Yavanna, the Valarian queen of the earth and all things that grow. Vána's special preserve is flowering plants: "All flowers spring as she passes and open if she glances upon them; and all birds sing at her coming." While Tolkien typically does not provide Vána with any mythology, there may be a hint of Persephone's marriage to Hades in Vána's marriage to Oromë, a Vala connected to Arawn, the Celtic god of the underworld.

PIPEWEED

Hobbits are the *spiritus mundi* of England. They are meant by Tolkien to be the Anglo-Saxon earth spirits who are most in touch with the land itself. They literally live in the earth and in so many ways are meant to define the essential elements of Englishness.

Hobbits are, after all, the *holbytla* (hole-builders and hole-dwellers), so it is logical that their first instinct is to work on the land. From their ground-level existence Hobbits have a profound understanding of plant and animal life. They can grow almost anything on farms and in orchards and gardens under conditions that humans would not even attempt to grapple with.

It is not surprising, then, that one of the most famous figures in Hobbit history was a horticulturist. The year 1070 SR is one date in their history that all Hobbits know, for it was in this year that the famous Hobbit farmer Tobold Hornblower of Longbottom succeeded in perfecting the cultivation and curing of sweet galenas.

The galena is a smoking herb akin to the modern nicotiana or tobacco plant, but apparently devoid of the unwholesome and poisonous aspects of modern tobacco. Popularly known as pipeweed, Old Toby's discovery was the beginning of an industry and tradition of which the Hobbits were proud inventors and most dedicated practitioners.

After Old Buck, Old Toby is the most famous ancestral Hobbit in their early history. The name, of course, is a typical Tolkien jest: he is suggesting that our word "tobacco" originated in the name Old Toby, the Hobbit who originated the practice of smoking.

PLATO (428/427–348/347 BC) Greek philosopher, best known for his dialogues (philosophical investigations in the form of conversations between various characters). He often used myths and his stories in his writing as part of his philosophical explorations, including the Myth of the Cave, the Ring of Gyges, and the story of Atlantis.

Plato was extremely influential in Tolkien's mythopoetic approach to literature, and references to Plato's dialogues and philosophical ideas are scattered throughout his writing. The most obvious inspiration provided by Plato is the philosopher's account of the legend of Atlantis as found in the *Timaeus* and, principally, in the *Critias*, which was the primary source of inspiration for Tolkien's the "Akallabêth" ("The Downfall of Númenor").

According to Plato, Atlantis was an island about the size of Spain in the western sea beyond the Pillars of Heracles. Its power extended over all the nations of Europe and the Mediterranean, but the overwhelming pride of these powerful people brought them into conflict with the immortals. Finally, a great cataclysm in the form of a volcanic eruption and a tidal wave resulted in Atlantis sinking beneath the sea.

See also: G Y G E S ' R I N G

POSEIDON In Greek mythology the mighty god of the sea, equated by the Romans with Neptune. Both Poseidon and Neptune were manifest in the form of giant bearded ocean lords who command earthquakes and tidal waves and ride sea chariots drawn by seahorses on the crests of great waves. Poseidon is only second in power to his brother Zeus (the Roman Jupiter) the king of the gods and the Lord of the Sky.

Poseidon was undoubtedly Tolkien's primary inspiration for the Vala Ulmo, Lord of Waters. Ulmo is second only to his brother Manwë, the king of the Valar and the Lord of the Air. In his manifestation as king of the Sea, Ulmo is described as fearful "as a mounting wave that strides to the land," speaks through the sound of water, and makes music using his great white sea-conch horns, the Ulumúri.

Ulmo's character, however, somewhat differs from Poseidon's, in that while Poseidon's mythology shows him as being above all vengeful and destructive, Ulmo is benevolent, and closely concerned with the affairs of Middle-earth.

PRINCESS AND THE GOBLIN, THE

A children's novel by the Scottish writer George MacDonald (1824–1905), published in 1872, and read by Tolkien as a child. The novel largely concerns itself with conflicts between diminutive Miners and Goblins in underground tunnels. In this respect it strongly foreshadowed the subterranean skirmishes between Tolkien's Hobbits and Goblins in *The Hobbit*.

Both Tolkien's Hobbits and MacDonald's Goblins appear to have been curiously preoccupied with their feet. MacDonald's Goblins' feet appear to be their only weakness: the iron-shod Miners eventually defeat the Goblins by stamping on their feet and singing magic spells. In Tolkien's story, by contrast, the Hobbits' oversized feet are seen as a strong and positive characteristic of the race and they go barefoot; his Goblins are the one who are iron-shod. MacDonald's story includes a ditty: "Once there was a goblin / Living in a hole; / busy he was cobblin', / A shoe without a sole." This rhyme is a kind of riddle, and one worthy of a Hobbit at that. Question: Why does the Goblin make a shoe without a sole? Answer: Because the Goblin is a creature without a soul! Iron-shod shoes protect Tolkien's Goblins, but they share MacDonald's Goblins' soulless condition, while Tolkien's barefoot Hobbits share MacDonald's Goblins' sole-less condition.

This foot obsession seems to have been a long-standing one for Tolkien: the first poem Tolkien is known to have published, as a teenage student at Oxford in 1915, was entitled "Goblin Feet."

PROMETHEUS In Greek mythology, a Titan who defies the

gods by stealing fire from heaven and giving it to human beings. Zeus punishes

Prometheus' crime by having him chained to a rock and sending an eagle to feed on his liver every day, only for it to always grow back. Prometheus is in many respects a trickster god, associated with craft and science and human ingenuity generally.

Tolkien's Sauron—who shares some of the features of trickster gods found in many mythologies—serves as a kind of mirror image of Prometheus, seemingly bringing secret knowledge to the Elves but in fact bringing death and darkness. When Sauron returns to Middle-earth after the defeat of his master Morgoth at the end of the First Age, he appears in disguise as the mysterious Annatar ("Lord of Gifts"). A Prometheus-like figure, he provides the Elven-smiths of Eregion with forbidden knowledge of fire and forge—rightfully the preserve of Aulë the Valarian Smith—and thus the power to create the Rings of Power. Only after the forging of the Rings do the Elves learn the terrible price of Annatar's gifts. While in Greek mythology Prometheus's gifts are freely given to help humankind, Annatar/Sauron uses the Rings of Power as part of his mission to enslave the peoples of Middle-earth.

PROSERPINE
See: PERSEPHONE

PTEROSAURS
Name given to extinct flying reptiles that existed some 228 to 66 million years ago. The word comes from the Greek *pterosaurus*, meaning "winged lizard."

When asked about the origin of the winged beasts that served as the horrific airborne mounts of the Ringwraiths, Tolkien acknowledged that they resembled pterosaurs and that, on Middle-earth, they might even be survivors from an older geological age. This seems to have been already hinted at in *The Lord of the Rings* where the fearsome steeds of the Nazgûl are nameless, though variously described by Tolkien as Fell Beasts, Hell-hawks, and Nazgûl-birds: "if bird, then greater than all other birds, and it was naked, and neither quill nor feather did it bear, and its vast pinions were as webs of hide between horned fingers; and it stank. A creature of an older world maybe it was."

The name of the Dark Lord, Sauron, may have worked on Tolkien's imagination when it came to supplying the Ringwraiths with their nightmarish winged steeds. Tolkien's name for his Dark Lord, "Sauron," may suggest "the abomination" in his invented language of Quenya, but in English it evokes the Greek *saurus* meaning "lizard." This, of course, is used as a suffix in the names of numerous species of reptiles and lizards, both living and extinct, including the dinosaurs ("fearsome lizards") and the pterosaurs themselves. Sauron's reptilian name already hints at the ancient evil he embodies.

PUCK In the ancient folklore of the British Isles, a mischievous hobgoblin or fairy, found as *púca* in Irish, *bucca* in Cornish, and in many other variations. This mad and merry sprite found his most famous incarnation in William Shakespeare's *A Midsummer Night's Dream* (1595/6), where the fairy Puck unleashes mischief on the human characters during their woodland wanderings.

Puck seems to have played a role in Tolkien's characterization of his Hobbits, who are often shown as having a mischievous, puckish streak (for example, Frodo's youthful theft of Farmer Maggot's mushrooms). It is no accident, then, that one of the founding fathers of the Hobbits is Bucca of the Marish. Here Tolkien implies that in the Hobbit Bucca he has revealed the original archetypal British sprite, while Puck is but a pale imitation, only vaguely understood by Shakespeare and others.

PUCK OF POOK'S HILL Children's book by the English writer Rudyard Kipling, published in 1906, which undoubtedly influenced Tolkien's conception of his Hobbits. Through a series of short stories, the book tells the tale of William Shakespeare's Puck as one of the last survivors of the People of the Hills. These small brown, blue-eyed, freckled folk measured just 2 or 3 feet in height and lived in secret dwellings beneath the ancient "hollow hills." In Kipling's tale we learn that Puck's people were once powerful pagan gods who came to Britain with the first oak, ash, and thorn trees but, now that all the great forests are gone, only a few survive to hide away in the hills and hollows of England.

The Battle of Pelennor Fields

QUENDI ("SPEAKERS") The umbrella term for "Elves," encompassing both the Eldar and the Avari. For Tolkien's complex categorization of his Elves, beginning with the inspiration he took from Norse mythology, *see* ELVES.

QUENYA The first language of the Elves and therefore the first language of Tolkien's world, as the Elves are the first race to speak aloud and to sing (hence their alternative name, Quendi, meaning "the speakers"), and indeed to give names to all things in the world. Later on the Elves are also the first to devise a written language. By the time of the First Age, however, Quenya is only in common use by the three High Elven kindred of Eldamar (the Vanyar, Noldor, and Teleri) in the Undying Lands. The common Elvish tongue in the mortal lands of Middle-earth is Sindarin, the language of the Sindar or Grey Elves of Beleriand.

In Middle-earth, Quenya, then, becomes a kind of Elvish Latin, largely employed in formal recitations, during ceremonial occasions, or for the swearing of sacred oaths. Linguistically, Tolkien took some of his inspiration for his invented Elvish language from Latin and Greek but, most especially Finnish.

See also: FINNISH LANGUAGE AND LITERATURE

QUETZALCOATLUS A species of prehistoric flying pterosaur, or "winged lizard," the fossils of which were discovered in 1971, two years before Tolkien's death. Named after the Aztec deity Quetzalcoatl, the "feathered serpent," this species is one of the largest pterosaurs ever discovered, standing 10 feet tall at the shoulder and with an astonishing wingspan of 40 feet.

While the discovery of *Quetzalcoatlus* came far too late to influence Tolkien's creation of the terrifying flying steeds of the Ringwraiths, it provides a curious instance of (prehistoric) life imitating art. When the fossilized remains of these ancient monsters were first uncovered in Texas, the *Quetzalcoatlus* was found to be a near-perfect match for the dimensions of Tolkien's "hell-hawks." It must have seemed as though a nightmare creature out of Tolkien's Middle-earth had entered the real world.

QUICKBEAM   An Ent, one of the younger of his kind, and notorious among them for being rather hasty in word and deed—a reputation he initially gains after answering "yes" to a question that a fellow Ent has not yet finished. He is the guardian of rowan trees, one of which he himself resembles. Naturally enough, he is the first Ent to resolve on an Entish attack on Isengard.

As is usually the case, Tolkien is playful in the inspirations he gathers into his names. "Quickbeam" is another English name for the rowan, a hardy tree that is one of the shortest-lived (and so the youngest) of European trees. The word "beam" leads to not only a "piece of timber" and the German word for tree, *Baum*, but also suggests the swiftness of a shaft of sunlight passing through a woodland canopy (an idea suggested by his Sindarin name, Bregalad, potentially meaning "sudden radiance" as well as "sudden tree"). The name, of course, gives us the Ent's personality in a nutshell.

R

Magical Ring

RADAGAST

One of the Istari, the five Maiar sent to Middle-earth in around 1000 TA to provide help to Elves and Men in their struggle against Sauron. Known as "the Brown" for the color of his garb, he is one of the "people" of Yavanna and is thus mostly concerned with tending to the flora and fauna of Middle-earth. Gandalf, at the Council of Elrond, calls him "a worthy wizard, a master of shapes and changes of hue; and he has much lore of herbs and beasts, and birds are especially his friends." His Quenya name Aiwendil indeed means "love of birds."

There has been much speculation about the inspiration for Radagast's name: from the Slavic god of hospitality, Radegast, to the Gothic King Radagaisus, to the Anglo-Saxon word *rudugást*, meaning "ruddy spirit." In his character we might look to the figure of the brown-robed Friar Saint Francis (1181/1182–1226), who in Roman Catholic legend is closely related to nature and animals, and is known for having preached to birds.

RAGNARÖK

In Norse mythology the great final battle-to-be between the gods and the giants, which will result in the cataclysmic end of the Nine Worlds of the cosmos. An account of the battle is given in the Old Norse poem *Völuspá*, part of the *Poetic Edda*.

This great conflict of elemental forces has a direct counterpart in Tolkien's Dagor Dagorath, the "Battle of Battles," an end-of-days conflict prophesied by the Vala Mandos in an early version of *The Silmarillion*, allusions to which can be found both in that book as published and elsewhere in Tolkien's writings. Both the Norse Ragnarök and Dagor Dagorath are clearly prefigured, however, in the author's history of the First Age in the cataclysmic Great Battle in the War of Wrath, as Tolkien himself acknowledged. This is the greatest battle ever fought in Middle-earth and shakes the very foundations of the world.

Just as the final battle of Ragnarök will begin with the sounding of the Horn of Heimdall, the Watchman of the Gods, so Tolkien's Great Battle begins with the blast of the Horn of Eönwë, the Herald of the Valar. In both great battles all the legions of good and evil—and all creatures, spirits, demons, and beasts—meet in one final terrible conflict. In Tolkien's version of Ragnarök, Morgoth, the Dark

Roäc the Chief Raven of Ravenhill. The Ravens were wise counselors and swift messengers of the Dwarves.

Enemy, releases one last great horror in the form of Ancalagon the Black, the first and greatest of a vast legion of Winged Fire-drakes. The attack of Ancalagon in the Great Battle has precedence in the *Völuspá*'s description of the coming of "the flying dragon, glowing serpent" known as Nidhogg (meaning "malice striker"). The dragon's appearance in the poem, many scholars argue, announces Ragnarök. In Tolkien's works, by contrast, Eärendil's slaying of Ancalagon marks the final defeat of Morgoth.

RED BOOK OF HERGEST

See: RED BOOK OF WESTMARCH

RED BOOK OF WESTMARCH

The name of the ancient manuscript written by Hobbits, which Tolkien "claimed" as the principal source of *The Hobbit, The Lord of the Rings,* and other related writings. A book in five volumes of red leather binding and casing, it was kept in Westmarch, an area in the far west of the Shire. In naming the *Red Book of Westmarch* as his major source of Elf-lore on Middle-earth, Tolkien was making a scholarly joke and an allusion to the fourteenth-century *Red Book of Hergest.* This vellum manuscript, currently kept in the Bodleian Library, Oxford University, includes the Welsh tales now collectively known as *The Mabinogion,* a collection whose supernatural hunters, beautiful maidens, enchanters, and magic rings provided inspiration for Tolkien's own tales of the Elves. Like the Shire's *Red Book,* it too has a red leather binding and was for several centuries kept at the manor of Hergest Court in the Welsh Marches, on the western edge of Herefordshire, in England.

RELIGION: CHRISTIANITY

For those who first encounter Tolkien's world by way of *The Hobbit* and *The Lord of the Rings,* the author's religious beliefs are not immediately apparent. While Tolkien was a deeply committed Roman Catholic, his fictional world is resolutely pagan. Indeed, Tolkien took pains to create a pre-Christian, even pre-religious, world. Middle-earth is an archetypal world "constructed in an imaginary time."

Tolkien, moreover, very much disliked heavy-handed Christian messages in literature, famously stating: "I cordially dislike allegory in all its manifestations, and have always done so since I grew old and wary enough to detect its presence." However, his tales nonetheless prefigure, to his mind, the Christian moral struggle between good and evil, as revealed in the most admirable aspects of heroic pagan men and women. This was the noble heroic struggle of Tolkien's Anglo-Saxon ancestors, and, as with Christian symbolism that would follow, there is a spiritual light that shines through in the telling of those pagan legendary quests and adventures.

In his lecture and essay "On Fairy-Stories," Tolkien links the world of myth and fairy tale with that of his Christian faith: "The Gospel contains a fairy story, or a story of a larger kind which embraces all the essence of fairy stories." Tolkien sincerely believed that, in the story of Christ, mythology and history met and fused: "Because this story is supreme and is true, Art has been verified. God is the Lord, of angels, and of men—and of elves." This was where the importance of ancient myth arose: it was only through the "prefiguration" of miraculous pagan tales that the human imagination could have been prepared to accept the true and historic miracle of Jesus Christ.

It was not until Tolkien's posthumously published *The Silmarillion* that his legendarium revealed the primal cause of his cosmos to be a single entity consistent with the God of Tolkien's Christian faith. Although not worshipped on Middle-earth in any formal religious sense, Eru the One is a deity who has much in common with the Yahweh or Jehovah of the monotheistic Jewish and Christian faiths. *The Silmarillion* also revealed Tolkien's wonder-filled creation story of a world sung into existence by Eru's angelic choir known as the Ainur, or Holy Ones. It is an original story filled with biblical language and undeniable grandeur that is much indebted to the Book of Genesis. As the respected Tolkien scholar Tom Shippey has observed, Tolkien's creation myth is comparable to "a summary list of doctrines of the Fall of Man common to Milton, to St. Augustine, and to the Church as a whole."

See also: LUCIFER; MICHAEL, ARCHANGEL; "ON FAIRY-STORIES"; VIRGIN MARY, THE

RHÛN The name of the regions of Middle-earth east of the Wilderland of Rhovanion and beyond the Inland Sea of Rhûn. The name simply means "East" in Sindarin, and in *The Lord of the Rings* it is described as characterized by "wide uncharted lands, nameless plains and forests unexplored." If we take into account Tolkien's explanation that the theater of his tales in the northwest of Middle-earth have a real-world equivalency to Europe, then Rhûn must have a real-world equivalency to Asia. The Inland Sea of Rhûn may have been inspired by the Black Sea.

However, if we look for a specific historic counterpart to the Easterlings of Rhûn, the most likely source of inspiration, at least linguistically, would be the Seljuk Sultanate of Rhum (or Rûm) that existed in Anatolia (Asia Minor) between the eleventh century and the beginning of the fourteenth. During this time the Sultanate of Rhum grew wealthy and had sufficient military power to drive out the Byzantines and repulse European Crusaders. Here we find echoes of the struggle of Gondor with the Easterling hordes.

RIDERS OF THE MARK Alternate name for the Riders of Rohan. In medieval times, the term "mark" or "march" (Anglo-Saxon: *mearc*; Old Norse: *mörk*) meant a "borderland" and referred to land occupied by an independent ally to serve as a buffer between two hostile nations. In Britain, the Romans established the Welsh Marches, which the Anglo-Saxons later called the "Mark" or the "Mearc." This became the kingdom of Mercia in the early Middle Ages, and became the most powerful in Britain.

RIDERS OF ROHAN
See: ROHIRRIM

RING OF DOOM
A gathering space outside the western gates of Valimar, the city of the Valarian "gods" of Arda, where important councils are held. Its Quenya name is Máhanaxar. Both Melkor and Fëanor face the judgment of the Valar here. This may be an echo of the Domhring, the Ring of Doom, a circle of monolithic stones that stood before the Temple of Thor, perhaps the most potent symbol of the law among the Vikings. In the center of this ring of stones was the Thunder God's pillar, the Thorstein. In the ninth century the Irish King Maelgula Ma Dungail was made captive in the Viking enclave of Dublin. He was taken to the Ring of Doom and his back was broken upon Thorstein. Of another such ring in Iceland, a scribe in the Christian twelfth century wrote that bloodstains could still be seen upon the central stone.

RINGS OF POWER
Magical rings forged by Sauron and the Elven-smiths of Eregion in the Second Age: "the Nine" for Men, "the Seven" for Dwarves, and "the Three" for the Elves. Sauron plans to use the Rings of Powers to control and enslave the peoples of Middle-earth, using the One Ring he later secretly forges in Mordor, on Mount Doom. Only the Three Rings, made exclusively by the greatest Elven-smith of Eregion, Celebrimbor, remain unsullied by his craft. Similar rings of power—rings that connote power as well as perhaps magically bestowing it—may be discovered in the myths and folklore of every civilization in the world, but are also very much a part of history itself.

No people in history were as obsessed with the symbolism of the ring as the Vikings. To those warrior people, the ring meant wealth, honor, fame, and destiny. Under its sign they charted unknown seas, waged barbarous wars, sacrificed man and beast, pledged their faith, made great gifts of it, and finally died for it. Their gods were ring lords of the heavens, and their kings were ring lords of the Earth. No earthly king or earl who was not a "ring-giver" held power for long. By these gifts of wealth and honor the warrior expected his reward for his faithfulness. Thus, often a kingdom's power might rightly be judged by the "ring-hoard" of the king.

The longship's figurehead was a ring clenched in a dragon's teeth. It broached the gray horizons of the North Sea and Dublin Bay, pointed the way to Spain, Italy, Tangier, and Byzantium across the blue Mediterranean, and swept through the icy seas of the North Atlantic and the fog banks of North America. For many, the Vikings' ring-prow ships heralded fire, death, and destruction.

It is no surprise, then, that rings play an important role in Norse religion and mythology. The rings of Norse mythology—like Tolkien's—were commonly magical rings forged by elfs or dwarfs. They were tokens of both power and eternal fame. They were also symbolic of the highest power: destiny and the cycle of doom. The most powerful ring of all belongs to Odin, the Norse king of the gods and ruler of the Nine Worlds. This "one ring," Draupnir, has the power to drip eight other rings of equal size every nine days. Its possession by Odin was not only emblematic of his dominion over the Nine Worlds but consolidated his accumulated powers by giving him a source of almost infinite wealth. Odin, in his darker guise as the Necromancer and "Lord of the Rings," is a model for the Dark Lord, Sauron, whose return to Middle-earth in the Second Age heralds an age of dominion, terror, and destruction.

Although the symbol of the ring was widespread and prominent in many far more ancient cultures, it was the Norsemen who brought the ring quest to its fullest expression, and to the very heart of their cultural identity. Virtually all ring-quest tales in myth and fiction in the Western world are deeply indebted to the Norse myths. Tolkien's *The Lord of the Rings*, although striking in its originality and innovation, is no exception.

RINGWRAITHS
See: NAZGÛL

RIVENDELL   The steep hidden valley and Elven refuge of Master Elrond Half-elven and his people. Considered the "Last Homely House East of the Sea," for four thousand years Rivendell (known as Imladris in Sindarin) is a refuge of wisdom and great learning for all Elves and Men of goodwill.

Rivendell, as a place of learning, takes some of its inspiration from Tolkien's own university city of Oxford, and, as a place of almost oracular wisdom and counsel, from ancient Delphi in Greece. Topographically, however, it seems to have been inspired—as shown in Tolkien's sketches and watercolors of Rivendell—by the spectacular deep-cloven Lauterbrunnen Valley, which the 19-year-old author-to-be encountered while on a walking tour in the Swiss Alps.

Perhaps the most convincing circumstantial evidence for this association might be a linguistic one. The river that cuts through Rivendell's steep valley is the Bruinen, a Westron name that Tolkien more often translates and refers to as the Loudwater River. Consequently, Middle-earth's Bruinen matches up rather well with the Swiss Lauterbrunnen: *lauter*, meaning "louder," and *Brunnen*, meaning "fountain, spring." Thus Lauterbrunnen, in one theory, simply translates as "louder water."

See also: D E L P H I

ROHAN   Inland kingdom to the north of Gondor, on the grasslands between the White Mountains and Fangorn Forest. It is the home of the horse people known as the Rohirrim, allies of Gondor. Just as the Rohirrim are a blend of both Goths and Anglo-Saxons, Rohan seems to be a blend of the grasslands of eastern Europe, home to the nomadic Goths, and the Anglo-Saxon kingdom of Mercia. Rohan is also known as the Mark, cognate with Mercia.

ROHIRRIM   A horse people from whom come the supreme cavalrymen of Middle-earth, the Riders of Rohan or Riders of the Mark. Like

Rohirrim

the historic Goth cavalrymen on the plains east and north of the Western and Eastern Roman Empires, the Rohirrim command the great plains of Rohan (formerly the Gondorian fiefdom of Calenardhon) and defend the passes into Gondor. Both the Goths and the Rohirrim are constantly prepared for battle and are similar in appearance and temperament. The charge of the Rohirrim in the Battle of Pelennor Fields in the War of the Ring is inspired by a historic Roman account of Goth and Lombard cavalry battle formations and actions.

Although historically the Rohirrim have much in common with the Goths, in their characterization they are almost entirely akin to the ancient Anglo-Saxons, except for the overwhelming significance of the horse in their culture. Essentially, in the Rohirrim we have Beowulf's people *plus* horses. Indeed, the language of the Rohirrim, Rohirric, as "translated" in Tolkien's writings, is almost entirely derived from Anglo-Saxon (specifically its Mercian dialect). Many names incorporate the Anglo-Saxon for "warhorse," *eoh*.

ROLAND
Frankish military leader and "lord of the Breton March" under Charlemagne (king of the Franks) who died in AD 778 during an ambush of the king's troops by the Basques while returning from a Frankish expedition in Spain. He was immortalized in a number of medieval and Renaissance literary masterpieces, notably the anonymous eleventh-century French epic *Chanson de Roland* (Song of Roland). In the epic, Roland is shown making his heroic last stand in the Roncesvalles Pass in the Pyrenees while under attack from the Saracens, here substituting for the Basques.

Tolkien's noble, deeply patriotic but flawed Boromir, the son and heir of Denethor, Ruling Steward of Gondor at the time of the War of the Ring, is to some degree modeled on Roland. Boromir's last stand and death, in particular, recalls the verses in the *Chanson de Roland* describing the Frankish hero's last stand and death:

Count Roland lifts the horn up to his mouth,
Then sets his lips and blows it with great force.

The hills are high; the horn's voice loud and long;
They hear it echoing full thirty leagues.

Faced with impossible odds, Roland, preoccupied with his honor and renown, repeatedly refuses to blow his oliphant (a hunting horn made of an elephant's tusk) to summon help from Charlemagne. Only when it is already too late does he finally take up his horn. We find elements here of Boromir, who also seems preoccupied with his own "will to power" and renown and, of course, is associated with his own hunting horn, the Horn of Gondor, which he blows *in extremis* to summon his Charlemagne-like companion Aragorn. Both heroes, too, are seen as redeemed in death, Roland finally showing humility by submitting his soul to God, and Boromir in dying to save the Hobbits Pippin and Merry.

ROMAN EMPIRE The vast territories ruled from the city

of Rome in the early centuries AD, encompassing much of Europe, West Asia, and North Africa. While its history was fraught with war, conquest, and internal strife, the Roman Empire became closely associated with "advanced" civilization in terms of culture, technology, politics, and the rule of law. At the end of the third century AD, it was divided into Western and Eastern Empires. While the former finally collapsed in AD 476 after wave after wave of Germanic invasion, the latter (as the Byzantine Empire) survived until 1453. The Western Empire was notionally restored in the Holy Roman Empire established by Charlemagne in AD 800.

The Roman Empire provides the most obvious historical precedent for Tolkien's fictional North- and South-kingdoms of Arnor and Gondor, which are closely associated with civilized values and the rule of law (even if they are often shown as imperfect). Tolkien's annals of his Dúnedain kingdoms are informed by his readings in the histories of the rise and fall of the Roman Empire, as well as its eventual resurrection in the form of the Holy Roman Empire. For example, just as the twin brothers Romulus and Remus laid the foundations of Rome, two brothers, Isildur and Anárion (although not twins), founded the kingdom of Gondor. Both kingdoms are depicted as "imperial" powers, establishing their rule over neighboring lands and "lesser" peoples, considered "barbarians."

The division of the Roman Empire can be matched to that of Gondor and Arnor. Like the Western Empire, Arnor eventually collapses under the combined weight of internal strife and external invasion while Gondor, like the Byzantine Empire, continues to survive throughout the Third Age, though, again like Byzantium, it gradually declines in power and splendor. In a letter, Tolkien explicitly called Gondor's latter-day capital the "Byzantine City of Minas Tirith."

By the end of the Third Age, after three millennia of conflict, Tolkien presents the reader with a remarkable hero (comparable to the historic Charlemagne) who is also the legitimate heir to the crown of the Reunited Kingdoms of Arnor and Gondor. In so doing, Tolkien implicitly suggests—and in a letter explicitly stated—that, in his chronicles of Middle-earth, the progress of the histories of Arnor and Gondor was based on the historic precedent of "the reestablishment of an effective Holy Roman Empire."

RUMPELSTILTSKIN
A fairy tale made famous by the Brothers Grimm with their 1812 edition of *Children's and Household Tales*. It was an ancient tale about a goblin or dwarf who spins straw into gold using a spinning wheel, but is tricked out of his golden hoard by the solving of a riddle. In many variations, it may be discovered in the folklore and myths in many parts of the world.

In *Rumpelstiltskin*, Tolkien observed the essential association of dwarfs with magic rings—here transmogrified into a spinning wheel—a fairy-tale version of the magical powers embodied in the dwarf-forged ring of the German *Nibelungenlied* and the Norse *Völsunga Saga*. This magical gold ring was known as Andvarinaut in Norse mythology, meaning "the ring of Andvari the Dwarf." It was also called "Andvari's loom" because of its power "to weave gold" and endlessly reproduce itself, a power linking it to Draupnir, the gold ring of Odin.

In the riddling contest between Bilbo Baggins and Gollum over the possession of the One Ring, we can perceive something comparable to the riddling and outwitting of the dwarf Rumpelstiltskin in the fairy tale.

sS

Steward of Gondor

S A M P O   A mysterious magical artifact forged by the immortal smith Ilmarinen the Eternal Hammerer, appearing in the Finnish national epic the *Kalevala*. The Sampo has been described as a bright artifact emerging from a forge that brings wealth and good fortune. By one account, it appears to be a kind of mill that perpetually grinds out salt, grain, and gold. And when it was stolen, it became the object of a disastrous quest comparable to J. R. R. Tolkien's similarly disastrous quest for the Silmarils.

The Sampo and the Silmarils were in some respects akin to the Greek Cornucopia, the medieval Holy Grail, Odin's ring, Draupnir, the Norse mill, Grotti, and numerous other mysterious objects of quests in the mythologies of Japan, India, and China. Tolkien believed the Sampo was both an object and an allegory. He saw it as the quintessence of Ilmarinen's creative powers, capable of provoking both good and evil. Similarly, his Silmarils were objects of obscure symbolism, the quintessence of Fëanor's creative powers, capable of provoking both good and evil.

See also: SILMARILS

S A M W I S E   G A M G E E   The companion and servant of Ring-bearer Frodo Baggins throughout the Quest of the Ring. The rough-cut working-class Samwise, as one of the Fellowship of the Ring, was what Tolkien called a typical "plain unimaginative, parochial" Hobbit. However, Sam's courageous heart and unswerving loyalty to Frodo more than once saves the day in their long quest. His deeds also displayed what Tolkien described as the most unlikely Hobbit characteristic of the "amazing and unexpected heroism of ordinary men 'at a pinch.'"

In a personal letter in 1956, Tolkien wrote that a good part of his characterization of his fictional Samwise Gamgee was derived from his experience as a signals officer in the First World War. "My Samwise is indeed largely a reflection of the English soldier—grafted on the village-boys of early days, the memory of the privates and my batmen that I knew in the 1914 War, and recognized as so far superior to myself." (Batmen were soldiers who were essentially manservants to British officers.) In the First

World War, British officers were from the upper-middle classes, or—as was Tolkien—university-educated men. Working-class men were recruited as privates and could only ascend to the rank of sergeant. Sam was a humble uneducated gardener and employee of the Master of Bag End.

In Samwise Gamgee, we discover a Hobbit's name serving as the key to his character. So just as we found his master's name Frodo, means "Wise," logically enough, we discover Samwise transliterated into Old English means "Half-wise" or "Simple." Sam's father's name, Hamfast, was equally descriptive because in Old English, it means "Home-stay" or "Stay-at-home." Both are unambiguous names for simple garden laborers.

The relationship between Frodo and Samwise was very much that of an Edwardian master and servant. Although not uncritical of the class structure and customs of that time, Tolkien was enough of an Edwardian himself to believe that within these roles a bond of mutual respect and loyalty to each other was possible and could be an ennobling thing. John Garth, the author of *Tolkien in the Great War*, has observed that as the quest progressed, the master–servant relationship largely became inverted: "[Frodo] presents the problems, Sam the solutions." And, that in the First World War "this process was far from atypical." It was a view that Tolkien observed and recognized in the fog of war that his batsmen might often prove "far superior to myself." *See also*: GAMGEE

SAREHOLE
See: HOBBITON

SARUMAN   One of the Istari, the five Maiar emissaries sent by the Valar to Middle-earth at the end of the first millennium of the Third Age. Very much in the tradition of Merlin and other Arthurian Wizards, Saruman was initially the highest ranked of the order of the Istari (meaning "Wise-ones"). Like Merlin—or the Norse god Odin or Greek god Hermes who also traveled the world in mortal guise—the Istari appeared as ancient travelers with long white beards, great cloaks, and their Wizard's staff, an emblem of the magician's power.

Saruman the White's name in Valinor was Curumo meaning "Cunning One" among the Valar. In the Undying Lands he was (like Sauron) a Maia of Aulë the Smith. Among the Elves he was known as Curunir "Man of Skill," while among Men upon Middle-earth he was known as Saruman. This was a linguistic construct derived from one of two Old English words: "*Searomann*" meaning "Man of Skill" (a good name for a White Wizard) or the similar "*Saroman*" meaning "Man of Pain" (a good name for a Black Wizard). Always the philologist, the hidden meanings of Tolkien's names always reveal hidden aspects of their character.

Upon arrival in Middle-earth, Saruman was the chief and greatest of the five Istari, but in seeking to overcome the evil power of Sauron, he became seduced by the quest for power itself. Ultimately, his secret desire was to take possession of the One Ring himself and supplant Sauron as the Lord of the Rings. Saruman's tragic tale has much in common with the ancient German legend of Faust, the Magus who became the subject of Christopher Marlowe's *The Tragic History of the Life and Death of Doctor Faustus* and Johann Wolfgang von Goethe's *Faust*.

Just as Faust made a bargain with the Devil by exchanging his immortal soul for the promise of unlimited knowledge and worldly power; so Saruman made a bargain with the Dark Lord by exchanging his immortal soul for the promise of unlimited knowledge and worldly power. Treebeard the Ent describes Saruman as having "a mind of metal and wheels" and a fascination with technology, which resulted in the sacrifice of humane values and life itself. Both Faust and Saruman passionately sought knowledge instead of wisdom.

And so the greatest of the Istari who had come to destroy the Dark Lord unwittingly became one of his greatest agents. For just as Faust was deceived by Mephistopheles, so Saruman become the ally and puppet of Sauron the Dark Lord. From his tower of Orthanc in his great ring-walled stronghold of Isengard, Saruman summoned legions of Orcs, Uruk-hai, Half-Orcs, and Dunlendings under a black banner marked with a White Hand to make war upon the Men of Rohan and Gondor.

Saruman's influence over others was in good part due to a melodious voice characterized as the "very sound an enchantment" with the power to hold his audience spellbound and enthralled. His speech was also filled with rhetorical tricks, subtle illusions, flattery, and charm that combined evil, malice, and lies. His speeches had much in common with the enthralling and deceptive discourses of Satan in John Milton's *Paradise Lost*.

Prince Éomer of Rohan, in full recognition of Saruman's deceptions, declares the Wizard "an old liar with honey on his forked tongue." This is much in tune with the biblical Satan who, as the great deceiver, was given the New Testament epithet "the father of lies." And yet, in the War of the Ring, all of Saruman's subtle powers and powerful alliances come to nothing after the March of the Ents on Isengard and the decisive Battle of Hornburg. The mighty ring walls of Isengard are torn down by the Ent tree herds, and the heroic Rohirrim, along with the vengeful Huorn tree spirits, annihilate his vast legions of Orcs, Uruks, Half-Orcs, and Dunlendings.

In the end, Saruman's Wizard staff was taken from him and broken. All his sorcerous powers were stripped from him and he was sent to wander in exile. So low did Saruman fall that looking for some petty vengeance he entered into the tiny realm of the Shire, where the Hobbits, the least of his enemies, resided. There Saruman, under the Orkish name of Sharkey (meaning "old man"), set himself up as a petty tyrant before finally being overthrown by the heroic brotherhood of Hobbits returning from the War of the Ring. Sharkey's squalid end was comparable with another tyrant recorded in an episode Tolkien knew well in *The Anglo-Saxon Chronicle*. That account, from AD 755 begins: "Here Cynewulf deprived Sigeberht of his kingdom" (Wessex, or present-day West Sussex), and concludes with the exiled usurper being slain by his formerly loyal servant, who in turn is chased and slain by a swineherd. Similarly, Sharkey was slain in a murderous rage by the last of his followers, his own servant, Gríma Wormtongue, who in turn is chased and slain by a Hobbit bowman. And so, the once great Saruman the Istari came to the same ignoble end as the tragic usurper Sigeberht, the once great king of Wessex.

SATAN

The personification of evil in Hebraic, Christian, and Islamic religions. Also known as the Devil, the name Satan means "accuser" or "adversary" and is seen as the primary hostile and malignant force in the world. Satan's portrayal in John Milton's *Paradise Lost*, as the Old Testament rebel archangel who provokes a war in heaven, was J. R. R. Tolkien's model for his portrayal of the Morgoth the "Dark Enemy of the World." Morgoth provokes a war with the Powers of Arda and, like Satan, proves to be the primary hostile and malignant force in Tolkien's world. Like Satan on his throne in Hell, Morgoth in his subterranean "Iron Hell" of Angband gathered about him other fallen rebel demons and a multitude of evil and twisted forms of life. Among Satan's great allies were Mammon, Beelzebub, Belial, and Moloch; while about Morgoth were Balrogs, Orcs, Trolls, Werewolves, and Serpents. Both Satan and Morgoth were loud in their defiance, and very much is the spirit of Satan's proclamation in *Paradise Lost*, both would "rather rule in hell than serve in heaven."

One might have admired these rebel angels if one believed their defiance was (as they claimed) in the name of liberty. However, both lie. Their rebellions were truthfully provoked by envy and the usurper's desire to become tyrants themselves. As Milton confirmed, Satan's true motive was to "set himself in glory above his peers." Both were primarily motivated by overweening pride and envy. It is worth noting in *Paradise Lost* how Satan's minions "Towards him they bend / With awful reverence prone; and as a God / Extol him equal to the highest in Heav'n." It is a description that is comparable to Morgoth enthroned in his subterranean halls, and reveals the true motive of both antagonists: to become God the Creator themselves. For, as Tolkien explains, Melkor's fall—like that of Satan—was a moral one: "From splendour he fell through arrogance to contempt for all things. . . . He began with the desire for Light, but when he could not possess it for himself alone, he descended through fire and wrath into a great burning, down into Darkness." Never were there two more natural tyrants than Satan and Morgoth.

SAURON THE RING LORD

Original Maia spirit of Valinor who was corrupted by Morgoth the Dark Enemy. In the First Age

Barad-dûr. Sauron's stronghold.

upon Middle-earth, he became known as Sauron Gorthaur, meaning "Dread Abomination," or Sauron the Cruel. By the Second Age, Sauron would rise up to become Morgoth's successor as the new Dark Lord of Middle-earth. In his creation of Sauron the Lord of the Rings, Tolkien drew on a wealth of ring legends and myths, Celtic, Greek, German, Finnish, and Norse among them. The tales with the strongest association to those of Sauron as Ring Lord were the myths and legends of the Vikings and, in particular, those tales related to their supreme god, Odin.

Necromancer, sorcerer, warlord, transformer, and ring lord, no figure in mythology more closely resembles Sauron than the Norse god Odin. In his desire for dominion over Midgard, Odin matches Sauron's thirst for dominion over Middle-earth. Their intentions were identical: to gain control of a magical all-powerful ring; the One Ring in the case of Sauron, and Draupnir for Odin. Just as the forging of the One Ring and the Rings of Power required the combined talents of Sauron and the Elven-smiths of Celebrimbor in Eriador, so the forging of Draupnir required the combined skills of Sauron and the Elven-smiths Sindri and Brok in Alfheim. Just as Sauron's One Ring controlled all the other Rings of Power worn by sorcerers and kings throughout Middle-earth, so Draupnir dripped eight other rings on every ninth day. Odin gave out these rings to sorcerers and kings whom he then bound to himself with oaths of loyalty and ultimately controlled throughout Midgard.

In the beginning, Sauron was not numbered among the rebel Maiar. His name was Mairon, meaning "the Admirable." He was a Maia of Aulë, the Smith of the Valar, who has an exact counterpart in the Greek god Hephaestus the Smith (the Roman Vulcan). As an apprentice to Aulë the Smith, Sauron gained such deep knowledge of fire and forge that in the Second Age, as the new Dark Lord of Middle-earth, he is able to forge Rings of Power. Appearing in the fair and "admirable" form of Annatar, "Lord of Gifts," Sauron is also able to seduce and corrupt the Elves of Eriador with his knowledge.

In Eastern mythology, there is a sorcerer-smith comparable to Sauron the Ring Lord who dwelt in a mountain kingdom akin to that of Mordor. This was Kurkar the Ring Lord, of the mountain kingdom of Hor. Like Sauron, this sorcerer's power over his hellish mountain kingdom was reliant on the supernatural power of a ring. However, Kurkar's ring was a massive iron mandala ring, which, we are told, contained the "life" or "soul" of Kurkar and all his ancestors. So long as it was kept within his mountain stronghold, Kurkar believed that his power and his life were safe, especially as the massive iron ring could not be melted or forged by any known means. This archetypal myth of a sorcerer-smith appears to share many of the properties of Sauron's One Ring, for even the fierce fire of the furnace cannot redden this ring. Kurkar the Ring Lord gathered demons and human allies about him in the mountain kingdom of Hor, just as Sauron the Ring Lord gathers Orcs and human allies about him in the mountain-guarded kingdom of Mordor.

It is difficult to determine whether the spirit of Sauron, after his re-manifestation as the Necromancer in the Third Age, is ever able to regain actual material form over the next millennia, either in Dol Guldur or, later, in Mordor. Tolkien gave only vague clues as to Sauron's physical and/or spectral manifestations. In *The Lord of the Rings* we are told of one fearful encounter that describes the Dark Lord's four-fingered "Black Hand," but whether this is a phantom shape or the actual material physical form of the Dark Lord is open to debate. However, the most common manifestation of the spirit of Sauron in the Third Age is as the fiery "Eye of Sauron," variously described as the "Red Eye," the "Evil Eye," the "Lidless Eye," or the "Great Eye." Certainly, Tolkien's son and literary executor Christopher eventually concluded that, in the War of the Ring, his "father had come to identify the Eye of Barad-dûr with the mind and will of Sauron."

In all cultures, eyes are believed to have special powers and are often said to be windows onto the soul. So, Tolkien's description of the Evil Eye of Sauron gives us considerable insight into the Dark Lord himself: "The Eye was rimmed with fire, but was itself glazed, yellow as a cat's, watchful and intent, and the black slit of its pupil opened on a pit, a window into nothing." This last phrase, "a window into nothing," reflects Tolkien's Roman Catholic, Augustinian philosophical standpoint that evil is essentially the absence of good, and that ultimately evil in itself is a soul-destroying nothingness.

Odin the Necromancer is the mythological figure who most obviously informed the identity of Sauron the Necromancer and who was—not coincidentally—also known as the One-Eyed God. In the Norse canon, Odin sacrificed one eye in exchange for one deep draft from the Mímisbrunnr, the "Well of Secret Knowledge." Thereafter, Odin—like Sauron—was able to consult and command wraiths, phantoms, and spirits of the dead.

In most of the world's mythologies, we find epic tales dealing with the cosmic battle between good and evil: the fate of the world is held in balance as the mass forces of evil threaten to overwhelm and obliterate the apparently doomed forces of good. In Tolkien's *The Lord of the Rings*, the climactic battle between good and evil is played out in the Battle of the Black Gate. In his epic novel, Tolkien combined the theme of the cosmic battle with another universal mythological motif, the "External Soul," known, in multiple forms, by "peoples from Hindoostan [*sic*] to the Hebrides," as James George Frazer observed in his famous *The Golden Bough: A Study of Comparative Religion* (1890). A warlock, giant, or other supernatural being, Frazer explained, "is invulnerable and immortal because he keeps his soul hidden away in some secret place [or object]; this secret is revealed to the hero, who seeks out the warlock's soul, heart, life or death (as it is variously called), and by destroying it, simultaneously kills the warlock."

In *The Lord of the Rings*, the mighty Sauron, who commands vastly superior armies and terrible supernatural powers, appears to be an unstoppable force in the final cosmic Battle at the Black Gate. However, at that very moment when total victory seems within his grasp, Sauron discovers that he is supremely vulnerable and mortally threatened as Frodo the Hobbit slips the One Ring onto his finger: "The Dark Lord was suddenly aware of him, the Eye piercing all shadows looked across the plain . . . the magnitude of his folly was revealed to him in a blinding flash, and . . . he knew his deadly peril and the thread upon which his doom now hung." The One Ring that effectively contains Sauron's "external soul" is on the hand of the Hobbit who now threatens its destruction in the volcanic fires of the Cracks of Doom.

SCATHA THE WORM The mightiest of the Cold-drakes of the Grey Mountains who slaughtered Dwarves and Men and took

possession of a great treasure hoard. Appropriately enough, Scatha's name was derived from an Anglo-Saxon word meaning "Assassin." Scatha's end at the hand of Fram the Éothéod Dragon-slayer was comparable to that of the Cold-drake that died at the hand of Wolfdietrich, the Langobard Dragon-slayer. Meanwhile, the slaying of Dain I, king of the Dwarves, by the Cold-drakes of the Grey Mountains is mirrored in the slaying of Ortnit, king of the Langobards, by dragons in the mountains of Lombardy.

After the War of Wrath, it is not until the twentieth century of the Third Age that the histories of Middle-earth speak again of Dragons. These monsters were akin to the dragons to be found in the eponymous High German epic poems *Wolfdietrich* and *Ortnit.*

Like Tolkien's tales of Dragons appearing in the Grey Mountains of Middle-earth, these thirteenth-century tales of the monsters infesting the mountains of Lombardy were like Cold-drakes, a somewhat less formidable breed of Dragon than either the Fire-drakes (like Tolkien's Glaurung) or the Winged Fire-drakes (like Tolkien's Ancalagon). And yet, even lacking the power of fire or flight, the great strength of these serpents, with their fangs, claws, and armor of iron scales, made them a terror of their times.

The Langobards were one of the many powerful German tribes who lived on the eastern European borderlands of the Roman Empire. These warrior people swept into northern Italy where they settled and gave their name to the region today called Lombardy. Described by Latin historians as the supreme horsemen of the German peoples, the Langobards were Tolkien's models for the Éothéod and their heirs the Rohirrim (the Horsemen of Rohan). Also, curiously enough, the tribal name "Langobards" translates directly into English as "Longbeards," the same name Tolkien gave to the Dwarves of Durin's Line, and to Dain I, the Longbeard king of the Grey Mountains.

Ortnit, the eponymous hero of the Langobard epic poem was the son Alberich, the legendary dwarf king of the Italian Alps. Just as Dain I's kingdom in the Grey Mountains was terrorized by Cold-drakes, so Ortnit's kingdom was terrorized by dragons in the Lombard Mountains. There, despite being a great warrior protected by dwarf-forged dragon-proof armor, Ortnit was slain by being crushed to death by a dragon. This appears to be comparable to the death of Tolkien's Dwarf King who, despite his formidable strength and his own Dwarf-forged, Dragon-proof armor, was crushed to death by a Cold-drake in the Grey Mountains.

SEVEN FATHERS OF THE DWARVES

The first of their race, these Dwarves were conceived and shaped by Aulë, the Smith of the Valar. It is Aulë, whom the Dwarves call Mahar (meaning "The Maker"), who fashions Dwarves from the substances of the deep earth. From Aulë comes the desire to search down into the roots of mountains, a search to discover the brightest of metals and the most beautiful jewels of the earth. And from Aulë also comes the desire to master crafts, such as the carving of stone, the forging of metal, and the cutting of gemstones. In their wrathful and violent nature, however, the Dwarves often appear to have more in common with the followers of the warrior cult of Thor, the Norse god of thunder. Unlike the smith gods Hephaestus and Aulë, Thor found glory in battle and honor in the hoarding of gold won by virtue of his war hammer, the dwarf-forged thunderbolt.

In their conception, Aulë's Seven Fathers of the Dwarves are in many ways similar to the creatures conceived by the smith god of the Greeks, Hephaestus. These appeared to be living creatures, but in fact were robotlike automatons designed to help him in his smithy to beat metal and work the forges. The original Seven Fathers of the Dwarves are in the beginning, like those automatons, incapable of independent thought or life. They can move only on command or by the thought of their master. It is Ilúvatar who gives the Dwarves the gift of true life, although he does not permit them to walk upon Middle-earth before the awakening of his own creations, the Elves. Hence the Seven Fathers of the Dwarves sleep through many ages until Varda, the star queen, fills the dark skies with starlight.

There can be little doubt of Tolkien's intentions here, for one of the many names for Varda is the High Elvish Fanuilos, which translates as "Snow White." This is somewhat disorienting. Having just got used to the revelation that the "Seven Dwarves" were the real "Sleepers" in Tolkien's version of the Snow White and the Seven Dwarfs fairy tale, we now discover

Shadowfax on the Plains of Rohan. Shadowfax the horse is tamed by Gandalf the White, and can outrun the winged beasts, the Nazgûl.

that it is Snow White who is actually responsible for the awakening of the Seven Dwarves.

SHADOWFAX

A horse of Rohan and chief of the *maeras*—the wild horses first tamed and bred by Eorl the Young, first king of Rohan. Like all of his kind, Shadowfax has almost miraculous intelligence, speed, and endurance. The *maeras'* reputedly "divine" origin—they are said to be descended from Nahar, the horse of the Vala Oromë—emphasizes Shadowfax's connections with divine mythological horses such as Odin's eight-legged horse Sleipnir.

SHAKESPEARE, WILLIAM

Arguably the world's most celebrated English-language poet and playwright, he was also an author J. R. R. Tolkien loved to hate. Tolkien rather enjoyed voicing the Englishman's heresy of hating William Shakespeare altogether. In fact, he went even further and tended to voice his dismissal of drama as a form of literature at all. In his lecture lecture and essay "On Fairy-Stories," Tolkien stated that more than any other form of literature, fantasy needs a "willing suspension of disbelief" to survive. In dramatized fantasy (like the Witches scene in *Macbeth*, 1606) Tolkien found "disbelief had not so much to be suspended as hanged, drawn and quartered." However peculiar Tolkien's dislike of Shakespeare and *Macbeth* in particular was, it proved to be a very fruitful hatred. As Tolkien himself explained the March of the Ents chapter in *The Lord of the Rings* was: "due, I think, to my bitter disappointment and disgust from schooldays with the shabby use made in Shakespeare of the coming of 'Great Birnam wood to high Dunsinane hill': I longed to devise a setting in which the trees might really march to war." Tolkien felt Shakespeare had trivialized and misinterpreted an authentic myth, providing a cheap, simplistic interpretation of the prophecy of this march of the wood upon the hill. And so Tolkien gives us the "true story" behind the prophecy in *Macbeth* in the epic March of the Ents on the realm of Saruman of the White Hand.

Tolkien tells us, in "On Fairy-Stories," "*Macbeth* is indeed a work by a playwright who ought, at least on this occasion, to have written a story, if he had the skill or patience for that art." Since Shakespeare was no longer available to take the advice, Tolkien decided to take on the job himself. In this effort, Tolkien extended himself by challenging Shakespeare's portrayal of Macbeth himself. Tolkien's evil Lord of the Ringwraiths—the Witch-king of Angmar (and later Morgul)—who sold his mortal soul to Sauron for a ring of power and the illusion of earthly dominion is meant to suggest to us a grand and ancient archetype for Macbeth's tale of a king possessed of a doomed and blasted soul.

So that none will mistake the comparison, or Tolkien's challenge to Shakespeare, the life of the Witch-king is protected by a prophecy that is almost identical to the final one that safeguards Macbeth. Tolkien's Witch-king "cannot be slain by the hand of man," while the similarly deluded Macbeth "cannot be slain by man of woman born." Again, Tolkien's challenge to Shakespeare is largely about what he considers a fairly limp fulfilment of the prophecy. In terms of convincing plot, one must acknowledge that the Witch-king's death, by a woman disguised as a warrior with a Hobbit as an accomplice, is a much better answer to the fatal riddle than Shakespeare's lawyer's loophole resolution to the riddle that someone born by caesarean section is not strictly speaking "of woman born."

The most important aspect of all this literary fencing is not really whether Tolkien actually succeeded in his challenge to Shakespeare, or anyone else. Nor does it particularly matter whether or not readers of *The Lord of the Rings* register the allusion. The result was that Tolkien's mind was provoked into creating original characters and events that resonate with a depth and power that they inherit from their source.

SHELOB The "last child" of the gargantuan Ungoliant the Mother of All Spiders of the First Age, in *The Lord of the Rings*. In the Second and Third Age, Shelob the Great and her offspring—"lesser broods, bastards of [her] miserable mates"—lived in the mountains of Mordor and forest of the Mirkwood. Ungoliant and Shelob's portrayals as monsters capable of paralyzing and killing their prey, and as females who in the act of mating cannibalize their male partners, have some valid basis in zoology. This is

Oromë Hunts the Monsters of Morgoth. The foul brood of Ungoliant are largely destroyed in the First Age, but Shelob survives almost until the end of the Third.

largely due to the appropriately named real world "Black-Widow" spiders, which have toxic venom that paralyzes or kills its prey, and the females which have the deeply unpleasant habit of occasionally devouring their much smaller male partners while in the act of mating.

Although Shelob (an Old English construct meaning "She-Spider") did not reach the majestic proportions of Ungoliant—referred to by Tolkien as "the primeval devourer of light"—she was the greatest and largest Spider of the Second and Third Age. In what could be described in biological terms as successive degeneration, Shelob was about as big as a plowhorse, while her offspring the Spiders of the Mirkwood in *The Hobbit* were "very much smaller and less intelligent."

Shelob was the guardian of Cirith Ungol (Elvish for "Spider Pass") where she occupied a complex of tunnels and fed off anyone of any race who attempted to enter Mordor by that route through Ephel Dúath (the Shadowy Mountains). In the year 3000 TA Shelob captured Gollum, but released him so he might bring her more victims. Nearly two decades later, in the middle of the War of the Ring, Gollum fulfilled his promise by leading Frodo Baggins and Samwise Gamgee to her lair.

The Hobbits' descent into Shelob's Lair has been described as comparable to the descent into the Underworld in Virgil's *Aeneid*. Gollum serves as Frodo and Sam's guide, just as the Sibyl serves as Aeneas' guide. Sam uses the Phial of Galdriel to overcome Shelob and escape, while a golden bough and a drugged cake are used to bypass Charon the Ferryman and Cerberus the three-headed Hell Hound. Tales of descent into the underworld are most often attempts by heroes to return loved ones to the world of the living. Aeneas cannot bring his father back to life, but Sam succeeds in reviving Frodo after Shelob's poison places him in a state resembling death.

Just as Ungoliant was the counterpart of Morgoth the Dark Lord, so Shelob was the counterpart of Sauron the Dark Lord. Neither were true spiders, but evil entities in spider form that are something akin to the medieval portrayal of the deadly sins of lust, envy, sloth, wrath, pride, gluttony, and greed. These monsters served in both Dark Lord's plans up to a point. However, ultimately, neither accepted a master. Ungoliant turned upon Morgoth, while Shelob proved equally ungovernable and served "none but herself."

Tolkien's arachnophobic characterization of his Great Spiders is consistent with the portrayal of India's eight-limbed Kali the Black One, the "Destroyer of the World," who dances on the slaughtered body of her lover. However, this is not in keeping with most of the world's mythologies. Despite the formidable reputation of the Black Widow, the fact remains that only thirty out of the forty-three thousand spider species in existence are capable of seriously harming humans.

In the ancient Mediterranean world, from Egypt to Babylon, Greece, and Rome, tales equate the spider with spinning and weaving, skills essential to all civilizations. Ultimately, spiders are personified as the Fates who spin the destinies of men and gods, the direct antithesis of Ungoliant and Shelob. In these cultures spiders are deities of creation. In Africa and the West Indies we have widespread variations on Anansi, the Ashanti spider god who is the creator god and a trickster in many folk tales. He is also transformed into Aunt Nancy in many children's "spider tales," which are essentially allegorical stories and moral lessons. The Hopi and Navaho have creation myths of the wise Spider Mother or Grandmother who weaves the world into existence. Other myths among North and South American (and some Oceanic) Indigenous peoples portray the spider god as a trickster and creator who weaves constellations of stars or the entire universe into existence.

SHIRE, THE
See: SHIRES

SHIRES
First created by the Anglo-Saxons in reference to counties in central and southern England under the authority of the "shire reeve" or sheriff. In modern times, the shires are rural or outlying counties not under the authority of a metropolitan council. Commonly, even today, the shires of the rural Midlands are considered strongholds of traditional rural culture. Tolkien's idealized childhood memories of the shires of the rural West Midlands inspired his fictional Hobbit

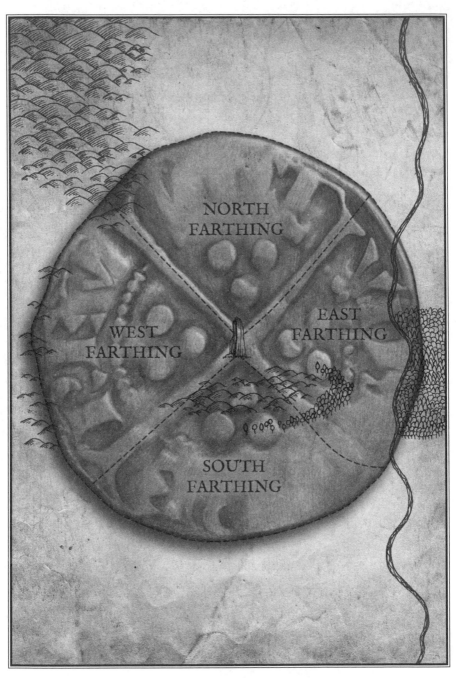

Map of the Shire

homeland of "the Shire" in *The Hobbit* and *The Lord of the Rings*. The Shire was Tolkien's romanticized analogy for the rural and preindustrial English shires of his late Victorian childhood. His Hobbits were styled on the yeomen of England's "green and pleasant land," and were to the tilled fields and rolling farmlands what Dwarves were to the mountains or the Elves to the forests: the genies, or guardian spirits, of the place. "The Shire is based on rural England and not any other country in the world," Tolkien once wrote. It was also, he added, "a parody of rural England, in much the same sense as are its inhabitants: they go together and are meant to. After all, the book is English, and by an Englishman." At the same time, there is a serious intent on Tolkien's part to create in his Hobbit homeland a place that embodies the enduring spirit of that ideal "little England" characterized by the lands and villages of the English shires.

The Shire is shaped like a child's wobbly drawing of the large front wheel of an old-fashioned penny-farthing bicycle and has a diameter measurement roughly equal to 40 or 50 leagues (120 to 150 miles). The four great spokes of the wheel radiate out from the hob and divide the Shire into four regions known as the Four Farthings. This is logical enough as a farthing comes from the Old English *feorthing*, meaning fourth or a fourth part. This is because the silver penny was marked with a cross on the reverse and each of these quarters was a farthing. The central hob of the Shire is marked geographically with a large standing stone, known as the Three-Farthing Stone.

SIDHE   The remnant of the once mighty prehuman race of Irish immortals known as the Tuatha Dé Danann or the "People of the Goddess Danu." The Sidhe (pronounced "Shee") or the Aes Sidhe, meaning "People of the Hills," were believed to be those immortals who withdrew from the mortal realm and most often hid themselves away inside "hollow hills" and ancient burial mounds. However, other Sidhe lived hidden away and trapped in time in enchanted woodlands and kingdoms beneath lakes and in rivers grottos.

Tolkien's theme of the dwindling power of the immortal Elves upon the mortal lands of Middle-earth has much in common with the Aes Sidhe "People of the Hills." With Tolkien's Elves, we have kingdoms and cities that are comparable to many of those in the legends of the Sidhe hidden away in all manner of places.

In the First Age the Sindar, Elves were found in the enchanted forest of Doriath and the glittering caverns of Menegroth. Noldor refuges were also hidden in the secret mountain passes of Gondolin, in precarious river gorges of Nargothrond, in the havens of Brithombar and Eglarest, and in the distant island refuge of Balar. The Second and Third Ages saw the establishment of the hidden realms of Lindon and the Grey Havens, the deep valley refuge of Imladris, and the enchanted golden forest of Lothlórien.

SIGURD

The hero of the Norse epic, the *Völsunga Saga*. The story of Sigurd the Völsung, the slayer of Fáfnir, the "Prince of All Dragons," was one of Tolkien's primary sources of inspiration for his Túrin Turambar, the slayer of Glaurung, the Father of Dragons in *The Silmarillion*.

Both dragon-slayers lay claim to broken dynastic swords that were reforged. Túrin's sword was given the name Gurthang, meaning "iron of death," while Sigurd's was Gram, meaning "wrath." But, even so armed, neither of these heroes understood that the Great Worms could not be slain by strength of arms alone. Courage and cunning were also talents required of dragon-slayers. Túrin chose to hide himself in a deep ravine at a river crossing, and when Glaurung attempted to cross over the gap, he drove his sword Gurthang upward and into the massive monster's underbelly. Sigurd the Völsung employed a similar tactic and hid himself in a covered trench dug into the narrow trail that the beast took each day to drink from a forest pool. So, when Fáfnir's great body passed over the trench, the Völsung hero drove his sword, Gram, up into the dragon's exposed belly.

SILMARILS

Three shining jewels forged from silima, a crystalline substance that captured and held the pure and sacred light of the two trees of Valinor. After the destruction of the trees, the struggle over the possession of the Silmarils or *Silmarilli* (meaning "radiance of pure light") resulted in the centuries-long war of the jewels, the central focus of Tolkien's *The Silmarillion*. As he once acknowledged, the Finnish national epic, known as the *Kalevala*, originally inspired *The Silmarillion*. In reference to *The*

Silmarillion, Tolkien wrote in a letter to W. H. Auden: "the beginning of the legendarium . . . Was in an attempt to reorganize some of the *Kalevala* . . . Into a form of my own." And just as the Silmarils were the central focus of *The Silmarillion,* the central focus of the *Kalevala* was the pursuit of a mysterious artifact called the Sampo.

The Silmarils were gems forged by Fëanor (meaning "spirit of fire"), the eldest son of Finwë the High King of the Noldor Elves of Eldamar. Fëanor was the greatest smith of the Noldor and the greatest of all the Eldar in gifts of the mind, body, and spirit. To some degree, Fëanor was comparable to the supernatural smith Ilmarinen in the *Kalevala.* Ilmarinen forged the Sampo, an artifact believed to be a kind of magic mill that grinds out salt, grain, and gold, bringing great wealth and good fortune to its possessor. The Sampo and the Silmarils were, in many respects akin, to the Greek Cornucopia; the medieval Holy Grail; Odin's ring, Draupnir; the Norse mill, Grotti; and numerous other mysterious objects of quests in the mythologies of Japan, India, and China.

Fëanor's Silmarils were the most beautiful and holy gems upon Arda, but so coveted they were first hidden away, and then stolen, and finally became the objects of a doomed quest to retrieve them. In that doomed pursuit of the gems into Beleriand, Fëanor was slain (and after six centuries of warfare) and the gemstones were lost: one deep in the seas; another in the bowels of the earth; and one in the upper air above the world. The fate of the Sampo was similar to that of the Silmarils. Once created, the Sampo was first locked away in an underground vault, then stolen, and finally became the object of a doomed quest to retrieve it. In the end, the Sampo was smashed and lost in the depths of the sea.

Yet, ultimately, Tolkien's use of these "Primeval Jewels" is symbolically ambivalent, as it is the desire for the possession of the gems that results in disaster, while the Silmarils themselves remain symbols of ultimate good, the last remnant of the pure and holy light of the Trees of the Valar. And indeed, the one Silmaril carried aloft into the sky in Middle-earth by Eärendil the Mariner became—in Tolkien's cosmology—the origin of the morning and evening "star" we know as the planet Venus.

SINDAR A kind of twilight race of Grey Elves in Beleriand in the northwest of Middle-earth. J. R. R. Tolkien's creation of races and realms of the Elves were to some degree guided by the Norse cosmology with its Light-Elves dwelling in Alfheim and the Dark-Elves dwelling in Svartalfheim. For in the far west of Tolkien's world, we have Caliquendi or Elves of Light of Eldamar; while in the east, we have the Moriquendi or Elves of Darkness of Middle-earth. In the Sindar "Grey People" or "Elves of the Twilight" in Beleriand, we have the sad history of a new category of Tolkien's own invention geographically located between the Light-Elves of the west and Dark-Elves of the east.

In the beginning, the first lord of the Teleri Elves rested with his people in their westward migration in the land of Beleriand. There the Teleri lord Elwë abandoned the Great Journey, for in Beleriand's great forest of Doriath, he fell under the spell of Melian the Maia, a beautiful and powerful spirit who once tended the flowering trees of the Lórien (meaning "dreamland") in Valinor.

In Tolkien's earliest drafts of *The Silmarillion*, his original name for Beleriand was Broceliand. This was a name was obviously inspired by Celtic and Arthurian romances relating to Brocéliande in a mythical (and actual) forest in Brittany. Tolkien's Beleriand—and his kingdom of Doriath in particular—was to a considerable degree modeled on Brocéliande. This was a vast forest realm with magical fountains, glittering grottoes, and hidden palaces, all protected by the powerful spell of an enchantress.

After years of enchantment, Elwë (the tallest of all the Elves) emerged from the forest of Doriath with silver hair and eyes that shone like stars. By the time of his reappearance, the greater part of the Teleri had departed for Eldamar. Those who remained behind and loyal to Elwë, now called Thingol or "Greymantle," were known as the Sindar, or "Grey Elves." And so, with King Thingol and his queen, Melian the Maia, the Grey Elves came to inhabit the enchanted forest kingdom of Doriath and the glittering mansions of the "Thousand Caves" of Menegroth.

The tales of the enchantments of Brocéliande were often somewhat less benign in nature. The best known of its enchantresses were Vivien, the Lady of the Lake, and King Arthur's sister, Morgan Le Faye. Both of these emerged from Celtic elements within the body of Arthurian romance.

The most famous single legend was that of Vivien, who came upon Merlin asleep beneath a thorn tree. There the enchantress ensorcelled the magician in a "tower of air" from which he could never emerge. It was a spell that rendered him invisible, but to this day, it is claimed, the faint and distant voice of the magician may be heard in that forest bewailing his fate.

King Thingol ruled as High King of the Elves of Beleriand through thousands of years in the Ages of Stars. There was peace and prosperity throughout the land, and in time Melian gave birth to the only child of Eldar and Maia blood, the incomparably beautiful Princess Lúthien. And all seemed safe within their realm, even during times of strife, as the Forest of Doriath was protected the "Girdle of Melian," a spell that prevented all from entering, save those given leave by King Thingol. This was a theme common in legends and fairy tales about enchanted forests ensorcelling hidden kingdoms and sleeping beauties in many mythologies throughout the world.

SINDARIN
The language of the Sindar Grey Elves, which became the common tongue of the Elves in the western lands of Middle-earth. The degree to which Tolkien's Elves were inspired by Celtic models is most obviously demonstrated by looking at his invented language of Sindarin. Tolkien himself noted that Sindar names for persons, places, and things were "mainly deliberately modeled on those of Welsh (closely similar but not identical)." Structurally and phonetically, there are extremely strong links between the two languages. A few words are identical: *mal* means "gold" in both the Welsh and Sindar tongues. Others are close: *du* means "black" in Welsh and "shadow" in Sindarin; *cal an* means "first day" in Welsh and "daylight" in Sindarin; *ost* means "host" in Welsh and "town" in Sindarin; *sam* in Welsh means a stone "causeway" and in Sindarin means a "stone" in a ford. There are many others close in spelling and/or meaning: "fortress" is *cacr* in Welsh and *caras* in Sindarin; *drud* in Welsh means "fierce" while *dru* in Sindarin means "wild"; *dagr* in Welsh means "dagger" while *dagor* in Sindarin means "battle." Others are the same words with different meanings: *adan* is "birds" in Welsh and "man" in Sindarin; *ucu* is "heaven" in Welsh

and "water" in Sindarin; *nar* is "lord" in Welsh and "sun" in Sindarin. And finally, here are some others that are strangely connected: *iar* in Sindarin means "old," while the Welsh *iar* means "hen." However, the Welsh word *hen* actually means "old." Coincidentally, a few of Tolkien's characters take their names directly from Welsh words. For example, Morweri means "maid," Bard means "poet," and Barahir means "longbeard."

See also: W E L S H

SLEEPING BEAUTY
A fairy tale of the Brothers Grimm briefly alluded to in the wake of Tolkien's Battle of Pelennor Fields, when the Witch-king of Morgal is slain by Éowyn the Shield Maiden of Rohan. Éowyn belongs to an ancient tradition of warrior women in the world of epic romance and saga. In the Norse *Völsunga Saga* and the German *Nibelungenlied*, we have comparable heroines in the twin figures of Brynhild and Brunhild. In the *Völsunga Saga*, Brynhild is a Valkyrie, a beautiful battle maiden who defied Odin, who subsequently pierced her with a sleep-thorn and imprisoned her in a ring of fire. Like Sleeping Beauty, a warrior awakens Brynhild from sleep, in this case, Sigurd the Dragon-slayer, with whom she falls in love. In the *Nibelungenlied*, Brunhild ("armored warrior maid") is the warrior-queen of Iceland, who falls for the Sigurd's medieval German equivalent, Siegfried. Both Brynhild and Brunhild are based on the historic and notorious Visigoth Queen Brunhilda. Just as there are elements in Brynhild/Brunhild to be found in Éowyn, so there are elements in Sigurd/Siegfried to be discovered in Aragorn. Likewise there is Brynhild/Brunhild's hopeless love for Sigurd/Siegfried, comparable to Éowyn's unrequited love for Aragorn. Siegfried, for example, is betrothed to another queen, Kriemheld, in the same way that Aragorn is betrothed to Arwen Evenstar. And as the warrior-queen Brunhild is transformed by marriage into the wife of King Gunnar, so too is Éowyn the Shield Maiden, through her marriage to Faramir, the future Steward of Gondor.

SMAUG THE DRAGON Inspired by the nameless dragon portrayed in the Anglo-Saxon epic poem *Beowulf*. Tolkien was one who searched for "dragons, real dragons, essential both to the machinery and the ideas of a poem or tale." He found elements of his Dragons in Germanic literature and mythology, but also very specifically in *Beowulf*, a poem that provided both the monster and much of the plot outline for his fairy-tale novel, *The Hobbit*.

"A dragon is no idle fancy," Tolkien once observed. "Whatever may be his origins, in fact or invention, the dragon in legend is a potent creation of men's imagination, richer in significance than his barrow is in gold." In the author's view this truly wonderful monster has such universal appeal that every man in every age may find him or her self, "caught by the fascination of the worm."

The Hobbit takes its basic plotline from *Beowulf* and his fatal encounter with a dragon. In that ancient poem, a thief enters the dragon's lair and steals a gold cup. In Tolkien's tale the thief is the Hobbit, Bilbo Baggins. And in both tales, the theft of a gold cup awakens a sleeping dragon that emerges from its lair to lay waste to a nearby kingdom. *The Hobbit* is essentially the *Beowulf* dragon story told from the thief's point of view. There is, however, one problem with *Beowulf*'s dragon. It is more the terrifying embodiment of an evil curse than an individual villain that happens to be a dragon.

All characters in a really good fairy-tale adventure must offer the reader something of a close-up, intimate feeling. This is true of all of an adventure's characters, even—or especially—the bad ones. The trouble with the *Beowulf* dragon is that the closer you come, the more it recedes. You cannot gain a hold on it. In fact, the monster is not even given a name. For Tolkien, this was a cardinal sin. Within the spheres of Middle-earth, names are the primary factors in all life forms and his chief motivation in the creation of all things. It may be suggested that Tolkien began to feel like the maiden in *Rumpelstiltskin* whose fate depended on discovering the creature's true name. With this end in mind, and a philological search through a series of Old English and prehistoric German words he arrived at the name "Smaug."

So Tolkien decided "Smaug the Golden," "Smaug the Magnificent," and "Lord Smaug the Impenetrable" would be the names of the greatest Dragon of the Third Age. Not simply a Cold-drake like those haunting the Dwarf

Smaug Destroys Esgaroth

mansions of the Grey Mountains, Smaug was to be a full-fledged golden-red Fire-drake.

Smaug had vast wings like a bat and a coat of impenetrable iron scales. Far better than a large but nameless lizard like *Beowulf*'s monster. The name "Smaug the Greatest of Calamities" carried the collective meaning of its composite parts in Old English: penetrating, inquiring, burrowing, worming into, and creeping through. These were all useful clues to a really slippery, intelligent, and nasty villain. Then, too, came an appropriate—if accidental—pun on "smog," which insinuates its way through a distinctive whiff of brimstone.

To all the sinister qualities gained by way of the naming of Smaug, Tolkien added a multitude of aspects in legendary dragons dating back to the ancient Greek Python of Delphi as a fierce guardian of treasure: a great serpent; a keeper of arcane knowledge; a monster with an inquiring mind, a terrifying glance, and a mesmerizing voice. It is certain that from this hoard of dragon lore, Smaug the Worm of Dread inherited its laser eyes, brilliant intellect, mesmerizing spells, and a few of its other more terrifying qualities.

And yet, as Tolkien famously wrote in his lecture and essay "On Fairy-Stories": "The dragon had the trade-mark of Faerie written plain upon him." This is perhaps why his dragons either appear in the ancient mythic world of Elves in *The Silmarillion* or the children's fairy-tale world of Hobbits in *The Hobbit,* but not in the epic high romance world of mortal Men in *The Lord of the Rings.*
See also: D R A G O N S

SMÉAGOL
The Westron translation of the original Hobbitish name *Trahald* for the cannibalistic ogre that became known as Gollum. Bilbo Baggins first encountered this repellent creature in the caverns beneath Goblin Town in *The Hobbit*. In the beginning, Sméagol was a Hobbit and his name largely defined his nature, as it means "burrowing, worming in." For even then, Sméagol was possessed by a restless and inquiring nature. He was always searching, and digging among the roots of things, burrowing, but also twisting and turning, this way and that. While fishing and exploring

Sméagol

Stoorish Hobbit river lands east of the Misty Mountains, Sméagol's cousin, Déagol (meaning "secret") discovered a gold ring lost on the river bottom.

Nonetheless, as the history of the One Ring is revealed, we eventually learn that Sméagol was immediately corrupted by its power. He murdered his cousin and took possession of the One Ring. Or, to be more accurate, the One Ring took possession of Sméagol and so began the transformation of Sméagol the Hobbit into Gollum the cannibalistic ogre. The evil power of the One Ring lengthened Sméagol's cursed life for centuries, yet it warped and corrupted him beyond recognition. Thereafter he was called Gollum because of the nasty guttural sounds he made when he spoke. Gollum became a murderous ghoul and cannibal, shunning light and taking grim solace in dark caverns and dank pools.

In *The Hobbit,* Gollum was merely one of a number Bilbo Baggins' obstacles in his quest to reach the Lonely Mountain of Erebor. The discovery and acquisition of a magic ring was a simple plot device to give the Hobbit hero enhanced powers comparable to those described in Plato's ancient Greek legend of the Gyges ring, a similar "ring of invisibility" that proved to be essential to the plot of that tragic tale. However, the true significance and history of the One Ring before he began work years later on *The Lord of the Rings* was no more apparent to the author at the time than it was to Bilbo Baggins or Gollum.

The evolution of the character of Sméagol to that of Gollum draws on a considerable body of mythology related to Ring Legends. In the *Völsunga Saga,* the most famous ring legend in Norse mythology, we have Fáfnir the son of the Dwarf King Hreidmar who murders his own father in his desire to possess a cursed ring and its treasure. This is comparable to Sméagol's murder of his cousin Déagol in his own desire to possess the One Ring. Retreating like Sméagol to a mountain cave, Fáfnir broods over his ring and eventually transforms into a monstrous dragon. Similarly Sméagol, who, through the power of the One Ring, extends his life over the centuries, transforms into a ghoul twisted in mind and body into the cannibalistic Gollum brooding over his "precious" ring. The Icelandic narrative poem *Völundarkviða* reveals a similar ghoul in Sote the Outlaw. Sote steals a cursed ring but so fears it may be taken from him that he has himself buried alive with it, and sleeplessly guards it with his weapons drawn.

In Sméagol–Gollum we have a classic case of a split personality, as first portrayed in Robert Louis Stevenson's *The Strange Case of Dr. Jekyll and Mr. Hyde* or in Charles Dickens' *The Mystery of Edwin Drood*. In Tolkien's case, it is not Jekyll and Hyde, but Sméagol and Gollum. When Sméagol is in control, he had pale eyes and referred to himself as "I." Gollum, however, was a green-eyed creature that called himself "we" because the Gollum and the Ring spoke collectively together. Just as in Stevenson's tale, it is this evil aspect of his being that was in perpetual conflict with that of the good. And just as in Stevenson's tale, the conflict leads to destruction of both Sméagol and Gollum.

SNOW WHITE A fairy tale first published in 1812 in the first volume of the Brothers Grimm's *Grimms' Fairy Tales*. It has become one of the most famous and best-loved collection of fairy tales throughout the world and, if we look to Tolkien's Middle-earth, we will discover its themes appearing in his tales. Indeed, many of Tolkien's heroic tales are presented as the histories of "true myths," which he believed had been reduced to the most basic and obvious of fairy tales in our world. He particularly liked to demonstrate to his readers how the writers of fairy tales often got their stories wrong. Certainly, in the enchanted forest of Lothlórien there contains virtually every element of the story of Snow White, including Arwen Evenstar, the beautiful dark-haired princess and Galadriel, the queen with the magic mirror. Arwen also had her prince charming, Aragorn, her long-parted lover whom she meets again in Lothlórien. Except, as Tolkien suggests, the fairy-tale version of Snow White got it all wrong. Queen Galadriel is Arwen's guardian and protector (and actually her grandmother), the enchanted forest a place of refuge and healing, and the magic mirror seems to be a combination of oracle and wishing well.

The Elven princess, also known as Arwen Undómiel (meaning "evening maid" or "nightingale") is comparable to Snow White in that both were dark-haired beauties with luminous white skin. He also quite pointedly links Arwen's beauty to that of the Varda Elentári, the Valarian queen of the stars, who is also known by the epithet "Fanuilos" or "Snow White."

Tolkien also makes another obvious nod to the fairy tale in a running debate between Prince Éomer of Rohan and Gimli the Dwarf over the relative beauty of

Arwen of Gondor and Galadriel of Lothlórien. So, Tolkien implies, it is easy to see how some mischievous teller of fairy tales might invent a story of a jealous queen asking her magic mirror, "Who is the fairest of them all?"

SOLOMON'S RING

The most famous ring legend in the Judeo-Christian tradition, wherein Solomon was not only considered a powerful king and wise man, but was also believed to be the most powerful magician of his age. These magician's powers were attributed largely to his possession of a magic ring. The legend of King Solomon's ring is certainly the one tale of the Judeo–Christian tradition that is closest to Tolkien's account of Sauron's use of the One Ring in the construction of his Dark Tower of Mordor.

There can be little doubt that Tolkien was familiar with this ancient biblical tale of a sorcerer-king who, like Sauron, used a magic ring to command all the demons

Dagorlad. A haunting recollection of the trenches of the Battle of the Somme.

of the Earth, and bent them to the purpose of his empire. Just as Solomon uses his magic ring to build his Great Temple on Mount Moriah, so Sauron uses the One Ring to build his great tower in the mountains of Mordor. Of all the biblical ring legends, Solomon's Ring most resembles the One Ring of *The Lord of the Rings.*

Solomon's Ring was a small gold ring marked with the seal of God: the five-pointed star of the pentalpha and the four letters of the name of Yahweh (YHWH). Sauron's Ring was also small and made of gold but was engraved with an evil spell of command: "One Ring to rule them all . . . " written in the Black Speech of the Orcs.

S O M M E

This was the site of the single most disastrous battle in the First World War, resulting in over a million casulties. Tolkien's Battle of Dagorlad was the site of the single most disastrous battle in the War of Sauron and the Last Alliance of Elves and Men. It was a battle authentically informed by the author's own real-life experience in the First World War and specifically as a soldier in the Battle of the Somme.

In that terrible conflict, Tolkien witnessed the total obliteration of the beautiful pastoral French landscape, which became a churned-up, treeless, blood-soaked wasteland filled with unclaimed rotting corpses. It was a futile battle wherein vast armies fought for months. In Tolkien's fictional Battle of Dagorlad (meaning "battle plain"), we can see the effect of Tolkien's real-life experiences with war— this fictional battle fought before the Black Gate of Mordor, wherein: "All living things were divided in that day, and some of every kind, even of beasts and birds." The fictional Dagorlad's terrible slaughter lasted for months. Beautiful, pastoral green fields became bloody treeless landscapes littered with thousands of unclaimed corpses.

S O T E T H E O U T L A W

A pirate in the Norse *Saga of Thorstein* who entered a barrow grave and discovered a treasure chamber filled with drifts of gold and gems. Yet most prized of all among that treasure was a gold ring, which he placed on his finger. And with that act, Sote the Outlaw became wed to darkness. Forever after, fearful other thieves might seize his ring and his treasure, Sote remained within the barrow grave armed with drawn sword and dagger. And there, Sote became the never-sleeping guardian who endlessly stalked the corridors and chambers of the tomb. This is the curse and power of the ring: in possessing the ring, Sote became possessed by it. Instead of simply looting the barrow grave, the Outlaw was condemned to haunt it as a demon and guardian, dwelling forever in darkness.

The legend of Sote the Outlaw has much in common with the story of the ring-obsessed Sméagol–Gollum in *The Hobbit* and *The Lord of the Rings*. And apart from being an example of the overwhelming power of magic rings, in the tale of Sote we see a likely source for the Hobbits' near fatal encounter with Barrow-wights in *The Lord of the Rings*. In Tolkien's novel, it is that peculiar spirit, Tom Bombadil, who effortlessly scatters the bones of the Barrow-wight and rescues the Hobbit adventurers. In the Norse version of the tale, however, the approach is more brutal and less humorous. Unlike the bizarre but wise Tom Bombadil, the Viking hero Thorsten is not immune to the terror and murderous intent of the Barrow-wight. Thorsten knows he must pay a price for his challenge, and there is nothing of Bombadil's comic exorcism in his actions. Thorstein simply depends on his vast strength of body and unquenchable spirit. The Viking descends into the passages beneath the barrow. The wailing screams of the tortured fiend and the bellowing of the warrior are heard. There is the sound of steel striking stone and bone, and the flickering of sorcerous flames can be seen within. Finally, however, Thorsten emerges from the barrow, bloodied and as pale as a ghost, but in his hand is the glint of the gold ring.

SPIDERS
See: SHELOB; UNGOLIANT

STOOR The largest and strongest of three Hobbit breeds and the most like humans. The Stoors were the first Hobbits to live in houses, and they tend to dwell near rivers and marshes. They are also the only Hobbits to use footwear (usually Dwarf boots) and to be capable of growing any kind of beard or facial hair. Stoors also distinguish themselves by being the only breed that is unafraid of water or even considers the idea of boating and swimming. Through their commerce on the river, the Stoors are among the wealthiest of Hobbits.

The name "Stoor" appears to be appropriately derived from the Middle English "stur" and the Old English "stor," meaning hard or strong. It also suggests "store" in the sense of being merchants, but even more in the sense that all Hobbits are hoarders with many storage spaces and rooms in their Hobbit holes or houses. Typical Stoorish names include Banks, Puddifoot, Cotton, and Cotman.

STRONGHOLDS
A fortified place used to defend a strategic site, to launch military campaigns, and, last but not least, as a symbol of power. In history, myth, and fiction, the castle, hill fort, citadel, or walled town is a dramatic manifestation of a ruler's or people's military might. It protects the seat of earthly power, the throne; it contains the symbol of heaven, the chapel; and it threatens its enemies with the symbol of hell, the dungeon. The character of that enclosed world is determined by the master who builds and commands it. It might be a place of peace and safety or a hell on earth. Whether as a place to storm, or a place to defend, the castle is the symbol of strength, spiritual as well as physical.

The castle in all its metaphoric implications was understood by all who lived in the great ages of castles—the medieval world. As Tolkien knew well enough, the oldest surviving morality play in English literature is the *Castle of Perseverance* (c. 15th century). Here, despite a besieging army made up of the Deadly Sins and the Forces of Hell, Mankind is secure. The evil Enemy, for all its might cannot overwhelm the Castle. So long as Mankind stays within it, he is safe, but if he is tempted to go outside, he may face eternal damnation. The meaning of the Castle is direct and unmistakable, and it is an allegory as much psychological as moral.

In the writings of Tolkien we have the most fully realized and extensive invented world of castle-kingdoms and fortified strongholds in modern fantasy fiction. Tolkien's world of Middle-earth was created by an imagination fueled by an extensive knowledge of mythologies and histories of the castle-kingdoms of Europe. Although Tolkien himself denied any allegorical intention in his work, his theme is that most ancient struggle, never to be resolved, between the powers of good and evil. In the wide lands of Middle-earth, the kingdoms of Elves, Dwarves, and Men are at war with the dread forces of Sauron, the Dark Lord of Mordor. The center and source of power in the mountain-ringed land of Mordor is the massive Barad-dûr, the Dark Tower of Sauron. From this tower Sauron commands his legions of Orcs, Uruks, Trolls, and the damned spirits of barbarian men.

Ultimately in the War of the Ring, against this sea of darkness, one stronghold stands fast, the citadel and walled city of Minas Tirith, "The Tower of Guard." It is here, before the seven-ringed walls of the White Tower, that the greatest battle rages and the tide of war finally turns against the Dark Lord. However, it is only when the Dark Tower itself is toppled and entirely obliterated that the War of the Ring would be ended. Only then would the White Tower become the center of a new world of peace and prosperity, a monument to all that is good and great in the world.

See also: MINAS TIRITH

SUTTON HOO   The largest and oldest-surviving Anglo-Saxon burial ground in existence. Covering more than 10 acres, its barrows and tombs had been a burial ground for nearly three millennia. Of the first three barrows opened at that time, the largest contained a ship 90 feet in length. This was longer than any previously known ship of the time. Monumental earthworks, stone circles, and barrow graves were often the focus of folktales and legends relating to the ancestors of the English people. Some of these stories have survived as myths or fairy tales. As the only substantial monuments built by the early Anglo-Saxons, barrow graves were immediately excavated by archeologists in the hope of discovering artifacts of this little-known and long-underestimated culture. Unfortunately, most known barrow graves were pre-Anglo-Saxon in origin, and excavations seldom produced artifacts of great significance. All that changed in the years immediately before the outbreak of the Second World War with the discovery of Sutton Hoo.

At about the time Tolkien was writing the opening chapters of *The Lord of the Rings*, archeologists began excavations in Suffolk in what was the historic equivalent of the fictional Barrow-downs of Middle-earth. It was also the richest treasure trove of Anglo-Saxon culture ever found. The Sutton Hoo revelation of the ancient Germanic world was as important as the discovery of Tutankhamen's tomb had been to our understanding of the ancient Egyptian world.

Tolkien does not appear to have visited Sutton Hoo, but we know he was familiar with many other long-barrow gravesites. One was a particularly impressive monument about 20 miles from Oxford, which Tolkien was known to have visited. This was locally known as Wayland's Smithy. Wayland was manifest in Tolkien's world in the figure of Telchar the Smith, who forged the blade Narsil. Both Wayland and Telchar were master swordsmiths who forged weapons with charmed blades, such as those discovered by the Hobbits in the Barrow-downs.

SVINFYLKING
Also "swine array." *Svinfylking* was a wedge-shaped shield-wall formation employed by the Vikings as a shock troop tactic by infantry carrying heavy armaments. This was the formation and tactic Tolkien had Thorin Oakenshield employ at a pivotal moment in the Battle of Five Armies in *The Hobbit*. Here Tolkien was borrowing from real-world military history, as shield walls were an effective infantry strategy in warfare for thousands of years. The *svinfylking* was a high-risk tactic used by Norsemen to break though enemy lines and create panic among the closed ranks of an army with superior numbers. It could be extremely effective, but it entirely depended on the initial monumental shock. If this flying wedge did not immediately break through enemy lines, the formation would soon collapse. Like many shield-wall tactics, it could often be outflanked and entirely encircled. And, indeed, this would likely have been the fate of Thorin Oakenshield and his warriors had it not been for the sudden unexpected appearance of Beorn the berserker skin-changer in the form of a gigantic black bear.

The Battle of Five Armies. During the culminating battle of *The Hobbit*, the Dwarves use a version of the *svinfylking*, a shield-wall attributed to the god Odin, and used by the Vikings.

Thorin

TANIQUETIL
The highest mountain in Valinor and home to the thrones of Manwë Súlimo, king of the Valar, and of his spouse, Varda Elentári, queen of the Stars. This holy mountain, whose name means "snow-high-peak," is also known as Amon Uilos ("white mountain") and Oiolossë ("everlasting snow").

Sacred mountains like Taniquetil can be found in real-world mythologies around the globe, from Mount Sinai in Egypt, where Moses received the Ten Commandments from the Hebrew God, to Mount Kailash in the East, considered the home of the Hindu gods Shiva and his spouse Parvati. Taniquetil, however, has a fairly direct counterpart in Greek mythology in the snow-capped Mount Olympus, where Zeus, king of the gods, was enthroned alongside his wife, Hera. Olympus is both a real mountain and a mythological place. Measuring 10,000 feet, it was the highest mountain in the ancient Greek world: Taniquetil is the tallest mountain in all of Arda, though Tolkien never tells us exactly how tall.

TELCHAR
A Dwarf of Nogrod in the Blue Mountains of Beleriand during the First Age and one of the greatest smiths of Middle-earth, famous for the forging of armor. Wayland, the greatest smith in Anglo-Saxon mythology who was similarly famous for forging the weapons and armor of heroes, probably in part inspired Tolkien's creation of Telchar.

Among Telchar's many creations are: Angrist ("the iron cleaver"), which Beren uses to cut the Silmaril from the iron crown of Morgoth; the Dragon-helm of Dor-lómin, worn by Túrin Turambar the Dragon-slayer; and Narsil, "the red and white flame," dynastic sword of the Dúnedain. Among Wayland's many works are Gram ("wrath"), the sword of Sigurd the Dragon-slayer, and the shirt of mail worn by Beowulf.

Coincidentally or not, Telchar's name also recalls the Telchines of Greek mythology, who were divine metalworkers associated with the island of Rhodes.

TELERI The Third Kindred of the Eldar to make the Great Journey from Middle-earth to Eldamar in the Undying Lands. For various reasons, large numbers of the Teleri do not reach Eldamar, but turn aside from the journey, forming subgroups, such as the Sindar (Grey Elves) and Laiquendi (Green Elves). Teleri of all kinds have a particular affinity with water and song. In the Bay of Eldamar the Teleri live on Tol Eressëa, one of whose port-cities, Avallónë, cannot but recall—as Tolkien surely knew—Avalon, the island-paradise of Arthurian legend.

TEMPLE OF MORGOTH A structure in Armenelos, the capital of Númenor, constructed late in the Second Age after Sauron the Dark Lord corrupted King Ar-Pharazôn and turned his people to the worship of darkness and the practice of human sacrifice. The temple was 500 feet in diameter and 500 feet tall, with walls 50 feet thick, and was "crowned with a mighty dome."

In one of his more obscure early works, the abandoned novel *The Notion Club Papers*, Tolkien has a rather sinister description of Oxford's Neoclassical-style Radcliffe Camera (completed 1749) that suggests it was the architectural model for his satanic Temple of Morgoth in the *Akallabêth*. Although constructed on a much smaller scale, the circular and domed Radcliffe Camera is quite similar in structure to the fictional temple. The Radcliffe Camera is the most distinctive of Oxford's buildings and probably the most frequently photographed.

Just why Tolkien might have chosen this architectural gem as the model for the Temple is something of a mystery. A possible explanation might be that Radcliffe Camera's Neoclassical architectural style was intimately linked with English Freemasonry. As a devout Catholic, Tolkien would certainly have known that for three centuries papal edicts have not only banned the faithful from belonging to the Freemasons, but have not infrequently condemned Freemasonry as a cult with links to Satanism. While it is unlikely that Tolkien would have subscribed to such a view, it is quite possible that he may have indulged in a private joke by modeling

Thangail

Númenor's satanic temple on a building constructed in an architectural style championed by the Freemasons.

In *The Silmarillion*, the Temple of Morgoth, along with the continent and population of Númenor, was destroyed and sunk into the Western Sea in the year 3319 SA.

THANGAIL
Sindarin word for "shield fence" and a defensive military formation consisting of a double rank of heavily armed knights, used in situations when soldiers are heavily outnumbered in close-up hand-to-hand combat. The name suggests that it was originally used by the Elves, though its only recorded use in the annals of Middle-earth is at the disastrous Battle of Gladden Fields, where it is a last brave but sadly unsuccessful strategy employed by the hopelessly outnumbered Númenórean troops of Isildur.

Here Tolkien was drawing on real-world military history, as shield walls have been used as an infantry strategy in warfare for thousands of years. However, the major weakness of the conventional shield wall is that it can be outflanked. This is the case in the wedge-shaped shield wall tactic used by Thorin Oakenshield at the Battle of the Five Armies (a tactic known to Norse warriors as the *svinfylking*, or "swine array"). Tolkien's *thangail* attempts to address this problem in that it is flexible enough to curve around on itself and form an unbroken circle of shields and spears, thus countering any attempt by the enemy to outflank the defenders. Roman legions had a somewhat similar closed-rank defensive formation known as the *testudo* (or "tortoise)" formation, akin to a turtle shell of shields on all sides and above.

THÉODEN
The seventeenth king of Rohan and son of Thengel, also known as the King of the Golden Hall. His name is Anglo-Saxon for "lord" or "king," and is related to the Old Norse title for "leader of the

Théoden. King of the Golden Hall.

people" or "king." In Tolkien's invented language of Rohirric, his name is Tûrac, which once again carries the meaning of "king."

Kingship is important in Middle-earth and seems to be considered part of the natural political order (there are no republics in Middle-earth). Kings are not like ordinary men and have a quasi-divine quality, as we see especially in the hallowed descent of Aragorn, destined by long lineage to ascend to the throne of Gondor. This is an old tradition in English thought, and Tolkien was a thorough royalist in his sympathies. As William Shakespeare wrote in *Hamlet* (approximately 1599), "divinity doth hedge a king." In Tolkien's world, even when a king goes utterly bad or evil, as with the Witch-king of Angmar, he retains his kingly quality and powers of leadership.

Although a king may become old and weak, like Théoden, his royal gift remains, and, as Tolkien reveals, he can shake off his enfeeblement and resume strength and command. Readers of George MacDonald's classic children's fantasy novel *The Princess and Curdie* (1883) will see a certain debt to the story there of an old king, long kept in a sort of stupor by his wicked servants. With Gandalf's aid, the old king's powers are revived, and he once again becomes "Tûrac Ednew," or "Théoden the Renewed," lord of the Éothéod.

THEODORIC I, KING OF THE VISIGOTHS (c. AD 390–451) The historic

figure in the Battle of the Catalaunian Fields (AD 451) whose life history is recorded in the *Getica*, the sixth-century Latin history of the Goths written by Jordanes. Theodoric's actions during that critical battle against the invading forces of Attila the Hun not only inspired Tolkien's account of the Battle of the Field of Celebrant led by Eorl, the first king of Rohan, but also the cavalry charge in the Battle of Pelennor Fields led by Théoden, the seventeenth king of Rohan, a thousand years later. Not only are the kings' names, Théoden and Theodoric, similar (they both carry the meaning "people-ruler" or "king") but also their victories in these critical battles came at the cost of their own lives, with both kings being crushed beneath their fallen steeds.

THESEUS
Greek hero and slayer of the Minotaur, elements of whose story resonate with that of Aragorn in *The Lord of the Rings*. As a badge of his kingship (he is the rightful heir of Athens), Theseus must retrieve his father's sword from beneath a huge rock. This motif calls to mind not only Arthur and the "Sword in the Stone," but the gifting of Andúril (the reforged Narsil) to Aragorn. The key parallel between the two heroes, however, lies in the motif of the black sails.

See also: ATHENS; BLACK SAILS

THINGOL
Name taken by the Telerin Elwë, as the silver-haired king of the Sindarin, or Grey Elves, and founder of the forest kingdom of Doriath, where he rules alongside his wife, the Maia Melian. In his own right and as the father of Lúthien, he is a key figure in the tales of Beleriand in the First Age.

Some of the events in his history echo those in myths and legends. His enchantment and disappearance after he meets Melian in the forest of Nan Elmoth recalls the enchantment and imprisonment of Merlin by Vivien in Arthurian legend. There is an important distinction, however. In Tolkien's works the enchantment arises out of mutual love—almost like *a coup de foudre*—while Vivien, in most versions at least, acts out of hatred.

Likewise, Thingol's refusal to give Lúthien in marriage to Beren, unless the latter succeeds in what seem the impossible task of retrieving a Silmaril from the iron crown of Morgoth, echoes any number of myths and fairy tales in which a jealous or fearful father prevents his daughter from marrying. We find the motif, for example, in the medieval Welsh legend *Culhwch and Olwen,* and in Greek mythology in the story of Pelops and Hippodameia, whose father, Oenomaus, will only allow a suitor to marry his daughter if he can beat him in a (rigged) chariot race.

Thingol's death at the hands of the Dwarves of Nogrod, in a conflict over a beautiful necklace, returns us to the brutal world of Norse mythology.

Tirion. The first and greatest city in Eldamar. "Tirion" is Elvish for "watch tower."

THORIN OAKENSHIELD

Son of Thráin, son of Thrór, and Dwarf King in the Blue Mountains in exile. Tolkien chose his name, Thorin, from the list of Dwarf names found in the twelfth-century *Dvergatal* or "Dwarf's Roll," in the *Prose Edda*. Appropriately enough for this daring and enterprising Dwarf, it means "bold." However, Tolkien also gave him yet another Dwarf name drawn from the Dwarf's Roll, *Eikinskjaldi*, meaning "he of the Oakenshield." This was a name Tolkien viewed as a kind of riddle, and provoked the author into inventing a complex piece of background history for his Dwarf hero of *The Hobbit*. Tolkien explains that, during a battle in the Goblin Wars, Thorin broke his sword but fought on by picking up an oak bough, which he used as both a club and a shield.

THREE-FARTHING STONE

A stone beside the East Road, roughly in the center of the Shire, marking the point where the Eastfarthing, Westfarthing, and Southfarthing meet. It was very probably inspired by the Four Shire Stone, a monument where four historic English counties and Tolkien's "homelands," so to speak—Warwickshire, Oxfordshire, Gloucestershire, and Worcestershire—once met.

THURINGWETHIL

See: VAMPIRES

TILION

The Maia spirit who guides the moon through the night skies of Arda. Once, Tilion was a hunter in the company of Oromë, the Huntsman of the Valar, but was chosen to be the guardian of the last flower of the Silver Tree of the Light, Telperion, after it was placed in a silver vessel and raised into the night sky.

Tilion shares this role as protector of the moon with the Norse god Mani (both Tolkien's and Norse mythology reverse the more common gender roles of a male sun and a female moon deity). Both Mani and Tilion later became the

Thrush. The ancient breed of Thrush that lived in Erebor had an alliance with the Men and Dwarves. One Thrush became famous as Thorin Oakenshield's messenger.

Treebeard

source of the folklore tradition of the "Old Man in the Moon," a figure about whom Bilbo composes a humorous song, performed by Frodo at the Prancing Pony Inn, in Bree.

In Tilion's role as a hunter armed with a silver bow, he recalls the Greek goddess Artemis (the Roman Diana), likewise associated with both hunting and the moon.

TITANOMACHY

In Greek mythology the primordial struggle for supremacy between the Olympian gods (representing order and civilization) and the monstrous Titans (representing chaos and barbarism). The story is told in Hesiod's *Theogony* as well as, probably, in a lost epic of the seventh century, the *Titanomachia*. Like the Gigantomachy, a myth with which it is often confused or conflated, the Titanomachy provides some of Tolkien's inspiration for the primordial wars between the Valar and Melkor/Morgoth.

TOBACCO

See: PIPEWEED

TOLLKÜHN The surname of the "original" Tolkien family, according to a not-so-serious family legend. One of Tolkien's German ancestors, the story went, had been an officer in the imperial cavalry of the Holy Roman Empire. His name was Georg von Hohenzollern, who, it was claimed, fought alongside Archduke Ferdinand of Austria against the invading Turks at the Siege of Vienna in 1529. The siege was broken only by an unexpected and ferocious cavalry charge that turned the tide of war, and in this von Hohenzollern took a flamboyant part, earning him the nickname Tollkühn, meaning "foolhardy."

This was a tale that Tolkien deprecated all his life (and indeed it seems to be completely unfounded), but it would seem that, secretly, it delighted him. He often retold the tale in disguised form so obscurely that virtually none of his readers or lecture audiences registered his private little joke. On several occasions he used the name Rashbold, while in the introduction to his famous lecture and essay "On Fairy-Stories," Tolkien apologized for being "overbold," claiming to be "Overbold by name" and "Overbold by nature."

Can it be chance that in Tolkien's vivid accounts of battles throughout the Third Age we find many of his cavalry commanders, such as Eorl the Young in the Battle of the Field of Celebrant and Théoden in the Battles of the Hornburg and Pelennor Fields, resorting to *tollkühn* stratagems that turn the tide of battle at its most critical moment?

TREEBEARD An Ent and, according to Gandalf, "the oldest living thing that still walks beneath the Sun upon this Middle-Earth."

At 14 feet tall, the "Shepherd of Trees" is among Tolkien's most original and eccentric heroes. Treebeard, or Fangorn (to use his Elvish name), resembles something between an evergreen tree and a man. The name Ent came from the Anglo-Saxon word *enta*, meaning "giant," while the portrayal of Ents (and of their wilder, more dangerous cousins, the Huorns) was inspired by Tolkien's extensive knowledge of the ancient lore and traditions of the Green Man.

Years after the publication of *The Lord of the Rings*, Tolkien in an interview acknowledged that the eccentric characterization of Treebeard

Huorns

was specifically meant as a good-humored lampooning of his friend and colleague C. S. Lewis, the author of *The Chronicles of Narnia*, complete with his booming voice, his absurd "Hrum, hroom" interjections, and the authority of a complete know-it-all who, irritatingly, usually did know it all.

The Ents were also meant as a gentle satire of Oxford dons and particularly hidebound philologists more generally. Like those academics, Ents "were long on the discussion of problems, but slow to take action." Often, however, in both Oxford and in Entwood, action ultimately proved unnecessary as the debates often outlasted the problems. Ent gatherings, or "moots" with their qualifications, additions, exceptions, and verbal footnotes on every point must have had a special savor for those who were familiar (as Tolkien was) with the editorial meetings of the compilers of the *Oxford English Dictionary*.

TROLLS/TROLLS
Huge humanoid monsters that can be discovered in the folklore and legends in every region of the world. They leave their footprints all over the landscape, move mountains, and change the course of rivers. In many folktales, large standing stones are believed to be Trolls that have been turned to stone after being exposed to sunlight. They appear to prefer living in mountain caverns or dark forest caves from which they emerge to prey on lost children and unwary travelers.

The Trolls of Middle-earth draw on two major troll traditions. One we might loosely call "Scandinavian," and the other "fairy tale." Tolkien's portrayal of Trolls in *The Hobbit* owes a great deal to the trolls of fairy tale where they are most often dull-witted creatures who are simply content with random, if brutal, acts of mayhem and mischief. The three Trolls encountered by Bilbo Baggins and Thorin and Company (Bert, Tom, and William Huggins) are very much of the comic fairy-tale variety (rather like overgrown louts), and the Wizard Gandalf's outwitting of the Trolls by keeping them arguing until the sun rises, and thereby turning them to stone, is clearly based on the Brothers Grimm tale "The Brave Little Tailor."

Elsewhere in the legendarium, however, Tolkien's Trolls are an altogether more serious matter. While they are still lumbering, vicious, and dull-witted, as tools in the hands of Morgoth in the First Age or Sauron in the Second and Third, they are extremely dangerous, by force of their massive strength alone. A Hill-troll kills Aragorn's grandfather, Arador; Cave-trolls attack the Fellowship of the Ring in Moria; and Mountain-trolls lead the assault on the gates of Minas Tirith. These Trolls, it seems, are largely inspired by Norse myths of the *jötnar*, a word often misleadingly translated as "giants" but which in fact were manifestations of the fierce powers of nature, of mountain, forest, and blistering cold. It's worth noting, too, that in the Anglo-Saxon epic *Beowulf*, the monster Grendel is described as a "water-haunting Troll."

TUATHA DÉ DANANN
In Irish mythology, a race of immortals who do not age or suffer from sickness or disease. They provided Tolkien with inspiration for his portrayal of the Eldar: just as the Tuatha Dé Danann are the "People of the Goddess Danu," Tolkien's Elves might similarly be described as the "People of the Goddess Varda," the Valarian queen of the Stars.

In their earliest days, the Tuatha Dé Danann live in a land of immortals much as did Tolkien's Noldor Elves in Eldamar. This is Tír na nÓg, "Land of the Ever Young," whose high king, Nuada, sails with his people over the western sea to the mortal shores of Ireland. There, High King Nuada burns his fleet of ships, so that none of the Tuatha Dé Danann might return to Tír na nÓg.

The Silmarillion tells us of the Noldor high king Fëanor who sails with his people over the Western Sea to the mortal shores of Beleriand. There, King Fëanor, too, burns the ships of his fleet, so that none of the Noldor might return to Eldamar. Both Nuada and Fëanor soon lead their people to victory in their first battle in this new land. In advance of the rising of the first sun, the Noldor win a great victory in the Dagor-nuin-Giliath, or "Battle-under-Stars," but in that battle Fëanor is slain. Similarly, Nuada of the Tuatha Dé Danann leads his people to victory in the First Battle of Magh Tuireadh. Even though he is not slain, his arm is severed and he can no longer rule as king.

So both peoples win their first battles in their new lands, but lose their king. The next high king of the Tuatha Dé Danann is the Dagda, who leads his people to victory in the Second Battle of Magh Tuireadh against the monstrous legions

Troll. Trolls may be stupid but have almost invincible strength.

Tulkas Chaining Morgoth

of underworld demons and giants known as the Fomorians. In Beleriand, the next high king of the Noldor is Fingolfin, who leads his people to a second victory in the Dagor Aglareb, or "Glorious Battle," against the Orcs, Trolls, and Balrogs, likewise demons of the underworld.

The Dagda's victory over the Fomorian legions gives the Tuatha Dé Danann an age of relative peace during which the king's sons, and those of his chieftains, establish fiefdoms over much of Ireland. In like manner, Fingolfin's victory over Morgoth's legions gives the Noldor nearly four centuries of relative peace. During that time Fingolfin's sons and those of his brothers, Fëanor and Finarfin, establish a dozen Noldor fiefdoms in northern Beleriand as a bulwark against their foes.

However, just as the appearance of the sun signals the beginning of the Age of Men (our historic human ancestors, Tolkien implies), it also signals the beginning of the end of days for the Noldor upon Middle-earth. This corresponds to the history of the Tuatha Dé Danann: as their time in the mythic age of Ireland nears its end, they are eventually superseded by the Milesians, a race of mortals believed to be the ancestors of the historic Gaelic people of Ireland.

Tolkien's theme of the dwindling power of the Elves upon Middle-earth has much in common with the fading of the Tuatha Dé Danann. The remnants of this once-mighty prehuman race eventually become known as the Aes Sidhe, or the Sidhe (pronounced "Shee"). The name means the "people of the hills," for it was believed that, as these people withdrew from the mortal realm, they hid themselves away inside "hollow hills" and ancient burial mounds.

In Tolkien's Noldor and Sindar Elves of Beleriand, we have kingdoms and cities that are comparable to the legends of the Sidhe hidden away in all manner of places: in glittering caverns like King Thingol's Menegroth; in secret valleys like Turgon's vale of Tumladen with its citadel, Gondolin; in precarious river gorges like Finrod's mighty Nargothrond; in havens like Círdan's Brithombar and Eglarest; and in distant islands like the refuge of the Isle of Balar.

TULKAS The most valiant and warlike of the Valar, whose name in Quenya simply means "strong." In this respect, Tulkas has a passing resemblance to the Norse god Magni, a name that similarly means "strong."

However, a closer counterpart can be found in the Greco-Roman Heracles (Hercules), whose primary attribute is his superhuman strength. Both are depicted as supreme wrestlers.

Both Tulkas and Heracles play a key role in cosmic, primordial struggles. Heracles becomes the champion of the gods in the Gigantomachy, killing the giants with his "rushing arrows." Similarly, Tulkas is the "Champion of Valinor," wrestling and overcoming Melkor, after long ages in which the Valar have been unable to contain his powers.

TÚRIN TURAMBAR

One of the greatest of Edain heroes of the First Age. In good part, Tolkien's tale of Túrin and his father, Húrin, was inspired by Sigurd the dragon-slayer and his father, Sigmund, the heroes of the *Völsunga Saga*, the Norse epic described by

Túrin Turambar

the designer and poet William Morris (1834–96) as "the great story of the North, which should be to all our race what the tale of Troy was to the Greeks."

Tolkien's tale and the Norse saga begin with the deeds of the fathers. Both Húrin and Sigmund survive the near-extermination of their dynastic houses. In the Dagor Nírnaeth Arnoediad (Battle of Unnumbered Tears), Húrin is the last man standing in the Edain rearguard and, by single-handedly slaying 70 trolls, saves the retreating Noldor army from certain annihilation. With equal courage, Sigmund slaughters scores of his foes in acts of bloody revenge for the murder of his entire clan, including his eight brothers. However, both are eventually defeated: Húrin when his war axe withers in the heat of battle, and Sigmund when his dynastic sword breaks in one last fatal duel.

Among the Elves and Men of Beleriand, Húrin the Steadfast is celebrated as "the mightiest warrior of mortal men" but, like the Norse hero Sigmund, he became even more renowned as the father of a dragon-slayer. Húrin's famous son is Túrin Turambar, the slayer of Glaurung, the Father of Dragons, while Sigmund's son is Sigurd the slayer of Fáfnir, the "Prince of All Dragons."

Both dragon-slayers lay claim to broken dynastic swords that are reforged: Túrin's sword is given the name Gurthang, meaning "iron of death," while Sigurd's is Gram, meaning "wrath." But, even so armed, neither of these heroes believe that these great worms could be slain by strength of arms alone. Courage and cunning are also required to defeat this terror. Túrin chooses to hide himself in a deep ravine at a river crossing, and when Glaurung attempts to cross over the gap, he drives his sword upward and into the massive monster's underbelly. Sigurd hides himself in a covered trench dug into the narrow road the beast takes each day to drink from a forest pool. When Fáfnir's great body passes over the trench the Völsung hero drives his sword Gram up into the dragon's exposed belly.

Tulkas in Utumno

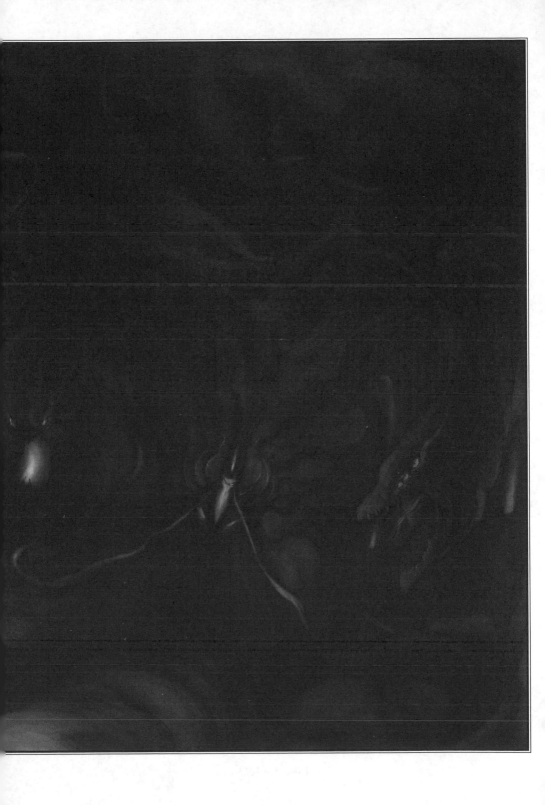

Ulmo, Lord of Waters

UINEN One of the Maiar who serves Ulmo, Lord of Waters and King of the Sea. Beloved by the Teleri Sea Elves, Uinen calms the waters before their ships in the wake of the sea storms and squalls stirred up by her tempestuous spouse, Ossë. We can find all manner of counterparts to this kindly sea spirit in the minor sea goddesses and sea nymphs (Nereids and Oceanids) of the ancient Greeks. These include figures such as the Nereid Galene, goddess/personification of the calm; Leucothea, the goddess who rescued sailors in distress; Brizo, a patroness of mariners worshipped on the island of Delos; or Thetis, the kindly Nereid. Uinen's intercession to Manwë for her spouse to be forgiven for his brief collusion with Melkor may remind us of the intercession of Thetis to Zeus on behalf of her son Achilles, in the *Iliad*.

See also: N Y M P H S

ULMO A mighty Vala, Lord of Waters, second only in his powers to Manwë, Lord of the Air. He dwells in the depths of the sea, rather than in Valinor, and has no spouse. He rarely takes on physical form, but when he does so it is often as a great warrior in silver-green armor with a foam-crested helm, terrible "as a mounting wave that strides to the land." For all that, he is the Vala who is friendliest with the peoples of Middle-earth. He is also closely associated with music by blowing his horns, the Ulumúri.

Ulmo has a direct counterpart in the Greek god Poseidon and the Roman Neptune, who were depicted mounted on a giant wave in armor and a chariot drawn by seahorses and accompanied by the merman "old Triton blowing his wreathed horn." In Celtic mythology, Ulmo is most akin to the sea god Manannán mac Lir, with his seaborne chariot. Manannán mac Lir features prominently in the legends of the Tuatha Dé Danann, though without that god's associations with the Underworld. In Norse mythology, Ulmo is most comparable to Njord.

Interestingly, Ulmo's name may remind us of the Christian martyr Saint Elmo, occasionally spelled Ulmo (died AD 303), the patron saint of mariners.

Corsairs of Umbar on the River Anduin

UMBAR
Port city to the south of Gondor and of the mouth of the Anduin River. For a thousand years a colony of Númenor, then a base for the Black Númenóreans, and later part of the Gondorian empire. By the time of the War of the Ring, Umbar had long been in the hands of the marauding Corsairs.

Umbar plays a similar role in the history of Gondor to the port-city of Carthage in the history of Rome. A colony of the mighty sea power of Phoenicia for a thousand years, Carthage rose to be an independent and significant power in the wake of the destruction of the Phoenician island city-state of Tyre in 332 BC (here a counterpart for Númenor). Just as Carthage and Rome vied for control of the Mediterranean, Gondor vied with Umbar for control over the vast Bay of Belfalas. The Black Númenórean Lords of Umbar (whose war fleets were the terror of the seas and whose powerful mercenary armies were buttressed by divisions of war elephants) were a torment over many lands. The lords of Carthage (whose mighty war fleets were the terror of the seas and whose powerful mercenary armies were buttressed by war-elephants) were a torment over many lands.

In the Third Age, after centuries of rivalry, the Ship Kings of Gondor engaged in century-long wars (933–1050 TA) on sea and land, which resulted in the eventual conquest and subjugation of Umbar and its Southron Empire of Harad. This is similar to the Rome's century-long Punic Wars (256–146 BC) on sea and land, which resulted in the eventual conquest and subjugation of Carthage and its North African empire. The Black Númenórean rulers of Umbar were slain or scattered, and the city and port served as Gondor's southern fortress controlling its vast Haradrim territories. The Carthaginians, too, were slain or sold into slavery, and its city and port served as Rome's southern fortress controlling its vast North African territories.

Subsequently, Tolkien's chronologies inform us that Umbar slipped from Gondor's grasp after five centuries. In the year 1448 TA Gondorian rebels and lords among the Haradrim captured Umbar. These new lords became known as the Corsairs of Umbar, and their mighty pirate fleets once again terrorized the seas, harassing and attacking Gondor and its allies.

Morgoth Ensnared by Ungoliant

UNGOLIANT A primordial monster in *The Silmarillion* that takes the shape of a gigantic female spider. Sometimes called the "Gloomweaver," Tolkien's monster weaves a web of darkness and horror from a substance that Tolkien calls the "Unlight of Ungoliant."

Ungoliant's exact origins in terms of Tolkien's cosmology are left obscure in his writings. We are told that she is from "before the world," which only serves to heighten the black vastness of her evil. While her spider form may remind us of Kali, the eight-limbed Hindu goddess of destruction, Ungoliant is, ethically speaking, far indeed from the goddess. Kali is ultimately a benevolent deity who *destroys* evil, and does not incarnate it. As the English prefix *un-* we find in her name suggests, Ungoliant is a personification of "Non-Being."

In Eastern Painted Scrolls, we find a "Master of Non-Being," an entity similar to Ungoliant, but in a male form that actually resembles Morgoth, the Dark Lord. Indeed, in this huge "Master of Non-Being," the identity of Morgoth and Ungoliant merge as one in this living form of darkness. The Master is a massive scorched black demon described as a "Black Man, as tall as a spear . . . the Master of Non-Existence, of instability, of murder and destruction." And just as Ungoliant and Morgoth together extinguish the sacred Trees of Light in the Undying Lands, the Eastern Master of Non-Being "made the sun and the moon die and assigned demons to the planets and harmed the stars."

The tale of Ungoliant provides a philosophical or theological account of the nature of evil. In Tolkien's Roman Catholic Christian view—rooted in the theology of Saint Augustine of Hippo (AD 354–430)—evil is nothing but the absence of good. In a letter, Tolkien explained: "In my story I do not deal in Absolute Evil. I do not think there is such a thing, since that is Zero."

In the end, in her insatiable hunger, Ungoliant devours herself. Ungoliant and Morgoth are destined to a self-devouring annihilation, a return to the Void, and the nothingness of "Non-Being."

See also: RELIGION: CHRISTIANITY; SHELOB

Uruk-hai. A race of "Super-Orc" bred in Mordor by Sauron. Besides being larger and stronger than the lesser Orcs, they have the advantage of being unafraid of light.

URD
(OR WYRD)

A Norse Norn, or Fate, who shares some aspects of her nature with Tolkien's Vairë the Weaver, the spouse of Mandos the Doomsman. Vairë dwells in the subterranean Halls of Mandos where she wove the story of the World in the tapestries that hung from its walls.

URUKS
(OR URUK
HAI) A swarthy-skinned and lynx-eyed warrior race that Sauron breeds and releases in the twenty-fifth century of the Third Age, as a new and more powerful breed of Orkish soldiery. They may have resulted from an interbreeding of Orcs and Men.

It has been suggested that these larger and more ferocious forms of Orcs may in part have been inspired by Tolkien's reading of the sixth-century Eastern Roman historian Jordanes and his

Utumno. The subterranean fortress of Melkor.

xenophobic description of the "scarcely human" Huns. Sauron's Uruks are Orkish in appearance and manner, but the size of Men and could endure and remain strong in sunlight. Jordanes' description of the soldiery of the Hunnic leader, Attila, the Scourge of God, might easily have been applied to Sauron's Uruks:"Their swarthy aspect is fearful, and they have pin-holes rather than eyes... Broad-shouldered, ready to use a bow and arrow. Though they live in the form of Men, they have the cruelty of wild beasts."

Like the Huns against the Romans, the Uruk-hai come forth in great numbers against the Men of Gondor. They lay waste to their capital, Osgiliath, and for the next five centuries of the Third Age, the Uruks fight in Sauron's alliance alongside lesser Orcs, Trolls, Easterlings, and Southrons.

UTUMNO
The mighty subterranean fortress of Melkor, the Black Enemy, beneath the Iron Mountains in the northern wastes of Middle-earth. Utumno means "hidden depths" in Quenya, while its Sindarin name is Udûn, meaning "dark pit." It is in Utumno that Melkor gathers rebel Maiar, monstrous demons, and other evil spirits about him and breeds the first Orcs in mockery of the Elves, and from which he wages war against the Valarian Powers of Arda before the first rising of the moon and the sun.

Utumno's various names connect it to Tartarus in Greek mythology. In the *Iliad* Homer situates Tartarus below Hades (the Underworld), so deep and dark that one would not reach its bottom for a year. Rather than being a *fortress* for evil and chaos, however, it is conceived of as their *prison*, into which Zeus, king of the gods, has thrown the Titans after he has defeated them in the Titanomachy, the primordial war between the Olympian gods and the rebel Titans.

In John Milton's *Paradise Lost* Tartarus is the name given to the subterranean fortress of Satan and the fallen angels and is, thus, a direct counterpart to Utumno.

Utumno. Melkor is the Dark Lord of Utumno, just as Milton's Satan is the Dark Lord of Tartarus. Both are tyrants who would "rather rule in Hell than serve in Heaven."

W

Eärendil's ship, Vingilótë

VAIRË

Vala known as the Weaver, spouse of Mandos, the Doomsman of the Underworld. In some respects she is comparable to the Greek Persephone (the Roman Proserpina), spouse of Hades (Pluto), lord of the Underworld. In the Halls of Mandos, Vairë weaves the story of Arda in tapestries that are hung on the walls. In this, she shares some aspects of her nature with the goddesses of fate found in other mythologies, such as the Norse Urd (or Wyrd) and the Greek Clotho, though both these are associated with spinning human destiny rather than weaving.

Vairë's art may also remind us of the Greek goddess Athena, who was the patron of weavers, and of her human rival, Arachne, with whom, in Ovid's *Metamorphoses*, she enters a weaving contest, creating tapestries showing stories of the gods.

VALAR (SINGULAR: VALA)

The fourteen ruling Powers of Arda, angelic beings who, after the creation of Arda, enter into its "circles" and shape various aspects of it. Many of the Valar are associated with a particular realm, such as the sea, starry night sky, rocks and mountains, and plants and animals. Most form male-and-female pairs ("spouses") and a few are siblings. Except in Tolkien's earliest writings, they do not have offspring.

Tolkien did not conceive of his Valar as gods, even if they sometimes seem to be perceived as such by Elves, Men, and others. They are not worshipped (even if they are revered or called upon), and there are few mythological stories attached to their names. They are above all manifestations of good creative power, nurturing order and stability in a world that is constantly threatened by the evil powers of disorder and chaos, manifested in Morgoth and Sauron.

Nonetheless, in creating his "pantheon," Tolkien was clearly influenced by both the Greco-Roman gods (and occasionally heroes) and Norse gods. The charts on pages 450 and 451 list the Valar and their possible/probable counterparts in Greco-Roman and Norse mythology.

Trees of the Valar. The "Trees of the Light" which Yavanna sings into being. These saplings grew into the largest of trees and light up Aman with gold and silver light. The silver tree is Telperion; the gold, Laurelin.

VALARAUKAR
See: BALROGS

VALINOR

In Tolkien's legendarium the land of the immortal Valar and Maiar in the continent of Aman, surrounded, except to the west, by the mighty Pelóri Mountains, also known as the Undying Lands. Ruled by Manwë and Varda, the king and queen of the Valar, Valinor is comparable to Asgard, the home of the Norse gods ruled by Odin and Frigg, the king and queen of the gods, as well as to any number of mythological lands of the immortals.

Geographically, Valinor's/ Aman's positioning to the far west of the continent of Middle-earth—at least in the First Age—recalls the continents of North and South America, which for Europeans during the early Age of Discovery (fifteenth to sixteenth century) was a New World full of wonders.

VAMPIRES

Blood-sucking creatures in folklore that feed on the blood of the living, usually taking the form of undead humans beings and sometimes as "were-bats." Considering their powerful hold on the European imagination, they play surprisingly little part in Tolkien's legendarium, perhaps because he felt that they belonged so distinctly to a territory already amply occupied by Bram Stoker's *Dracula* (1897).

Batlike demons do, however, make a passing appearance in *The Silmarillion*, where they serve Morgoth. One especially powerful Vampire or bat-demon has a name, Thuringwethil, the "Woman of Secret Shadows," who inhabits the haunted tower of Tol-in-Gaurhoth. In the First Age, too, Sauron also sometimes takes on a batlike form, dripping blood as he passes. Otherwise, these beings largely disappear from Tolkien's stories of later ages.

VÁNA

The Vala of spring flowers and birds of the forest. Of the golden-haired Vána we are told, "all flowers spring as she passes and open if she glances upon them; and all birds sing at her coming." She is called "the Ever Young."

Aspects of Vána's nature appear to be adapted from a combination of the Anglo-Saxon spring goddess Eostre and the Norse goddess of eternal youth Idunn; and likewise Persephone, the Greek goddess of spring, and Hebe, the Greek goddess of youth.

VANDALS

A historic Eastern Germanic people who in 439 AD captured Carthage from the Romans, founding a powerful kingdom in North Africa. From this ancient city, they were able to exert power over much of the Western Mediterranean and, with their mighty pirate fleets, to harass and attack Rome and its allies.

The history of the Vandals of Carthage and their pirate fleets is comparable to that of the Corsairs of Umbar whose pirate fleets terrorize the waters and coastlands of the Bay of Belfalas for much of the Third Age. Just as after seven centuries Rome lost its grip over Carthage, so after five centuries Gondor lost its grip on Umbar. In 1448 TA rebels in Umbar allied with the Haradrim drove Gondor loyalists from Umbar. These new lords became known as the Corsairs.

Aragorn II (the future King Elessar of Gondor) ultimately destroyed the Corsairs of Umbar in his quest to win control of the seas and reunite the North- and South-kingdoms of Gondor and Arnor. Suffering a similar fate, the historic Vandals of Carthage were ultimately destroyed by the Byzantine general Belisarius (c. AD 500–65) and the Emperor Justinian the Great (c. AD 482–565) in their quest to win control of the seas and reunite the Eastern and Western Empires of Rome.

VANYAR

The first Kindred of Elves to enter Eldamar, and the noblest and fairest of all the Eldar. Their king is Ingwë, who plays a role similar to Moses in leading his people to a "promised land." He is close to the king of the Valar, Manwë, dwelling on the slopes of Taniquetil, as Moses comes close to God on Mount Horeb. The name Vanyar in Quenya carries the meaning "fair" in reference to the race's golden hair. It is also derived from the word *vanya* meaning "light or pale," so perhaps is an allusion to the Light Elves of Norse mythology.

VARDA

The most beloved of the Valar among Elves and Dwarves, Varda is the maker of the stars. Her importance is shown in her large number of epithets: she is Elentári (star-queen) and Tintallë (star kindler), Quenya titles that translate as Elbereth and Gilthoniel in Sindarin. The white light of the stars is also evoked in other names, such as Fanuilos, meaning "Ever-white."

While her position as queen of the Valar and spouse to Manwë give Varda a comparable position to the Greek Hera and the Norse Frigg, Tolkien's main inspiration for Varda appears to have come from his own Christian tradition, in the figure of the Virgin Mary. Indeed, in *The Lord of the Rings*, Tolkien's Elvish song *A Elbereth Gilthoniel*—meaning "O Varda the Star-kindler" in Sindarin—has been linked in theme and mood to the

Varda, Queen of the Stars

Roman Catholic devotional hymn to the Virgin that begins: "Hail, Queen of Heaven, the Ocean Star, / Guide of the wanderer." Varda is called upon by Elves in extremis, just as Roman Catholics call on the Virgin to intercede in time of need.

There may be a link between Varda and the "White Goddess," an ancient Celtic goddess of the Moon hypothesized by the English poet Robert Graves in his book of that name published in 1948, though there is no evidence for Tolkien having read this work.

VARIAGS OF KHAND

An Easterling race that comes under the influence of Sauron the Ring Lord in the Third Age and who in the second millennium join together with Southrons and Wainriders in a failed attack on Gondor. They return again in service of Mordor in the War of the Ring, just over a millennium later, this time most prominently in the service of the Witch-king in the Battle of Pelennor Fields.

Tolkien took his inspiration for the Variags from the Varangians of Ukraine. Worshippers of Odin, the Varangians were Viking river traders, pirates, and raiders who settled in the Dnieper–Volga region in the eighth century. They drove out the Khazar rulers from Kiev, adopted the culture of the region's Slavic population, and became known as Rus's (later, the Russians).

VENUS

The brightest "star" in the night sky, long before it was understood to be a planet. It was frequently referred to as two separate stars: the Morning Star and the Evening Star. To the Greeks, Venus as the morning star was Phosphorus and as the evening star it was Hesperus. In Tolkien's world, the bright light of Venus comes from the sacred Silmaril jewel bound to the brow of Eärendil the Mariner who travels through the sky in his flying ship *Vingilótë*. This story was inspired by Tolkien's interpretation of a line in the Anglo-Saxon poem known as *Crist II*, written by Cynewulf: "Hail Earendel, brightest of angels, over Middle-earth to men sent."

A Viking. King Völsung was the eponymous founder of the Völsung dynasty.

Tuor and Voronwë Seek Gondolin. To deliver Ulmo's warning of the city's destruction.

By contrast, Venus, the Roman goddess of love—after whom the planet is named—has no counterpart among Tolkien's somewhat chaste Valar. Sexuality, generally, is largely absent from Middle-earth.

VIKINGS
See: NORSEMEN

VIRGIN MARY, THE   In Christianity, the biblical Mary, the mother of Jesus, mother of God, and queen of Heaven. Roman Catholics especially revere the Virgin as a protector and intercessor, and in this respect she shares similarities with Varda, "Queen of the Stars," to whom Elves, Men, and Hobbits may call in hours of need. Frodo, for example, calls out two of Varda's titles ("O Elbereth! Gilthoniel!") when he is under attack from the Nazgûl on Weathertop. As "Our Lady of Sorrows" (the Mater Dolorosa), the Virgin Mary also colors Tolkien's portrayal of the Vala Nienna, who weeps for the griefs of the world.

VÖLSUNGA SAGA   Icelandic saga, composed in the late thirteenth century but based on much older material, telling the story of the decline of the Völsung clan and encompassing the story of Sigurd and Brynhild. William Morris, the nineteenth-century translator, artist, author, and poet described it as "the great story of the North, which should be to all our race what the tale of Troy was to the Greeks."

The heroic age for all the nations of northern Europe was the chaotic fifth, sixth, and seventh centuries AD, the time after the collapse of Rome and before the rise of the Holy Roman Empire. The historic chieftains of those times became the subjects of oral traditions that elevated them to mythic status. It was a heroic age equivalent to the chaotic eleventh, tenth, and ninth centuries BC of the ancient Greeks after the collapse of the Mycenaean civilization and before the rise of classical Greece, a period that generated the epics *Iliad* and *Odyssey*.

The probable destruction of Troy in around 1200 BC was the catastrophic event that inspired the literary masterpieces of the Greek people. In northern Europe there was an equivalent catastrophe, the annihilation of the Burgundians in AD 436 by a contingent of Huns under the leadership of Attila, acting as mercenary agents for the Roman Empire. The memory of this catastrophic end to an entire warrior elite—and the near-extermination of a once-powerful people—was recalled vividly by the neighboring Franks. The story of the Burgundians on the Rhine was told and retold by the Visigoths, Saxons, Ostrogoths, Lombards, Austrians, and Norsemen. Over the next millennium the Burgundian tragedy became the most influential catastrophe in European literature since the fall of Troy.

Those who doubt this might consider just a small part of the literature inspired by this event. Besides being the catalyst for the *Völsunga Saga*, the national epic of Norway and Iceland, it also provided the basis for the *Nibelungenlied* (c. 1200), the national epic of the Germans. The latter also provided the inspiration for Richard Wagner's opera cycle, *The Ring of the Nibelung* (first performed as a cycle in 1876).

All three works, saga, epic, and opera cycle, have a single common motif in the ring quest, and all three, along with the original historic event, had a profound influence on Tolkien's *The Lord of the Rings*. The *Völsunga Saga*, however, was the most influential of the three on Tolkien's creative writing in general, and on *The Silmarillion* in particular. Certainly, the heroes Húrin the Steadfast and his son, Túrin the Dragon-slayer, were undoubtedly inspired by the *Völsunga Saga*'s heroes, Sigmund the Völsung and his son, Sigurd the Dragon-slayer.

VULCAN The Roman god of blacksmiths, metalworkers, and artificers, from early on identified with the Greek god Hephaestus. He also seems to be related to the Etruscan deity Velchanus, whose primary association is with fire but also with the underworld. In Tolkien's "pantheon" of Valar, Vulcan most resembles Tolkien's Aulë the Smith and Maker of Mountains.

Aulë, Maker of Mountains. Aulë, like Vulcan, is associated with mountains.

W

Gandalf the Wizard

WAINRIDERS In Tolkien's histories of Middle-earth, a nation of Easterlings that for nearly a century—1851–1944 TA—invaded and conquered Gondor's eastern fiefdoms. The fictional accounts of Gondor's wars in its eastern territories owe something to historic accounts of the century-long Roman conflict with the Ostrogoths (East Goths) and its culmination in the Battle of Adrianople in AD 378. Tolkien's Wainriders are a nomadic confederacy of people who travel as an army and nation in vast caravans of wains (wagons) and war chariots. This certainly is comparable to the nomadic Ostrogoths whom Roman historians described as not just an invading army but also "an entire nation on the move in great wains."

WALES A rugged, western country of Great Britain that has remained one of the homelands of the Celtic people, sometimes known as the ancient Britons. It provided Tolkien with a geographic model for Tolkien's maps of the Elven kingdom of Lindon in the Second and Third Age; a treasure trove of Celtic and medieval tales (most notably as collected in *The Mabinogion*) and also, in the Welsh language, a rich linguistic seam he could mine as he elaborated his Elvish language Sindarin.

Historically, Wales and Cornwall were the last refuges of the true "British" (the Britons) as distinct from the "English" (the Anglo-Saxons). Similarly, the fictional North and South Lindon, to the west of the Shire, were the last true refuges of the Noldor and Sindar Elves of Middle-earth. The history, myths, and languages of ancient Welsh and Tolkien's fictional Elves are absolutely intertwined. Sindarin, Tolkien's invented language of his fictional Grey Elves, was "mainly and deliberately modeled on those of Welsh." The choirs of Wales are renowned throughout the world, while Lindon was "the land of song" or, more precisely, "the land of sacred song."

Tolkien also acknowledged that his fictional Elvish tales and mythology were in good part inspired by the tales and mythology of the Britons. These were sophisticated and highly civilized Welsh-speaking Celts who settled the land at least two millennia before the arrival of the relatively primitive English (Anglo-Saxon) tribes in the fifth century AD.

WARGS A breed of demonic wolf in Middle-earth. From the First Age to the Third Age, Wargs work in alliance with Goblins and Orcs, most obviously as steeds for the Orc Wolf-riders in battles and as scouts for Sauron or Saruman.

As Aragorn the Ranger succinctly observes in *The Lord of the Rings*: "Where the warg howls, there also the orc prowls." The Wargs of Middle-earth are not only more fierce and frightening than ordinary wolves, but there is something supernatural in their nature that makes them more akin to werewolves. Just how sentient and communicative Wargs are is not made clear, though Tolkien does speak of the "dreadful language of the Wargs."

Tolkien derived the word "Warg" from the Anglo-Saxon *warg* or *wearg*, meaning "strangler" or "choker" but also "outlaw" or "criminal." The Wargs' close association with the forces of Sauron the Necromancer underlines the latter's connections with the Norse god Odin who was accompanied by two wolves, Geri and Freki, both names meaning "greedy."

WARS War and battle play a leading, even the dominant, role in Tolkien's legendarium. Ranging from cosmic primordial struggles between "angelic powers" through to carefully depicted, realistic battles between multiple armies, with numerous more minor skirmishes in between, war and conflict are almost the status quo in Middle-earth. Long-term peace exists only in otherworldy "utopias," such as Valinor or Númenor, or in the eucatastrophe at the end of *The Lord of the Rings*, in which King Elessar establishes a reign of harmony and reconciliation.

For his wars, Tolkien took inspiration from his deep study of mythology, history, and literature. The "war in heaven" is a common motif in many world mythologies, from the Titanomachy of the Greeks to Ragnarök of the Norse. It is also the staple of history writing in such classical works as Thucydides' *History of the Peloponnesian War* (begun 431 BC) and Julius Caesar's *Commentaries on the Gallic War* (58–49 BC). In literature we find it in such diverse sources as *Beowulf*, the *Nibelungenlied*, and *The Song of Roland*.

The ubiquity of war in Tolkien's studies is not quite enough, however, to explain its predominance in his fictional world, nor the extraordinary power

The Battle of Azanulbizar. The last battle in the War of Dwarves and Orcs.

Wargs. Wargs served as steeds for Orcs.

of its depiction. It is above all his own traumatic experience as a soldier in the First World War that energizes his dismay, horror, and terror at the brutality and sorrow of the battlefield.

See also: GIGANTOMACHY; RAGNARÖK; SOMME; TITANOMACHY

WAYLAND THE SMITH

The greatest smith, inventor, and craftsman in Anglo-Saxon and other Germanic mythologies. Known as Weiland to the Germans and Völundr to the Norsemen, he was famous for the forging of the weapons and armor of many of the heroes of sagas, epic tales, and romances. He is sometimes depicted as a mortal prince, sometimes as the son of a giant, and sometimes even as a god. Whatever his origin, the stories associated with him emphasize not only his skill but also his sorrows. The Anglo-Saxon poem *Deor* recorded: "The stout-hearted hero endured troubles / had sorrow and longing as his companions / cruelty cold as winter – / he often found woe."

In Wayland the Smith we find aspects of the archetypal gifted but cursed smith and craftsman, who in Tolkien is manifest both in the Noldor king, Fëanor, the creator of the Silmarils and his grandson, Celebrimbor, the forger of the Rings of Power. However, he is most often compared to Tolkien's fictional Telchar the Smith, the supreme Dwarf-smith of Nogrod in the Blue Mountains of Beleriand.

WAYLAND'S SMITHY

An ancient long barrow and chamber tomb about 20 miles from Oxford visited by Tolkien and his family on at least one occasion during the period he was writing *The Lord of the Rings*. Wayland's Smithy is the oldest and best-preserved pre-Celtic burial site monument in Britain. It is also just a half-hour's walk from the famous White Horse of Berkshire, Britain's largest and oldest chalk-cut hill figure.

The Neolithic barrow grave located near The Ridgeway, an ancient road running along the Berkshire Downs, was the likely inspiration for Tolkien's

Werewolf

haunted Barrow Downs of Middle-earth in *The Lord of the Rings*. Although this Neolithic monument was constructed several millennia before the arrival of Wayland's Saxons in Britain, the name of Wayland has been linked to this site for the last thousand years. The legend of Wayland the Smith as the forger of ancestral weapons may also have suggested the presence of the charmed blades discovered by the Hobbits and wielded by the terrible Barrow-wights.

WELSH

A language belonging to the Britonnic branch of the Celtic family, still widely spoken in Wales today, which inspired Tolkien's invented Elven tongue of Sindarin.

As a child in the rural Midlands, Tolkien became interested in the strange language written on the sides of Welsh coal trucks. It was the beginning of a life-long fascination with the language. Tolkien purchased a Welsh grammar book and studied the language while still a student at Oxford. Then as a university lecturer at Leeds, he taught medieval Welsh for five years in the early 1920s.

In 1955 Tolkien gave the inaugural O'Donnell lecture, entitled "English and Welsh" (later published as *Angles and Britons*) in which he argued that Welsh was as important as Norse and French to linguists studying English. He also spoke of his adherence to the theory of phonaesthetics: an aesthetic sense of language based on the beauty (or ugliness) of words and phrases unrelated to meaning. Even during his childhood when he heard Welsh spoken and sung in church choirs, Tolkien had little doubt that he had discovered one of the world's most beautiful and musical of languages. If his Elves were to have a language, Tolkien believed that it was logical to look for its inspiration in Welsh, the language of the original Britons.

Tolkien himself noted that Sindar Elves' names for persons, places, and things were "mainly deliberately modeled on those of Welsh (closely similar but not identical)." Structurally and phonetically, there are strong links between the two languages. A few words are identical in meaning: *mal* means "gold" in both the Welsh language and Sindarin. Others are close in meaning: *du* means "black" in Welsh and "shadow" in Sindarin. There are many others that are close in spelling and/or meaning: "fortress" is *cacr* in Welsh and *caras* in Sindarin; *drud* in Welsh means "fierce" while *dru* in Sindarin means "wild."

Still others are the same words but with radically different meanings: *adan* means "fin of a fish" in Welsh and "man" in Sindarin; *ucu* is "heaven" in Welsh and "water" in Sindarin. Some others are strangely connected: *iar* in Sindarin means "old," while the Welsh *iar* means "hen." However, the Welsh word *hen* actually means "old." Coincidentally, a few of Tolkien's characters take their names directly from Welsh words: Bard means "poet"; Barahir means "longbeard."

WEREWOLVES
The belief in lycanthropy—of humans who intermittently change into wolves, often at full moon—is part of the folklore and mythology of every civilization that interacts (or has once interacted) with wolves. Wolves and werewolves also loom large in Tolkien's legendarium.

In Tolkien's *The Silmarillion* we are informed that, of all Morgoth's "creatures that walked in wolf-shape" upon Middle-earth, the first is Draugluin, the Father of Werewolves.

The name Draugluin means "blue wolf," at once bred by Morgoth and the bodily form of a corrupted Maia spirit, chosen to be the sire of all the Werewolves of Middle-earth. Draugluin is also the sire of the gigantic

Woses. Wildermen of the Drúadan Forest, the Woses were a fair-skinned, pygmy race of hunters. In the War of the Ring, they guided the Rohirrim cavalry through their forests to fight in the Battle of Pelennor Fields.

Carcharoth, meaning "red maw," the greatest of the Wolves of Middle-earth and the unsleeping guardian of the gates of Morgoth's underground kingdom of Angband.

However, it is Sauron the Cruel who is the Werewolves' master in the First Age, sometimes taking on the shape of a great wolf himself. In Beleriand, Sauron and Draugluin come to dwell in the tower of Tol-in-Gaurhoth, the "Isle of Werewolves." It is from this horrific Werewolf-haunted tower and dungeon that Lúthien rescues her imprisoned lover, Beren, during the Quest for the Silmaril.

Although not prominent in the histories of the Second and Third Ages of Middle-earth, Draugluin's descendants may have been present among the Wolves and Wargs that allied themselves with Orcs, Trolls, Wraiths, and other dark forces.

WESTERNESSE   A fictional kingdom of King Almair in the Middle English romance of *King Horn* that has been associated with the real-world location of the Isle of Man, among other locations. In one of his letters, Tolkien acknowledged his borrowing of the name from *King Horn*: "I have often used Westernesse as a translation. This is derived from rare Middle English Westernesse (known to me only in MS. C of King Horn) where the meaning is vague, but may be taken to mean 'Western lands' as distinct from the East inhabited by the Paynim and Saracens." Westernesse in Tolkien's fictional writing was the name in his (invented) common tongue of Westron for the island-continent of Númenor: his conscious attempt to reinvent the ancient Greek legend of Atlantis. Tolkien's reworking of the Atlantis myth is another example of a "legend on the brink of fairy tale and history."

WHITE HORSE OF BERKSHIRE   The oldest chalk-cut hill figure in Britain and a historic site Tolkien knew well. On at least one occasion it was the destination of a family outing. A half-hour walk away is Wayland's Smithy. This gleaming white pictogram of a horse cut into the green turf of White Horse Hill measures well over 300 feet in length and in height. The

White Horse monument was originally cut into the chalk hillside well over three thousand years ago in the late Bronze Age.

Just 20 miles from Oxford on the border of Mercia, there can be little doubt that this White Horse inspired the image of the white horse on a green field on the banners of Tolkien's fictional Kings of Rohan, also known as the Mark, an ancient real-world name for Mercia.

See also: H O R S E S

WHITE LADIES

In the mythology of the ancient Welsh, spirits of the forests who were guardians of sacred fountains, wells, and grottoes, much like the Greek nymphs. Perceived by mortals as having eyes like stars and bodies that shimmer with light, they often lived in glowing crystal palaces beneath water or floating in air. To reach the forest refuges of the White Ladies, it was often necessary to pass through or across water and their domains, like other worlds in Welsh and Celtic mythology, they existed outside of time.

In *The Lord of the Rings*, the domain of Lothlórien is the fairest and most mysterious Elf-kingdom on Middle-earth, ruled by the Noldor Lady Galadriel, and the Sindar Lord Celeborn. "Tall and beautiful, with the hair of deepest gold," robed in white and with her magical mirror of water, Galadriel is the very incarnation of a White Lady.

WHITE SHIP DISASTER

An infamous historic event in the twelfth century that extinguished any clear heir to the English throne. The *White Ship* or *La Blanche-Nef* was a royal vessel that sank in the English Channel off the Normandy coast on November 25, 1120, drowning William Adelin (born 1103), the only legitimate son and heir of King Henry I of England, as well as his half-brother Richard and his half-sister Matilda. This historic real-world disaster provided Tolkien with a comparable disaster in his fictional world of Middle-earth with the wreck of a white Elven swan-ship in 1975 TA and the drowning of Arvedui, the last king of Arthedain—and the last king of the North-kingdom of Arnor.

Winged Beast

The resulting English crisis of succession eventually resulted in a prolonged period of invasion, civil war and the total breakdown of the rule of law—an era of English history that is aptly known as the Anarchy (1135–53). Similarly, the death of Arvedui in Middle-earth resulted in the extinguishing of the line of the kings of Arnor and an era of anarchy in the North-kingdom lasting many centuries.

WILD HUNT

In Germanic folklore a procession of ghostly horsemen or supernatural huntsmen riding through the forests and fields in a mad pursuit of some unnamed quarry. In Anglo-Saxon, it was known as "Herla's Assembly," in the Norse tradition it was the "Ride of Asgard," and in Swedish the "Hunt of Odin." The master of the hunt was variously named after old pagan gods such as Wotan, cursed biblical figures such as Cain, legendary kings such as Arthur, or even historical figures such as Charlemagne. Witnessing the Wild Hunt was thought to presage some catastrophe such as war or plague, or, at best, the death of the one who saw the cavalcade.

In Tolkien's world, these supernatural Wild Huntsmen most resemble the Witch-king and the Nazgûl Black Riders, whose presence certainly presages disaster and death. However, also somewhat akin to the Wild Hunt are the expeditions of Oromë, Huntsman of the Valar, to Middle-earth when it still lies in darkness, as he tracks down the evil beings that lurk there. Oromë's name Araw connects him with Arawn, lord of the dead in Welsh mythology, who conducts his own hunt with a pack of hounds as he rounds up wandering spirits to take them to the otherworld of Annwn.

WINGED BEASTS OF THE NAZGÛL

See: NAZGÛL; PTEROSAURS; QUETZALCOATLUS

WITCH-KING OF ANGMAR

Lord of the Nazgûl, the Nine Ringwraiths who appear in *The Lord of the Rings* as the terrifying phantom black horsemen and slaves of Sauron the Lord of the Rings.

Also known as the Black Captain, earlier in the Third Age this all-powerful Wraith becomes the Witch-king of Angmar (meaning "Iron Home"), a realm on the northern borders of Eriador in the foothills of the Misty Mountains.

In terms of influence, the Witch-king is most interesting in terms of his death. At the Battle of Fornost (1975 TA), the great decisive battle between the forces of Angmar and of Crown Prince Eärnur of Gondor, Tolkien weaves into his tale a direct allusion to William Shakespeare's riddling prophecy of the doomed Scottish warlord Macbeth as one who cannot be slain by the hand of a man "of woman born." As the Witch-king vanishes from the battleground in the gathering dark, the High Elf lord Glorfindel makes his own riddling prophecy: "Do not pursue him! He will not return to these lands. Far off yet is his doom, and not by the hand of man will he fall."

Indeed, the phantom horseman's doom proves to be a distant one. For just five years after the Battle of Fornost, the Witch-king reappears in all his evil glory in the Black Land of Mordor. There, he is joined by the other Ringwraiths, and over the next seven decades the Nine launch massive attacks on Gondor that result in the capture of its eastern fortress of Minas Ithil and the death of Gondor's last king. Minas Ithil becomes Minas Morgul, the "Tower of Black Sorcery," and over the next millennium, just as the prophecy foretold, no man survives the Witch-king of Minas Morgul on the field of battle.

For Tolkien's inspiration for the death of the Witch-king we must once again look to the plays of William Shakespeare. First, there is Tolkien's choice of date for the Witch-king's imminent death on March 15: the Ides of March, the first day of the old Roman calendar that was also the fatal date of Julius Caesar's assassination. The Witch-king, as he turns from Gandalf and the gate to join battle on Pelennor Fields, would have been well advised by Shakespeare's soothsayer to "Beware the Ides of March." And second, in Tolkien's portrayal of the Black Captain and Lord of the Ringwraiths, we have a mortal man who has sold his immortal soul to Sauron for a Ring of Power and the illusion of earthly dominion. This tragic exchange, set within

Willows. The Willow spirits numbered among the Huorns, and their will was bent on destroying enemies of the forests.

the context of his epic fantasy world, is exactly comparable to Shakespeare's *Macbeth* (1606), the tale of a king who has lost his doomed and blasted soul.

The life of the Witch-king is protected by a prophecy that is almost identical to the final one that safeguards Macbeth. Tolkien's Witch-king "cannot be slain by the hand of man," while the similarly deluded Macbeth "cannot be slain by man of woman born." The Witch-king is, of course, not slain by the hand of man but by the shield-maiden Éowyn of Rohan.

WIZARDS
Practitioners of magic found in the mythologies, folklore, and fairy tales around the world, often endowed with powers over the natural world and sometimes with the gift of prophecy. While wizards are often conceived as benevolent and wise (the etymological root of the word), their great power lays them open to corruption and the temptation of necromancy.

In traditional folklore and fairy tales, wizards are most commonly portrayed as solitary wanderers wearing a broad-brimmed hat and a long traveler's cape and carrying a tall staff. Traditionally, too, these wanderers tend to be bearded and world-weary individuals of distant or unknown origin. They do not appear to have any personal wealth or material support; they do not have definable status or social position; nor do they have families or homes. They are literate in many languages and customs as well as founts of wisdom and good counsel.

The wizard's garb—a combination of clothing that was best suited to traveling in all weathers—is the same costume worn by nearly all pilgrims, traders, and professional travelers since antiquity. It is also how the Greek god Hermes (the Roman Mercury) was portrayed in his guise as the god of travelers and merchants, while the Norse god Odin, too, frequently appeared on Earth as an ordinary traveler, his divine power and majesty hidden beneath his cloak and hat. Significantly, both these gods were also closely associated with magic and arcane knowledge.

Both the wizards of fairy tale and folklore—Hermes and Odin—inform Tolkien's portrayal of the Wizards of Middle-earth, especially the figure of Gandalf the Grey. While in *The Hobbit* Gandalf seems most akin to the avuncular, "professorial" wizards often found in fairy tales, in *The Lord of the Rings* he grows in stature and power, eventually to be "reborn" as Gandalf the White. Indeed,

Tolkien's "Order of Wizards," known as the Istari (meaning "the wise" or "those who know"), are divine in origin, mighty Maiar spirits of Valinor who, like Odin in Midgard, appear on Middle-earth in the Third Age in disguised and diminished human form. In Saruman, the chief of the Istari, meanwhile, we see the temptations that lie in the possession of great powers.

WOLVES
A species (*Canis lupis*) of the canine genus once common throughout Europe that play a key role, in various guises, in Norse and Germanic mythology, as they do in Tolkien's Middle-earth.

The heraldic beast of Odin, the one-eyed Necromancer and king of the gods, was the wolf. As Odin was the god of battles, his wolves were the creatures that always profited from the slaughter of war. When Odin presided in the Hall of the Slain, two great wolves, his bodyguards, lay at his feet. But by far the most terrifying wolf in Scandinavian legend was Fenris, brother of Hel, the goddess of the underworld. He was of such monstrous size that his opened jaws stretched from the Earth to the uppermost heavens. Kept by the gods in fetters, when the doomsday of Ragnarök arrives, the monstrous Fenris will break loose and challenge Odin in single combat before devouring the king of the gods himself.

In *The Silmarillion*, the greatest wolf legend is that of Carcharoth, meaning "red maw," the unsleeping guardian at the gates of Angband who ensures that none can pass unchallenged into the underworld kingdom of Morgoth the Enemy. In Carcharoth we can see mythological parallels with other guardians at the gates of underworld kingdoms: in the Norse Garm, the guardian of Helheim, and the Greek three-headed Cerberus, the terrifying watchdog of Hades.

WOSES
Name given to the Drúedain—the Wild Men of the Woods—by the Rohirrim. Short and stumpy and unlovely as they are, and possessing a "primitve culture," they nonetheless have an innate goodness and are skilled at the arts of healing. They may have been inspired by the European notion of "noble savages" who dwelt in the New World, untouched by the corruption of modern civilization.

^xX ^yY ^zZ

Eru

YAHWEH One of the names of the Hebrew God in the Bible, considered by the sixth century BC to be the one and only God and creator. Jehovah is another Hebrew name for God.

Yahweh provides some inspiration for Tolkein's Eru, meaning "The One," in that he is the only true god in Tolkien's imagined cosmos: transcendent, omnipotent, omniscient, the only true creator. The Valar and other spirits are not gods, but independent manifestations of Eru's thoughts (much like the biblical angels), and they create only through his power and with his permission. While Eru exists beyond and outside Arda, like Yahweh, he is depicted as occasionally intervening (often dramatically) into its history, as in the remaking of the world at the end of the Second Age.

Like Yahweh, too, Eru is conceived of as male and as a divine father. He is also known as Ilúvatar ("All-father"), and the Elves and Men are called the children of Ilúvatar. Unlike Yahweh, however, Eru does not receive worship.

See also: RELIGION: CHRISTIANITY

YAVANNA In Tolkien's legendarium, the Valarian queen of the Earth (Kementári) who watches over all living things. In the form of a woman, she is described as tall and clothed in green, though "Some there are who have seen her standing like a tree under heaven, crowned with the Sun; and from all its branches there spilled a golden dew upon the barren earth." Her younger sister is Vána, the Ever Young, who brings forth blossoming flowers.

Yavanna has a direct parallel in the Greco-Roman pantheon, in the earth-mother goddess Demeter/Ceres. In Demeter's grief for her daughter Persephone (who bears some resemblance to Vána), which causes nature to go into hibernation, there is a parallel with the Sleep of Yavanna. After the destruction of the Two Lamps, the queen of the Earth walks "in the shadow of Middle-earth, grieving because the growth and promise of the Spring of Arda was stayed" and causes the animals and plants to go into a slumber that lasts many years.

ZEUS The Greek king of the gods, equated by the Romans with their god Jupiter. To a degree, he is Tolkien's inspiration for Manwë, Vala king of Arda. Manwë, the Lord of the Air, rules from his throne and temple on top of Taniquetil, the tallest mountain in the world, while Zeus rules from his throne and temple on the top of Olympus, the tallest mountain in the Greek world. The eagle, likewise, is sacred to both Zeus and Manwë. While Manwë and Zeus are both considered all-wise, all-seeing, and all-just, Manwë is quite without Zeus' more human frailties, as seen in Zeus's numerous love affairs with nymphs and mortal women, and his fathering of a good many heroes.

ZIRAKZIGIL The great peak above the Dwarven city of Khazad-dûm that contains the Endless Stair and Durin's Tower, and at whose summit Gandalf and the Balrog fight their three-day battle, which ends with both their deaths. The name means "silver spike" in Khuzdul, the language of the Dwarves, while the Elves call it Celebdil the White. A clue to Tolkien's real-world inspiration for this peak is revealed in its Westron translation of the Elvish name, "Silvertine" or "Silverhorn," a match for a peak in the Swiss Alps known as the Silberhorn. Tolkien confirmed this in a letter to his son Michael, describing the Silberhorn as "the Silvertine of my dreams."

The pinnacle of Zirakzigil

CHARTS

Tolkien's imaginary world is of enormous complexity and richness and encompasses thousands of years of history, a detailed (and changing) geography, and a diversity of peoples, cultures, and languages. For all that, his major fictional works—*The Hobbit, The Lord of the Rings,* and *The Silmarillion*—wear this "world-building" lightly, for newcomer and initiate alike; the details of Tolkien's legendarium can sometimes bewilder, even as it fascinates and beguiles.

The following pages bring together a number of charts, tables, and chronologies that will help the reader negotiate the byzantine byways of Middle-earth with all the ease and wisdom of Elrond of Rivendell. There is a chronology of the major events from the Creation to the beginning of the Fourth Age, as well as others tracing the histories of the Rings of Power and Gollum. There are charts showing the "evolution" of various kindreds—among the Elves, Men, Hobbits, and Dwarves—and still others detailing the astonishing wealth of flora and fauna that Tolkien created for his world. Two tables detail the connections between Tolkien's Valar and Maiar and the gods of the Norse and Greco-Roman pantheons.

While mastery of such detail is hardly necessary for an appreciation of Tolkien's greatness as a writer of narrative and fantasy fiction, it does nonetheless contribute to our sense of the immensity of the feat of the imagination that is Middle-earth, and of the mythological, philological, historical, and literary sources that underlie it—buried, so to speak, within its geology.

A CHRONOLOGY OF
THE UNDYING LANDS

CREATION

Eru the One ("He that is Alone")

Ainur conceived

Timeless Halls fashioned

Music of the Ainur

Vision of Eä

Creation of Arda

SHAPING OF ARDA
YEAR 1: 1ST VALARIAN AGE

Valar and Maiar enter Arda

Arda shaped by Valar

First War

Arda marred

Melkor expelled

AGES OF THE LAMPS
YEAR 5000: 5TH VALARIAN AGE

Lamps of the Valar forged

Spring of Arda begins

Valar found Almaren

Great Forests of Arda grow

Melkor founds Utumno

Rebel Maiar enter Arda

Lamps and Almaren destroyed

Spring of Arda ends

AGES OF THE TREES
YEAR 10,000: 10TH VALARIAN AGE

Years of Bliss

Valinor founded

City of Valimar founded

Trees of the Valar created

Eagles conceived by Manwë

Yavanna visits Middle-earth

Ents conceived by Yavanna

Oromë visits Middle-earth

Varda gathers light for Stars

Melian departs to Middle-earth

Oromë reports awakening of Elves

Valar depart for War of Powers

Chaining of Melkor

Peace of Arda begins

Summons of the Valar

Vanyar and Noldor settle in Eldamar

City of Tirion founded

Teleri arrive on Tol Eressea

Teleri build first ships

Haven of Alqualondë founded

Noldor forge Elven jewels

Silmarils forged

Melkor unchained

Peace of Arda ends

Trees of the Valar destroyed

First kinslaying of Elves

Flight of the Noldor

FIRST AGE OF SUN
YEAR 30,000: 30TH VALARIAN AGE

Moon and Sun fashioned by Valar

Melian the Maia returns to Valinor

Valar depart for War of Wrath

Melkor/Morgoth Expelled

SECOND AGE OF SUN
YEAR 30,600: 31ST VALARIAN AGE

Avallónë founded

Valar create Númenor

Ban of the Valar

Númenor–Elves alliance

Gift of Palantíri to Númenor

Númenórean Armada

Destruction of Númenor

Change of the World

THIRD AGE OF SUN
YEAR 34,000: 34TH VALARIAN AGE

Long peace of Valinor begins

Istari chosen from Maia Spirits

Istari depart for Middle-earth

Eldar ships from Lothlórien arrive

Eldar ships from Dol Amroth arrive

Valar reject Sauron's spirit

Ringbearers' ships arrive

FOURTH AGE OF SUN
YEAR 37,000: 37TH VALARIAN AGE

Last Eldar Ship of Arrives

A CHRONOLOGY OF THE MORTAL LANDS OF MIDDLE-EARTH

CREATION

Eru the One ("He that is Alone")

Ainur conceived

Timeless Halls fashioned

Music of the Ainur

Vision of Eä

Creation of Arda

SHAPING OF ARDA
(YEAR 1—1ST VALARIAN AGE)

Valar and Maiar enter Arda

Arda shaped by Valar

First War

Arda marred

Melkor expelled

AGES OF DARKNESS
YEAR 1: DARK AGE
(YEAR 5000 VALARIAN AGE)

Melkor in Utumno

Melkor's Lord of Middle-earth

Sleep of Yavanna Begins

Melkor builds Angband

Balrogs and Great Spiders appear

Werewolves and Vampires appear

Dwarves conceived by Aulë

AGES OF STARS
YEAR 1: STAR AGE
(YEAR 10,000 VALARIAN AGE)

Varda rekindles Stars

Elves awakened

Ents awakened

Dwarves awakened

Orcs bred in Angband

Trolls bred

Dwarves found Khazad-dum

Great Journey of Elves begins

Melian the Maia in Beleriand

Great Journey of Elves ends

Dwarves found Nogrod

Dwarves found Belegost

Sindar found Doriath

Sindar delve Menegroth

Laiquendi enter Ossiriand

FIRST AGE OF SUN
YEAR 1: FIRST AGE
(YEAR 30,000 VALARIAN AGE)

Moon and Sun first appear

Men awaken in East

War of Jewels begins

Men appear in Beleriand

Dragons bred in Angband

Noldor kingdoms destroyed

Sindar kingdoms destroyed

War of Wrath and Great Battle

Morgoth cast into Void

SECOND AGE OF SUN
YEAR 1: SECOND AGE
(C. YEAR 30,600 VALARIAN AGE)

Gil-galad founds Lindon

Círdan founds Grey Havens

Edain arrive in Númenor

Sauron established in Mordor

Elven-smiths found Eregion

The One Ring is forged

War of Sauron and Elves

Eregion destroyed

Refuge of Rivendell secured

Nazgûl Ringwraiths appear

Downfall of Númenor

Last Alliance of Elves and Men

Defeat of Sauron and Mordor

THIRD AGE OF SUN
YEAR 1: THIRD AGE
(C. YEAR 34,000 VALARIAN AGE)

The One Ring lost

Easterling invasions begin

Rise of Ship Kings of Gondor

Sauron the Necromancer reappears

Hobbits first recorded in histories

Witch-king in Angmar

Great Plague

End of North Kingdom of Arnor

Balrog appears in Moria

The One Ring found

Uruk-hai and Olog-hai bred

Dragons reappear in north

War of Dwarves and Orcs

Death of Smaug the Golden

War of the Ring

Sauron's Final defeat

Ringbearers' Ships sail west

FOURTH AGE OF SUN
YEAR 1: FOURTH AGE
(C. YEAR 37,000 VALARIAN AGE)

Dominion of Men begins

Last Elven Ships sails west

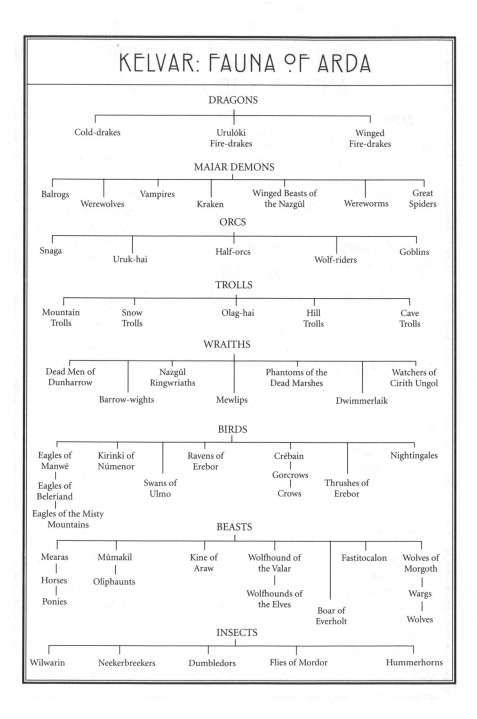

KELVAR: FAUNA OF ARDA

DRAGONS

Cold-drakes | Urulóki Fire-drakes | Winged Fire-drakes

MAIAR DEMONS

Balrogs | Werewolves | Vampires | Kraken | Winged Beasts of the Nazgûl | Wereworms | Great Spiders

ORCS

Snaga | Uruk-hai | Half-orcs | Wolf-riders | Goblins

TROLLS

Mountain Trolls | Snow Trolls | Olag-hai | Hill Trolls | Cave Trolls

WRAITHS

Dead Men of Dunharrow | Barrow-wights | Nazgûl Ringwriaths | Mewlips | Phantoms of the Dead Marshes | Dwimmerlaik | Watchers of Cirith Ungol

BIRDS

Eagles of Manwë | Kirinki of Númenor | Ravens of Erebor | Crébain | Nightingales
Eagles of Beleriand | Swans of Ulmo | Gorcrows | Thrushes of Erebor
Eagles of the Misty Mountains | Crows

BEASTS

Mearas | Mûmakil | Kine of Araw | Wolfhound of the Valar | Fastitocalon | Wolves of Morgoth
Horses | Oliphaunts | Wolfhounds of the Elves | Wargs
Ponies | Boar of Everholt | Wolves

INSECTS

Wilwarin | Neekerbreekers | Dumbledors | Flies of Mordor | Hummerhorns

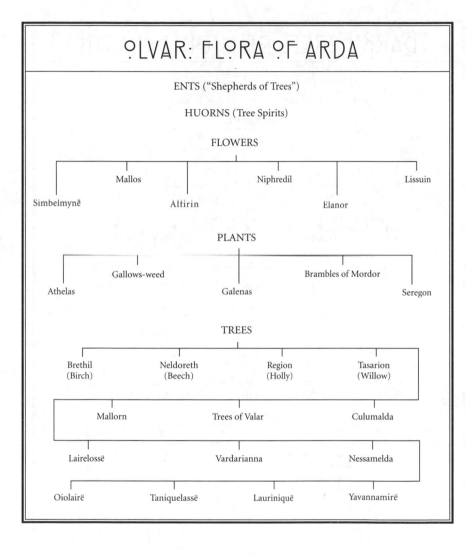

ǑLVAR: FLǑRA ǑF ARDA

ENTS ("Shepherds of Trees")

HUORNS (Tree Spirits)

FLOWERS

| Mallos | Niphredil | Lissuin |

| Simbelmynë | Alfirin | Elanor |

PLANTS

| Gallows-weed | | Brambles of Mordor |

| Athelas | Galenas | Seregon |

TREES

| Brethil (Birch) | Neldoreth (Beech) | Region (Holly) | Tasarion (Willow) |

| Mallorn | Trees of Valar | Culumalda |

| Lairelossë | Vardarianna | Nessamelda |

| Oiolairë | Taniquelassë | Lauriniquë | Yavannamirë |

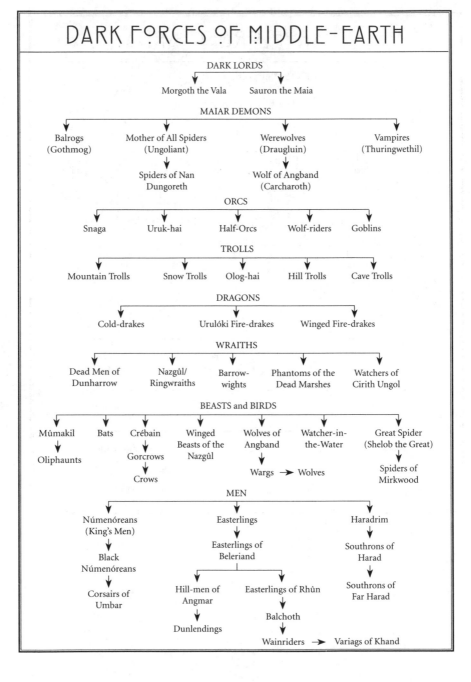

DARK FORCES OF MIDDLE-EARTH

DARK LORDS

Morgoth the Vala   Sauron the Maia

MAIAR DEMONS

Balrogs
(Gothmog)

Mother of All Spiders
(Ungoliant)

Spiders of Nan
Dungoreth

Werewolves
(Draugluin)

Wolf of Angband
(Carcharoth)

Vampires
(Thuringwethil)

ORCS

Snaga   Uruk-hai   Half-Orcs   Wolf-riders   Goblins

TROLLS

Mountain Trolls   Snow Trolls   Olog-hai   Hill Trolls   Cave Trolls

DRAGONS

Cold-drakes   Urulóki Fire-drakes   Winged Fire-drakes

WRAITHS

Dead Men of
Dunharrow

Nazgûl/
Ringwraiths

Barrow-
wights

Phantoms of the
Dead Marshes

Watchers of
Cirith Ungol

BEASTS and BIRDS

Mûmakil   Bats   Crébain   Winged
Beasts of the
Nazgûl

Wolves of
Angband

Watcher-in-
the-Water

Great Spider
(Shelob the Great)

Oliphaunts

Gorcrows

Crows

Wargs → Wolves

Spiders of
Mirkwood

MEN

Númenóreans
(King's Men)

Black
Númenóreans

Corsairs of
Umbar

Easterlings

Easterlings of
Beleriand

Hill-men of
Angmar

Dunlendings

Easterlings of Rhûn

Balchoth

Wainriders → Variags of Khand

Haradrim

Southrons of
Harad

Southrons of
Far Harad

HISTORY OF SMÉAGOL—GOLLUM

2430 *Birth of Sméagol Stoor Hobbit of River-folk Near Gladden Fields*

2463 *One Ring found at Gladden Fields*
Sméagol murders cousin Déagol and takes the One Ring

2470 *Exiled Sméagol takes "precious" Ring*
Hides in caves in Misty Mountains

c. 2600 *Corrupted by One Ring*
Sméagol morphs into Gollum, a mad and paranoid ghoul

c. 2800 *Gollum hunts the deepest tunnels in caves of Goblin-town*

2941 *Loss of the One Ring in a Riddle Game to the Hobbit Bilbo Baggins*

2944 *Leaves Misty Mountains in search of One Ring*

2951 *Gollum travels to south and east towards Mordor*

2980 *Gollum enters Morgul Pass and encounters Shelob the Great*

3010 *Gollum enters Mordor captured by Sauron*

3017 *Released from Mordor Gollum captured by Aragorn*
Imprisoned by Wood Elves

3018

20 June *Gollum escapes from Wood Elves after Dol Guldur attack*

c. 1 August–December *Trapped in his refuge in the of Mines of Moria*
Hunted by both Elves and Sauron

3019

13 January *In Moria, discovers and stalks Frodo Baggins the Ring-bearer*

16 February *Tracks down Ring-bearer and Fellowship as they depart from Lórien*

29 February *Frodo and Sam descend from Rauros Falls and capture Gollum*

1–2 March *Gollum guides Ring-bearer through the Dead Marshes*

4–5 March *Gollum, Frodo, and Sam reach Black Gate of Mordor and turn away to the south*

7 March *Faramir at Henneth Annun captures, then releases Gollum*

9 March *Gollum guides Ring-bearer on to the Morgul Road*

12 March *Gollum betrays Ring-bearer, leads him into Shelob's Lair*

14 March *Gollum stalks Sam and Frodo after their escape from Shelob and Orcs of Tower of Cirith Ungol*

24 March *Gollum follows Frodo and Sam across Mordor to Mount Doom*

25 March *Gollum seizes the One Ring Falls to his death in the fires of Cracks of Doom*

BREEDS OF HOBBIT

	HARFOOT	FALLOHIDE	STOOR
NAME	Harfoot: *English surname* Hare-foot. Hare-foot: *Anglo-Saxon epithet or nickname usually meaning* fast runner *or* nimble as a hare.	Falo-hide: falo—*Old High German:* pale yellow. hide—*English:* skin or pelt. Fallow Hide: fallow—*Old English:* ploughed land. hide—*Old English:* measure of land.	Stoor: stur *(Middle English)* stor *(Old English)* strong *(Modern English)*
JOKE	Harfoot ➔ Hare-foot ➔ Hair-foot.	Follow-Hide: game of Hide and Seek.	Stoor ➔ stower ➔ store.
TYPICAL NAMES OF BREEDS	Brown and Brownlock are descriptive of the hair and skin color of Harfoots. Other names such as Sandheaver, Tunnelly, and Burrows suggest the construction of hole-dwelling Harfoot Hobbit homes. Names such as Gardner, Hayward, and Roper tell us of typical Harfoot occupations.	The fair-haired Fallohides are suggested by family names such as Fairbairn, Goold, and Goldworthy. Their unconventional and independent nature and their intelligence are suggested by names such as Headstrong and Boffin.	Puddifoot is a Stoorish name as it suggests "puddle-foot," or someone who enjoys seeing in water. However, as an English surname, it was originally Puddephat (or Pudding Vat, or otherwise Bulgy Barrel), meaning a man with a fat belly. So we get these images at once: large, fat, and water-loving. Banks appears to be a name for Hobbits who liked to live on river banks. Other names like Cotton, Cottar, and Cotman may have been Stoorish names in origin because they all mean "Cottager" and the Stoors were the first Hobbits to emerge from their holes and live in houses.

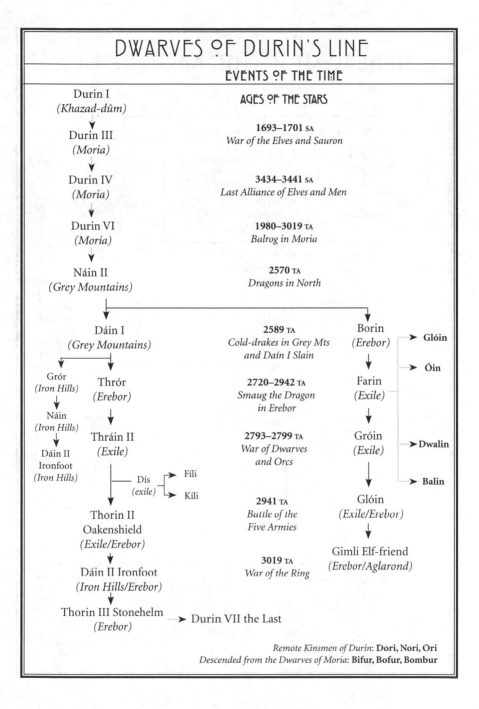

DWARVES OF DURIN'S LINE

EVENTS OF THE TIME

Durin I
(Khazad-dûm)

AGES OF THE STARS

Durin III
(Moria)

1693–1701 SA
War of the Elves and Sauron

Durin IV
(Moria)

3434–3441 SA
Last Alliance of Elves and Men

Durin VI
(Moria)

1980–3019 TA
Balrog in Moria

Náin II
(Grey Mountains)

2570 TA
Dragons in North

Dáin I
(Grey Mountains)

2589 TA
*Cold-drakes in Grey Mts
and Daín I Slain*

Borin
(Erebor)

→ **Glóin**

→ **Óin**

Grór
(Iron Hills)

Thrór
(Erebor)

2720–2942 TA
*Smaug the Dragon
in Erebor*

Farin
(Exile)

Náin
(Iron Hills)

Dáin II
Ironfoot
(Iron Hills)

Thráin II
(Exile)

2793–2799 TA
*War of Dwarves
and Orcs*

Gróin
(Exile)

→ **Dwalin**

Dís
(exile)

→ Fíli

→ Kíli

→ **Balin**

Thorin II
Oakenshield
(Exile/Erebor)

2941 TA
*Battle of the
Five Armies*

Glóin
(Exile/Erebor)

3019 TA
War of the Ring

Gimli Elf-friend
(Erebor/Aglarond)

Dáin II Ironfoot
(Iron Hills/Erebor)

Thorin III Stonehelm
(Erebor)

⤑ Durin VII the Last

Remote Kinsmen of Durin: **Dori, Nori, Ori**
Descended from the Dwarves of Moria: **Bifur, Bofur, Bombur**

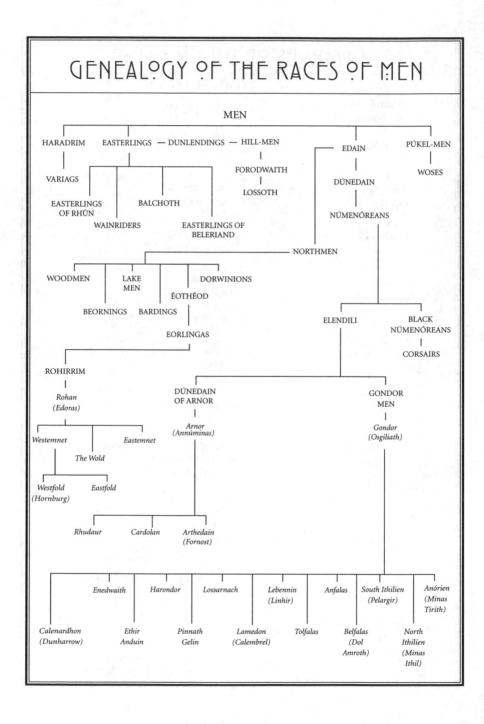

GENEALOGY OF THE RACES OF MEN

MEN

HARADRIM — EASTERLINGS — DUNLENDINGS — HILL-MEN — EDAIN — PÚKEL-MEN

VARIAGS — FORODWAITH — WOSES

EASTERLINGS — LOSSOTH — DÚNEDAIN
OF RHÛN

BALCHOTH — NÚMENÓREANS

WAINRIDERS — EASTERLINGS OF
BELERIAND

NORTHMEN

WOODMEN — LAKE — DORWINIONS
MEN

ÉOTHÉOD

BEORNINGS — BARDINGS

EORLINGAS — ELENDILI — BLACK
NÚMENÓREANS

ROHIRRIM — CORSAIRS

Rohan
(Edoras)

DÚNEDAIN — GONDOR
OF ARNOR — MEN

Westemnet — Eastemnet — Arnor
(Annúminas)

Gondor
(Osgiliath)

The Wold

Westfold — Eastfold
(Hornburg)

Rhudaur — Cardolan — Arthedain
(Fornost)

Enedwaith — Harondor — Lossarnach — Lebennin — Anfalas — South Ithilien — Anórien
(Linhir) (Pelargir) (Minas
Tirith)

Calenardhon — Ethir — Pinnath — Lamedon — Tolfalas — Belfalas — North
(Dunharrow) — Anduin — Gelin — (Calembrel) — (Dol — Ithilien
Amroth) — (Minas
Ithil)

GENEALOGY OF THE RACES OF ELVES

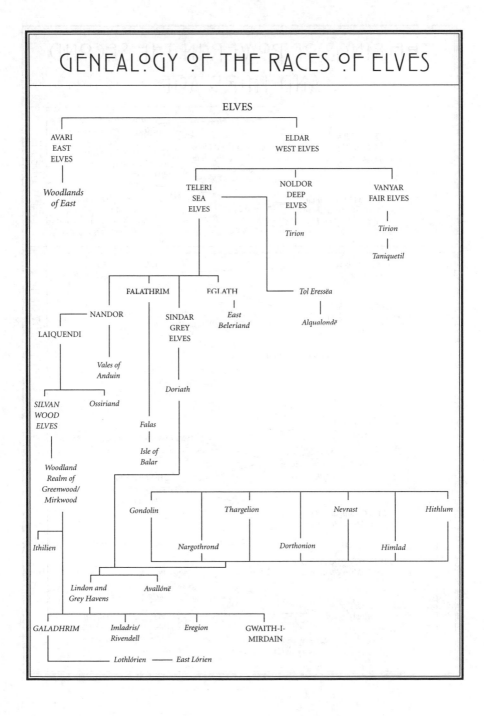

THE RINGS OF POWER IN THE SECOND AND THIRD AGE

1500 *Rings of Power forged by Sauron and Elven-smiths of Eregion (Three Elf Rings, Seven Dwarf Rings, Nine Rings for Men)*

1600 *Sauron forges One Ring in fires of Mount Doom*

1693 *War of Sauron and Elves. Three Elf Rings hidden (Círdan in Grey Havens, Gil-galad in Lindon, Galadriel in Lothlórien)*

2251 *Ringwraiths, slaves of the Nine Rings, come to serve Sauron*

3430 *Last Alliance of Elves and Men formed*

3441 *One Ring cut from Sauron's hand. Mordor falls. Sauron and Ringwraiths vanish*

1 *Gil-galad's Elf Ring goes with Elrond to Rivendell*

2 *Battle of Gladden Fields One Ring lost in Anduin River*

1000 *Sauron, in Mirkwood, secretly gathers Rings*

1050 *Wizards come to Middle-earth. Círdan gives Elf Ring to Gandalf*

1200 *Ringwraiths reappear in north*

1300 *Lord of Ringwraiths becomes Witch-king of Angmar*

1975 *Angmar destroyed*

1980 *Ringwraiths dwelling in Mordor*

2002 *Witch-king begins rule in Minas Morgul*

2463 *One Ring found by Gollum in Anduin River*

2470 *Gollum takes One Ring into Misty Mountains*

2845 *Sauron seizes last of Seven Dwarf Rings*

2941 *Bilbo Baggins finds One Ring in Misty Mountains*

3001 *Bilbo Baggins gives One Ring to Frodo Baggins*

3018 *Fellowship of the Ring formed*

3021 *The War of the Ring begins. One Ring destroyed. Mordor falls. Sauron and Ringwraiths vanish forever*

3021 *Keepers of the Three Elf Rings sail to Undying Lands*

CELEBRIMBOR AND THE FORGING OF THE RINGS OF POWER

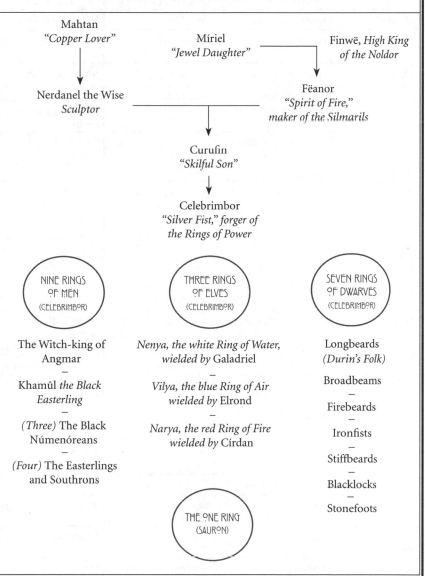

Mahtan
"Copper Lover"

Míriel
"Jewel Daughter"

Finwë, *High King of the Noldor*

Nerdanel the Wise
Sculptor

Fëanor
"Spirit of Fire," maker of the Silmarils

Curufin
"Skilful Son"

Celebrimbor
"Silver Fist," forger of the Rings of Power

NINE RINGS OF MEN
(CELEBRIMBOR)

THREE RINGS OF ELVES
(CELEBRIMBOR)

SEVEN RINGS OF DWARVES
(CELEBRIMBOR)

The Witch-king of Angmar

–

Khamûl *the Black Easterling*

–

(Three) The Black Númenóreans

–

(Four) The Easterlings and Southrons

Nenya, the white Ring of Water, wielded by Galadriel

–

Vilya, the blue Ring of Air wielded by Elrond

–

Narya, the red Ring of Fire wielded by Círdan

Longbeards
(Durin's Folk)

Broadbeams

–

Firebeards

–

Ironfists

–

Stiffbeards

–

Blacklocks

–

Stonefoots

THE ONE RING
(SAURON)

VALAR AND MAIAR AND THE NORSE GODS

VALA/MAIA	MAIN FUNCTION/NAME	RELEVANT ASSOCIATIONS	NORSE GOD/HERO
Manwë	King of the Valar	All-seeing	Odin, king of the gods
Varda	Queen of the Valar	Stars and starlight	Frigg, queen of the gods
Ulmo	Lord of the Waters	Seas and storms	Njord, God of the seas
Aulë	Lord of the Earth, mountains, and smithing	Skill, craft	Völundr, divine or hero smith (Wayland the Smith)
Yavanna	Queen of the Earth and Giver of Fruits	Fertility	Sif, goddess of the harvest
Vairë	The Weaver	Fate	Urd
Nienna	Lady of Mercy	Mourning, sorrow, consolation	Hlín, protective goddess; Nanna, goddess who grieves
Oromë	Huntsman of the Valar	Horses, hunting	Odin, king of the gods; Ullr, god of hunting
Vána	The Ever Young; Lady of Blossoming Flowers	Fruits and flowers	Idunn, Goddess of youth
Estë	The Gentle	Healing, rest	Eir, Goddess of healing
Tulkas	The Strong; Champion of Valinor	Strength, courage	Magni, god/personification of strength; Tyr, warrior god
Nessa	The Dancer	Forest wilderness, speed	Skadi, goddess of the hunt
Eönwë	Herald and banner-bearer of Manwë	Messenger	Heimdall, watchman of the gods
Ilmarë	Handmaiden of the Varda		Fulla, handmaiden of Frigg
Arlen	Guide of the sun		Sunna, goddess of the sun
Tirion	Guide of the moon		Mani, god of the moon
Mairon/Sauron	Dark Lord	Skill, cunning, necromancy	"Black" aspects of Odin
Curumo/Saruman	Istari (Wizard)	Skill, cunning	"Black" aspects of Odin
Olórin/Gandalf	Istari (Wizard)	Wisdom, foresight	Odin

VALAR AND MAIAR AND THE GRECO-ROMAN GODS

VALA/MAIA	MAIN FUNCTION/NAME	RELEVANT ASSOCIATIONS	GREEK/ROMAN GOD/HERO
Manwë	King of the Valar	The sky and eagles; all-seeing	Zeus/Jupiter, king of the gods
Varda	Queen of the Valar	Stars	Hera/Juno, queen of the gods
Ulmo	Lord of the Waters	Seas and storms	Poseidon/Neptune, God of the seas
Aulë	Lord of the Earth, mountains, and smithing	Earth, minerals, metallurgy	Hephaestus/Vulcan, Smith-god
Yavanna	Queen of the Earth and Giver of Fruits	Growth, nature	Demeter/Ceres, Goddess of the harvest
Mandos	Judge of the dead; Doomsman of the Valar	Doomsman	Hades/Pluto, god of the underworld
Vairë	The Weaver	Fate	Clotho/Nona, one of the Fates
Nienna	Lady of Mercy	Virginity	Hestia/Vesta, goddess of the hearth and home
Oromë	Huntsman of the Valar	Forests, hunting	Orion, huntsman hero
Vána	The Ever Young; Lady of Blossoming Flowers	Blossoming flowers	Persephone/Proserpine, goddess of the spring; Hebe, goddess of youth
Irmo/Lórien	Master of Dreams and Visions	Rest, visions	Morpheus, God of dreams
Estë	The Gentle	Healing, rest	Hygieia, goddess of health and healing
Tulkas	The Strong; Champion of Valinor	Strength	Heracles/Hercules, greatest Greeek hero
Nessa	The Dancer	Dancing, deer (not portrayed as a huntress)	Artemis/Diana, goddess of the wilderness and hunt
Eönwë	Herald of the gods	Heraldry	Hermes/Mercury, god of heraldry, merchants, trickery
Ilmarë	Handmaiden of Varda		Hebe/Juventas, handmaiden of Hera/Juno, goddess of youth
Ossë	Protector of Inner Seas	Beaches	Nereus and other sea gods
Uinen	Lady of the Sea	Rescuer of sailors	Leucothea and other sea goddesses/nymphs

BATTLES

B A T T L E S From the creation of J. R. R. Tolkien's world of Arda until the end of the War of the Ring—some 37,000[1] years later—cataclysmic wars punctuated by crucial battles have determined the course of that world's evolution and history. In the recording of these events upon Middle-earth and the Undying Lands, Tolkien takes a similar approach to that of a real-world historian.

Like those of their real-life historic counterparts, the annals of Tolkien's races and nations record each civilization's achievements in the creative arts, the architecture of its great cities and the genius of its technologies, but they also give weight to the pivotal role of great battles that result in the rise and fall of empires.

For undeniably it is in battles and wars that the fates of nations and races are finally determined. And for all nations (both real and imaginary), it is in these crucial battles that the courage and wisdom of their most celebrated heroes are ultimately tested. Furthermore, these wars are also the crucial themes of all the great civilizations' national epics: Greece's *Iliad*, Germany's *Nibelungenlied*, Norway and Iceland's *Poetic Edda*, India's *Mahabharata*, Mesopotamia's *Epic of Gilgamesh*.

In Tolkien's Middle-earth, *The Lord of the Rings* is certainly comparable to Greece's *Iliad*. However, the difference is that Homer—unlike Tolkien—did not have to invent an entire world's evolution, geography, history, and mythology before even beginning his tale of the Trojan War.

---

[1] This estimation of 37,000 years is based on one early version of Tolkien's own chronology. However, there is another (and possibly earlier) account by Tolkien that suggests a 57,000-year history. That said, the disputed 20,000 years occur so early in Arda's history that virtually no specific events take place. Consequently, I have chosen to stick with Tolkien's first published time span.

BATTLE OF DAGORLAD

The single greatest battle of the Second Age was fought in Sauron's War with the Last Alliance of Elves and Men on a treeless stony plain between the Dead Marshes and the Gates of Mordor. It was a battle fought over months, rather than days, with hundreds of thousands of casualties. Tolkien's fictional Battle of Dagorlad was authentically informed by his own experience as a soldier in the equally bloody real-world Battle of the Somme during the First World War. When the Last Alliance of Elves and Men marched on Mordor in 3434 of the Second Age, Tolkien framed the conflict in Arthurian terms.

In 2013 Tolkien's unfinished poem *The Fall of Arthur* was published, illuminating similarities between his conception of the Arthurian legends and the battles of the Second and Third Ages of Middle-earth. Many stanzas are strongly redolent of the threat of Sauron: "The endless East in anger woke / and black thunder born in dungeons / under mountains of menace moved above them." For the Battle of Dagorlad and the Siege of the Dark Tower, Tolkien seems to have drawn particularly on the legend of the Last Battle of Camlann. At Camlann, Arthur destroyed the forces arrayed against him, only for he and Mordred to slay each other in climactic single combat; the Alliance experienced a similarly pyrrhic victory as their armies triumphed but Gil-galad and Elendil received mortal wounds as they finally overcame Sauron.

After Arthur's death, it was the duty of one surviving knight to retrieve the king's sword. In Tolkien's Middle-earth, it was left to Elendil's son Isildur to retrieve (the shards of) the king's sword and with it cut the One Ring from Sauron's hand.

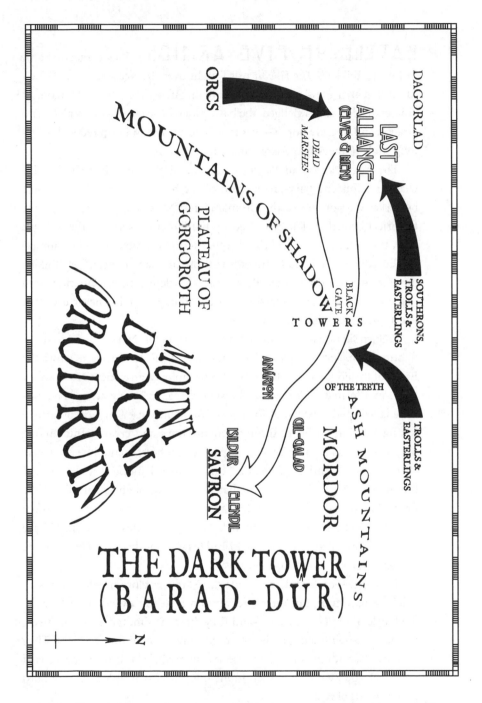

Battle of Dagorlad. This is an artist's impression of the Battle of Dagorlad and the Siege of the Dark Tower. For Tolkien's account of the battle, *see The Silmarillion*, "Of the Rings of Power and the Third Age."

BATTLE ꝋF FIVE ARMIES This climactic battle

in J. R. R. Tolkien's *The Hobbit* was fought over the treasure of the Lonely Mountain after the slaying of its guardian, Smaug the Golden Dragon. As Tolkien readily acknowledged, the basic plot of *The Hobbit*—complete with Dragon and treasure horde—was largely informed and inspired by his life-long study of the Anglo-Saxon epic poem *Beowulf*.

The huge Northman Beorn, Chieftain of the Beornings, is a "skin-changer": Tolkien's fairy-tale version of the bear-cult hero of the real-life berserker warrior cult of the Germanic and Norse peoples. Although the historical berserkers felt possessed by the ferocious spirit of the enraged bear, these states were only rituals attempting to imitate the core miracle of the cult: the incarnate transformation of man to bear. Yet Tolkien provides the real thing when Beorn has a battlefield transformation from fierce warrior into an enraged were-bear (though Tolkien never uses that word)—an event that turns the tide of battle.

Tolkien's Dwarves resembled the warriors of Norse myth in their fighting style. For example, in Thorin Oakenshield's sudden entry into the Battle of the Five Armies, the Dwarf-king employed an ancient Norse shock tactic in a formation known as the *svinfylking*, or "swine array." This was a wedge-shaped shield-wall formation frequently used by heavily armed Viking warriors to break through enemy lines and create panic among the closed ranks of an army with superior numbers. It could be extremely effective, but it entirely depended on the initial monumental shock. If this flying wedge did not immediately break through enemy lines, the formation would soon collapse. Like many shield-wall tactics, it could often be outflanked and entirely encircled. And, indeed, this would likely have been the fate of Thorin Oakenshield and his warriors had it not been for the sudden arrival of an unexpected ally.

The Eagles of Middle-earth are generally not prominent players in Tolkien's narratives, but their intervention is nearly always crucial—as in the Battle of the Five Armies—and they arrive at times of desperate need, frequently when rescue can be achieved only by the power of flight. They are part of a tradition of eagle-emissaries in myth, leading from the birds of the Greek god Zeus (the Roman Jupiter) to the vassals of Manwë, the Lord of the Winds of Arda.

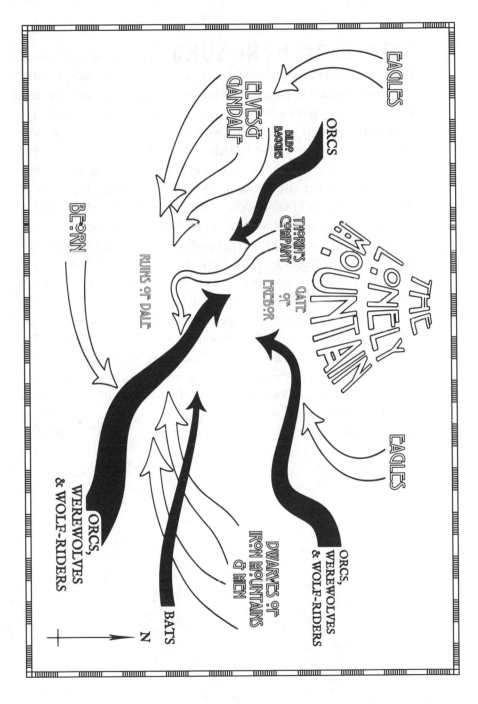

Battle of the Five Armies. This is an artist's impression of the Battle of Five Armies. For Tolkien's account of the conflict, *see The Hobbit*, Chapters XI and XVII, and *Unfinished Tales*, Part Three, Chapter III.

BATTLE OF HORNBURG

This was one of the most decisive battles in the War of the Ring. Here the army of the White Hand of Saruman the Wizard was set against Théoden the King of Rohan's defenders of the Hornburg. Also known as the Battle of Helm's Deep, the Hornburg's impressive earthwork walls and trench—known as Helms Dike—was defended two centuries earlier by Helm Hammerhand, the Ninth King of Rohan in the first Dunlending–Rohirrim war. That mighty Rohan king was modeled on the historic eighth century Anglo-Saxon King Offa of Mercia: the architect of Offa's Dyke, a massive earthwork wall and trench that marked (and still marks) the border between England and Wales. However, in the War of the Ring, Helm's Dike was breached by Saruman's hordes of Dunlendings, Orcs, Half-Orcs, and Uruk-hai that then stormed the Deeping Wall and smashing the gates of the Hornburg fortress itself. While a faction of Rohirrim retreated into Helm's Deep, the tide of battle was turned by the unexpected charge of King Théoden's cavalry that drove the invaders from the high walls of Hornburg out onto the battleground of Deeping-comb. There the fleeing enemy forces were driven directly into the path of a second charging army of Rohirrim led by Gandalf the Wizard and Erkenbrand the Lord of Westfold. In the crush of battle, the Dunlendings either fought to the death or surrendered; while the Orcs and Uruks were driven into the forest where they were slaughtered by a legion of those wild giant tree spirits known as Huorns.

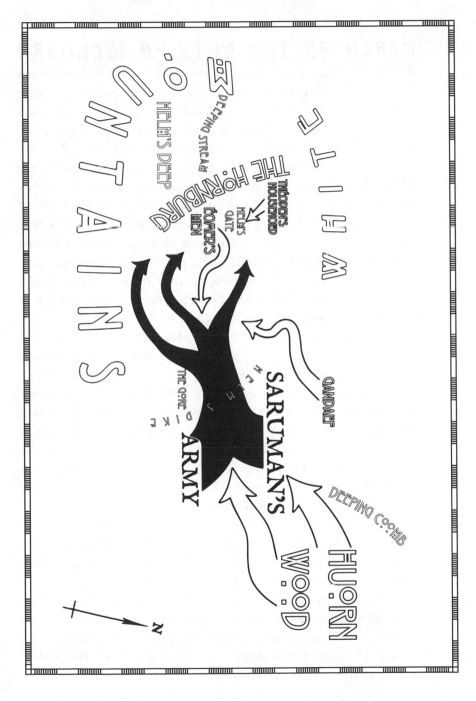

Battle of the Hornburg. This is an artist's impression of the Battle of the Hornburg. For Tolkien's account of the battle, *see The Lord of the Rings*, Book III, Chapter VII.

MARCH OF THE ENTS ON ISENGARD

Beyond *ent* being an Anglo-Saxon name for "giant," the inspiration for Tolkien's March of the Ents came about in a rather negative way: through his dislike and, indeed, disapproval of William Shakespeare's treatment of myths and legends. His greatest abuse was heaped on one of the playwright's most popular plays, *Macbeth*. The creation of the Ents, Tolkien explained, "is due, I think, to my bitter disappointment and disgust from schooldays with the shabby use made in Shakespeare of the coming of 'Great Birnam wood to high Dunsinane hill': I longed to devise a setting in which the trees might really march to war." Tolkien felt Shakespeare had trivialized and misinterpreted an authentic myth, providing a cheap, simplistic interpretation of the prophecy of this march of the wood upon the hill. So in *The Lord of the Rings* Tolkien did indeed devise such a setting. And certainly, in his own March of the Ents, the fundamental opposition between the spirits of the forest and of the mountain was revealed and portrayed in a way that lends power and dignity to the archetypal miracle of a wood marching on a hill.

To find beings of myth who do correspond directly to the Ents, Tolkien had only to look back into English folklore, where the Green Man plays a distinctive part. Green Man stories and carvings were common in Tolkien's beloved West Midlands and the Welsh Marches just beyond. He was a Celtic nature spirit and tree god who represented the coming of new growth in victory over the powers of ice and frost. Essentially benevolent, he could also be powerful and destructive.

The semi-sentient Huorns represent the wilder, more dangerous aspect of the Green Man: an inhuman power tapping the deepest sources of the natural world where fowls, animals, and even children were sacrificed to placate the demonic spirit of certain trees.

The appearance of Huorns brought terror to their foes. They may have been Ents who in time had grown treeish, or perhaps trees that had grown Entish, but they were certainly wrathful, dangerous, and merciless. In the Huorns, we have a dramatization of an avenging army of "Green Men" making an attack on all creatures who are hostile to the spirits of forests.

March of the Ents on Isengard. This is an artist's impression of the March of the Ents on Isengard. For Tolkien's account of the fall of Isengard, *see The Lord of the Rings*, Book III, Chapters IX and X.

THE BATTLE OF THE PELENNOR FIELDS

This is the most richly described conflict in the annals of Middle-earth, and the most dramatic, if not the final, battle of the War of the Ring. As such, it draws on many aspects of real-world military history, ranging over a thousand years of European warfare.

In his chronicles of Gondor and Arnor, Tolkien links the history of the Dúnedain kingdoms to many comparable aspects in the history of the ancient Roman Empire. However, by the time of the War of the Ring, in Aragorn's attempt at restoration of the Reunited Dúnedain Kingdom of Arnor and Gondor, Tolkien has drawn on the historical precedent of the warrior king Charlemagne, who reunited and restored the Roman Empire to its former glory in the form of the Holy Roman Empire in the eighth century.

In a letter to a publisher, Tolkien makes direct reference to this Carolingian motif in *The Lord of the Rings*: "The progress of the tale ends in what is far more like the reestablishment of an effective Holy Roman Empire with its seat in Rome."

And certainly, in its physical geography, Tolkien saw the Reunited Kingdom as an expanse of land comparable to Charlemagne's empire. The action of *The Lord of the Rings* takes place in the northwest of Middle-earth, in a region roughly equivalent to the Western European landmass. Hobbiton and Rivendell, as Tolkien often acknowledged, were roughly intended to be at the latitude of Oxford.

By his own estimation, this put Gondor and Minas Tirith some 600 miles to the south in a location that might be equivalent to Florence. This would suggest that Mordor might be approximately comparable to the mountainous regions of Romania or Bulgaria and the basin of the Black Sea.

In terms of enemies as well as allies, Charlemagne and Aragorn have much in common. At the Battle of the Pelennor Fields, the Gondor and Rohan cavalry encounters an enemy in the form of the Southron cavalry of Harad. This is comparable to battles in which Charlemagne's cavalry fought their historic enemies: the Moors of Spain and the Saracens of North Africa. Other foes of Gondor and Rohan were the ancient, rebellious Dunlending tribesmen who had their historical counterparts in the rebellious Basque tribesmen who ambushed Charlemagne's chevalier, Roland, in Roncesvalles Pass in the Pyrenees.

However, with the appearance on the Pelennor Fields of the warriors mounted on Mûmakil—equivalent to Hannibal's Carthaginian war elephants—and companies of Easterlings bearded like Dwarves and armed with great two-handed axes—equivalent to the late Byzantine axe-bearing infantries—Tolkien introduces troops and weaponry drawn from both much earlier (third century BC) and much later periods (twelfth century AD) of European warfare.

And, as already noted, Tolkien's dramatic charge of the Rohirrim in the Battle of the Pelennor Fields has parallels with the fifth-century AD Roman account of an historical Gothic cavalry action in the Battle of Châlons in AD 451. This was an alliance between the Roman general Flavius Aetius and the Gothic King Theodoric that proved to be the salvation of Western Europe from the seemingly unstoppable invading hordes of Attila the Hun.

Similarly, among earlier allies of Mordor, we are told, there were the Easterlings of Rhûn who were perhaps inspired by the twelfth-century Seljuk Turks of Rhum (Anatolia). Meanwhile, among those fighting on Gondor's eastern borders were the Variags of Khand; these were perhaps inspired by the tenth- or eleventh-century Variangians of the Khanate of Kiev, who were also known as the Rus—and, later, the Russians.

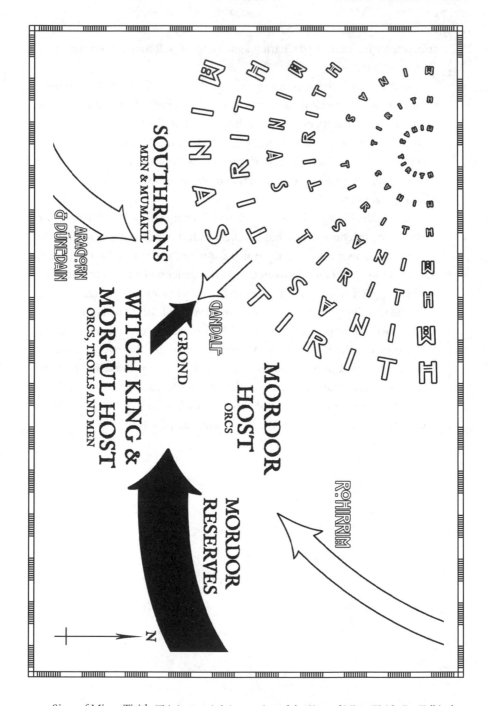

Siege of Minas Tirith. This is an artist's impression of the Siege of Minas Tirith. For Tolkien's account of the siege, *see The Lord of the Rings,* Book V, Chapter IV.

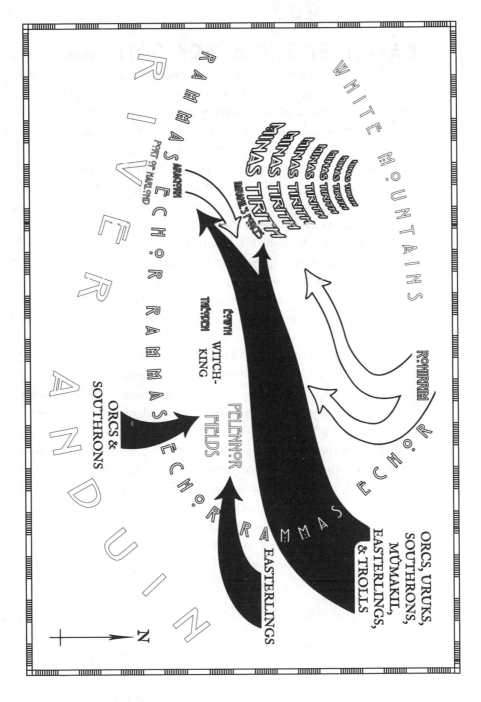

Battle of Pelennor Fields. This is an artist's impression of the Battle of Pelennor Fields. For
Tolkien's account of the battle, *see The Lord of the Rings*, Book V, Chapters V and VI.

BATTLE OF THE BLACK GATE

Morannon the Black Gate was not only the entrance of that cursed and hellish realm of Mordor, but it was specifically the entrance to the region known as Udûn, meaning "black pit, hell." Certainly, Tolkien meant the Black Gate to be Middle-earth's equivalent to the Gate of Hell in Dante's inferno with its motto: "Abandon all hope, ye who enter here." Tolkien may have been inspired by the medieval images in his conception of a massive iron gate with its two mighty "Towers of the Teeth." This would certainly be in keeping with the ancient Anglo-Saxon vision of the "Hellmouth": the entrance of hell as the gaping the jaws of a huge monster.

In the War of the Ring, the Black Gate was the site of the final last stand of Sauron the Ring Lord against the Army of the Captains of the West. Victory for the evil forces of Sauron appeared certain as the few thousand Gondor men-at-arms were outnumbered by "forces ten times, and more than ten times their match." However, the battle at the Black Gate proved to be a tactical distraction; while others worked secretly to bring about the Necromancer's downfall by destroying the One Ring of Power. In German Romance, there was one named Janibas the Necromancer who, like Sauron, lived in a mountain kingdom where he commanded demonic armies of giants, men, and monsters. And just as Sauron's power was invested in a ring, Janibas's power was invested in a black tablet. Janibas's downfall came in the midst of battle, when suddenly his tablet was snatched from his grasp and smashed. The destruction of Janibas's tablet not only destroyed his necromancer's power, but also caused all his demonic armies of giants, men, and monsters to become like him a mere phantom dispelled by the wind. This was the fate he shared with Sauron the Ring Lord. The mighty foundations of his palaces cracked and the very mountains of his realm collapsed in ruin.

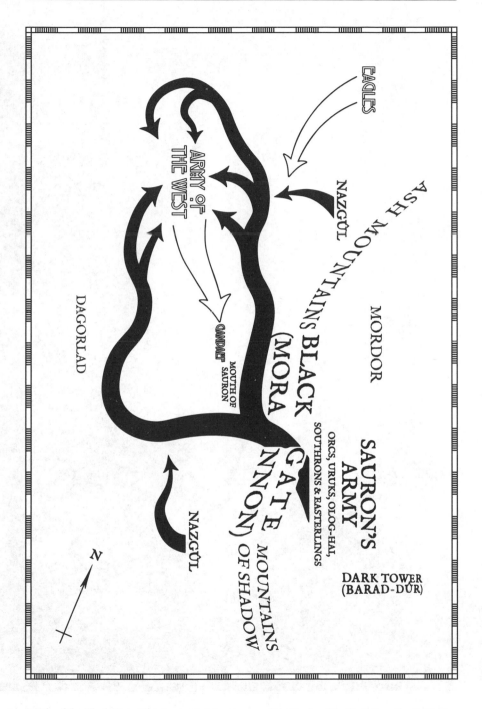

Battle of the Black Gate. This is an artist's impression of the Battle of the Black Gate. For Tolkien's
account of the conflict, *see The Lord of the Rings*, Book VI, Chapter X.

Battle of Azanulbizar. Dwarves make dangerously persistent enemies, as proved by this battle—
a conflict with echoes in various mining cultures, where goblins or demons have been said to
sabotage miners in tunnels, hindering their work out of sheer malice and spite.

THREE PRIMARY

RING LEGENDS

NORSE RING

Völsunga Saga

GERMAN RING

Nibelungenlied

WAGNER'S RING

The Ring of the Nibelung

NORSE RING

Völsunga Saga

The most famous ring legend of the Norsemen is told in the *Völsunga Saga*. The epic tale is one of the greatest literary works to survive the Viking civilization. Within the *Völsunga Saga* is the history of many of the heroes of the Völsung and Nibelung[1] dynasties. In the nineteenth century William Morris—British textile designer, writer, and translator—wrote of the epic: "This is the great story of the North, which should be to all our race what the tale of Troy was to the Greeks."

The fates of the Völsung and Nibelung dynasties were bound up with that of a magical ring called Andvarinaut. This was the magical ring that once belonged to Andvari the Dwarf. Its name means "Andvari's loom" because it "wove" its master a fortune in gold; and with that wealth went power and fame. The tale of Andvarinaut has become the archetypal ring legend. It is primarily concerned with the life and death of the greatest of all Norse heroes, Sigurd the Dragon-slayer.

It is this legend of Sigurd and the Ring as told in the *Völsunga Saga* that in various forms survives in the modern imagination as *the* Ring Legend. William Morris brought the first satisfactory direct translation of the *Völsunga Saga* into the English language. His later long epic poem *Sigurd the Völsung*, Henrik Ibsen's play *The Vikings of Helgeland*, and—above all—Richard Wagner's great opera cycle *The Ring of the Nibelung* brought the epic tale into the popular European imagination in the nineteenth and twentieth centuries.

In this retelling of the *Völsunga Saga*, it should be noted that the full-length epic is a collection of over forty linked but individual saga tales. These were the final outcome of an oral tradition of diverse authorship composed over many centuries. The resulting texts therefore often result in a somewhat irregular plot structure, although the overall outline is clear. In this retelling, those parts of the saga concerning the ring are emphasized in detail, while peripheral adventures (particularly those that precede the appearance of Sigurd) are told in synopsis form. Readers will find many parallels between the *Völsunga Saga* and Tolkien's *The Lord of the Rings* and *The Silmarillion*, along with the legends of King Arthur, Charlemagne, Dietrich von Berne, and numerous other heroes and traditions including the medieval German *Nibelungenlied* and a score of Brothers Grimm fairy tales.

---

[1] In earliest recorded sagas, the Nibelungs were called the Guikings. However, the names appear to be used interchangeably. Iceland's Snorri Sturluson, in the thirteenth-century *Younger Edda*, states: "Gunnar and Hogni were called Nibelungen or Guikings; therefore the gold is called the Nibelungen hoard." To minimize the confusion in view of later Germanic traditions, I will use the Nibelung name for the dynasty.

The *Völsunga Saga* begins with the tale of the hero Sigi, who is the mortal son of Odin. He is a great warrior who by his strength and skill becomes king of the Huns. King Sigi's son is Reric, who is also a mighty warrior, but cannot give his queen a child and heir. So the gods send to Reric a crow with an apple in its beak. Reric gives this apple to his wife, who eats it and becomes heavy with child. But the child remains in his mother's womb for six years before he is released by the midwife's knife. This child is Völsung, who becomes the third in this line of kings.

Völsung is the strongest and most powerful of all the kings of Hunland. He is a man of huge physical size and he sires ten sons and one daughter. The eldest of his children are the twin brother and sister, Sigmund and Signy.

One day a gray-bearded stranger with one eye appears in the great hall of the Völsungs in the middle of a great gathering of Huns, Goths, and Vikings. Without a word, the old man strides over to Branstock, the great living oak tree that stands in the center of the Völsung hall. He draws a brilliant sword from a sheath and drives it up to its hilt in the tree trunk. The ancient stranger then walks out of the hall and disappears.

No mortal man could have achieved such a feat, and all know that this old man can be none other than Odin. All the heroes in the great hall desire this sword, but only Sigmund has the strength to draw it from Branstock. All acknowledge that, armed with Odin's sword, Sigmund is the god's chosen warrior.

With this sword, which can cut stone and steel, Sigmund wins great fame, yet terrible tragedy soon befalls the Völsung family. Sigmund's sister Signy is married to the king of Gothland, who treacherously murders their father King Völsung at the wedding feast. He then imprisons Völsung's ten sons by placing them in stocks in a clearing in the wild wood. There, each night for nine nights a werewolf, revealed as the witch-mother of the king of Gothland, devours one of the sons. However, on the tenth night, Sigmund—with the help of his sister Signy—manages to trick the werewolf and slays her by tearing out her tongue with his teeth. Sigmund escapes and lives for many years as an outlaw in an underground house in the wild wood. His sister Signy's desire for vengeance is so great that, while remaining the wife of the king of Gothland, she casts a spell on Sigmund. When she comes to his underground house, he does not know she is his own sister and makes love to her. Months later, Signy has a child from this incestuous union. The child is called Sifjolti, and when he is grown, Signy sends him to Sigmund in the wild wood, so that together they may avenge the deaths of King Völsung and his nine sons.

After many trials, including stealing and wearing werewolf skins and being buried alive in a barrow-grave, Sigmund and Sifjolti set fire to the great hall of the Goth king. Signy secretly returns Odin's sword to Sigmund, and all who attempt to escape the fire are slain. Seeing the Goth king and his kin slain, Signy confesses the price she has paid to exact her revenge, including incest with her brother, and leaps into the flames.

Sigmund returns with Sifjolti to his homeland and claims his father's throne as king of Hunland. He rules successfully for many years, although his son Sifjolti dies by poisoning. Shortly after King Sigmund marries Princess Hjordis, two armies of Vikings ambush Sigmund. However, they fail to slay him because of his supernatural sword. Into the fray of battle comes an ancient one-eyed warrior. When Sigmund strikes this old man's spear shaft with his sword, the blade shatters. Sigmund knows his doom has come. The ancient warrior can be none other than Odin, and Sigmund's enemies strike him down. Mortally wounded, Sigmund does not despair for he has lived long and he knows that his queen is heavy with child. The dying Sigmund tells his wife she must take the shards of Odin's sword, for Sigmund knows the prophecy that he will sire a son who, with the sword reforged, will win a prize greater than that of any mortal man. Sigmund's queen flees the battleground and after a long journey finds refuge in the court of the king of the Sea Danes. There, the exiled queen gives birth to her son, Sigurd, and raises him in secret under the protection of the Danes.

Now in the realm of the Sea Danes is a master smith. He is called Regin, and from his long, toiling hours at the forge, his powerful body is hunched and stunted like a dwarf's. Yet from his fire and forge comes much beauty in jewels and bright weapons. Swords, spears, and axes shine with a bright sheen. None know their equal and no one knows Regin's age or his past. He entered the land of the Danes before the memory of the oldest king. He is no lord of fighting men, but a smith and a master of other crafts as well. He is filled with the wisdom of runes, chess play, and the languages of many lands.

But Regin casts a cold eye on life, and none knows him as a friend. So the Sea-Dane king is much surprised when Regin offers to foster Sigurd and then becomes his tutor. There never was a pupil like Sigurd, so quick and eager to learn. He is well taught by the smith in many arts and disciplines, though in the warrior's skills he excels the most. Teacher and pupil make a strange pair. Some say Regin is too cold-tempered, while others say Sigurd was born too hot. Whatever the reason, over the years of learning, master and apprentice thrive but never form a bond of love or a close friendship.

Wise though Sigurd becomes with Regin's teaching, there is something in his blood that beckons him to learn matters that are even beyond the smith's teachings. So Sigurd often goes to the forest for many days of wandering. On one such solitary journey, Sigurd meets an ancient man in a cape and a wide-brimmed slouch hat. The old man's bearded face has but one eye, and he uses a spear as a walking stick. Sigurd has encountered the god Odin, who grants Sigurd a gift: he may choose any horse he wishes for himself from his herd in the meadow.

When Sigurd chooses a young gray stallion, the old man smiles. "Well chosen. He is called Grani, meaning 'gray-coat' and he is as sleek as quicksilver, and will grow to become the strongest and swiftest stallion ever ridden by a mortal man. For Grani's sire was the immortal Sleipnir, the eight-legged stallion of Asgard, who rides storm clouds over the world."

Not long after his visitation from Odin, Regin sends for the youth. "You have grown large and strong, Sigurd. Now is the time for an adventure," says Regin. "I have a tale to tell." The two then go out onto the green grass before Regin's hall. By an oak tree there is a stone bench on which the smith settles, while the huge youth sits on the grass at his feet.

"Know me now, young Sigurd, for what I am. Not a man, but one born in a time before the first man entered the spheres of the world. This was a time almost before there was Time. Giants and dwarfs were filled with terrible strength, and there were magicians of such power that even the gods feared to walk alone across the lands of Midgard.

"In this time, the gods Odin, Honir, and Loki went on an adventure into Midgard and dared to enter the land of my father, Hreidmar, the greatest magician in the Nine Worlds. On the first day, the three gods came to a stream and a deep pool. Resting, they soon saw a lithe brown otter swimming in the pool. Diving deep, the otter caught a silver salmon in its jaws and, reaching the far shore, struggled to drag his prize out of the water. It seemed an opportunity not to be missed. Without a word, Loki hurled a stone and broke the otter's skull.

"Loki rejoiced at having won both otter and salmon with a single stone. He went to the otter and skinned it. Taking up their double prize of salmon and otter skin, the three gods walked on until evening, when they came to a great hall upon a fair heath. This was Hreidmar the Magician's hall, which stood on the Glittering Heath just above the dark forest called the Mirkwood.

"When the three gods entered the hall, they made a gift of the salmon and the otter skin to their host. The magician immediately flew into a rage, and bound the gods at once with a deadly spell. Then he called to me to bring my fire-forged chains of unbreakable iron. And he called to my brother, the mighty Fafnir, to bind these gods tightly with my chains and his pitiless strength. Once this was done, no one but the Magician-King might ever free those three gods.

"Although my father much admired my craft and Fafnir's strength, it was his third son that he loved best. This son was the magician's eyes and ears. He was a shape-shifter who traveled often in many forms of bird and beast, and told my father what went on in the wide world. He was called Otter after his favorite guise.

This was the reason for the Magician-King's terrible wrath. The otter that the gods slew at the pool, then unknowingly offered as a gift, was the flayed skin of their host's favorite son.

"For this outrage, the magician was intent on the destruction of all three who slew his son. But Odin spoke persuasively, saying truthfully that Otter was slain in ignorance; and that in such cases, payment of weregild instead of blood was just and honorable compensation. Though much grieved, the Magician-King laid the terms. "Fill my son's skin with gold and cover him with it too. Do that and I will spare you," he demanded, grimly.

"Since Loki had cast the fatal stone, he was chosen to find the weregild, while the others remained bound. Odin advised him to quickly find Andvari the Dwarf, who was renowned for his wealth. Andvari possessed a hoard of gold that he kept hidden in a mountain cavern beneath a waterfall. Yet Odin warned that Andvari was also a shape-shifter who hid his identity. Most often, he took the form of a great pike that lived in the pool beneath the falls, so he might better guard his watery treasury door.

"Loki was not long in finding the waterfall. He stared hard into the clear pool and saw the great pike hiding in eddies under the rocks. He dragged the pike to the land where, gasping, it took on Andvari's true shape and begged for mercy. Loki was not gentle. He twisted the dwarf until his screams drowned out the sound of the water. Finally Andvari gave up his golden treasure to Loki, but the dwarf begged that he might be allowed to keep just one red-gold ring for himself. Guessing at the ring's importance, Loki snatched the ring from Andvari as well, and hurried on his way.

"Now this was the ring called Andvarinaut, which means 'Andvari's loom,' for by its power gold comes, and treasure increases ever more. This golden ring breeds gold, though this was but one of its powers; many of its other powers are unknown. This one, small red-gold ring that Loki stole was worth all the rest of treasure together.

"The dwarf screamed after him: 'I curse you for this! The ring and the treasure it spawned will carry my curse forever. All who possess the ring and its treasure for long will be destroyed!'"

"Loki returned to the magician's hall with the gold hoard and stuffed Otter's skin tight with it, and piled gold over all. The price in weregild seemed to be made, but the Magician-King looked keenly at the treasure and pointed to one whisker that still protruded. Loki smiled grimly then, and let fall the ring Andvarinaut, which he had held back. The ring covered the last hair and the payment was made.

"The Magician-King packed up the treasure in great oak chests, but took the ring Andvarinaut and placed it on his hand. Then he released the bonds of his spell, commanded Fafnir and me to unlock the chains, and the gods were given safe passage out of his land.

"For a short time, all seemed well, but the mere sight of the ring was a torment to Fafnir. And so, one night Fafnir crept to our father's bed and cut his throat while he slept. He placed Andvari's ring on his own hand, then appeared at my bedside with his bloody dagger.

"'Come,' he said, 'I have need of you.' Fearfully I did as I was told and dragged the treasure out across the Glittering Heath and beyond to a cavern under a mountain deep in the Mirkwood.

"'You make a good porter, my brother. You've earned your life, but little else. If you turn now and run, I will not slay you. Put this gold from your mind, for it shall never be left unguarded.'

"So it was that Fafnir won the ring and the treasure of the Dwarf Andvari with the blood of our father. Over that treasure, he ever after brooded. Hateful lust has poisoned his heart and mind, and all who have come his way by chance or intent, he has murdered. For now his outward form has matched his inner evil, and he has become a serpent—a huge dragon—the mightiest of this or any age."

Sigurd now sees his destiny and takes up Regin's challenge: "Slay me this dragon to avenge my father, and win for yourself great glory. Help me to my share of the weregild, and besides glory you shall have Andvari's ring and the greater part of the treasure, as well."

For such a mission, the valiant Sigurd desires a weapon to match his strength, and so goes to his mother and claims the shards of his father's sword that had been the gift of Odin. These shards he gives to Regin in his smithy. Regin sets furiously to work, heating them in the hottest fire, reforging the blade, and tempering it in the blood of a bull. The sacred runes above the hilt recover their brightness, the rings engraved on the steel gleam like silver, and as the smith carries the sword out into the daylight, it seems that flames play along its edge.

Sigurd takes the weapon in his strong hands and swings it fiercely at the smith's anvil. The sword slices clean through the iron and the wooden stock below it, as well. Yet the blade is unblemished by the stroke.

"This truly can be no other but the sword called Gram, the gift of Odin, which my father swore would one day be reforged and be given to his only son," says Sigurd, smiling. So armed and mounted on his steed Grani, Sigurd rides on his quest with Regin. They come at last to the fire-scorched and desolate outlands of what was once the Glittering Heath. Now this place is wild and blasted heath on the edge of the evil forest of the Mirkwood. It is a scorched wasteland where many a hero was slain by the dragon. Upon this heath is cut a deep path of stone that is the slime-covered track of the dragon road that leads to Fafnir's serpent cavern deep in the Mirkwood. There the dragon made his bed upon the golden treasure that was the ring-hoard of Andvari the Dwarf.

Fafnir left his golden bed only once each day, when he traveled his road to the foul pool on the heath where he drank at dusk.

"Dig a trench in the dragon's path and hide in it," advises Regin. "When he comes over you thrust your sword up into his soft belly. You cannot fail."

While Sigurd is digging, Regin makes off across the heath and hides himself in the Mirkwood. A shadow falls over the pit and Sigurd whirls around. It is the same one-eyed, bearded old man who had given Sigurd his gray horse.

"Small wisdom, short life," murmurs the old man, leaning on his spear. "The dragon's blood will sear your bones. Dig several pits, and hide in the one to the left. Then you may thrust your blade into the worm's heart, while the boiling, poison blood falls into another pit."

By evening the work is done, and just in time. The stinking dragon comes down to drink, roaring horribly and slavering poison over the ground. Biding his time, Sigurd thrusts Gram's blade into the dragon's breast up to the hilt. The scalding, corrosive blood floods into the ditch, and Fafnir collapses. His writhing coils shake the earth. His roaring fills the air with flame and venom. His jaws snap at an enemy he cannot reach, as he curses the hero who has slain him and the brother who betrayed him.

When Sigurd emerges from his pit, Regin too comes from his hiding-place and feigns both sorrow and joy. Claiming that he wishes to remove any bloodguilt from Sigurd for the slaying of Fafnir, Regin asks Sigurd to cut the dragon's heart from its body and roast it. Regin claims that by eating the dragon's heart, he alone might be brought to account for its death. Sigurd does as Regin tells him and builds a fire and spits the heart over the flames. But as the dragon's heart cooks, its juice spits out and scalds the young man's fingers. He puts his fingers in his mouth and, upon tasting the monster's heart's blood, at once finds he can understand the language of the birds in the trees about him.

The birds speak with sorrow, for they know of Regin's treachery and how the smith will gain great wisdom and bravery by eating the dragon's heart, and that he then plans to slay Sigurd in his sleep. The birds know that Regin will never share the golden treasure, or the ring with the brave youth, despite his sworn oath. They know as well that Regin wishes to steal Sigurd's sword and steed.

Hearing this talk among the birds, Sigurd moves swiftly. With his sword Gram, he strikes the false smith's head from his shoulders. Then Sigurd eats the dragon's heart himself and sets to work clearing out Fafnir's lair.

It is a whole day's work, for the cave floor is carpeted with drifts of gold. No three horses however strong could have stood beneath such a load, but Grani carries this with ease. The extra burden of Sigurd, now wearing golden armor, seems to cause him no effort at all.

So laden, with the Ring of Andvari on his hand, Sigurd the Dragon-slayer goes out of that burnt wasteland in search of more adventures. He seeks and achieves further honor, for he makes war on the kings and princes who murdered his father and his kinsmen, and slays them every one.

Many other adventures the youth has as well, but then he goes south into the lands of the Franks. Traveling long one night he sees, like a beacon, a great ring of flames on a mountain ridge. The next morning he rides over the ridge of the Hindfell, where he sees a stone tower in the middle of the ring of flames.

Sigurd does not hesitate. He urges Grani into the ring of fire. Nor does Grani flinch. His leap is as high as it is long, and though his tail and mane are scorched, he stands quietly once they are through. There is an inner circle next: an overlapping ring of massive war shields, their bases fixed in the mountain rock. Sigurd draws Gram and shears a path through the iron shield wall.

Beyond this is the stone tower, and within it is the body of a warrior on a bier. Or so it seems. When Sigurd takes the helmet from the warrior's head, he sees that this is a beautiful woman and that she is not dead, but sleeping. As he gazes on her sleeping form, Sigurd sees she is of a warrior's stature but blessed with a woman's grace. He also sees a buckthorn protruding from her neck. When Sigurd draws it out, this sleeping beauty sighs and wakes, and the shield maiden's steady gray eyes look up at him with love.

This sleeping beauty is Brynhild, who was once a Valkyrie, one of Odin's own battle maidens—his beautiful angels of death—who gathered the souls of heroes as they fell in war and carried them to Valhalla. But once, she set her will against Odin in the matter of a man's life. For this, Odin pierced her with a sleep-thorn and set her in a tower surrounded by a ring of fire.

Only a hero who did not know fear would be able to pass through the ring of fire. When Brynhild opens her eyes, she knows Sigurd for the hero he is, and Sigurd knows that in this Valkyrie he has met his match for courage and his master in wisdom. And when Sigurd becomes the Valkyrie's lover, within the ring of fire, he learns what twenty lifetimes might never teach a mortal man. For in that embrace of love, many things in Sigurd are awakened and filled with the wisdom of the gods; while in Brynhild many things are put to sleep, and filled with the unknowing of mortals.

Sigurd, as the lover of the Valkyrie, knows that he must embrace strife and war, which give a warrior immortal fame. Painful as it is, Sigurd knows he must leave Brynhild and go out of the ring of fire into the world of men again, where he might earn glory enough to be worthy of his bride. This Sigurd resolves to do, but as a token of his eternal love and as a promise of his return, he places the Ring of Andvari upon Brynhild's hand. And then, as Brynhild sleeps, Sigurd rises at dawn, mounts Grani, and passes out of the ring of fire.

When Brynhild wakes, under a spell, she remembers nothing of Sigurd, or Odin, or any of her past before that day. Upon her hand is a gold ring, though she does not know its significance. All she knows is that she must await the coming of a warrior who knows no fear and can pass through the ring of fire. To this man, and this man alone, she will be sworn in marriage.

As for Sigurd, great though his love is for Brynhild, he knows that his fate is that of a warrior. Like his father, he was chosen by Odin, and in the god's service Sigurd travels to many lands, and slays no less than five mighty kings in battle.

In time, Sigurd comes to the Rhine lands of the Nibelungs. The Nibelung king welcomes the now-famous hero, Sigurd the Dragon-slayer, with great warmth and camaraderie. In time, Sigurd and the king's three sons—Gunnar, Hogni, and Guttorm—become the closest of friends and allies in both war and peace. Sigurd and Gunnar swear unbreakable oaths of friendship, and become blood brothers.

Seeing how Sigurd's friendship has increased the power and wealth of their realm, Gunnar's mother Grimhild, queen of the Nibelungs, wishes to keep him within their realm. To this end, she hopes Sigurd might marry her daughter, the beautiful Gudrun. However, though she knows Gudrun loves Sigurd, she also knows Sigurd loves another.

And yet, Grimhild is not without hope for she is also secretly a great witch capable of casting spells and making powerful potions. So in the feasting-hall one evening, Grimhild gives Sigurd an enchanted drink. This potion robs Sigurd of his memory of the Valkyrie whom he swore to love always, and at the same time fills him with desire for the beautiful Gudrun.

Obedient to the spell, Sigurd soon asks for Gudrun's hand and with great pomp and ceremony they are wed and blessed by all. Many seasons pass, Sigurd and Gudrun are happy and content, and the power and glory of the Nibelungs grows and grows. Yet tales of a strange and beautiful maiden held captive in a ring of fire on a mountain reach the court. These tales mean nothing to Sigurd, but Gunnar wishes to win this maiden and make her his queen. His mother, Grimhild, is wary of this adventure and asks Sigurd to accompany and protect his blood brother. Sigurd does this gladly, but Grimhild arms Sigurd with another secret potion. By this potion's power Sigurd may change his appearance to that of Gunnar.

Gunnar and Sigurd ride away and at last come to the ridge of the Hindfell and the mountain with the tower ringed in fire. Gunnar sets his spurs to his horse, but the beast turns away at each attempt, and the flames rear higher and more fiercely at every failure. Even though Sigurd lets him mount Grani, Gunnar gets nowhere.

Gunnar despairs at ever winning his queen, so he begs Sigurd to try in his place. Sigurd uses Grimhild's potion and changes his appearance to that of Gunnar. He then mounts Grani and charges straight into the ring of fire. Sigurd's boots catch fire and Grani's mane and tail are alight. Horse and rider seem to hang in that inferno forever, deafened and blinded by its heat, but finally they pass through the flames.

Next is the barrier of the wall of shields but, as before, Sigurd shears through the iron wall with his sword. Behind this wall in the tower sits the beauty that is Brynhild all in white upon a crested throne, like a proud swan borne up on a foaming wave.

"What man are you?" asks Brynhild of the one standing before her. Memories of her past are gone from her mind, yet something deep within her tells her something is wrong.

"My name is Gunnar the Nibelung," says the rider, "and I claim you as my queen." Passing through the ring of fire was the price of Brynhild's hand, and she cannot refuse such a hero. Nor is there any reason for her to do so, for the man before her is handsome enough; and in traversing the wall of fire and the wall of steel has proved himself to be brave and strong beyond the measure of ordinary mortals.

So Brynhild embraces him and places the gold Ring of Andvari upon his hand with a pledge her eternal love. Then within the tower she takes him to bed and lays with him for three nights, though these nights were strange to her. For each night the hero places his long sword on the bed between them. He must do this, he says, for he will not make love to his new queen until they both return to the great halls of the Nibelungs. In this way the disguised Sigurd conspires, so he might not betray Gunnar and dishonor the bride.

When the marriage of Brynhild and Gunnar takes place in the hall of the Nibelungs, it is the true Gunnar who weds Brynhild and takes her to bed. In the land of the Nibelungs all seems to be content. But one day while bathing in a stream the two young queens set to quarreling. Brynhild boasts that Gunnar is a greater man than Sigurd by virtue of his feat of passing through the ring of fire and the ring of steel.

Gudrun will have none of this, for Sigurd has foolishly told to his wife the true tale of that adventure. So the young queen cruelly reveals the truth to Brynhild; and as proof reveals the gold ring upon her hand. At its sight Brynhild is crushed, for this was the ring Andvarinaut that she thought she had given to Gunnar that day on the mountain, but in fact Sigurd had taken and given to his own wife.

Now all the secrets are out, and poison runs in Brynhild's heart when she learns of how she has been deceived. Outraged, she can only think of vengeance. Brynhild turns to Gunnar and his brothers Hogni and Guttorm. She taunts and threatens her husband.

"All the people now laugh and say I have married a coward," mocks Brynhild. "And now my disgrace is your disgrace, for they say not only did another man win your wife for you, but also took your place in the wedding bed. And no use is there to deny this, for the Ring of Andvari—which Sigurd gave your sister—is proof that this is so."

"Sigurd shall die, then. Or I shall," swears Gunnar. But he has neither the heart nor the courage to act alone, and slay his friend. Instead he and Hogni inflame the heart of their youngest brother, Guttorm, with the desire to slay Sigurd. That night Guttorm creeps into the chamber where Sigurd lies sleeping in Gudrun's arms. Young Guttorm thrusts his sword down with such force that it pierces the man and the bedstead too. Waking to death, Sigurd still finds strength enough to snatch up Gram and hurl it after his killer. The terrible sword in flight severs the youth in half before he reaches the door. Guttorm's legs fall forward, but his torso drops back into the room.

When Brynhild hears Gudrun's scream she laughs aloud, but there is no joy in her terrible revenge. For that night, Brynhild takes Sigurd's sword and slays herself. True to her Valkyrie passion, she resolves that if she cannot be wed to Sigurd in life she will be wed to him in death. Once again and finally, Sigurd and Brynhild lie side by side—with Odin's bright sword between them—as the fierce flames of their funeral pyre slowly devours them.

So ends the life of Sigurd the Dragon-slayer, but this is not the end of the tale of the Ring of Andvari, nor of the dwarf's treasure. For the ring remains on Gudrun's hand and the treasure is taken by her brothers Gunnar and Hogni, and hidden by them in a secret cavern in the Rhine River.

Gudrun is filled with horror at Sigurd's death at the hands of her brothers, but she does not grieve long before her mother Grimhild comes to comfort her. Once again the old witch has prepared a potion, which secretly she gives to Gudrun to make her forget her grief and the evil her brothers have done. Instead, the potion fills her with love and loyalty to her brothers in all matters.

Still, Gunnar and Hogni wish to have Gudrun gone. They also wish to increase the power and glory of the Nibelungs, and believe they might do so by an alliance with the mighty Atli, the king of the Huns. And so the brothers send Gudrun to Atli. Under her mother's spell, Gudrun must obey her brothers' wishes. She weds the king of the Huns and becomes his queen.

Now Atli the Hun is a powerful man, but one who is filled with greed. He has heard much of the huge treasure that Sigurd the Dragon-slayer once won, and that the Nibelungs have taken this hoard by a foul murder. Each time Gudrun walks before the Hun king, her gold ring glints, and Atli finds he can think of nothing else but that great golden treasure.

Time passes and Gudrun gives the king of the Huns two young sons, but all the while Atli plans an intrigue and finally he acts. King Atli invites Gunnar and Hogni and all the Nibelung nobles to a great feast in his mead hall. But when the Nibelungs come to the feasting hall, they discover that a huge army of Huns has surrounded them. The great hall becomes a slaughterhouse. Although the Nibelungs slay ten for every one they lose, finally they are overwhelmed and all are murdered, save the brothers Gunnar and Hogni. These two are bound with chains and held captive.

The Hun king has Gunnar brought before him in chains, and promises to spare his life if he will give up the golden horde that was taken from Sigurd the Völsung. But Gunnar says that he and Hogni have hidden the treasure in a secret cavern beneath the Rhine, and swore blood oaths that neither will reveal it while the other lives. At once Atli gives an order and within the hour a soldier returns. In his hand is Hogni's heart, torn from his living breast.

Gunnar greets this loathsome act with cruel laughter. There had been no oath, he explains. Gunnar had been fearful that Hogni might surrender the treasure to save his life. But now that his brother is slain, only Gunnar knows the secret, and he will never surrender it. In rage, Atli has Gunnar bound and cast in a pit where serpents filled with venom finally still that warrior's stubborn heart.

The Hun king's wife, Queen Gudrun, is filled with grief at the death of her brothers and the obliteration of the Nibelungs. Although Andvari's treasure is lost, Andvari's ring still carries the dwarf's curse while it remains on Gudrun's hand. And Gudrun—as the last of the Nibelungs—resolves to have bloody retribution for Atli's treachery.

Though the battle with the Nibelungs has cost Atli dearly and profited him little, the king of the Huns calls for a victory feast in his great hall. Secretly, Gudrun makes her own preparations for the feast. She murders her own two children, Atli's sons. From their skulls, she makes two cups. Their innocent blood she mixes with the wine; and their hearts and entrails she spits and roasts as his meat. All these she serves up to the unknowing Atli at the feast. Then later that night, Gudrun takes a knife and cuts the Hun King's throat while he sleeps. Not yet sated, she creeps away, bars all the doors from without, and sets the Hun's great hall to the torch. This is the greatest funeral pyre ever seen in the land of the Huns, for all Atli's soldiers and vassals perish in their sleep in that fire.

Before that inferno, Gudrun stands and stares with mounting madness, for the leaping flames bring back many terrible memories. She flees the land of the Huns and wanders until she comes to a high cliff overlooking the sea. There, Gudrun glances once more upon the glinting gold Ring of Andvari on her hand; then she fills her apron with stones and leaps into the sea.

GERMAN RING

Nibelungenlied

The *Nibelungenlied* is the national epic of the German people, written by an anonymous poet around 1200 for performance in the Austrian court. Although, more precisely, this Austrian poet was just the last poet to contribute to the *Nibelungenlied*, for the work was the product of a heroic poetic tradition that began sometime in the fifth century AD. The heroic age for all the Teutonic (Germanic and Scandinavian) races of northern Europe was the chaotic fifth and sixth centuries, when the authority of the Roman Empire was collapsing before the migrating Teutonic tribes. The chieftains of those times became the subjects of oral traditions that elevated them to mythic status. The events in the *Völsunga Saga* and the *Nibelungenlied* are both based on the historical events surrounding the catastrophic annihilation of an early Germanic people known as the Burgundians in AD 436 by the Huns of Attila who were acting as mercenary agents for the Roman Emperor.

Although many medieval hero cycles use elements of the Norse *Völsunga Saga*, the *Nibelungenlied* is the most direct rendering of that particular tale. Siegfried is definitely the Norse Sigurd, Gunther is Gunnar, Kriemhild is Gudrun, Brunhild is Brynhild, and Hagen is Hogni. Besides employing the German names, rather than Norse names, the *Nibelungenlied* represents much more of a courtly medieval world than the more primitive Norse world of the Völsungs. Historically, the *Nibelungenlied* concerns itself with the Burgundian kingdom on the Rhine near Worms that at the time was under Roman rule. In the year AD 436 the Burgundians rose up in rebellion against the Roman governor Aetius. By AD 437 they had been all but exterminated by a contingent of Huns acting on behalf of the Empire. What remained of the annihilated Burgundians fled westward from the Rhine to the Rhone (roughly that part of France now called Burgundy). The memory of this catastrophic end to a once powerful German tribe was retold by the neighboring Franks on the Rhine around Cologne. The story was adapted by their Norse neighbors and integrated into the Völsung legend, then—centuries later—was readapted and reclaimed by medieval Germans in the epic tale of the *Nibelungenlied*.

Although Attila was certainly the Hun king at the time of the Burgundian uprising, he did not participate in the quelling of the revolts, and was elsewhere at the time. However, as the legend grew, inevitably, Attila became part of the tale as Atli in the Norse version and Etzel in the German retelling. The source of the death of Atli, the Völsung Hun king, at the hands of his wife is undoubtedly related to the historical events surrounding Attila's death in the year 453 AD. Reliable historical accounts tell us that Attila died of a throat hemorrhage after drinking and feasting on the first night of his marriage to a German princess called Hildico. Immediately there sprang up a belief that Hildico had killed Attila in revenge for the Burgundian massacre.

The names of the two great queens of the *Nibelungenlied* are in fact etymologically connected with this historical German princess. Hildico means "Little Warrior Maiden," which is fairly close to both Kriemhild or "Helmed Warrior Maiden," and Brunhild or "Armored Warrior Maiden." The characters of Brunhild and Kriemhild—and much of the plot of the *Nibelungenlied* and the *Völsunga Saga*—are also shaped by the deeds of another historical character, the notorious Visigoth Queen Brunhilda.

Born about AD 540, Brunhilda was married to King Sigebert of the Eastern Franks. King Sigebert's brother Chilperic was king of the Western Franks and married to Queen Brunhilda's sister. In the ensuing war between the brothers, King Sigebert was murdered through intrigue in AD 575, and Brunhilda was made a captive. Her life was saved and her freedom won, however, by her captor's son, who took her as his wife. She soon became a powerful force among the Franks, and over the thirty years of her influence she brought about the murders of no less than ten royal noblemen. Finally, in AD 613, a group of Frank noblemen decided to put an end to her intrigues. They tortured Brunhilda for three days, had her torn apart by wild horses, and then burned her on a pyre—a spectacular and barbaric end to a remarkable historical character.

There are aspects of the medieval *Nibelungenlied* that obviously differ from the more worldly ones portrayed in the *Völsunga Saga*. One is that the ring-hoard of the *Völsunga Saga* has suffered severe inflation by the time it reaches the *Nibelungenlied*. Gold among the Norsemen was a rare commodity. We find the golden hoard that Sigurd's horse Grani carried in the *Völsunga Saga* is so inflated in the *Nibelungenlied* that a baggage train consisting of hundreds of wagons is required to transport it.

There are also other curious variations. In the *Völsunga Saga*, the historical Attila as Atli is a savage and treacherous tyrant. However, in the *Nibelungenlied*, the Hun king as Etzel is portrayed as a humane and sympathetic character. This is certainly because of the politics of the Austro-Hungarian court for which this final version of the *Nibelungenlied* was composed.

Christian morality and chivalric tradition also resulted in changes. The supreme courtly behavior of the knights and the coyness concerning the defloration of Brunhild is at odds with the more direct Norse version. Also, there is undoubtedly a war-of-the-sexes aspect to the epic. Siegfried makes this clear in his battle with the Amazon queen: "If I now lose my life to this girl, the whole sex will become uppish and never obey their husbands forever after." It does not seem to matter that Siegfried and Gunther cheat and lie to this obviously superior warrior woman in the arena and in the bedroom. It all serves the high moral purpose of keeping women subservient. This double standard is also vividly demonstrated in the last remarkable scenes of the *Nibelungenlied*.

The *Nibelungenlied* displays perspectives that sound strange to the modern reader since the epic is not primarily a vehicle for the hero Siegfried, as, for example, the *Iliad* is for Achilles. It also appears that our sympathies with the valiant Siegfried in the first half are supposed to shift in the second half to the heroic deeds of his murderers, Hagen and Gunther. The epic is not even a history of a single dynasty or race. The Nibelungs are first one people, then another, then a third, depending on who controls the Nibelung treasure, which has become separated from the ring. As Richard Wagner concluded in his studies of the epic: "The Hoard of the Nibelungen, as the epitome of earth power, and he who owns it, who governs by it, either is or becomes a Nibelung."

The *Nibelungenlied* begins with a prophetic dream visited upon the young Princess Kriemhild of the Burgundians. In that dream a falcon is mounted upon Kriemhild's jeweled wrist. This falcon is without equal; it is the most cherished of all things that Kriemhild calls her own. Yet, without warning, two eagles strike the bird in flight. Before Kriemhild's eyes, the eagles tear her falcon to pieces and glut themselves on its flesh. A troubled young Kriemhild seeks solace from her mother who is a woman wise in the reading of dreams, but to her child she could give no comfort. The falcon is a prince whom Kriemhild will love and marry, while the eagles are two murderers who would destroy that prince. And so, because of this dream, Kriemhild swears she will wed no man. Though many chivalrous knights desire her and sing her praises, she will wed no one. Nor are there any who might force her to wed, for now she rules as queen jointly with her brothers, Gunther, Gernot, and Giselher, the three powerful kings of Rhineland.

Yet fate will not allow Kriemhild to keep her vow. North of the kingdom of the Rhine are the Netherlands and the great city of Xanten. There lives the hero Siegfried, the son of King Siegmund and Queen Sieglind. This is the mighty warrior who gained fame by traveling far to the north into the land of the Nibelungs, the richest kingdom in the world. There, Siegfried slays the twelve guardian giants of Nibelungenland, and takes from their armory that ancient sword called Balmung. With it, he defeats seven hundred men of Nibelungenland. Then, at last, he duels with the two mighty kings of the Nibelungs themselves and, in the din of combat, slays them both.

But the great treasure of the Nibelungs has one last guardian, more subtle and dangerous than all the rest. This is the ancient dwarf, Alberich, who not only possesses huge strength but also wears the Tarnkappe, the Cloak of Invisibility. So Siegfried now must wrestle an invisible foe that he finally locks in his grip, and wins from Alberich both the magic cloak and the Nibelung treasure. So vast was the Nibelung treasure that it would take one hundred baggage wagons to carry away the precious stones alone; though these were but a scattering over the mounds of red gold that were heaped on the floors of the secret cavern where it was kept.

By force of arms, Siegfried becomes master of the Nibelung treasure and lord of Nibelungenland. And although Siegfried returns to Xanten to rule the Netherlands, he is acknowledged as the king of Nibelungenland as well. However, this is not the end of Siegfried's deeds, for besides countless duels with other men-at-arms, this hero also slays a mighty dragon. Further, by this deed Siegfried wins him not just fame but invincibility. For after slaying the monster, he bathes in the dragon's blood, and his skin grows tough as horn so that no weapon can pierce him.

When Siegfried rides south in search of adventure, he ultimately comes to the land of the Burgundians, and there the three kings of the Rhine greet him with honor. For the best part of a year Siegfried remains in Rhineland in the great city of Worms, and with King Gunther swears an oath of friendship. Still, there is another reason for Siegfried's journey. He has heard of the beauty of Kriemhild, and hopes he might win her as his queen.

Siegfried has reasoned well, for from her tower Kriemhild has often watched the hero from afar in pageants and in combat. By the sight of him alone, she is filled at once with love, and her resolve not to give her heart to any man is soon discarded. As the year of Siegfried's visit approaches its end, there is a call to arms. The combined armies of the king of the Saxons and the king of the Danes are joined in a huge force to make war on the Burgundians. Siegfried champions the Burgundian cause. So great is Siegfried's valor that although he leads a force of only one thousand knights, he crushes an army of twenty thousand Saxons and Danes in a single day.

Shortly after this great service to the Burgundians, Siegfried asks Gunther for his sister's hand in marriage. With gladness Gunther agrees, for he knows that his sister's heart is filled with love for this man, and that his kingdom has no stouter ally and friend. However, Gunther explains, one obstacle still stands before this union might he blessed. As Gunther is the eldest royal son and high king of the Rhine, the laws of the land insist he must he wed before his sister.

Now Gunther reveals that he has become enamored of another beautiful maiden-queen who rules in Iceland. The only problem is that Queen Brunhild is no ordinary woman. She is a warrior-queen blessed with supernatural strength, and she swears that she will wed no man unless he can defeat her in three feats of strength. If a suitor tries and fails, he will be put to death. Many suitors have tried to win Brunhild, and all have failed and died.

So a bargain is struck: King Gunther will grant Queen Kriemhild's hand to Siegfried, if Siegfried helps Gunther win the beautiful Queen Brunhild. Siegfried and Gunther set sail for far Iceland. They take with them only two of Gunther's brave vassals: Hagen of Troneck and his brother Dancwart. This is a suitor's quest, and so they take no weapons of war, but array themselves in their finest clothes.

Queen Brunhild's fortress-city has eighty-six towers and three palaces, and her royal hall is built of sea-green marble. This proud and beautiful queen of Iceland graciously receives the royal travelers. On her hand Brunhild wears an ancient red-gold ring and about her waist is a girdle adorned with precious gems: a splendid orphrey of jewels and fine silk braid from Nineveh.

Gunther's heart goes out to Brunhild at once. But it is to Siegfried that Brunhild speaks first, for the queen assumes that Siegfried is the most noble of her visitors, and that it is he who has come as suitor. Here is the first of Siegfried's deceptions. To Brunhild, Siegfried falsely claims that he is a vassal to King Gunther, who is the greatest and strongest of heroes, and it is Gunther who comes to compete for her hand. With some reluctance the queen accepts Gunther's challenge and agrees to the contest.

Queen Brunhild stands alone in the vast arena, surrounded by an iron ring of seven hundred men-at-arms who will judge the contest. The warrior-queen dresses herself in steel armor adorned with gold and gems. It takes four strong men to lift the Queen's bright shield, and three men to carry her spear: both of these she takes and wields like childish toys. Then into that arena marches her suitor and challenger, King Gunther of the Rhine. However, though he appears to stand alone against the warrior-queen, this is not so. The wily Siegfried has covered himself in Tarnkappe, the Cloak of Invisibility, but which has a second power, that of increasing the strength of its wearer twelvefold.

So, when the contest of the javelin is made, it is the invisible Siegfried who stands between Gunther and his shield and stops the force of the queen's throw. Certain death would have been delivered to Gunther alone, for even with Siegfried's twelvefold strength, both heroes are staggered when the spear strikes and a tongue of flame leaps from the pierced shield. Brunhild is amazed when Gunther does not fall. Instead, Gunther appears to lift up her spear and, turning the blunt end to the fore—so as not to slay the maid—throws the weapon with such force as to drive her to the ground. But here Brunhild is deceived by appearances, for it was the invisible hand of Siegfried that hurled the spear.

Then come the next two tests: the casting of a great stone and the long leap. The stone is so heavy it takes twelve men to carry it into the arena. Without hesitation, Queen Brunhild lifts the stone and throws it the length of those twelve men laid end to end; then she makes a mighty leap that overshoots the distance of the stone.

In silent reply, Gunther goes to the stone and appears to lift it effortlessly, but once again it is the invisible Siegfried who does the deed and hurls the stone far beyond Brunhild's mark. Then, lifting Gunther by his waist, Siegfried leaps, carrying Gunther with him through the air, landing far beyond their stone-cast.

So, by the strength and cunning of Siegfried, Gunther has won a bride, and to the kingdom of the Rhine comes the proud Queen Brunhild. In Gunther's court at Worms there is much celebration and joy. There are to be two royal marriages: Gunther to Brunhild and Siegfried to Kriemhild.

Wedding guests receive gifts of bracelets, lockets, and rings, while an iron ring of armed knights solemnly stands about the betrothed couples as they swear their holy vows. Joyfully, Gunther and Siegfried march out of the chapel with the two loveliest of brides. As night comes, they retire to their wedding beds, as their guests revel on.

In the morning, Siegfried and Kriemhild are radiant with their mutual love while Gunther seems distraught, and Brunhild distant and aloof. Gunther has none of the bridegroom's natural joy and pride. Indeed, that very afternoon, Gunther comes to confide in Siegfried and tell him of his humiliation. On their wedding night Brunhild tells Gunther that although he has won her hand by his skill in the arena, she will not willingly give up her body to him. For to give herself to a man would break the spell of her warrior's strength, which she wishes to keep all her life. When Gunther tries by force to claim his nuptial rights, Brunhild merely laughs at him. She binds him up with her braided girdle, and hangs him like a slaughtered pig from a peg on the wall until dawn.

Once again, Siegfried is drawn into an intrigue against the warrior-queen. That night in darkness, using Tarnkappe, the Cloak of Invisibility, Siegfried enters Brunhild's room. In Gunther's place he lies in Brunhild's bridal bed. Thinking it is Gunther in the dark, Brunhild strikes Siegfried with such force that blood leaps from his mouth and he is thrown across the room.

Wrestling with the hero, Brunhild grips Siegfried's hands so tightly that blood spurts from his nails and he is driven against the wall. Yet finally, aided by the twelve-fold power of Tarnkappe, Siegfried's huge strength prevails. He lifts her from the ground, throws her down upon the bed, and by main force crushes her in his gathered arms so fiercely that all the joints of her body crack at once. Only then does she submit and cry out to her conqueror to let her live.

Now most who tell this tale say that at this moment Siegfried is an honorable friend to Gunther and does not rest in the lovely cradle of Brunhild's long limbs that night. But whatever the truth of the matter, in one way at least Siegfried does dishonor this proud woman. For in the darkness, Siegfried sees the dull glint of red gold. It is Brunhild's ring, and in his pride of conquest, he takes the ring from her hand. Then, as he leaves the marriage bed, he also takes the jeweled girdle of woven Nineveh silk as well.

In stealth, Siegfried flees the dark chamber, and Gunther comes to the bed of the vanquished bride who no longer dares to resist his advance. When the dawn comes, Brunhild is as pale and meek as the mildest bride. For with the loss of maidenhead and her ring, Brunhild's warrior strength flees her body forever. She becomes a good and submissive wife to King Gunther.

Now twelve years pass happily. Siegfried and Kriemhild live and rule over the Netherlands and Nibelungenland from their palace in Xanten while Gunther and Brunhild live and rule over the Rhinelands and their palace at Worms. Then Gunther invites Siegfried and his sister to come to a festival in his court.

Perhaps the ancient power of the ring is at work, or perhaps the fault was in Siegfried's pride. Whatever the reason, Siegfried makes a tragic error, for in Xanten he gives to Kriemheld as a gift the ring and the silken girdle he took from Brunhild in her wedding bed. And, even more foolishly, he reveals to Kriemhild the secret of the winning of them.

One day the two queens meet at the cathedral door and a dispute arises between them as to who should enter first. Brunhild is rash and maintains that Kriemhild has displayed unwarranted arrogance toward her; for obviously Siegfried is nothing more than a vassal of Gunther. Kriemhild will not stand for this insult. She argues that Siegfried is the greater man and no man's vassal. Filled with exasperation, Kriemhild's discretion is abandoned. To Brunhild, she holds up the stolen ring of red gold, and then reveals the jeweled girdle of braided Nineveh silk that Brunhild once wore.

Contemptuously, before all who will listen, she claims that Brunhild had been Siegfried's concubine before she wed Gunther; and that Siegfried had taken these trophies after he had been the first to enjoy her body upon the bridal bed. The humiliated Brunhild flees to Gunther with this tale and demands that he redeem her honor. Full of anger, Gunther calls Siegfried to him. Alarmed at this scandalous talk, Siegfried tells Gunther that what his wife has said is untrue and that he had not so used Brunhild that night.

With no gentleness, Siegfried chastises his wife, and demands that she apologize for this shameful argument. In his haste to make amends so that Brunhild should not discover the other stratagems by which he deceived and subdued her, Siegfried orders an iron ring of knights to form about him, and swears a sacred oath that all these tales are black lies.

This false oath is the final seal on Siegfried's fate. His honor is despoiled. For although it seems that most accept this denial, the proof of the gold ring and the girdle cannot be withdrawn and rumor of the scandal of the marriage bed spreads. To Brunhild comes the steadfast Hagen of Troneck, the queen's champion and the king's stoutest vassal. Brunhild inflames Hagen's heart, and these two persuade Gunther that only blood vengeance can restore their honor.

At this time rumors of war with the Danes again arise in the Rhine, and Siegfried once again makes ready for battle, but Kriemhild has dire forebodings. Artfully, Hagen comes to Kriemhild, saying that he too has heard evil omens concerning her husband but that he cannot believe these omens, as all know that the spell of dragon's blood protects Siegfried. It is then that Kriemhild reveals the secret of Siegfried's mortality. For when Siegfried bathed in dragon's blood, a lime leaf covered one place between his shoulder blades. In this place alone, Siegfried can he pierced with sharp steel. On Hagen's instructions, Kriemhild secretly sews a tiny cross on Siegfried's doublet over his one mortal place. Then Hagen swears he will always be at Siegfried's back, and will guard the hero from any unexpected blow.

The very next day, Hagen, Gunther, and Siegfried go hunting in the royal forest. When Siegfried lies down to drink from a stream after a long chase, Hagen drives his spear into the cross and through Siegfried's back to his heart. Mortally wounded, Siegfried is like a wild, dying beast flailing in the air. But after Hagen strikes, Gunther seizes Siegfried's weapons and flees, so the hero might not wreak vengeance with his final breath.

When at last Siegfried's life's blood spills out upon the forest floor and he breathes no more, the assassins return. They take up his body and carry it to the court, proclaiming lawless highwaymen have treacherously murdered Siegfried. With Siegfried's death, Brunhild believes her husband Gunther and her champion Hagen have upheld her honor. Not only has she brought death to the man who deceived her, but also now the proud rival queen who had humiliated her is brought to despair. Further, because Kriemhild is without a husband, Gunther takes her under his protection, and with this pretext plunders her inheritance: the Nibelung treasure.

In this treacherous way, the Burgundians win the Nibelung treasure. For days and nights an endless caravan of wagons filled with gold and jewels carries the huge treasure into the walled city of Worms where Gunther and Brunhild rule. This treasure entirely fills the city's greatest tower. Yet, so rich is this hoard that King Gunther mistrusts its keepers and others who might steal it. Stealthily over the years, under the cover of night, Gunther and Hagen pillage all that huge treasure and take it to a secret place on the Rhine. In that place, Gunther and Hagen find a deep river cavern and sink all that vast treasure of gold and gemstones, so only these two alone know where it is hidden.

For a time the power and strength of Gunther's people are without parallel. With the Nibelung hoard in their possession, they are renowned as the wealthiest of nations. Indeed, because that famous treasure now rests in their land, the Burgundians of the Rhine soon become known by all people as the Nibelungs: possessors of the Nibelung treasure and the luckiest of men.

Not all within the kingdom are content. The grieving Kriemhild for one is not deceived by the tale of Siegfried's death. She guesses well enough the truth of his murder. Gradually her despair is replaced by a desire for revenge. Daily she stares at the gold ring on her hand that reminds her of the dispute that was the reason for her hero's treacherous murder.

At last Brunhild decides she can no longer have Kriemhild within the royal court, for she rightly fears that Siegfried's widow might ferment revolt. As chance would have it, Etzel, emperor of the Huns of the Danube, has sent word to the Nibelung court. The noble and elderly ruler of the Huns wishes to make the fair Kriemhild his queen. He has often heard of her beauty, and further he would be honored to marry and protect the widowed queen of Siegfried the Dragon-slayer.

To this proposal Gunther gives his blessing. He gives the hand of his sister to the Emperor Etzel and sends her to the Hun city of Gram on the banks of the Danube. Now Gunther believes that he and Brunhild might live forever, secure from retribution for the slaying of Siegfried.

This is not to be. For although Kriemhild is taken to the mighty royal city of Gram and the palace of Etzel on the banks of the Danube, her desire for vengeance is never forgotten. Although the generous Etzel gives to her every luxury and she feigns happiness in his presence, Kriemhild works always toward one end.

The Emperor Etzel is quite unaware of Kriemhild's intrigues, and seems little concerned as his queen comes to command greater and greater power among the Huns. She gains the sworn allegiance and obedience of great numbers of Etzel's vassals. Many knights, out of compassion, love, or greed, swear loyalty to Kriemhild above all others. After many years, when Kriemhild believes that her power is great enough, she persuades Etzel to invite all her kinsmen on a midsummer visit to the city of the Huns.

So open-handed and fair has Etzel always been with the Nibelungs that they suspect no evil intent. So to Gram come the three Nibelung kings: Gunther, Gernot, and Giselher. There also come the dauntless Hagen and his brother Dancwart, the mighty warriors Volker and Ortwine, and a thousand more heroic men as well. No nobleman is left within the walls of Worms, and from her tower Brunhild and her servants watch them go.

In the emperor's city, the midsummer celebrations are filled with pageantry and pomp. There are tournaments, games, and festivals of song and dance. Yet the Nibelungs do not take part in the celebrations, for Gunther and Hagen see the fierce light of hatred that is in Kriemhild's eyes. Well they know its source, although they had hoped she had long ago laid her hatred to rest. Then, too, they have received ill omens on their long journey to the land of the Huns.

On the twelfth day of the journey, they came to the wide banks of the Danube. There Hagen came upon the swan maidens, those fatal river women some call Nixies, and others call Water Sprites. From them Hagen was given a prophetic vision: all the Nibelungs by fire and sword would perish, and none would live to return to Rhineland.

So although all the Nibelungs had hoped that the Nixies had delivered to Hagen a false vision, the dreadful look of Kriemhild forewarns them of their doom. Thereafter they go about fully armed among the revelers. They do not have long to wait. That very night Kriemhild acts while all the Nibelung knights sit in the feasting hall. Secretly, without Etzel's knowledge, Kriemhild sends a force of armed men to the quarters of the Nibelung squires, and all those valiant youths are slaughtered. When news of the slayings reaches the hall, Hagen leaps to his feet at the feasting table. With relentless savagery, he draws his sword and strikes off the infant head of Ortlieb, the emperor's only child, as he plays upon his father's lap.

Then Hagen calls out to the Nibelungs, telling them they have fallen into a trap, that like the squires they too would all be slain. The Nibelung knights leap into battle and the hall becomes a slaughterhouse. Though Etzel and Kriemhild escape, two thousand Huns fall in that battle in the hall.

Much to Etzel's distress, Kriemhild urges on more of the Hunnish legions and allies. The feasting hall is transformed. The tables are covered with severed limbs and heads, silver dishes are filled with human entrails, and gold cups are filled to the brim with human blood. Kriemhild too is transformed; once the gentlest of women, she is now an avenging angel of death. Relentlessly, she urges the Huns into battle, and although more than half the Nibelungs have been slain, they hold the doors to the hall until a wall of bodies blocks the entrance, and the Huns have to clear their own dead to renew the fight.

Filled with fury, Kriemhild calls for torches and has the hall set ablaze to drive the Nibelungs into the open. But the fire does not drive the Nibelungs out, though many perish by flame and heat and smoke. They fight on through the blazing night. Taking refuge beneath the stone arches of the hall while the wooden structures burn about them, they battle on and drink the blood of the dead to slake their thirst.

Through the horror of that night a number of the Nibelungs survive, but with the dawn, the queen calls forth many more grim Hunnish men-at-arms. These vengefully attack the Nibelungs in the burnt wreckage of the feasting hall. Yet these warriors find even the remnants of the Nibelung knights a terrible foe, and many fall before their pitiless weapons.

Some of the Nibelungs might yet have lived had not that mighty hero, Dietrich, king of Verona, come to the aid of the Huns. Dietrich has no great desire to stand against the valiant Nibelungs; however, too many friends and kinsmen have now died at their hands. He knows he must act, so he sends his noble lieutenant Hildebrand with his men before him into the ruined hall. He asks Hildebrand to make some treaty between the Nibelungs and the Huns, so he himself need not be drawn into this feud.

But this act of reconciliation fails; the truce erupts at once in a bloody dispute that entirely eclipses both Dietrich's army and the ragged remainder of the Nibelungs. Only the wounded Hildebrand lives to return with the disastrous news. Grimly Dietrich arms himself and comes to the ruined hall to find that only the exhausted but defiant Gunther and Hagen remain alive of all the Nibelungs. In a rage of despair, Dietrich uses his mighty strength to drive the exhausted Gunther and Hagen to the wall. It might have been the ghost of Siegfried himself that had come, so great is Dietrich's might. The weapons of the Nibelungs—even the sword Balmung, which Hagen had usurped—are struck from their hands, and they are subdued and bound.

Still, Dietrich is a man of compassion and he implores Kriemhild to have pity on these brave knights. For a moment, it seems that Kriemhild will hold back her wrath. In truth, Kriemhild has now become an avenging fiend gone far beyond redemption. In the throne room she declares that there is yet the matter of her rightful inheritance to be resolved: the Nibelung treasure must be brought to Etzel's court.

In secret, Kriemhild has already been to the cells. She meets Hagen and makes to him a false promise of freedom if he will tell her where the Nibelung treasure is hidden. Hagen is a dark and stoic man, and he trusts not a word that Kriemhild speaks. Hagen tells the queen he has sworn an oath never to reveal where the Nibelung treasure is buried while his lord, Gunther, lives.

Queen Kriemhild orders Hagen to be brought in chains to the throne room. Then, to the horror of all, Kriemhild throws the severed head of her brother King Gunther upon the floor. The Emperor Etzel and the hero Dietrich are aghast at the queen's savagery, but the fierce Hagen of Troneck defiantly laughs aloud. There had been no oath of silence. Hagen had provoked the slaying because he feared that Gunther would trade his life for the treasure. But now that Gunther is gone, Hagen alone knows where that hoard is hidden, and no torture will ever make him tell. For if he cannot return the treasure to his Queen Brunhild, he can now at least deny that reward to her rival. Hagen laughs aloud, boasting that he would gladly suffer death and damnation to keep this last rich victory locked within his heart. Hagen's defiance so enrages Queen Kriemhild that in an instant she takes into her hands Hagen's sword: the Balmung that was once Siegfried's. Then, before the emperor or his courtiers can recover from the first shock of the unnatural murder of Gunther, Kriemhild strikes off the head of Hagen of Troneck as well.

All now see the monstrous being Kriemhild has become. At this last act of treachery, all the royal court recoil in horror. All know that no greater shame can befall a knight than to be slain by the hand of a woman. It is Dietrich's lieutenant, Hildebrand, who acts out the will of all the assembled nobles when he leaps forward with his drawn sword. In a deed that might almost have been merciful, he ends the tortured life of Queen Kriemhild with a single stroke.

With the death of Hagen, the last Nibelung lord is slain and the Nibelung treasure is gone forever from the sight of men. The Nixies and Water Spirits of the Rhine alone know where it lies, and they have no use for gold or gems. The ancient ring that was the cause of all this despair is buried with Queen Kriemhild who was once the gentlest of women; while her rival Queen Brunhild, who was once the strongest of her sex, is now broken by the loss of husband, champion, and all wealth. She mourns the disaster that has extinguished all her noble men-at-arms and left her alone in a ruined and empty realm.

So ends the tale of the rivalry of the two queens.

Dwarves Masked

WAGNER'S RING

The Ring of the Nibelung

The first performance of the four operas comprising Richard Wagner's *The Ring of the Nibelung* (also called simply the Ring Cycle) in 1876 has often been cited as the first great expression of the identity of the recently unified German nation. Certainly, Wagner saw art as a political as well as an aesthetic act, and with his Ring Cycle he was attempting to claim a mythological heritage and a national art. For Wagner, art and myth were linked. He believed that true art must arise from the primordial depths of the *Volk* (a people's collective being). His Ring Cycle was a purposeful act of making a statement of German identity and claiming the root of that identity was to be found in the Germanic epic tradition of the ring quest myths.

Criticized as Wagner may be for his manipulations and distortions of Norse myth and medieval German literature (*see also* TOLKIEN'S RING *The Lord of the Rings*), it was his genius that recognized the significance of the ring myth, and the importance of reclaiming it for his own time. Furthermore, one must recognize that Wagner's Ring Cycle brilliantly conveys the huge spirit of this ancient tale on a truly epic scale. Just as the *Völsunga Saga* and the *Nibelungenlied* were interpretations of the quest appropriate to their times, so Wagner's interpretation was true to the spirit of his.

In the second half of the nineteenth century, there was an awakening and flowering of interest in the Teutonic mythologies in Europe, and the ring quest emerged as a major theme in European literature. It was William Morris who (with Eiríkr Magnússon) gave the English the first full-blooded translation of the *Völsunga Saga* in 1870. Morris proclaimed the Icelandic epic the *Iliad* of northern Europe. Later, Morris followed this up with his own epic-length poem, *Sigurd the Völsung*, which appeared in 1876, the same year Wagner's Ring Cycle was first staged at Bayreuth.

The playwright and critic George Bernard Shaw saw Morris's *Sigurd* as one of the most monumental poems of the century. Shaw also wrote what must be the most brilliantly eccentric examination of Wagner's four operas in his pamphlet *The Perfect Wagnerite*. Shaw saw *The Ring of the Nibelung* as an allegory about socialism, with the working class of Manchester being the hell-born, miserable dwarf-slaves of the evil dictatorial corporate stockholder Alberich.

The Norwegian dramatist Henrik Ibsen adapted the *Völsunga Saga* in his early play *The Vikings at Helgeland*, and later used many of the same elements and themes in such mature works as *Peer Gynt*. During this period, the English poet, Matthew Arnold, wrote his *Balder Dead*; while Andrew Lang, George MacDonald, and Henry Wadsworth Longfellow were among the many who popularized Teutonic myth and legend in the English-speaking world. Another German, the poet and dramatist, Christian Hebbel wrote a trilogy based on *Die Nibelungen*, and Jacob Grimm wrote a monumental and massively influential study entitled *Teutonic Mythology*.

However, of them all, it is Wagner's *The Ring of the Nibelung* that is the ring legend of the age. In these four operas, we see all of what comes before: mythically, historically, and spiritually. It was Wagner who, in the four operas of his Ring Cycle (*The Rhinegold, The Valkyrie, Siegfried*, and *The Twilight of the Gods*) reforged the ring for his time.

I. THE RHINEGOLD

ACT I
SCENE I

In the depths of a river, the three water nymphs—the Rhine maidens— play and sing in the limpid green waters. These beautiful daughters of the Rhine River are spied on by Alberich the Nibelung. The ugly Dwarf has made his way down into their watery realm, where he lustfully and fruitlessly pursues the teasing nymphs. Enraged by their mocking, the Dwarf is suddenly overcome by a brilliant golden glow. Rays of sunlight catch on a gold pinnacle of rock that fills the murky river with shimmering gold light. The nymphs sing praises to this treasure. It is the *Rhinegold*, a golden stone that, if forged into a gold ring, would allow its master to become lord of the world. However, the *Rhinegold* can be taken and mastered only by one who is willing to curse love and renounce all love's pleasures. Since Alberich is too ugly to win love anyway, he will take power: he swears an oath renouncing love. Alberich the Nibelung then snatches the *Rhinegold* from the pinnacle and flees into the dark.

SCENE II

Dawn comes to a mountain height above the Rhine Valley where Wotan, the king of the gods, and Fricka, his queen, sleep. In the distance stands a magnificent castle with gleaming battlements, up on an impossibly high peak. Fricka wakes Wotan, and the god is filled with delight at the sight of the newly completed kingdom of the gods. This was a realm built by the brute force of giants, but conceived in Wotan's dreams. Unfortunately, the price promised to the giants Fasolt and Fafner for building this kingdom was the hand of Fricka's sister, Freia, the goddess of youth. However, with the loss of Freia the gods will also lose the golden apples of immortality of which she is guardian, and without this fruit they will soon grow old and die. When the giants come for their payment, Donner, the god of thunder, Froh, the god of spring, and Loge, the trickster god of fire, come to side with Wotan to defend Freia. However, the bargain cannot be broken, as Wotan has sworn to make payment upon his sacred spear of law. It is up to Loge to come up with an alternative payment. The giants agree: they will have the Ring of the Nibelung that Alberich has forged from the stolen *Rhinegold*, along with all the golden treasures he has amassed through its power. Loge also reveals that if the ring is not soon taken from Alberich, he will rule over all of them anyway. The giants take Freia as a hostage as Wotan and Loge descend into the bowels of the Earth in search of the realm of Alberich the Nibelung.

SCENE III

The subterranean caverns of Nibelheim, the home of the Nibelung Dwarfs, are a vast stone labyrinth of tunnels and chambers. This is a dark and sinister world lit only by the red glow of furnace and forge. Here, Alberich, the ring lord, torments Mime, his enslaved brother, who has just completed the forging of the magic helmet called Tarnhelm on Alberich's orders. Tarnhelm has the power to make the wearer invisible or change him into whatever form he desires. It can also transport him to any place he wishes. Alberich places the Tarnhelm on his head and immediately vanishes. The invisible Alberich then cruelly kicks and beats Mime until he cries out for mercy. Delighted with his new toy, Alberich goes off to terrorize his other enslaved Dwarfs. Mime continues to bewail his enslavement, as the gods Wotan and Loge enter the cavern. Alberich soon returns, driving his treasure-bearing Dwarfs before him. They pile up a huge hoard of purest gold. Alberich contemptuously greets his guests, and arrogantly reveals how he will build up such vast wealth and power that he will eventually overthrow the gods and rule the world. Wotan can barely contain his anger, but crafty Loge flatters Alberich and asks him about the powers of Tarnhelm. He asks if it can really transform him into any shape. Certainly, Alberich replies, and immediately becomes a huge dragon. Loge feigns fear and astonishment, but then suggests that it would surely be more impressive if the Dwarf could become something really small, like a toad. Alberich foolishly obliges and transforms himself into a tiny toad. Wotan immediately seizes the tiny toad, while Loge snatches up Tarnhelm. When Alberich resumes his usual shape, he is bound and dragged off as a captive.

SCENE IV

Alberich is taken to the misty mountain height above the Rhine where the bargain with the giants was struck. In order to win his freedom, Alberich is forced to give up his hoard of gold, Tarnhelm, and his magic ring. The enraged Dwarf refuses, but finally everything is taken from him. Once the humiliated Alberich is released, he wrathfully places a curse of disaster and death on anyone who commands the ring. Soon after, all the gods gather with the giants, Fasolt and Fafner, and their hostage Freia. Fasolt is in love with Freia, but agrees to accept gold only if it completely hides her from his sight. The gods pile all the gold around her, but Fasolt can still see the sheen of her hair, so Loge gives up Tarnhelm to cover it. She seems entirely covered, but Fasolt cries out that he can still see the starlike glint of one of her eyes. The giants demand the ring to seal the crack, but Wotan is enthralled by the ring's power and will not give it up. Loge meanwhile claims it for its rightful owners, the Rhine maidens. In the middle of the quarrel, the earth splits open and Erda, goddess of the Earth, arises out of the ground. She is the spirit of the world and the prophet of the gods. She commands Wotan to surrender the ring or the gods and the entire world will be doomed. Almost immediately the curse of the ring strikes when the giants quarrel over its possession. Fafner brutally murders Fasolt and takes both the ring and the treasure. After Fafner's departure, Donner walks into the mountain mists, where the thunder of his hammer is heard and flashes of lightning are seen as he forges a rainbow bridge. It arches through the air and leads up to the great castle of the gods that Wotan now names Valhalla. Wotan leads the godly procession over the rainbow bridge to Valhalla, while far below the Rhine maidens cry out for the loss of their gold.

II. THE VALKYRIE

ACT ONE
SCENE I

A storm is raging and the hero Siegmund the Walsung enters the great hall of the warrior-chieftain Hunding. In the middle of the dwelling is the trunk of a huge ash tree, the limbs of which support the roof. Siegmund, wounded and exhausted from pursuit by enemies through the forest, collapses on a bearskin before the fire in the enormous stone hearth. Hunding's wife Sieglinde enters the house and, seeing the now unconscious Siegmund, takes pity on him and revives him. Instantly, there is a powerful attraction between the two.

SCENE II

Hunding arrives home and reluctantly offers shelter and food to Siegmund. When he asks Siegmund his name, the youth gives his outlaw name, Wehwalt the Wolfing. His name means "Woeful" as his father Wolfe, his mother, and his twin sister were all either brutally slain, or hopelessly lost to him. As he describes his latest disasters, it is soon revealed that his enemies are Hunding's kinsmen. Hunding tells his guest he is safe for the night, but in the morning he must find a weapon and they will duel to the death.

SCENE III

Alone in the great hall, Siegmund is soon joined by Sieglinde, who has given Hunding a sleeping potion. Sieglinde tells Siegmund how she had been orphaned as a child, and as a captive was given as a reluctant bride to Hunding. But a stranger—an old man dressed all in gray with a slouch hat and a single glittering eye—came to the wedding. That old man brought a bright sword and drove it into the mighty ash tree that holds up the roof of Hunding's house. Many heroes since that time have tried to draw it out, but none could do it. When Sieglinde confesses her unhappiness, Siegmund swears his love for her and promises to free her from her forced marriage. As Sieglinde swears her love in return, they tell each other more about their past lives. When the hero reveals that his father's real name was Walse, Sieglinde suddenly realizes that Siegmund is her long-lost twin brother, and their mutual passion redoubles. Siegmund draws the gleaming sword from the great ash tree as the two lovers rejoice in this union of Walsung blood. They then rush out into the night.

ACT II
SCENE I

In a craggy mountainous wilderness, the mighty Wotan talks to his Valkyrie daughter, Brünnhilde, and tells her she must go into battle and give a just victory to his mortal son, Siegmund the Walsung, over Hunding. Joyfully, she obeys him and departs, just as Wotan's wife, Fricka, arrives upon a chariot drawn by two rams in the wake of a storm. Queen Fricka, who is also the goddess of marriage, insists that Hunding's sacred marriage rights must be defended and the Walsungs punished for adultery and incest. Wotan is forced against his will to uphold the law, for his power will leave him if he does not. Wotan swears an oath to command the death of Siegmund the Walsung. Queen Fricka celebrates her victory over Wotan and rides off in her chariot.

SCENE II

Angered and saddened, Wotan now tells the Valkyrie Brünnhilde how Valhalla was bought with the ring, and how the Dwarf and Rhine maidens doubly cursed the ring. To prevent disaster, Wotan went to the goddess Erda, with whom he conceived the nine Valkyries who would gather in Valhalla with a vast army of heroes to help defend the gods in their hour of need. Yet the fate of the world is dependent on Alberich's ring, for the Dwarf of Nibelheim still plots continually to seize it from the giant Fafner, who broods over his golden treasure and guards it night and day. If the Nibelung eventually seizes the ring, the fate of the gods will be sealed. For by its power, Alberich will turn Wotan's heroic army against him and overthrow the gods. Wotan is forbidden the ring, and only Alberich who has cursed love can command its power, so the only hope for the gods is to be found in a mortal hero who is brave and strong enough to slay the giant and seize the ring on their behalf. To this end, the mortal hero Siegmund the Walsung was conceived and given a godly sword called Notung. But the curse of the ring is at work, for the laws of Fricka dictate that Wotan must order Brünnhilde to slay Siegmund.

SCENE III

The Valkyrie Brünnhilde sees Siegmund and Sieglinde approaching a rocky gorge and slips away. Siegmund comforts his sister-bride, who hears the hunting horn of Hunding in pursuit and tells Siegmund to leave her and flee. Siegmund will not and swears to protect her with his sword, Notung, and tenderly comforts her until she falls into an exhausted sleep.

SCENE IV

Brünnhilde appears as if in a vision to Siegmund, leading her horse. Only warriors condemned to die can see the Valkyries, and Brünnhilde tells Siegmund that she will take him to Valhalla. Siegmund says he will not leave his sister-bride for the warrior's heaven. The Valkyrie tells him he has no choice, but Siegmund says he will make sure they are together in death. He takes out his sword with the intention of slaying both Sieglinde and himself. The Valkyrie stays his hand and swears she will violate the will of Wotan and give victory to Siegmund the Walsung.

SCENE V

Siegmund leaves the sleeping Sieglinde and goes in search of Hunding. As the storm clouds flash and roar, the battle between the heroes commences on a distant mountain ridge. Sieglinde wakes and is tormented by the sight of the conflict. Siegmund is protected by the Valkyrie's shield and Hunding is driven back. But just as Brunnhilde guides Siegmund's sword in what would certainly be a fatal blow; the storm clouds part and throb with fiery light. The fierce Wotan appears; he stands over Hunding and blocks Siegmund's stroke with the shaft of his spear. Siegmund's sword shatters and Hunding immediately plunges his own spear into the unarmed Siegmund's breast. Brünnhilde, seeing the hero lost, swiftly lifts Sieglinde onto her steed and rides away. Wotan remains sadly looking over the body of his mortal son Siegmund. Hunding pulls his spear from Siegmund's body, but stands too near the god. With a contemptuous wave of his hand, Wotan strikes Hunding dead and then vanishes in a flash of lightning.

ACT III
SCENE I

On the craggy heights of the Valkyrie Rock, the Valkyries arrive one by one with dead warriors slung across their saddles. The eight shield maidens gather to await Brünnhilde before they ride off to Valhalla. They are astonished when they see the rebel Valkyrie arriving with a living maiden across her saddle. Fear fills them when they are told what has occurred. Sieglinde despairs and does not wish to live until Brünnhilde tells her that she is carrying Siegmund's child. For this Sieglinde is thankful and determined to live. She takes the shards of the hero's sword from the Valkyrie, who also tells her that her son's name is to be Siegfried meaning "victorious" and "free." Brünnhilde tells Sieglinde to escape into the pine forest below the rock because Wotan avoids this place. In it lives the evil giant Fafner, who after long years of brooding over his treasure and his ring has become a great dragon. Sieglinde flees, while Brünnhilde bravely awaits Wotan's wrath.

SCENE II

Wotan appears before the nine Valkyries in a flash of fiery red light. In his fury he condemns Brünnhilde to lose all her supernatural powers and become a mortal man's wife. The other Valkyries are filled with horror at their sister's fate, and beg Wotan to have pity on her. Wotan silences them and drives them away by threatening them with the same terrible fate.

SCENE III

Wotan and Brünnhilde remain alone on the rock. She claims that in defying his command she was actually doing his will and protecting his favorite mortal children, the Walsungs. But Wotan cannot take back his judgment. He tells her he will cast a spell of sleep on her. She will be left upon this rock for any mortal man to find and when she is awakened, she will be his prize. Sadly, Wotan tenderly kisses Brünnhilde's eyes and she falls into an enchanted sleep. Wotan lays her gently upon the ground, closes the visor of her helmet over her face, and places her Valkyrie shield over her breast. Invoking Loge's fire, Wotan encircles the rock where the sleeping beauty lies with its wall of flame. Striking the rock as he departs, Wotan invokes a spell forbidding the rock to anyone who fears his spear.

III. SIEGFRIED

ACT I
SCENE I

A large cave on the edge of a deep wood serves as a smithy for the Dwarf
Mime, the ill-humored brother of Alberich. Mime toils at the forge,
complaining about his ungrateful foster son, Siegfried. The greedy Dwarf
has no love for the powerful youth, but his plan is to get Siegfried to slay
the dragon Fafner, who lives nearby, and so win the ring and treasure
for Mime. The problem is that Mime doesn't have the skill to reforge the
sword Notung, and all the swords he makes are not strong enough for the
youth. Dressed in skins, the young Siegfried enters the smithy leading a
huge bear on a rope, and jokingly has the bear chase the smith around the
cave until he gives him his new sword. Once again, when Siegfried tries
the blade, it breaks, and the youth scolds the Dwarf. Siegfried wonders
at his own dislike of this Dwarf, who has nurtured him. But something
has always told him that Mime is evil. After threats from Siegfried, Mime
finally tells the youth of how Sieglinde, his mother, died in childbirth.
Siegfried demands proof, so Mime shows him the fragments of the sword
Notung. Siegfried rejoices and orders Mime to reforge the sword.

SCENE II

An ancient one-eyed man in a dark blue cloak and a large broad-brimmed
hat enters the smithy. He is weary from his travels and uses a spear as a
staff. He is called the Wanderer, but is actually Wotan in his earthly guise.
He asks the inhospitable Mime for shelter. The Dwarf tries to turn the
traveler from his door, but the Wanderer challenges him to a contest of
riddles that will conclude with the loser forfeiting his head. The Wanderer
easily answers Mime's three riddles: who lives under the Earth (the Dwarfs
or black-elves of Nibelheim); on it (the giants of Reisenheim); and above
it (the gods of Valhalla). In return, Mime answers two of the Wanderer's
riddles: the name of the family that Wotan loved best yet treated most

harshly (the Walsungs) and the name of the sword of the Walsungs (Notung). However, when the Wanderer asks him to name the one who can reforge Notung, Mime is beaten. The answer to the riddle is: only one who has never known fear. To that same man, the Wanderer says, as he departs, he will leave the forfeit of Mime's head.

SCENE III

Siegfried returns for his sword and finds it not yet made. Mime now understands that Siegfried is the "one who has never known fear" and desperately tries to teach him the "meaning of fear." This proves impossible, so Mime suggests that they go to visit Fafner the dragon, so the youth might learn about fear. Siegfried is keen to learn this new sensation, but decides that he must reforge his father's sword, as Mime cannot. With sheer barbaric energy and demonic strength, Siegfried succeeds where Mime has failed. As he works at the forge, the Dwarf cooks up a sleeping potion for the youth. He believes that the youth will now slay Fafner the dragon, so the only way Mime may win the ring and save his life is to drug the youth and slay him while he sleeps. At last, the frenzy at the forge comes to a halt. Siegfried holds up the brilliant reforged blade of Notung. Then, with a single stroke, he splits the anvil in two.

ACT II
SCENE I

In the depths of the forest of the Mirkwood in the dark of night, Alberich the Nibelung watches Fafner's cave and broods over the ring. Wotan the Wanderer greets him in the dark. Alberich immediately recognizes him, but the god assures the Dwarf that he is not after the ring. He warns Alberich that his real rival is his brother Mime. The young Siegfried knows nothing of the dragon's gold and the ring, and Wotan is banned from informing or helping him. Then the Wanderer calls out to wake the dragon. Both the Wanderer and Alberich offer to save Fafner's life in exchange for the ring, but the dragon finds this a ridiculous offer. He fears no one and goes back to sleep. Wotan laughs as he departs, telling Alberich he woke the dragon only to show the Dwarf how fate cannot be altered.

SCENE II

As day breaks, Siegfried and Mime the Dwarf climb to a knoll above the mouth of the dragon's cave. Mime leaves Siegfried alone and the youth blows his horn and wakes the dragon. Surprised, but not alarmed by Fafner's size, Siegfried jokes with the monster, and then asks him if he might teach him fear. The dragon grows impatient with the cocky youth and a titanic struggle ensues. The battle ends when Siegfried pierces the monster's heart. As Fafner dies, he warns the youth of the ring's curse. He also tells the hero that because of the ring, Siegfried will also soon die. Some of the dragon's blood drips on Siegfried's fingers and he puts them in his mouth. He finds, at once, that he can understand the language of birds. The Woodbird tells Siegfried about the dragon's gold, the magic helmet Tarnhelm, and the Ring of the Nibelung, to be found within the monster's cave.

SCENE III

The Dwarf brothers Alberich and Mime emerge from hiding. Seeing Fafner dead, they begin at once to argue over who will claim the treasure. Siegfried emerges from the dragon's cave with the ring on his hand and Tarnhelm tied to his belt. The Woodbird now warns him about Mime's plot. When Mime approaches and offers Siegfried a poisoned drink, the young hero cuts the Dwarf's head off. Alberich laughs in the distance as Siegfried blocks the door to the treasure cave with the body of the dragon. He then sets out on a new adventure when he is told by the Woodbird about a sleeping maiden who is to be found surrounded by a ring of fire on Valkyrie Rock.

ACT III

SCENE I

In a wild mountain pass, Wotan in his earthly guise as the Wanderer summons the prophetic goddess Erda and demands to learn the fate of the gods. When Erda will not give an answer, Wotan accepts that the doom of Valhalla is near. His remaining hope lies with the young hero Siegfried, who now holds the ring, and with Brünnhilde. He bequeaths the world to the Walsungs and the race of mortal men.

SCENE II

In the middle of the god's reverie, Siegfried approaches. The Wanderer detains him and blocks his path. With a single stroke of the reforged Notung, Siegfried shatters Wotan's spear shaft. Thunder and lightning flash at his deed and the Wanderer vanishes. Siegfried goes on his way, but the wall of fire soon confronts him. He blows his horn and plunges fearlessly into the flames.

SCENE III

Siegfried emerges from the flames at Valkyrie Rock, where he finds an armored warrior asleep. However, when he removes the armor, he discovers the maiden Brünnhilde, and is overwhelmed by her beauty. For the first time, he claims to understand what fear is, but he controls his trembling and wakens the sleeping beauty with a long kiss. Brünnhilde awakens to her lover. She soon realizes that by surrendering to Siegfried, she will lose her immortality, but she does so joyfully.

IV. THE TWILIGHT OF THE GODS

PROLOGUE

Flames light up the Valkyrie Rock where the three fatal sisters, the Norns, sing of the ancient days of Wotan's great deeds, as they weave the golden cord of fate. They sing of the shattering of Wotan's spear of law and how this released Loge, the god of fire, whose flames will soon consume Valhalla. They attempt to learn when the end will come, but the cord snaps. They understand that their own end has come, and they flee in terror to the caverns of Erda. As dawn arrives, Siegfried and his bride Brünnhilde emerge from their cave. Although she is afraid that she may lose her lover, Brünnhilde knows how a warrior's heart yearns for adventure. She gives him her armor and her horse Grane to help in his quest. Siegfried swears his eternal love and gives Brünnhilde the Ring of the Nibelung as his constant pledge before he sets off into the Rhine Valley.

ACT I
SCENE I

Gunther, the king of the Gibichungs, and his sister Gutrune sit enthroned in the vast hall of their castle on the Rhine. They are in council with their dark, brooding half-brother Hagen, who advises them how they may increase the Gibichung dynasty's wealth and power. He tells them they both must soon marry: Gunther to the wise and beautiful Brünnhilde, and Gutrune to Siegfried the Dragon-slayer, who possesses the treasure of the Nibelung gold. This can be achieved only by guile. They agree that when the approaching hero comes, Gutrune will give him a magic potion that will make Siegfried forget Brünnhilde and fall in love with her.

SCENE II

Siegfried's horn sounds from a riverboat as he approaches the castle. Hagen and Gunther welcome him with friendship and honor, and Gutrune brings to him a cup with the fatal magic potion. Though he toasts them in the name of his lover Brünnhilde, the moment the drink touches his lips he opens his eyes and heart to Gutrune. He swears his undying love for her and asks for her hand in marriage. Gunther agrees on the condition that Siegfried win for him the fair Brünnhilde, whose name now means nothing to the drugged Siegfried. Hagen advises Siegfried that they may achieve their aim with the Tarnhelm, by whose magic he may change his shape to that of Gunther. Gunther and Siegfried swear blood oaths of brotherhood and ride off on their quest.

SCENE III

On the Valkyrie Rock, Brünnhilde calls out a greeting of welcome to a sister Valkyrie, but the Valkyrie brings news of disorder and degeneration in Valhalla since Wotan's spear was shattered. Wotan has no authority to rule or act, and nothing will lift the curse of the ring except its return to its rightful guardians. However, Brünnhilde angrily refuses to return the ring to the Rhine maidens, and drives her sister away. The ring is the token of Siegfried's love and nothing will make her part with it. After the Valkyrie's departure, however, a strange man penetrates the flames of the wall of fire. It is Siegfried wearing Tarnhelm, which has changed him to Gunther's form. As Gunther the Gibichung, he claims Brünnhilde as his bride because he has passed the test of the ring of fire. After he seizes the ring from her hand, Brünnhilde has no power to resist him. He carries her off into the cave as his bride, but resolves to lay his sword between them as they sleep, so as not to dishonor his blood brother.

ACT II
SCENE I

In front of the Gibichung hall on the bank of the Rhine, Hagen, armed with spear and shield, is leaning against a doorpost, asleep. It is dark, but in the moonlight Alberich the Nibelung appears to Hagen in a dream. It is revealed that Hagen is the son of Alberich from a loveless union with Gunther's mother. Alberich makes his unhappy son swear that he will win back the Nibelung's ring.

SCENE II

As dawn breaks, Hagen awakens and Siegfried joyfully returns and greets him and Gutrune with the news that he has won Brünnhilde for King Gunther. He tells how he remained faithful that night, and then how on the journey back Gunther came and took Siegfried's place. Siegfried then returned to his own form and rode back to reach the Gibichung castle.

SCENE III

Hagen has summoned all the vassals of the kingdom to welcome King Gunther and Brünnhilde as their new queen. They offer up sacrifices to the altars of the gods and swear to uphold Queen Brünnhilde's honor.

SCENE IV

When Gunther arrives to present his new bride, Brünnhilde sees Siegfried with the ring upon his hand. She realizes at once that Gunther treacherously won her by deception. Siegfried the Walsung, she tells all, is her true husband. Siegfried swears upon the point of Hagen's spear that he has never known this woman as a bride. Brünnhilde is inflamed with a sense of betrayal and swears that his oath is false and that his sword hung on the wall, not between them. Siegfried denies the charge and leaves with Gutrune, although the vassals clearly believe Brünnhilde's story.

SCENE V

Brünnhilde is devastated and bent on vengeance for her betrayal. She turns to Hagen, and tells him that Siegfried is protected from all weapons by a magic spell she wove. There is one way Siegfried may be slain, however. Because she knew he would never flee from battle, the spell does not protect his back. So if Hagen drives his spear blade into Siegfried's back, he will die. Brünnhilde's taunts and Hagen's promises of wealth and power eventually persuade Gunther to join in the conspiracy to murder Siegfried as his wedding procession passes by.

ACT III
SCENE I

In a wood on the banks of the Rhine, the three Rhine maidens lament their lost gold. When Siegfried, who is out hunting, appears, they plead that he give back the ring, but he refuses. They warn him that if he does not return the Ring of the Nibelung to the Rhine, he will be slain this day.

SCENE II

When the rest of the hunting party arrives, Hagen and Gunther urge Siegfried to entertain them with tales of his childhood with Mime and his slaying of Fafner the Dragon. Finally, after giving him a drink to revive his memory, Hagen persuades him to tell of the wooing of Brünnhilde. With the pretense of moral outrage, Hagen drives his spear into the hero's back. Calling out his love for Brünnhilde with his last breath, Siegfried dies.

SCENE III

In front of the Gibichung hall in the moonlight, Gutrune, awakened by an evil dream, is anxiously waiting. Hagen comes to tell her that Siegfried has been killed by a wild boar. However, when his body is carried in, Gutrune will have none of it. She accuses Gunther of murder, but Gunther denies it and curses Hagen. Hagen defiantly admits the murder, but says it was justice. Then he claims the golden ring for himself. When Gunther disputes his right, Hagen slays him. Yet, when he is about to seize the ring, the dead Siegfried's hand rises threateningly against him. Hagen falls back in fear, as Brünnhilde commands all to stand back from the hero. She orders a funeral pyre to be made for Siegfried. She takes the ring and places it on her own finger, torches the pyre, and calls on the Rhine maidens to retrieve the gold from her ashes. She then rides Grane into the flames. The Rhine overflows its banks as the Gibichung hall is also consumed in the flames. The Rhine maidens rise with the river. They joyfully seize the ring, and vengefully drag the damned Hagen down to a watery grave. The flood subsides to leave only the burnt ruin of the hall, but in the distance, in the heavens, Valhalla can be seen catching alight, as it is finally entirely engulfed in flames.

Alberich the Nibelung

TOLKIEN'S RING

The Lord of the Rings

In the twentieth century special circumstances or "accidents of history" made Tolkien's *The Lord of the Rings*, as a re-creation of the ring quest, not only relevant and meaningful but to some degree prophetic. That is not to say that *The Lord of the Rings* is an allegory of our time. Tolkien rightly rejected the allegorical view as too narrow for his tale. He especially abhorred questions of the "Are Orcs Nazis or Communists?" kind. Tolkien's purpose was both more specific and more universal.

He once wrote: "I think that many confuse 'applicability' with 'allegory,' but the one resides in the freedom of the reader, and the other in the purposed domination of the author." In *The Lord of the Rings*, Tolkien gives us an adventure in the form of a ring quest with a simple human moral truth at its center. However, the nature of that adventure and that moral position were undeniably "applicable" to the most dramatic conflicts of the twentieth century.

Although Tolkien did not intend to mimic the events of his time, he did acknowledge when he began writing *The Lord of the Rings* in 1937 that something of the impending conflict with Nazi Germany was discernible in the dark atmosphere of its composition. Furthermore, as the bulk of the book was written through the dark years of World War II, there were aspects of the real war that were inevitably comparable to his "War of the Ring."

It is interesting to note Tolkien's own comments on this in his wartime letters to his son, Christopher, stationed with the British forces in South Africa. He sent chapters in serial form to Christopher as he wrote them, along with personal letters with constant references to Hobbits, Orcs, and Rings, as similes for individuals and issues relating to actual events in the conflict with Germany.

"Well, there you are: a hobbit among the Uruk-hai," Tolkien wrote. "Keep your hobbitry in heart and think that all stories feel like that when you are in them." However, this did not mean that real events in the war shaped Tolkien's invented war. His "War of the Ring" was about ideals, not political realities. It essentially revolved around a human moral crisis, which he perceived in the real war, but not just in the enemy.

In one letter to Christopher, Tolkien wrote: "We are attempting to conquer Sauron with the Ring. And we shall (it seems) succeed. But the penalty is, as you will know, to breed new Saurons, and slowly turn Men and Elves into Orcs. Not that in real life things are as clear-cut as in a story, and we started out with a great many Orcs on our side . . . "

Clearly, Tolkien's war had its own direction to follow, which had no parallels in the war with Germany. This is not to say that Tolkien was neutral in his view of Hitler and Nazi Germany—far from it. In 1941, he wrote to another son, Michael, who was at the time an officer cadet at the Royal Military Academy at Sandhurst.

> "I have spent most of my life, since I was your age, studying Germanic matters (in the general sense that includes England and Scandinavia). There is a great deal more force (and truth) than ignorant people imagine in the 'Germanic' ideal. . . . Anyway, I have in this war a burning private grudge— which would probably make me a better soldier at 49 than I was at 22: against that ruddy little ignoramus Adolf Hitler. Ruining, perverting, misapplying, and making for ever accursed that noble northern spirit, a supreme contribution to Europe, which I have ever loved, and tried to present in its true light. Nowhere, incidentally, was it nobler than in England, nor more early sanctified."

Indeed, one might even perceive that this "grudge" against Hitler might have had something to do with Tolkien's ambitions in writing a new version of the ring quest. In the nineteenth century, Richard Wagner recognized the absolute centrality of the ring quest in the vast mythological themes of European and especially Germanic peoples. He consciously seized upon the ring as a symbol of the German identity, heritage, and state. In the twentieth century, the music of Wagner's *The Ring of the Nibelung* became so closely allied with the Nazi Party and the rise of the Third Reich that they became synonymous in the popular mind. During World War II, the grand themes and traditions of the ring quest were usurped (or, as Tolkien saw it, ruined, perverted, and misapplied) by the German state with which Tolkien's nation was at war.

On one level, *The Lord of the Rings* is certainly an attempt by Tolkien to reclaim the ring as a symbol of "that noble northern spirit," which had fallen into such disrepute in Germany. With some justification, Tolkien blamed Wagner and his heirs for the dimming of the "true light." Although Wagner's genius was indisputable, his politics were repugnant. The great musician's family and heirs were not innocent dupes of the Nazi Party. Wagner's ideological stance may to some degree be evaluated by the fact that he chose to dedicate his collected works to Arthur de Gobineau, the father of Aryan racialist theory—a theory that Tolkien correctly rejected as being as intellectually ridiculous as it was morally repellent.

To Tolkien's credit, he saw from the beginning the nature of the Nazi obsession with Wagner's Ring Cycle. What appealed to the Nazis in the ring quest was an idealization of the pursuit of power for its own sake. Tolkien appreciated the ring quest tradition on many levels, but having already lived through one World War, he understood the nature of the curse of the "ring of power" as well as any man could. He believed that even for the good man the pursuit of power was in itself an evil that would enslave the human spirit and soul. And, in the Third Reich, there were not many "good men" to start with.

There can be little doubt that part of Tolkien's deeply felt motivation in writing *The Lord of the Rings* was a desire to set the record straight by reclaiming the ring quest tradition, and presenting the "noble northern spirit" of Europe in its "true light." Just as Tolkien chose on minor points to "challenge" Shakespeare's use of myth and history in *Macbeth* (1606), so on a much grander scale he "challenged" Wagner's use of myth and history in his Ring Cycle operas by writing *The Lord of the Rings*.

Tolkien understood the deep moral crisis at the center of the ring quest as Wagner perceived it. He saw the devastation that the Iron Age mentality of the ring quest had wreaked in the world, and chose to reshape the ring quest fundamentally for the twentieth century. He did this by turning the quest on its head. The ring of power was "unmade" by reversing the spell. The hero of the quest does not seize the ring but destroys it by dropping it into the inferno where it was made.

In 1937, Tolkien began to forge his "One Ring" imaginatively as a symbol for an absolute power that morally and physically contaminated all who touched it. He could not even have guessed how soon history would catch up with his dark vision and make his tale appear almost prophetic. He certainly could not have imagined how the scientists of the real world would soon create something that was every bit as powerful, evil, and contaminating as the "One Ring" of Sauron the Dark Lord.

Although *The Lord of the Rings* was largely written during the war years, it was not published until 1954, and, by this time, the atomic bomb had seized the popular imagination. The public was less likely to equate Sauron with

Hitler than the One Ring with the Bomb. It was difficult for many to believe that the idea of the One Ring was not inspired by the Bomb. Surely, some suggested, no place could look more like a nuclear testing ground than the ash-laden land of Mordor?

There is no doubt that Tolkien was very much against the atomic bomb. On August 9, 1945, he wrote to Christopher: "The news today about 'Atomic bombs' is so horrifying one is stunned. The utter folly of these lunatic physicists to consent to do such work for war purposes: calmly plotting the destruction of the world!"

Still, Tolkien was at pains to point out that the One Ring was fully formed long before he had any idea of the activities of atomic scientists. In a letter written in 1956, he found it necessary to state: "Of course my story is not an allegory of Atomic power, but of Power (exerted for Domination)." However, he had to acknowledge that in a larger sense the message or moral of his novel certainly did not exclude atomic power.

Indeed, Tolkien's views on nuclear weapons would not have been at all out of place at any CND (Campaign for Nuclear Disarmament, begun in the UK in 1957) or Ban the Bomb meeting or protest march.

"Nuclear physics can be used for that purpose [bombs]. But they need not be. They need not be used at all. If there is any contemporary reference in my story at all it is to what seems to me the most widespread assumption of our time: that if a thing can be done, it must be done. This seems to me wholly false. The greatest examples of the action of the spirit and of reason are in abnegation.

"When you say Atomic power is 'here to stay' you remind me that Chesterton said that whenever he heard that, he knew that whatever it referred to would soon be replaced, and thought pitifully shabby and old-fashioned. So-called 'atomic' power is rather bigger than anything he was thinking of (I have heard it of trams, gaslight, steam-trains). But it surely is clear that there will have to be some 'abnegation' in its use, a deliberate refusal to do some of the things it is possible to do with it, or nothing will stay!"

Even retrospectively, however, it still seems very unlikely that such a self-confessed "old fogey" of an Anglo-Saxon professor, writing about a remote imaginary world filled with an impossibly obscure invented mythology, could suddenly find a huge American campus cult following in the middle of the radical, politically charged 1960s. Tolkien was nobody's idea of a radical campus professor, so what was it in his writing that was suddenly so relevant to the lives and politics of the youth culture of the 1960s, catapulting him into the category of one of the most popular authors of the century?

The answer was that Tolkien's approach to the ancient grand theme of the ring quest was as unconventional and inventive as his unlikely heroes, the Hobbits. In fact, *The Lord of the Rings* proved to be the perfect student counter-culture book. It was full of action and adventure, but it appeared ultimately to hold an anti-establishment, pacifist message. Frodo Baggins might not have been exactly a Hobbit Gandhi, but he did reject the temptations of worldly power to an almost saintly degree. The student antiwar and ban the bomb movements of the sixties found an empathetic antihero in the Hobbit's humble values, as did the back-to-the-land hippy dropout culture. Tolkien could not have touched more bases with the youth culture of the sixties if he had commissioned a market survey.

If Tolkien was ambiguous about the "meaning" of his tale, there is no doubt that the parallels between the One Ring and the Bomb were not missed by activists in the late sixties and early seventies. One need only read Robert Hunter's *The Greenpeace Chronicles* to see how closely allied the counterculture was with Tolkien's world. Greenpeace came into being in 1969 in Vancouver, Canada, as an ecological guerrilla organization that attempted to stop American nuclear testing on Amchitka Island in Alaska. To this end, it chartered its first ship and attempted to prevent the bomb from being exploded by sailing into the test area.

Writing about this maiden Greenpeace voyage, Hunter tells how they had arrived at a point where even the stout hearts of his shipmates saw their task as rather comically hopeless. "There was something superbly comical about it: here we were, eight green-clad amateur seamen, on our way to confront the deadliest fire of the age, like Hobbits bearing the ring toward the volcano of Mordor."

It was a comparison that carried them a long way. Like exhausted Hobbits, they persevered. If Hobbits could overcome the forces of Sauron, why couldn't a ragtag handful of hippies overthrow the US military-industrial complex? At one point the valves and pistons of the old engine of their rather battered vessel required such coaxing and constant care on their long voyage along the north Pacific Coast that the activists dubbed themselves the "Fellowship of the Piston Rings."

In Tolkien's tale, when the One Ring is finally destroyed, the subsequent volcanic eruption closely resembles a nuclear explosion—but an explosion that destroys only the evil forces of the Ring Lord. One might also see in that explosive "unmaking" of the One Ring the reversal of the traditional ring quest in a moral sense as well. That Iron Age mentality of "might equals right," which made the ring quest for power so important, ends with the nuclear age—when possession of such power entails only mutual destruction.

It was Albert Einstein who warned the world: "The unleashing power of the atom has changed everything except our way of thinking . . . we need an essentially new way of thinking if mankind is to survive."

Tolkien's reversal of the ring quest demonstrates this "new way of thinking." Its version of the quest represents a desire to change power structures. Tolkien saw the results of the pursuit of pure power in two wars, and rejected it. In his private mythic world, he understood a human truth that modern technology has brought home to mankind with a terrible vengeance in the form of the nuclear bomb. If ever there was a manifestation of the ultimate power of the One Ring, the Bomb was it. The "Cold War" was the result of the grudging admission that power of the kind represented by nuclear weapons was ultimately self-destructive.

Tolkien also displayed this "new way of thinking" in his inspired choice of heroes. One must not forget the importance of his Hobbits; it would do no good to change the nature of the quest without changing the nature of the hero. Not only did Tolkien turn the ring quest on its head; he also reversed many of the characteristics usually expected of the quest hero. He wrote:

"The Hobbits are, of course, really meant to be a branch of the specifically human race (not Elves or Dwarves) . . . They are entirely without nonhuman powers, but are represented as being more in touch with 'nature', and abnormally, for humans, free from ambition or greed of wealth. They are made small partly to exhibit the pettiness of man, plain unimaginative parochial man . . . and mostly to show up, in creatures of very small physical power, the amazing and unexpected heroism of ordinary men 'at a pinch.'"

Ultimately, the greatest strength of Tolkien's Hobbits in their epic struggle against all odds is their basic human decency. It is their essential humanity, their simple but pure human spirits, which allowed them to triumph in the end. And it is this human element, combined with the grandeur and pomp of a magnificently conceived mythic world that has been the key to Tolkien's continued popularity.

Characteristically, however, Frodo Baggins the Hobbit actually does live up to the classic "hero" image at the time of the ultimate test. At the last moment, on the edge of the Crack of Doom, the Hobbit's resolve fails and he refuses to destroy the One Ring. Virtuous though Frodo is, it is not the strength of his will that allows the One Ring to be destroyed and Middle-earth to be saved, it is Frodo's unprovoked and almost foolish charity toward an undeserving enemy. Out of a sense of mercy, the Hobbit allows the treacherous Gollum to live. Reason should tell Frodo that Gollum will betray him again, but the Hobbit chooses to obey his heart. In the end, the One Ring is destroyed exactly because Frodo takes pity on his enemy, and Gollum survives long enough to betray him again. On the edge of the Crack of Doom, Gollum wrestles with the Hobbit. Finally, he overcomes the weakened Frodo. He viciously bites off the Hobbit's ring finger. Then, seizing the One Ring, Gollum topples backward into the fiery abyss. The One Ring is destroyed.

In Frodo the Hobbit, Tolkien found a twentieth-century Everyman who has, and will continue to have in the twenty-first century, universal appeal to people of any time and any place. In Tolkien's *The Lord of the Rings* the Hobbit teaches us that "attempting to conquer Sauron with the ring" is no longer the goal of the quest. In the end, it is not the power of the mind, nor the strength of the body, but the instincts of the human heart that save the world. It is the simple human capacity for mercy that finally allows evil to be overthrown.

INDEX OF SOURCES

This index refers the reader from the entries in the Dictionary of Sources to Tolkien's original texts. The following abbreviations have been used:

S—*The Silmarillion*
H—*The Hobbit*
LR—*The Lord of the Rings*
TB—*The Adventures of Tom Bombadil*
UT—*Unfinished Tales*
BLT (1)—*Book of Lost Tales I*
BLT (2)—*Book of Lost Tales II*
LB—*Lays of Beleriand*
SME—*Shaping of Middle-Earth*
LRD—*The Lost Road*

Roman numerals indicate parts, and arabic numbers chapters or sections.

DAVID DAY

INDEX

Page numbers in *italic* type refer to illustrations and captions; page numbers in **bold** refer to charts and maps.

A

Aegir 17
Aeglos ("snow point" or "icicle") 17
Aeneas 17–18
Aesir 18
Aglarond 18–19
Ainur (Holy Ones) 19
    Music of 262
Akallabêth 19–20, *20, 144*
Alberich the Nibelung *523*
Alcuin of York 21
Alfheim 21
Alfirin 21–2
Ali Baba 22
Alighieri, Dante 13
Allfather (Ilúvatar) 200
Ancalagon the Black 22–3, *23*
Anduin *390–1*
Andúril 23–4
Andvari 24
Angband 24–5, *26–7, 78*
Angels 25
Angmar 25–9, *269,* 426–30
Annatar 29
Ar-Pharazôn 31–3, *32*
Aragorn II *28, 29, 133*

Arawn the Huntsman 30
Arda 30, *83,* **440, 441**
Arien 30–1
Armageddon 31
Artemis 33
Arthur 34
Arwen Evenstar 34, *218*
Asgard 35
Asmodeus 35
Asteria 35
Athelas 35–7, *36*
Athens 37
Atlantis *38–9,* 40
Aulë the Smith 40–1, *41, 43, 411*
Avallónë 41
Avalon 41–2
Avari 42
Azanulbizar *415,* 468–9

B

Bag End 45
Baggins 45–7
    Bilbo 63–4
    Frodo 150–2, *151*
Balchoth 47, *48–9*
Balor of the Evil Eye 47–50
Balrog of Moria *51,* 50–2
Balrogs of Angband 52–3
Barad-dûr *330*
Bard the Bowman 53
Barrow-downs 53–4
Barrow-wights 54–5, *54–5, 151*
Bats *44,* 55
Battle of Azanulbizar *415,* 468–9

Battle of Dagorlad 454, **455**
Battle of Hornburg 458, **459**
Battle of Pelennor Fields *296, 306–7,* 462–3, **465**
Battle of the Black Gate 466, **467**
Battle of the Five Armies *362–3,* 456, **457**
Battle of the Somme *356,* 357
Battle Plain (Dagorlad) 91–2, *356*
battles 56, *56, 167,* 414, 453–69 (*see also* wars)
Belegaer 57
Belegost *104, 106–7*
Beleriand 57
Beorn 57–8, *59*
Beowulf 58–60, *60*
Beren 61–2, *193, 230*
berserkers 62
Bifröst 63
Bilbo Baggins 63–4
Black Gate 64, 466, **467**
Black Númenóreans 65–6, *65*
Black Riders 66, *68–9*
Black Sails 67
Black Tower *204–5*
Boromir 70
Brambles of Mordor *263*
"The Brave Little Tailor" 70–1
Bridge of Nargothrond *270*
Brísingamen 71–2
Brocéliande 72–3
Brownies 73

Gollum Falling into Mount Doom